Christian Doctrine

"The Faith . . . Once Delivered"

William J. Richardson

General Editor

STANDARD PUBLISHING
Cincinnati, Ohio   88588

Sharing the thoughts of their own hearts, the authors may express views not entirely consistent with those of the publisher.

Library of Congress Cataloging in Publication data:
Christian doctrine.

1. Theology, Doctrinal—Addresses, essays, lectures.
I. Richardson, William J., 1921-
BT80.C47   1983   230'.044   82-25598
ISBN 0-87239-610-X

TABLE OF CONTENTS

CONTENTS

FOREWORD

I am greatly honored to write the foreword for this new book on Christian doctrine, and I am excited about the impact I am sure it will have on the various segments of the restoration movement. Those of us who have labored for many years in the movement, believing devoutly that the effort begun by the pioneer preachers is the proper approach to the problem of denominationalism, have prayed for the day that our brotherhood would be united in meaningful fellowship on the basis of our faith in the Lord Jesus Christ. It is exhilarating to read the chapters in this book and see the authors' faith and common love for truth as expressed in the Word of God amidst their different understandings about the implications of that faith and truth. In a time when the restoration movement is at a low ebb, it is refreshing to see a volume published that is so filled with the spirit of love and concern for genuine unity among those of a common heritage. The time has come for a large-scale effort at unity among us based upon a genuine acceptance of the meaning of such slogans as "In matters of faith unity; in matters of opinion liberty; in all things love." (This slogan appears on the face of a bulletin regularly published by a large evangelical church of my acquaintance not connected with the restoration movement at all.) Uniformity has never been an option for churches that do not espouse an authoritarian approach to church leadership. Among thinking people, it is not even a desirable option. There is both beauty and joy in the freedom granted to disciples through the realization that law was given through Moses, but grace and truth have come in the person of Jesus Christ. That spirit is contagious in the pages of this volume.

I am especially delighted to observe the high quality of work in these essays and that it is not only the pioneer preachers and teachers of our history that are being dealt with, but contemporary scholarship in the broad Protestant and Evangelical world as well. This will demonstrate both the competence and earnestness of the authors, and will make the volume a bridge between the restoration movement and the Evangelical world in general. These essays make a real contribution to the pursuit of truth in a non-sectarian atmosphere. It represents some of the clearest thinking I have seen from the pens of restoration-minded scholars. It is not important whether I or any other reader agree with every point made in the book. What is important is that "in matters of opinion there be liberty," and that love direct the course of those who pursue truth.

This work will stand in the tradition of J. S. Lamar's *Organon of Scripture* and J. D. Thomas' *We Be Brethren*. Its format will allow it to address much broader concerns, however, and its cross section of restoration scholars will cause it to be viewed as an effort to practice the concerns that the restoration movement espouses in theory. I can only lament the fact that a similar volume was not produced years ago for use in the college classrooms, but also equally suitable for in-depth reading by devout church members who are seeking a well-reasoned and carefully researched foundation for Christian doctrine.

John McRay
Professor of New Testament
Wheaton College Graduate School
Wheaton, Illinois

The Use of a Text in Teaching Christian Doctrine: One Person's Experience

William J. Richardson

I do not regard my style of teaching Christian doctrine as a model. There may be, however, some elements in my experience that will be helpful to the prospective user of this text, particularly as my experience relates (1) to the matter of choosing a text and (2) to the way of making use of it.

As a teacher of this subject to undergraduates, I felt it would be unfruitful to select for a text a work with which I fundamentally disagreed. At the same time, even where I approve of a text, there would be areas where I might not agree with the point of view expressed by the author. This provided the opportunity to indicate to students where I disagreed and to set forth the grounds of my disagreement—either in the author's presuppositions or in his use of, or interpretations of, data. By this procedure, I could contend for what I believed to be the clearer statement of the truth and at the same time reinforce a style of thinking I was encouraging in my students—one that distinguishes between the facts an author puts forward and the author's theories. This approach made it possible for me to use texts whose overall presentation had great value even though I perceived flaws at certain points.

The use of a text almost always posed the problem of correlating the author's outline of a chapter with my own outline of the subject it covered. In some instances I had points to emphasize on a particular theme of doctrine that were omitted from the author's presentation, or my order of presentation was different. Hence I faced the necessity of devising a scheme which avoided either using the author's outline exclusively or the alternative of not using it at all. The procedure I adopted was to develop a composite outline of the theme of the chapter, which combined the points I wished to emphasize with the points in the text to which I wanted to call attention. It was then a simple matter to identify these points of the outline drawn from the text by the use of some appropriate symbol. This style allowed me to take advantage of the insights of the text while being free to advance my own, thus making for more versatility in the treatment of the subject. It also guided students in their preparation and gave direction to class lecture and discussion.

CONTRIBUTORS

William J. Richardson is the general editor of this work and the author of chapter 1. He is professor of church history at Emmanuel School of Religion and holds the following degrees:
B.Th., Northwest Christian College,
B.D., Butler University,
M.A., Butler University,
Ph.D., University of Oregon.
He is also the author of *Social Action Vs. Evangelism: an Essay on the Current Crisis* (William Carey Library, 1977).

Fred P. Thompson, Jr., author of chapter 2, is the president and professor of Christian doctrine at Emmanuel School of Religion. He holds the following degrees:
B.A., Pacific Christian College,
B.A., Pepperdine University,
B.D., Butler University,
S.T.D., Milligan College.
He is the author of *What the Bible Says About Heaven and Hell* (College Press, 1982).

Leroy Garrett, editor of *Restoration Review*, authored two chapters in this work, chapters 3 and 4. He holds the following degrees:
B.S., Abilene Christian University,
M.A., Southern Methodist University,
Th.M., Princeton Theological Seminary,

CONTRIBUTORS

Ph.D., Harvard University.
He is the author of *The Stone-Campbell Movement* (College Press, 1981).

Robert F. Hull, Jr. is an associate professor of Bible at Emmanuel School of Religion and the author of chapter 5. His academic degrees include the following:
B.A., Milligan College,
M.Div., Emmanuel School of Religion,
Ph.D., Princeton Theological Seminary.

Ronald E. Heine, author of chapter 6, is professor of church history and theology at Lincoln Christian Seminary. He holds the following degrees:
A.B., Lincoln Christian College,
M.A., Lincoln Christian Seminary,
B.D., Lincoln Christian Seminary,
M.A., University of Illinois,
Ph.D., University of Illinois.
He translated Origin's *Homilies on Genesis and Exodus* (Catholic University of America Press, 1982).

David A. Root, professor of New Testament at Northwest Christian College, is the author of chapter 7. He holds the following degrees:
B.S., Pacific Christian University,
B.D., Emmanuel School of Religion,
Ph.D., Emory University.

Burton B. Thurston, professor of Middle Eastern studies at Bethany College, has written chapter 8. His degrees are as follows:
B.Th., Northwest Christian College,
B.A., Transylvania University,
B.D., Butler University,
M.A., Butler University,
Th.D., Harvard University.

Knofel Staton, president and professor of New Testament at Pacific Christian College, is the author of chapters 9 and 18. He holds two academic degrees:
B.A., Lincoln Christian College,
M.Div., Southern Baptist Theological Seminary.
A prolific author, he has written three books to be published in July, 1983: *Check You Home-life, Check Your Morality,* and *Check Your Life in Christ* **(Standard Publishing)**.

Frederick W. Norris, professor of Christian Doctine at Emmanuel School of Religion and editor of *Patristics,* is the author of chapter

10. He holds these degrees:
B.A., Milligan College,
B.D., Phillips University,
M.Th., Phillips University,
M.Phil., Yale University,
Ph.D., Yale University.

Ron Durham, author of chapter 11, is a special assignment writer for
Word, Inc. He holds three academic degrees:
B.A., Eastern New Mexico University,
S.T.B., Abilene Christian University,
Ph.D., Rice University.

Edwin S. Nelson, author of chapter 12, is the director of the Mesa
Extension Program, Central Christian School of Ministry of Pacific
Christian College. He holds the following degrees:
B.A., Platte Valle Bible College,
M.Div., Lincoln Christian Seminary,
M.Th., Gordon Conwell Theological Seminary,
Ph.D., Boston University.

James G. Van Buren, professor of humanities and Christian doctrine at
Manhattan Christian College, is the author of chapter 13. His de-
grees include the following:
A.B., Butler University,
B.D., Butler University,
D.D., Milligan College,
Ph.D., Kansas State University.
He has also written *What the Bible Says About Promise* (College
Press, 1980).

David R. Reagan, evangelist with Lamb and Lion Ministries, is the
author of chapter 14. He holds the following degrees:
B.A., University of Texas,
M.A., Fletcher School of Law and Diplomacy of Tufts and Harvard
Universities,
M.A.L.D., Fletcher School of Law and Diplomacy of Tufts and Har-
vard Universities.
He currently conducts the radio program, *Christ in Prophecy.*

Robert O. Fife, author of chapter 15, is the executive director of the
Westwood Christian Foundation. He holds the following degrees:
A.B., Johnson Bible College,
M.Div., Butler University,
Ph.D., Indiana University.
He is the author of *Teeth on Edge* (1971, now out of print).

CONTRIBUTORS

John Mills, minister of the First Church of Christ in Painesville, Ohio, wrote chapter 16. His degrees follow:
B.A., Milligan College,
M.Div., Phillips University,
D.Min., McCormick Theological Seminary.

Mont Smith, author of chapter 17, is professor of church growth and Biblical studies at Pacific Christian College. He holds three academic degrees:
B.Th., Northwest Christian College,
M.A., Butler University,
D.Miss., Fuller Theological Seminary.
He is also the author of *What the Bible Says About Covenant* (College Press, 1981).

PREFACE

Several years ago, I was asked to submit to Standard Publishing a manuscript for a book on Christian doctrine based on insights gained from twenty-three years of teaching this subject at Northwest Christian College. Circumstances made it impossible to undertake such a project at that time. The new book committee accepted my suggestion that we prepare a symposium using the skills of a number of writers. The present work is the fruit of this combined effort.

Inasmuch as patrons of Standard Publishing are familiar with such works as Alexander Campbell's *Christian System*, Robert Milligan's *Scheme of Redemption*, and other similar works, it may be asked, "Why another book on Christian doctrine?" A number of factors can be cited. On the one hand, there are circumstances that call for such an organization of Christian teaching as is offered here. Each generation needs to have the Biblical message articulated in ways that communicate it effectively, even though the results of these efforts must be constantly corrected by reference to Scripture. Although we affirm the completeness and sufficiency of Biblical faith, we still may grow in our understanding of its meaning and should share that understanding with others. In addition, new issues may arise that need to be considered in the light of the teaching of Scripture. Again, we may enlarge our perception of the areas of human experience to which the Biblical faith applies, especially in the fast-changing world of today in which the church lives and must carry out its mission.

A further need is that of taking into account developments in the world of scholarship concerning the text and meaning of the Scriptures which convey the content of Christian faith. Where perceived as valid, these scholarly insights must be incorporated into our understanding and organization of Christian truth. It may be that some scholarly findings will lead to a recasting of the way we organize our presentation of that truth. An example of this ongoing scholarship is the debate among scholars concerning Christian baptism, begun in 1943 with Karl Barth's lecture, *Die Kirchliche Lehre von der Taufe* (Eng. trans., 1948, *The Teaching of the Church Regarding Baptism*), and extending to the present, with results encouraging to those interested in a recovery of the New Testament concept of the ordinance of initiation.*

This symposium seeks to embody the objectives stated above. Its authors are alert to the need of the Christian community for a clear statement of the nature and meaning of the Christian faith. They are alert also to the questions that capture the attention and concern of believers today. They have sought to be aware of what is going on in the world of Biblical scholarship and to evaluate those developments in the light of their commitment to Biblical faith. They distinguish between faith in the person of Jesus Christ and faith in doctrines; hence they do not view their essays as creedal statements, much less tests of orthodoxy.

The chapters are unequal in length, due in part to the nature of their subject matter and in part to the mode of treatment chosen by their authors. Some essayists present as comprehensive a treatment of their theme as is possible in a symposium. Others focus their treatment upon issues that have arisen in current theological discussion or church practice. The body of each chapter is styled to address the general reader without his having to refer to the backnotes, which are provided as a means of discussing technical matters or supplying additional references for those interested in pursuing the subject in greater depth.

The informed reader will note that the format of the present

*See note 20, chapter 12, for an extended listing of these writings

volume cannot claim originality. Emphasis upon the Word of God as first an act of God, then as present in the proclamation of the Gospel, in the word of teaching, in the community of faith, and in the Scriptures, has been a tradition from the earliest days of the movement to restore New Testament Christianity. However, the attempt is made here to explicate matters of doctrine in the order in which one new to the faith encounters the Christian message: A proclamation about Jesus (Part I); the nature of the disclosure of God in Christ (Part II); the teaching given for the edification of the believer (Part III); the nature of the community to which the believer has been added (Part IV).

The authors of these essays have in common a deep commitment to Biblical faith. Each places his own mark on the style of the symposium. There are some differences, not radical, in points of view expressed. The reader may profit from analyzing and evaluating these differences where they occur. The retention of these differences in this volume reflects two convictions: (1) the Christian faith is not primarily an affirmation of doctrine, but rather a confession of Jesus as Lord, and (2) fellowship among Christians does not depend on their achieving the same level of understanding of doctrine.

It is hoped that these essays will lead the reader to a deeper awareness of some of the implications of Biblical faith for life today.

William J. Richardson

INTRODUCTION

SECTION OUTLINE

1. FAITH AND THE FAITH: THE ROLE OF CHRISTIAN
   DOCTRINE TODAY
   A. The Relation of Proclamation and Teaching
   B. The Role of Christian Doctrine
      Implementation of evangelism
      Exposition of the nature of faith
      Defense of the faith
      Guidance of the life of faith
   C. The Epistle to Rome as an Example of the Role of
      Christian Doctrine

2. THE WORD OF GOD
   A. The Nature of Language
   B. The Strangeness of the Word
      What "Word of God" implies
   C. God's Word as God's Act
   D. Jesus as The Word of God
   E. Scripture—The Word of God Written
      Inspiration of Scripture
      Authority of the Bible
      The Interpretation of Scripture

CHAPTER

1

FAITH AND THE FAITH: THE ROLE OF CHRISTIAN DOCTRINE TODAY

By William J. Richardson

The distinction between "faith" and "the faith" in the title of this chapter corresponds to the nature of revelation contained in the Bible. Revelation did not come all at once, but consisted of acts of God (including speech) in which He disclosed His nature, purpose, and will. He spoke to the fathers by the prophets "in many portions and in many ways" and now has spoken to us "in His son" (Hebrews 1:1, 2). These occasions of divine self-disclosure involved the revealing of aspects of His nature and will in accordance (1) with the needs of His people at a given time, and (2) with their state of readiness to receive His word—all in keeping with a program of progressive revelation culminating in Christ, the Word Incarnate.

The term *faith* describes the response of persons to the recitation of the acts of God *(kerygma)* referred to above. The expression *the faith* refers to the whole of the revelation summed up in the teachings of the New Covenant and embodied now in Scripture. The further elaboration of this distinction is the purpose of the first portion of this chapter. The remainder of the chapter considers the function of Christian doctrine in the light of this understanding of *the faith*.

The Relation of Proclamation and Teaching

For nearly a half century, Biblical studies have been stimulated by the question, "Can the materials of the New Testament be classified according to a distinction such as that suggested by C. H. Dodd in his *Apostolic Preaching and Its Developments* (1973)?" In these lectures, Dodd rather sharply distinguished *kerygma* (proclamation) from *didache* (teaching). By *kerygma*, he meant the proclamation of the inauguration of the reign of God in the person of, and through the ministry, death, and resurrection of, Christ.[1] By *didache*, he meant the ethical teaching given as accompaniment of the gospel to those who received the faith.*

Responses to Dodd have been varied. Some have found evidence in the epistles of a more abbreviated form of the proclamation than that in Acts, on which Dodd based his summary. Some contend that *kerygma* is part of *didache*, others that *didache* is part of *kerygma*. Still others see no difference in content between the two, holding that the terms teaching and preaching are interchangeable or are without distinction in their application.[2] More serious yet is the question whether *kerygma* is a "recital" of historical events relating to the person of Christ or a reference to preaching itself as an event in which persons are summoned to faith.[3]

There is a long standing tradition in the restoration movement for distinguishing between the gospel, as the facts concerning Christ, and doctrine, as the exposition of the meaning and implications of the gospel. For example, Alexander Campbell, in his debate with N. L. Rice (1843), summarized the content of the gospel in terms that anticipate Dodd's description of the *kerygma* referred to above. Peter's sermon on Pentecost (Acts 2), Campbell declares,

> is . . . a synopsis of the whole evangelical economy. It is based on three facts which transpired on earth—the death, burial, and resurrection of the Messiah, and three facts which transpired afterwards—his ascension, coronation and reception of the Holy Spirit, for the consummation of the objects of his reign. The precepts are also three—believe, repent, and be baptized. The promises are three—remission of sins, the Holy Spirit, and eternal life.[4]

*Chapter 4 of this symposium provides a more detailed discussion of this subject and also calls for a sharp distinction between *kerygma* and *didache*. A still different view is expressed in chapter 18.

While, in Campbell's view, the most prominent aspects of the gospel are those that pertain to the passion and resurrection of Jesus, the message includes the whole of His life and ministry. "To enumerate the gospel facts would be to narrate all that is recorded of the sayings and doings of Jesus Christ from his birth to his coronation in the heavens."[5]

Campbell's study of the New Testament convinced him that the most frequent use of "Word of God" in sacred Scripture is in reference to the gospel.

> The phrase "the Word of God," is used in a restricted sense in the apostolic writings. From the ascension of Jesus it is appropriated to denote the glad tidings concerning Jesus. ... Out of thirty-four times which it occurs, from Pentecost to the end of the volume, it thirty times obviously refers to the gospel. ... or proclamation of mercy to the human race.[6]

Campbell, of course, did refer to the Bible as the Word of God. He recognized, however, that prior in time to the written word was the apostolic proclamation of the Word of God incarnate in Christ.

Although familiar with the nomenclature of the Greek New Testament, Campbell preferred to use the term *fact* rather than *kerygma* to refer to the content of the proclamation; *fact* has to do with the person and mission of Jesus, particularly with His death and resurrection. The proclamation of the facts (the gospel) becomes the source and substance of the faith of Christians. Belief of these facts and acknowledgement of the Lordship of Jesus in obedience was for Campbell the only legitimate ground for establishing Christian status and hence is the basis for unity among Christians. "The belief of this ONE FACT ['that Jesus the Nazarene is the Messiah'], and submission to ONE INSTITUTION expressive of it ['baptism into the name of the Father, and of the Son, and of the Holy Spirit'] is all that is required of Heaven to admission into the church."[7] Like his father, Thomas Campbell, he affirmed that unity does not consist in the attainment of a given level of understanding of Christian doctrine. The Campbells' complaint against creeds was not that they necessarily contained error but that they were statements of doctrine that, when used as tests of communion, presumed a fixed level of understanding on the part of believers. The church, said Thomas Campbell, would always comprise the young as well as the old in faith; hence it was contrary to its

23

nature as the family of God to expect all its members to have achieved the level of understanding presumed by the various doctrinal statements of Christendom.[8] Illustrative of the younger Campbell's view of the nature of Christian faith as personal, and his denial of doctrinal consensus as the basis of unity, is the following assertion made in a series of letters to J. Wallis of England:

> To convert men to a party, to a tenet, and to a person, are very different projects. . . . In this our day . . . we have much reason to think that many confound conversion to a doctrine, to a theory, or to a party, with conversion to Christ. . . .
> The Christian religion is indeed a *personal* concern. It is confidence in a person, love to a person, delight in a person. It is not confidence in a doctrine, nor love to a party. Jesus Christ is the object on which the Christian's faith, hope, and love terminate; and to be with Christ is the Christian's heaven. Therefore, conversion is a turning to the Lord—in order to which Christ must be preached, and nothing else.[9]

Campbell, however, did not minimize the role of doctrine. He wrote many articles on doctrinal subjects as well as a book, *The Christian System*, devoted to an exposition of the religion of Christ. His definition of doctrine, given in this work, emphasizes the relation of fact and meaning in understanding the message of the Bible.

> The Bible . . . is a book of awful facts, grand and sublime beyond description. The facts reveal God and man, and contain within them the reasons of all piety and righteousness, or what is commonly called religion and morality. *The meaning of the Bible facts is the true biblical doctrine* [italics mine].[10]

If the good news focuses upon the person and mission of Jesus, it is proper to distinguish between that activity (preaching) and content (the gospel) that aim at evoking faith in Jesus as the Christ and that activity (teaching) and content (doctrine) whose aim is to inform the understanding and guide the behavior of those who affirm this faith.[11]

The faith evoked by the evangel involves a determination to bring all one's life into obedience to Christ; this is the basic meaning of repentance (*metanoia*: "change of mind"). It is this relationship of faith that motivates and guides the changes of outlook and life-style that believers are called upon to make. For example, the third chapter of Colossians contains a set of exhortations for a Christlike style of living (Colossians 3:5-17), all clearly grounded upon the relation of the believer to Christ in response to the good news. You "have died" and "have been raised up with Christ" in baptism (Colossians 3:1-4; cf. 2:12); therefore, "put to death" the old, put on "the new" (Colossians 3:5, 12). These converts did not come into the church fully informed of the meaning of the faith or of its implications for their lives. Believers were expected to grow in understanding and in their obedience (Romans 12:1, 2; Philippians 2:12); hence, one finds in the New Testament references to levels of teaching given to followers of Christ. Several epistles, for example, classify these levels of teaching by the distinction "milk" and "solid food" (1 Corinthians 3:2; Hebrews 5:12-14; 1 Peter 2:2).

However, this distinction between the proclamation and the teaching does not mean that they are exclusive of each other or do not function in relation to each other. On the one hand, the proclamation of the gospel involves factors that belong to the category of doctrine. While the kerygma centers primarily upon the acts of God in Christ, the elements in that message involve questions—such as the meaning of Lord and Christ as applied to Jesus—the understanding of which is important for the hearers' appropriation of the message. Clarification of these questions of meaning is an aspect of the proclamation itself.

On the other hand, the teaching function, aimed at the edification of believers, is inseparable from the content of the proclamation. If teaching is understood as the meaning of the facts (the gospel), then the gospel is the ground of every teaching situation and of all subject matter taught. This correlation is evident from the reading of the epistles. They are not primarily evangelistic in purpose or kerygmatic in content. They presume the presence of faith in the readers whom they are instructing. Yet in their instruction and exhortation, the epistles show their basis in the gospel.[12] Again, the content of the gospel is set in the context of the church assembled for worship and edification. This is very evident at the Lord's Table, where the facts of the gospel are recounted (1 Corinthians 11:26). All teaching and exhortation given to believers will be grounded in the content of the message that first called them to faith. As Floyd Filson writes: "The teaching will include the basic gospel message, though it will deal more with the understanding and living of the Christian life in the light of that basic gospel."[13]

In what we have stated above, the most appropriate use of the term *faith* is in application to the proclamation concerning Jesus and the response it evokes in its hearers. However, the term can also be used to denote the whole of the new covenant, which proceeds from the life and ministry of Christ—including not only belief in Him but also the precepts, institutions, and teachings that comprise the tradition of Christ. Such is our meaning when we speak of "the Christian faith." This usage is appropriate in light of the fact that every aspect of the religion of the New Testament has its focus in and derives its meaning from the reality we acknowledge when we confess "Jesus is Lord."

A careful analysis of Paul's use of the term *faith* in Galatians 3:15—4:31 reflects both the aspects named above. The apostle's most frequent use of the term *faith* is, of course, in reference to belief in Christ.[14] Such faith is the ground of justification (Galatians 2:16; 3:24); it is evoked by the proclamation of the gospel (Romans 10:17; Galatians 3:2). Paul, however, speaks not only of faith in Christ but also of "the faith" (Galatians 3:23, 25), which in Galatians 3:15-24 stands in contrast to the law, because the law as such could not fulfill the promise of righteousness and inheritance made to Abraham (Galatians 3:18, 21). Now, in chapter four, Paul illustrates the superiority of the gospel to the law; thus, in both these chapters of Galatians, he contrasts the law and the gospel. But where in Galatians 3:15ff, the term *covenant* is applied only to the promise to Abraham (vs. 15, 17), in Galatians 4:21-31, it is applied to the law and the gospel as well, the fact of which may be illustrated as follows:

Galatians 3
COVENANT (promise) to Abraham (vv. 15, 16) not fulfilled in the LAW (vv. 18, 21) but in
The GOSPEL (the faith, v. 23ff)

Galatians 4
Abraham's wives—an allegory (v. 24)
Hagar represents the OLD COVENANT
(Law—vv. 24, 25)
Sarah represents the NEW COVENANT
(Gospel—vv. 26, 28)

Hence, "the faith" that comes in the place of the law in Galatians 3:23, in order to consummate the promise to Abraham, is the same as the new covenant in Galatians 4:21-31, in which believers enjoy the freedom of the "Jerusalem that is above." Therefore, just as "the law" can refer to the whole of the old covenant made at Sinai, with its precepts, institutions, and teachings, so "the faith" can refer to the whole of the new covenant initiated in and by Christ. Thus, when Paul writes: "now that faith [literally, *the faith*] has come," he is referring to the whole of that which centers in and proceeds from belief that Jesus is Lord. Understood in this sense, *the faith* includes both the proclamation, "Jesus is Lord," and the teaching which is grounded in this confession.

We may distinguish, then, between (1) the proclamation of the gospel, the function and message that elicits faith in Jesus as the Christ, and (2) teaching, the function that instructs believers in the meaning of that confession and its implications for their individual or corporate life. One focuses upon the need for faith, the other upon the need to grow in the faith. We turn now to a more detailed examination of the aspects of this second function.

The Role of Christian Doctrine
Implementation of Evangelism

The overlapping of proclamation of the good news and teaching of "the faith" has already been mentioned; so one ought not to suppose that teaching has no role in winning persons to commitment to Christ. Indeed, teaching may have both a direct and indirect role, each vital, in carrying out the mission.

On the one hand, teaching may be directly related to a person's decision to receive Jesus as Lord. The New Testament indicates that there were times in the missionary situation when consideration of the claims of the gospel involved the problem of the meaning of the new faith over against the religious background and expectations of the hearers, especially at the point where the decision had to do with the issue of their basic allegiance. The critical factor in faith was that of identifying the authority under whom one would live his life. While converts were not expected to understand all the moral implications of the faith at the moment of their acceptance of it (as Romans 6:11-14; 12:1, 2; Colossians 3:4-17 clearly indicate), a

27

determination to submit themselves to the Lordship of Christ was crucial to that faith. Hence, there was the necessity of teaching concerning the nature of that commitment. It is likely that the first principles alluded to in Hebrews 6:1, 2 (teachings about baptisms, laying on of hands, resurrection of the dead, eternal judgment) were foundational, if not to the decisions of persons of Hebrew background to accept the new faith, at least to the initial stages of their life in this new obedience. Likewise, the manner in which Paul describes the decision of the Thessalonians to turn "to God from idols" (1 Thessalonians 1:9) suggests that teaching concerning the nature of one's allegiance was part of the missionary message. The clarification of the relation of John's baptism to Christian baptism was an aspect of Paul's mission at Ephesus (Acts 19:2-6). In such instances as these, teaching is a necessary concomitant of the gospel itself and is, therefore, an aspect of evangelism.

Teaching is also involved in evangelism through its role of developing the quality of discipleship needed for service in the body of Christ (Ephesians 4:11, 12; 2 Timothy 3:16, 17). All believers, as an aspect of their priestly status, share responsibility for extending the gospel (1 Peter 2:9, 10). It is important, then, that they have insight into the nature of the faith in order to be more effective in fulfilling this ministry. (1) Christian doctrine serves to clarify the nature of the gospel and the meaning of the institutions associated with it. Paul's declaration of the content of the gospel, as, for example, in Romans 3:21-31; 1 Corinthians 15:11 ff., is not intended to convert his readers but reflects the importance he lays upon correct understanding so that believers may meet the challenge of the culture, whose transformation is the task given to them. The instruction given to Apollos by Priscilla and Aquila concerning the nature of Christian baptism was aimed at increasing his effectiveness as an evangelist (Acts 18:24-28). (2) Again, the understanding of Christian teaching will help believers to answer challenges to the faith, whether in defense of their own commitment (1 Peter 3:15) or as an aspect of declaring the gospel to others, after the manner of Paul at Thessalonica (Acts 17:1-4). (3) Furthermore, the insight afforded by Christian doctrine will serve to clarify the role of the proclaimer of the good news and that of the person who is the object of that mission. For example, in his essay on regeneration, Alexander Campbell justifies his extended exposition of the process of being born again on the ground that it is needed by those "employed in the work of regenerating others"; in other words, the understanding of the process of regeneration will help delineate the proper role of proclaimers of the gospel. The theory of regeneration, as such, does not regenerate; rather it is the *"declaring of the testimony of God"* that produces faith and resultant new birth.

> I would hope . . . to be the means of regenerating one person in one year, never once naming regeneration, nor speculating upon the subject, by stating and enforcing the testimony of God, than by preaching daily the most approved theory of regeneration.[15]

However, insight into the nature of regeneration is important for the believer—in helping to clarify his task of communicating the gospel to others. The same may be said of Christian teaching in general. Rightly understood, it should better equip believers for the ministry of evangelism.

Exposition of the Nature of Faith

The most basic function of Christian doctrine, as reflected in the New Testament, is that of setting forth the nature of faith. The faith of new converts centered in the person of Christ, whom they confessed as Lord. In their obedience to this confession, believers were given new identity expressed by the phrase "in Christ." A vital factor in the growth of believers in this new identity is the understanding of the reality that had been disclosed in Christ: What did this confession suggest about such matters as the nature of His person, the nature of God, the continuing activity of God through His Spirit, God's purpose and action in history, the nature of man and of his relation to God, the meaning of salvation, the nature of the Christian community, and the outlook for the fulfillment of God's purpose (the Christian hope)? Christian doctrine addresses itself to such themes as these.

The basic ground for understanding these matters is the same. However, the basis for such understanding must, of necessity, be quite varied in view of the disparate backgrounds of those brought to a new style of living in Christ. For example, Christians of Jewish extraction had a background for understanding much of the concepts and nomenclature of the new faith because of its rootage in events of Old Testament revelation. The idea of a covenant community brought into existence through the elective grace of God and the Exodus as a redemptive event (Exodus 6:6) was quite familiar to them, but they had further need to understand the meaning of what God had now done in Jesus of Nazareth. Not often did believers of Gentile background have such a rootage for their faith. While there is evidence that the early evangelists, especially Paul, used terms familiar to the religious vocabulary of their Gentile hearers, they nonetheless set forth the understanding of the Christian faith as the culmination of what God had begun earlier in the call of Abraham.

Jesus as the Christ is for New Testament writers the hermeneutical key to understanding the being of God and His design for man, insofar as these can be understood within the limits of our being in time and space. God is the Father of our Lord Jesus Christ. God's glory has been exhibited in the life, death, burial, and resurrection of Jesus. He has wrought redemption through the Christ. He has brought into existence the community of the new covenant, given its character by its identity in Christ. He has disclosed in Christ not only the image of His own nature but also that of the nature of man, which He is at work in history to restore. The hope to which He calls man is the hope of one day being "conformed to the image of His Son" (Romans 8:29). To set forth these aspects of the nature of faith is the basic objective of Christian doctrine. This purpose is very evident in the epistles, but is evident in the Gospels as well. Although the events of the gospel preceded the church's coming into being, the Gospels were written within the context of the existing church and serve its need for instruction in the faith, as do the epistles.

There are few, if any, instances where the New Testament systematizes the teaching of the apostles on the themes listed above. Individual books are addressed to specific concerns and, hence, state only those aspects of the meaning of the faith appropriate to those needs. No New Testament book sets forth in as much detail as does Romans the relation between God's action in events of Old Testament revelation and what He has since done in Christ. Likewise, the relation of the law to the gospel is treated more fully in Romans and Galatians than elsewhere, principally because of the occasions that called forth these epistles. The nature of the person of Christ, while fundamental to all New Testament teaching, is set forth more explicitly in books such as Ephesians, Colossians, Hebrews, and 1 John than in others. Some books give greater insight into the nature of the church. We may infer that a similar difference of emphasis upon subject matter was involved in occasions of oral teaching such as that to which Paul alludes in 1 Corinthians 11:23 ff. and 15:1-4.

Defense of the Faith

Closely related to the function of setting forth the meaning of faith is that of defending the faith in its various aspects. In some respects, this is an unexpected feature of the New Testament teaching. We commonly associate apologetics with efforts to validate the truth claims of Christianity in the centuries following the apostolic age. Moreover, one would not expect to find an emphasis upon apologetics in writings addressed to persons already committed to belief in Christ. Avery Dulles has shown, however, that New Testament writings contain "reflections of the Church's efforts to exhibit the credibility of its message."[16]

Apologetical materials of the New Testament vary in content according to the types of challenges encountered by the early church. Some were directly related to the proclamation of the gospel. Believers were reassured that their faith was grounded in fact (Luke 1:1-4). The Gospels also reflect a purpose of arming believers to meet Jewish objections to the proclamation. Other apologetical materials served to strengthen the Christian life in such matters as (1) grounding believers in the tradition of Christ,[17] (2) demonstrating the superiority of the Christian system as the consummation of a process begun in the call of Abraham, and (3) resisting the "moral degradation of the pagan world" resulting from idolatry. Again, (4) an apologetic purpose was served in teaching directed against deviant tendencies in the church.[18]

The question naturally arises: can we speak of an apologetic role for Christian doctrine today? Will it be relevant in an age that poses new challenges to the Christian faith and where types of unbelief do not take the same forms as in the first century? We can answer affirmatively provided that we make due allowance for differences in the nature of the challenge. Despite the variety of circumstances and types of challenge, the element that is constant in apologetics is the faith itself. The understanding of the faith embodied in New Testament teaching provides the basic structure needed to give shape to any apologetics, whether aimed at outright rejection of the gospel or at deviations in the church resulting from capitulation to the spirit of the age in which we live.

Guidance of the Life of Faith

The uses of Christian teaching treated above share a common orientation, namely, the quality of life lived in keeping with the new identity given to men in Christ. What Jesus once said of the Sabbath may be said of Christian doctrine: it was given for the benefit of man. God uses His authority with a view to liberating man to participation in the full meaning of his creaturehood made in the image of God. The goal of redemption, of bringing man again into familial relation to God, is the restoration of that image. Becoming a Christian is not a matter of sloughing off our humanity, but of regaining it by being restored to relation to God.

Christian teaching thus functions to guide the people of God in fulfilling the stewardship given to them as a correlate of this new identity. Indeed, redemption conceived in Biblical terms as restoration of sonship may be understood as being also the recovery of stewardship (Hebrews 2:6-10)—the overcoming of the distortions that man experiences in consequence of his separation from God. The maxim "Love not the world" (1 John 2:15) does not mean the removal of oneself from involvement in the created order of existence, or the despising of that order. Rather, it means that the created order must not stand in place of God as the object of man's reverence. The alternative between idolatry (where the creature claims man's loyalty) and retreat from the world is stewardship, the use of the created order in keeping with the purpose of God. God has not relinquished His claim on the world; by His call to believers to present their bodies as a living sacrifice (Romans 12:1, 2), He is staking that claim. This point is reinforced by the fact that sonship means being an heir (Galatians 4:7; Romans 8:15-17). While the promise of the earth as an inheritance awaits eschatological consummation for its complete fulfillment, the believer lives now as an heir, guided by this expectation in his use of the temporal world. Teaching in the New Testament should be viewed as a means of guiding men in the fulfilling of this stewardship.

Another important aspect of the teaching in the New Testament is the ethical outlook given to believers. Here again the close relation of teaching and preaching is evident. There are two points of reference that serve to motivate and guide Christian behavior. One is the gospel itself. The believer has been restored to relation to God by the cross and resurrection of Jesus; moreover, he finds in Him the model of the new humanity he is urged to put on (Romans 13:14). At the same time, he looks ahead to the consummation of the potential of this relationship, which is the destiny appointed to him by the Father (Romans 8:29; Philippians 3:20, 21; 1 John 3:2). Both these foci—the gospel and the consummation—appear in New Testament teaching concerning the way of life of the believer (cf. Romans 6:3-13; Colossians 1:12, 13; 3:1-4).

Christian faith, because it is a decision to commit one's life to Christ, is an act of sanctifying oneself (Acts 26:18). This sanctification (holiness) needs to be perfected, or brought to completion (2 Corinthians 7:1). Thus, the Christian life is a growth in which one seeks to fashion his life in obedience to the new identity he has been given in Christ. Paul's travail for the Galatian Christians was that Christ be formed in them (Galatians 4:19). Much of the teaching of the New Testament is devoted to stimulating and guiding growth toward this goal.

Interpersonal relations must also bear the imprint of this new identity. Baptism into Christ creates a relationship that overcomes the barriers that history and culture develop among men (Galatians 3:27, 28; Colossians 3:9, 10). Believers must incorporate this reality into their interpersonal relations. But it is not only relations toward fellow believers that undergoes transformation. The verdict of human worth given in the gospel must affect the believer's attitude toward all men, whether or not they are members of the household of faith (Galatians 6:10). As an implication of their faith, disciples of Christ must conduct themselves toward all men in the light of the estimate God places upon them.

The implications of faith, however, apply not only to the life of believers individually but to their corporate life as well. Large portions of Scripture express concern for the life and conduct of the church as the body of Christ. While no New Testament writing is devoted to church order alone, it is also true that no one New Testament book is devoted alone to the life of believers apart from their life in the community of faith.

The teaching addressed to the church parallels that given to individual believers. On the one hand, the motivation for its conduct is similar. The church was called into being by the gospel: Christ "loved the church, and gave Himself up for it" (Ephesians 5:25). At the same time, the church lives in anticipation of the hope set before it—to be presented to Christ as "a glorious church" (Ephesians 5:27).

Teaching is directed to the church in order that it may be true to its identity as the body of Christ and thus equipped to carry out its task. The church is a fellowship; relationships within the body must reflect the fact that participation in Christ acknowledges no limitations based upon the race, social class, economic status, or sex of its members. The church is a worshiping community; its manner of observance of the ordinances must reflect the intention of Him who instituted them. The church is a commissioned community with the charge to communicate the gospel to the world; it must carry out this charge in faithfulness to the mandate given by the Lord.

The Epistle to Rome as an Example of the Role of Christian Doctrine

Because of the variety of problems and of occasions of writing of the parts of the New Testament, one does not find its teachings organized strictly along the lines suggested here, nor will many books contain all these aspects of Christian doctrine. However, one book, the epistle to the Romans, stands out as containing materials serving practically every function described above and may be cited as an example of the variety of roles served by doctrine in the New Testament.

In Romans, Paul explicitly asserts that the Christian message centers in the person of Jesus Christ (1:1-5) and the history associated with Him (10:9, 10). The gospel is the message of salvation in Christ (1:16, 17).

The major portion of Romans is devoted to setting forth the nature of the faith. The whole of chapters 3-11 may be summarized generally as explaining the relation of what God has now done in Christ to the Old Testament history of redemption. This section of the epistle also contains elements that are apologetical in purpose: the exposure of pagan idolatry (chapter 1) and answers to Jewish objections to the gospel (chapters 2, 3, 6, 7, 9-11).

Romans is concerned with evangelism 1:5, 15:14-28) and clarifies the nature of the response men make to the gospel

(10:5-17). Those sections that expound the way of salvation (chapters 5-8) give insight that serves to equip believers for participation in the task of sharing the gospel with others.

In this epistle, there is much that deals with the implications of the faith for the Christian life. It is a way of life built upon the new status of the believer (chapters 5-8), motivated by the redemptive acts of God—especially the cross (12:1, 2), with which the believer is identified by baptism (6:3-6)—and the hope of consummated salvation (13:11). Specific implications of the meaning of faith, both individual and corporate, are drawn in chapters 12-15. Here attention is given to the corporate character of the response of faith to the person and mission of Christ. As a fellowship, the church consists of persons of widely differing scruples in regard to matters of conduct and worship (chapters 14, 15). Where no instruction has been given concerning conduct in such matters, believers are free in their actions, bound only by the mandate to love and edify one another (15:1-7). The church is the body of Christ, whose several ministries function mutually to fulfill the tasks and needs of the community (12:3-8). An understanding and appreciation of Paul's authority and mission are vital to the church's participation in the mission of Christ, which has been committed to the church by the apostle (15:14-30). Moreover, the church must maintain its integrity as a community in order to carry out that mission (16:17-20).

The church today lives in circumstances quite unlike those of the first century. It is often called upon to respond to situations for which no precedent exists in the New Testament. Christian doctrine was first given in the context of first-century political, social, economic, religious arrangements and, hence, reflects aspects of that culture. This does not mean, however, that New Testament teaching is no longer relevant. It is the genius of the Christian message that it speaks to conditions of life in times and places other than those of the first-century world. In dealing with the challenge of that culture and in fulfilling its role in that world, the church was urged to shape its obedience in terms of the good news of God in Christ (the incarnation) and the identity given the church as the body of Christ. The church today, although facing a different culture, with new and different challenges, still has the same role as that given to the people of God in the beginning. It, too, must form its life—in fellowship, worship, and mission—in the light of that same identification with the gospel, of which the New Testament serves as source and norm.

NOTES

[1]Dodd's summary of the early *kerygma* includes the following particulars: (1) The dawning of the age of fulfillment foretold by the prophets, (2) which has been introduced by the death and resurrection of Jesus; (3) the exaltation of Jesus at the right hand of God; (4) the gift of the Holy Spirit "in the church" as the "sign of His present power and glory;" (5) the consummation of the present age in the return of Christ; (6) the "appeal for repentance, the offer of forgiveness, the gift of the Spirit, and the promise of salvation." *Apostolic Preaching and its Developments* (New York: Willet, Clark and Co., 1937), pp. 25-29.

[2]This is the position of Robert C. Worley, *Preaching and Teaching in the Earliest Church* (Philadelphia: Westminster Press, 1967). Worley also gives a helpful summary of the wide range of responses to C. H. Dodd in the first thirty years following the appearance of the latter's work on this subject.

[3]Examples of attempts to deal with this question follow: William Baird, "What is the Kerygma? A Study of I Corinthians 15:3-8 and Galatians 1:11-17," *Journal of Biblical Literature*, LXXXVI (1957), pp. 182-191; Jurgen Moltman, *The Church in the Power of the Spirit* (New York: Harper and Row, 1977), p. 210; Wolfgang Pannenberg, "Dogmatic Theses on the Doctrine of Revelation," *Revelation as History* (New York: Macmillan, 1969), p. 155.

[4]Alexander Campbell, N. L. Rice, *Debate on Christian Baptism* (Lexington: 1844), p. 435.

[5]Alexander Campbell, *The Christian System* (Cincinnati: **Standard**), p. 91.

[6]Alexander Campbell, "The Voice of God and the Word of God," *Millenial Harbinger* (1830), p. 124.

[7]Campbell, *Christian System*, p. 101.

[8]See Thomas Campbell, *Declaration and Address*, propositions 6-8.

[9]Alexander Campbell, "Letters to England—No. II," *Millennial Harbinger* (1837), pp. 317, 318.

[10]Campbell, *Christian System*, p. 6. Elsewhere Campbell is even more emphatic in defending the above distinction between proclamation and teaching. See his "Address at the Annual Meeting of the Christian Missionary Society" (1857), *Popular Lectures and Addresses*, pp. 536, 537.

¹¹Albrecht Oepke declares that the boundary line between missionary preaching and later instruction "is clearly the decision of the hearers to receive the faith." *Die Missionpredigt des Apostels Paulus,* p. 9, cited by Johannes Munck, "The Missionary Preaching of Paul," *New Testament Studies* 9, 2 (Jan., 1963), pp. 95-110.

¹²Cf. Jochaim Jeremias, *Sermon on the Mount,* tr. Norman Perrin (London: 1961), p. 21.

¹³Floyd Filson, *Three Crucial Decades* (Richmond: John Knox Press, 1963), p. 42.

¹⁴Altogether, Paul uses the term *faith* in five distinguishable ways: (1) personal commitment to Jesus as Lord (Rom. 10:9, 10); (2) one's role in the body of Christ (Rom. 12:3, 4); (3) confidence in the propriety of one's behavior in matters of indifference where no mandate has been given (Rom. 14:22); (4) miracle-working faith (1 Cor. 12:9; cf. 13:2); (5) faith as designating the new covenant (Gal. 3:23; 25; 4:21-31).

¹⁵Campbell, *Christian System,* p. 239.

¹⁶Avery Dulles, *A History of Apologetics* (Philadelphia: The Westminister Press, 1971), p. 19.

¹⁷See F. F. Bruce, "The Kerygma of Hebrews," *Interpretation* XXIII, 1 (Jan., 1969), p. 15.

¹⁸Dulles, *History of Apologetics,* p. 12. Chapter I of this work gives a helpful analysis of the types of apologetics and their respective roles.

CHAPTER

2

THE WORD OF GOD

By Fred P. Thompson, Jr.

Christian faith rests squarely on the conviction that God has revealed its nature and truth. The church has always rejected the view that the prophets and apostles can be accounted for solely in terms of genius. These men and women are believed to have been in a special way confronted by God and addressed by Him. Their message came from beyond themselves by revelation from the Spirit of God. Biblical faith is grounded on objective data, not merely on the noble insight of gifted seers and mystics.

God's self-revelation cannot be authentic if it never really took place in history. To interpret the language reporting revelatory events as description of subjective experiences without counterpart in objective reality is to becloud and confuse the issue. "Revelation" does not refer to states of mind or feeling, but to world-changing disclosures made by God to man. These disclosures are intensely personal in nature, of course, since He is the supreme Person and since He makes himself known to persons. But they have an *event* character that distinguishes them in significant ways from purely subjective imaginings.

These revelatory events were described and their meaning interpreted by members of the Hebrew and Christian communities, who committed their message to writing. Scribes, prophets, apostles, and other human beings participated in this historical process. It has always been the faith of the church that the Holy Spirit superintended this long process by which canonical Scriptures came into existence. As the apostle Peter puts it, "No prophecy was ever made by an act of human will, but men moved by the Holy Spirit spoke from God" (2 Peter 1:21). Thus, what was recorded by these holy men is, indeed, more than a mere record of certain occasions in Hebrew history. It is the inspired and living Word of God.

So we take note of the fact that *Word of God* is the characteristic Judaeo-Christian expression by which revelatory phenomena are distinguished from religious experiences and numinous feelings. Something comes to a person from outside his own psyche. Something is given and received. What that "something" is we must inquire into. In the Scriptures of the Hebrew and Christian traditions, the expression *Word of God* takes the reader at once into the sphere of revelation. It refers to a reality that is not a human invention.

The Nature of Language

To identify with some degree of preciseness the Word of God requires a brief consideration of the nature of language and the function of words. God's Word reaches us through human words. We ought, therefore, to know how words are used in the communication of truth and meaning.

Conventional wisdom holds that language is merely the clothing worn by ideas in their communicable form. Forms of speech, composition, and grammar are determined by the application of logic to language. Words are useful, if arbitrary, things that have no intrinsic relation to being, that is, no ontic reality. They are scarcely more than labels to which the human community assigns stipulated meanings for the sake of communication.

Contemporary linguistic study shows this understanding of language, words, to be inadequate. Words and being are inextricably and consequentially related.[1] Every schoolboy knows the power of the teacher's spoken reprimand to embarrass and humilate, as well as the exhilarating effect of words of praise. Life is enhanced or devalued by the impact of cheering or chiding words from those we respect. Words are agents through which the world comes to us and we affect the world.

God spoke—the heavens and the earth appeared. God spoke—and light expunged the darkness. By His Word, God brought into being the created order. Word and being have been linked together ever since. The definitive manifestation of that linkage is the Word (Logos) made flesh in Jesus Christ, God's only begotten Son. Incarnation signifies, among other things, the readiness of God to use human elements as conduits of the divine message of redemption.

Indispensable among these elements is language, words, which the incarnation credentials as capable of mediating reality and truth to human consciousness. One of the marks of this capacity is the power of language to make the past present. When we observe the Lord's Supper, we do not think the present tense of the verb inappropriate: "This is my body." The word of Scripture and symbol speaks of a present communion of believers with the living Lord. Historical fact and present reality merge in the everlasting contemporaneity of the Word.

Language has many genres and many uses (as Ludwig Wittgenstein has pointed out[2]). We know the meaning of a word by observing how it is used in context.[3] The reader is obliged to consider the intent and concern of the writer if he is to understand the message. For language is rooted in experience—it is more than a sign or a mere verbal correspondence to a real entity. Language is not primarily descriptive but relational. It brings about encounter with a subject, establishing a relationship between persons (as Gerhard Ebeling has observed[4]). This interpersonal bond created by words sent forth and received constitutes the primary means by which we come to know persons.

It needs also to be noted that language is not just one art among many. Language is the fundamental art through which all other arts, skills, and truth are learned. It is the medium in and through which all other teaching and learning takes place, the element in which they live.[5] But even when vocabulary is stretched as far as erudition can reach in an effort to convey feelings or emotional experiences, we are aware of the fact that some things lie too deep in our hearts for words to express. So we make words point to more than they can actually say, to suggest what cannot be described.

All of this we must keep in mind when we come to consider what Christians mean when they speak of the "Word of God." Words are rich, creative, and mysterious. It is a mistake to assume that we know exactly what words are, what language is, simply because we have consulted a dictionary and a textbook on grammar. We are obliged to take into account the whole of human experience if we are to make sense of the phenomenon of human language.

Nevertheless, if we are willing to make the effort, the linguistic deposit that marks the story of human cultures will open to us its treasures. Of no document, or set of documents, is this more true or important than of the Bible, God's written Word. Holy Scripture is the inspired account in language that all can understand, with appropriate seriousness of purpose, of God's history-long program of world redemption.

The Strangeness of the Word

All words used by human beings are empirical entities. They are of this world. Every child learns to speak a human language. There are no words from a Heavenly sphere, distinct in size and shape from the mundane words he hears. He always encounters a human word.

Even when the child is taught about transcendent realities—God, Christ, Holy Spirit, angels—ordinary mortal language is used. He is told the Christmas story in English, German, Chinese, or some other living language spoken by Mother and Father. The words which describe God's entry into historical time and space are plain human words.

How do plain human words come to be received as the "Word of God"? Karl Rahner has suggested that

1. This symbol (Word of God) refers to the cognitive encounters between God and man in which His person and will are revealed. In other words, it refers to God's self-revealing acts in history.

2. Word of God means the presence of God with His creatures in ways which convey meaning and offer support. God discloses himself as benevolently disposed toward His children.

3. Word of God stands for the manifestation of God's power to heal and save His human children. Revelation has centrally to do with redemption.

4. Word of God points to the givenness of our knowledge of God. We do not discover God by human wisdom. God comes to us and speaks His word to us.[6]

What "Word of God" Implies

(a) The term *word* means that God speaks. He is not

forever silent. The mystery of eternity is not unrelieved. His word takes historical physical form.

(b) God *spoke*, reminding us that the Hebrews were an auditory culture. Speech preceeded writing. Memory performed the functions of script in the Hebrew community. Greek culture, in comparison, was visually orientated. Sight was the Greeks' principal sense by which knowledge was obtained.

(c) In the Old Testament, God calls, addresses man, through His word *heard*. The sensation is specifically an auditory one. This is especially seen in the prophets. The word here is not merely a written transcript of a message written down, but a living phenomenon, a sound inducing to action.[7]

(d) In ancient oral-aural culture, stories were remembered and passed down for generations with remarkable accuracy. The story varies little in the retelling, but the words always do. That is, the essential character of the story remains unchanged although linguistic variations occur in each telling. Verbatim memory is not as important as thematic memory in these cultures.

(e) This phenomenon is difficult for us to understand because of centuries of dependence on the written word in society. In order to have a reliable record of transactions and happenings, we trust the record to paper and ink. Our skill in subtlety, bending and twisting the meaning of words when it suits our purpose to circumvent their original intention (as in legal contests and religious debate), makes us deeply suspicious of purely oral tradition. We increasingly require the exact words of documents to be put in evidence before we will accept them.

(f) However, having the exact words does not necessarily mean that one has the exact meaning of the author. Our understanding in the present depends upon the current use of the language involved. But that language may have undergone considerable change in the course of the centuries. As Walter Ong has noted, "The word as record depends for its meaning upon the continuous recurrence of the word as event."[8]

(g) Sound conveys meaning more accurately and powerfully than sight. Written words are more likely to be misunderstood than spoken words. We convey much of ourselves in speech. Not only the word, the verbal form, but the inflection of the voice, the intonation, and the volume all give clues to the meaning of the message being communicated. The spoken word thus has more power than the written word to do what the word is meant to do—to communicate. Far less ambiguity is possible in the encounter in which speech and hearing occur than in the encounter of the eye with the printed page.[9]

(h) Words reduced to writing become objects in space, one remove from actuality. They are thus less real—less active—than when spoken. Words with sound (presence) are more real than written words. They have a persuasive power that far exceeds that of script. I am sure this is the reason for the emphasis on preaching in the New Testament. God's good news is most effectively presented by the human voice, the sound of which is received by other ears.

Still, no rational person expects God to repeat for every generation the decisive revelatory acts in which His redemption is made known to man. The record of those acts is kept in the memory of mankind. It is also committed to writing in order that a reliable transcript of testimony to the saving acts of God may be available to all future generations. This process is guided by the Holy Spirit, who insures that the end-product is not a human word but is in very truth God's Word. It is on the basis of what is written that the contemporary generation preaches the Word of God in order that men may hear as well as read the good news.

But before writing, in historical sequence, came the deed. The "Word of God" is in the first instance the act of God.

God's Word as God's Act

Scripture often uses *word* to refer to a historical event seen as God's act. In the dramatic acts in which God himself is engaged, disclosure of God's character and purpose takes place. When inspired men and women understand this disclosure as an action of God, revelation occurs. Revelation then takes the form of words spoken in interpretation of the event under the inspiration of the Spirit of God and, when appropriate, includes the preservation of the revelatory disclosure in writing.

Texts that combine the act and word of God in a single process abound in the Bible. For example, in Psalm 33:6-9 it is stated,

> By the word of the Lord the heavens were made, and by the breath of His mouth all their host. He gathers the waters of the sea as a heap;

He lays up the deeps in storehouses. Let all the earth fear the Lord, let all the inhabitants of the world stand in awe of Him! For He spoke, and it was done; He commanded, and it stood fast.

Here God's Word is the instrument of His creative work. The event described is that in which our known universe was given existence by the divine word. Speech and being are here linked in the primordial occasion of creation. By God's Word creative, the earth stood forth; and by God's Word written, we know of that unique event.

In a different context, Psalm 107:20 recalls the merciful ministration of God to the wandering Hebrew tribes after their release from Egypt. Some of them became sick and God "sent forth His word and healed them, and delivered them from their destructions." The Word of God was His gracious act of healing.

In the prayer dedicating the temple he had built to the glory of the Lord, Solomon refers to the faithfulness of God to his father David. He acknowledges that God has kept His covenant and showed steadfast love to His servants. Then He says, "Thou hast spoken with Thy mouth, and hast fulfilled it with Thy hand as it is this day" (1 Kings 8:24). Note the linking of the divine speech with the action of the divine hand. What God says, He does; and what he does reveals who He is. His word of explanation makes this clear.

The Pentecostal event following the resurrection of Jesus gave opportunity to the company of Jesus' disciples to preach the gospel to great multitudes of Jews from many lands. Precisely what all the apostles spoke after the descent of the Holy Spirit upon them we do not know. Luke gives us a brief outline of the address of one of them, Simon Peter, on that occasion. But before Peter began to speak, the multi-lingual crowd had its attention arrested by an astonishing linguistic phenomenon: tongues of fire descending on the apostolic company. In Acts 2:11, these Jews of the dispersion remark, "We hear them in our own tongues speaking of the mighty deeds of God." The gospel of salvation and the works of God mesh in splendid inextricability. The good news of grace and the mighty works of God are one reality. Together they constitute the Word of God.

These texts and many others of similar character make it quite clear that the Word of God is a dynamic event. It is not the naked speech of metaphysical information, nor is it simply a series of propositional statements that convey divine truths and injunctions in abstraction from the real life of history. The word of God is alive and active, as the writer of Hebrews reminds us (Hebrews 4:12).

G. Ernest Wright has demonstrated that because it is the Word of God given through historical acts of grace and judgment, the Bible cannot be reduced to a philosophy of values, as modernism tended to do.[10] Nor is it properly understood as a compendium of religious truths and maxims, propositions and commandments, non-historically understood and applied without reference to historical data, as in the case of much contemporary fundamentalism. The Bible is neither a source text for idealist philosophy nor a Christian Koran.

On the contrary, the Word of God normally accompanies historical events and interprets them. If we are to understand the Bible as the Word of God, then, we must give primary attention to history. Every bit of information we can glean about the historical circumstances in which God acted and spoke, judging or redeeming His people, is germane to our proper understanding of His Word. Professor Wright says,

> While dealing with actual events and traditions, Biblical history is centered in its Creator and Director. By means of human agents God provides each event with an accompanying word of interpretation, so that the latter is an integral part of the former, and both together serve as the guide to the understanding of future events. God is thus known by what He has done. The so-called 'attributes' of God are inferences drawn from the way He has acted. His righteousness, justice, love, grace, jealousy, and wrath are not abstractions with which we are to deal abstractly—that is, apart from history. They are all descriptive of the way God has directed history; and hence it is inferred that they all find their unity in Him.[11]

We come to know who God is by what He has done. This is the reason for the large space given to narrative in the Scriptures. God's plan to redeem mankind is unfolded in the history of a special people chosen to be messengers of His truth and grace to the whole world. The recital of the acts of God contained in these Scriptures is an indispensable component of the Word of God. Israel's faith in God was a response to His word-acts in electing and directing them as His witnesses in the world. Their confession of God's name was a recital of their story (cf. Deuteronomy).

This Biblical story is the context for, as God is the source of, all ethical and religious teachings contained in the Biblical accounts. Prophets were raised up from time to time in order to denounce, challenge, prophesy, and instruct God's people in the matrix of the events of their immediate and more remote past. The ongoing march of historical events demonstrated the faithfulness or infidelity of God's people to their Lord. These factors determined the tenor of the prophetic word at any given time and colored the way this word was heard. God has always treated history as real and our participation in the continuing life of mankind as genuine. All human beings, whether Jews, Christians, Muslims, or whatever, are called to live out their lives in the sphere of the time-space world. Whatever God does by way of redemption or revelation, by deed or by word, He does for us within this framework.

God's Word comes to man in the form of address whereby He enters into vital relationship with His creatures. As address, God's Word is confrontation, meeting—an agonizingly disquieting experience. The divine intention and will is conveyed with a directness that disturbs us.

The Word of God penetrates to the depths of our existence. It is an existential word, which questions the quality and value of our lives. It is not concerned with theoretical questions but with the question of our being and acting in the world. The Word judges our selfishness and parochial vision.

The Word of God establishes again the original relationship between God and man. This is its reconciling purpose and character. By the Word of God, we are turned toward Him and brought once again into His fellowship. The restoration of the purpose of creation is accomplished by the Word

The Word of God is God's pledge of himself to be man's future—His pledge to meet man on his way through time as the End of all times. His Word is the fulfillment of our lives. It is the final word by which assessment of ourselves is undertaken and the correction of our course through time is made. It is the Word that welcomes us when we come to the end of the way.

Jesus as the Word of God

In the well-known prologue to John's Gospel, Jesus is presented as the eternal *Logos* or Word of God becoming incarnate and entering into the history of the world. He is the Word made historical person. His functions as the Word of God may be set forth quite simply.

First, it is He who declares the Father. To look into the face of Jesus is to see what God is like. The infinite and Wholly Other condescends to our finitude and sinfulness, coming within reach of our senses. Jesus opens up for us sinners access to the Father in faith. He is and speaks the word of grace and salvation.

Second, it is He who proclaims the kingdom of God. To be sure, it is a strange kingdom with a single, comprehensive law, the law of love. The kingdom has no policemen to coerce, intimidate, or incarcerate the guilty. "My kingdom is not of this world" (John 18:36).

The expression "kingdom of God" speaks of the nearness of God's rule. The phrase suggests the joy of imminent meeting with the Father and entering into the new creation that is being fashioned by Jesus Christ.

Further, "the kingdom of God" speaks of the clarity of God's will as it is made known in Jesus Christ. Two aspects of Jesus' kingdom teaching are especially noteworthy: (1) He taught the necessity of going beyond the demands of the law, and (2) He taught as one having authority. His teachings are simply stated and easily understood, though exceedingly demanding in performance.

Third, the kingdom of God voices a call to discipleship. This is the unique summons of Christian faith. We are called to be with Christ, to follow Christ, to learn of Him. In His close fellowship, we experience joy, freedom, and the absence of anxiety.

It is to these splendid particulars that Jesus witnesses as the true and faithful witness of God.

Jesus as the Word is also the basis of faith. He is seen and declared to be the Son and Word of God by His resurrection from the dead. The resurrection is a historical event. The same Jesus who was crucified has now been raised from the dead and lives forever. In raising Him from the dead, God validates the word of the cross—the message of grace and judgment that the cross silently utters.

The incarnation, ministry in behalf of the kingdom, death, and resurrection of Jesus constitute a new Word spoken by God to the condition of man. This is the final Word of salvation God utters. All the words of the Old Testament have no more than penultimate character in relation to this ultimate and decisive Word spoken in the life and deeds of Jesus Christ, the incarnate Word. This Word fulfills and transcends and judges all previous words spoken by God and heard by men. It does not make those words untrue, but it does show them to be incomplete disclosures of the truth of God and His will for human life. Now that the perfect light has come, the broken and flickering lamps by which we previously discerned our way through the maze of historical circumstance are seen to be preliminary provisions of limited usefulness. Their truth remains, but it is now taken up and infinitely enlarged in the great flawless light of the personal Word of God, who assumed flesh and dwelt among us.

Scripture—the Word of God Written

The supreme treasure of written language lies in the commitment to writing of the history-borne Word of God. The Bible is, contains, and becomes the Word of God. It *is* the Word of God because it faithfully presents the words spoken by God to and through holy men and women. It *contains* the Word of God within a story inclusive of the words and ideas of other beings, Satan himself among them. It *becomes* the Word of God in that some who hear it (or read it) become convicted by the Holy Spirit and open their minds to receive its good news of redemption. Of the one unchanging Word of God all this is affirmed. The Bible *is* true, and it becomes true *for me* when I perceive the saving truth.

Holy Scripture is God's Word in man's language (as Eugene Nida reminds us[12]). Not only language must be considered, but historical circumstance also, if we are properly to receive the Word. Revelation attested in the Biblical accounts was always communicated in specific times to specific people on specific occasions. There are no timeless truths in Scripture (i.e., truths that are unrelated to the temporal process). There are truths given in time that endure through time. There are truths that precede time and outlast time—the preexistence of Christ and the ascension of Christ, for example. But all Scriptural truth is time-related and circumstanced. We have to know the times and circumstances, the words and ideas, the concerns and problems, the politics and art, of the particular people to whom the Word of God came in the first instance if we are discerningly to hear it in our own time. More attention will be given this matter in the discussion of hermeneutics.

The Inspiration of Scripture

Christians have always distinguished the Bible from other literature by acknowledging its inspiration by the Holy Spirit. They have not always agreed on the nature and purpose of this inspiration. Canonical writings claim to issue from God's initiative in addressing man. Precisely what is involved in that communication process is the subject of hot debate in contemporary theology.

The Christian theologians of the second and third centuries, e.g., Athenagoras, Clement, and Origen, affirmed the inspiration of the Biblical books but were mainly interested in the doctrine as it concerned the Old Testament: how does the church maintain the importance of the Old Testament for its own life? This question prompted their consideration of the source of these documents, which they agreed was God. Athenagoras held that "the prophets 'spoke out what they were in travail with, their own reasoning falling into abeyance and the Spirit making use of them as a flutist might play upon his flute.' "[13]

Clement of Alexandria spoke of the prophets as "the organs of the divine voice."[14] Origen also believed that the inspiration of the true prophets made them "the organs of the divine voice."[15] Prophetic writings were thus called "sacred books."[16] Both the literary works and the persons of the prophets were understood to be inspired. God, therefore, is the real author of Scripture; the prophets are only His instruments. In Justin Martyr, the bare instrumentality of the prophets and other inspired writers of Scripture is very strongly stated. The human participation in the production of the Bible is purely mechanical, consisting of recording words spoken to men by God.[17]

R. P. C. Hanson has called attention to the effort of Origen to come to a more comprehensive understanding of Biblical inspiration without surrendering confidence in its divine character and authority. In place of a dictation theory, Origen contends that the writers "voluntarily and consciously collaborated with the word that came to them."[18] Inspired New Testament writers could and did express their own opinions, and, at least in the case of the Gospel of John, described events from their own point of view. In this way, Origen sought to account for the differences in the gospel narratives. He further distinguished between that which was revealed in the New Testament documents and commentary on that disclosure by

50

the inspired writer. Origen, thus, was one of the earliest Christian thinkers to discern both the divine and human aspects of Scripture and to insist on an examination of the texts themselves (in their total context) as essential to understanding how these aspects are related.

Little attention was given to the question of inspiration from the time of the Fathers to the Reformation. Thomas Aquinas wrote at some length on the subject but did not move the discussion along to any great degree. Inspiration meant, for him, the empowering by God of apostles and prophets in such a way as to enhance their own faculties. Divine enlightenment enabled the inspired spokesmen to know God's truth and to make it a part of their own awareness. Thomas, it should be noted, was more concerned with the grace of prophecy than with the inspiration of Scripture.[19]

Not until 1870 was there an official statement of a General Council of the Roman Catholic Church on the nature of the inspiration of Scripture. The First Vacation Council issued in that year the following statement, amplifying the brief words of Trent:

> The Church holds [these books] to be sacred and canonical not, indeed, because having been prepared by human industry alone they were later approved by her authority; nor only because they contain revelation without error; but because having been written under the inspiration of the Holy Spirit they have God as their author, and as such they have been committed to the Church.[20]

There can be little doubt that this pronouncement comes down solidly in favor of the view of inspiration called "verbal."

Reformation understanding of the nature of Scripture does not appear to differ markedly from this Catholic dogma. Luther speaks frequently of the Bible as the book of the Holy Spirit.[21] Calvin termed the writers of Scripture "secretaries of the Holy Ghost."[22] As Roland Bainton has observed, "Calvin could speak of the 'style' of the Holy Ghost."[23]

Neither Luther nor Calvin, however, believed that inspiration insured the correctness of Scriptural narrative in every minute detail. Both were careful and honest Biblical scholars who recognized that textual problems in the Bible do exist. An example of the kind of difficulty Luther noted is the speech of Stephen recorded in Acts 7 compared with the Genesis account

(Genesis 46). Luther simply acknowledged the problem but affirmed his confidence in the testimony of Scripture to the salvation wrought by God in Christ. He saw no need to suspend faith until all questions of harmony were resolved. Calvin took a similar position, refusing to hold the Holy Spirit responsible for every misplaced "yod" or tittle.[24] In any case, both knew that such problems constituted only a fraction of the vast material in Scripture and none was of doctrinal importance.

The followers of Luther did not follow their leaders in this perception, however. By the seventeenth century, they had hardened their position on Scripture into a five-point creed as follows: (1) the text of the Bible was regarded as infallibly authoritative in and of itself. (2) The Bible was received as the literal Word of God. Human "authors" participated only as stenographers for the Holy Spirit. (3) Every minute particular of the Bible—every word, letter, and vowel point—was given by God. Nothing was contributed by human intelligence. (4) The Bible speaks with infallible authority on such matters as geography, science, and history as well as religion and ethics. It is accurate and truthful in everything it reports and records. (5) All parts of the Bible are equally inspired and equally authoritative. One could appeal to any text to prove a relevant doctrinal point.[25]

Both Roman Catholic and Protestant views on the inspiration of Scripture as insuring the infallibility of the text thus became orthodox dogma in the post-Reformation era. With the advent of historical and textual criticism in the nineteenth and twentieth centuries, important modifications of this understanding of inspiration developed.

Alexander Campbell's thinking on inspiration and the nature of Scripture clearly differs from the Biblical positivism of the seventeenth century. Campbell had a high view of Scripture. He regarded the Bible as "but a specific embodiment of the Holy Spirit."[26] He spoke often of Scripture as the word (or oracles) of God. There is no doubt about his complete confidence in the Bible as the inspired record of God's revelation of His will through the history of Israel and, especially, through His Son, Jesus Christ.

But he would have had difficulty with the Lutheran statement cited above. Campbell recognized the inescapable mingling of human and divine elements in the articulation of God's Word. Words are human things. They are not perfect or infallible. Yet God speaks to His prophets through words. How else can cognitive (informational) communication take place? Further, Campbell saw the large place history occupies in divine disclosure. He did not think inspiration affected the writers of historical and factual material except to sharpen their memories.

Verbal discrepancies in parallel Biblical accounts did not bother Campbell. For him, revelation was the communication of supernatural truth. Inspiration by the Holy Spirit was the only possible source for this kind of information. Here even the words used were taught the writers by the Spirit. But in all other kinds of Scriptural data, the words are those of human beings deriving from the vocabularies of the many different writers. Their message, in the latter case, is entirely true and trustworthy even though verbal details are not always perceived as entirely accurate. He thought it completely natural, and to be expected, that the Gospels should differ from each other.[27]

Historical study of the documents comprising Scripture has greatly accelerated since Campbell's time. And this study has largely supported the understanding of inspiration with which he worked. We now have a much firmer grasp on the *historical* character of revelation, with all that implies for written records. To be truly historical means to be a genuine part of the ongoing human experience. Historicity does not eliminate the miraculous, despite Bultmann and his school. But historical criteria do insist on the intelligible relationship of miracle to history since history is the arena in which God's purposes are being worked out. Contemporary scholars also call attention to the economy of the supernatural (miraculous) in historical manifestation, God obviously preferring to work through ordinary (natural) processes wherever possible.

Just as inspiration did not absolve Paul from the necessity of hard thinking, so it need not be postulated that inspiration miraculously cleanses Scripture of all that is human and lifts the whole canon to the status of supernatural literature. God inspired (breathed on) men through the Holy Spirit to proclaim and preserve His Word. The literary deposit of the Word that we call Scripture is an astonishingly reliable and thoroughly authentic record of revelation history.

Liberal scholars have accepted Hume's analogical argument that since miracles do not occur in the present time, we may safely assume that they never occurred in any past time, either. Eliminating the miraculous in this way eliminates revelation as well. The Bible is reduced to the story of the Hebrews' quest for God and the development of religious rites and ceremonies as part of that quest. God has not spoken and Jesus has not been raised from the dead.

Conservative scholars affirm with one voice belief in the miraculous delivery of Israel from Egypt, the miraculous entry into history of the Son of God, and the miracle of inspiration in the creation of Holy Scripture. Conservatives are not of one mind on the nature of the inspiration of Scripture, however.

Some hold that the Holy Spirit is literally the author of every word and sentence in the Bible. The Spirit has accomplished this work through men whose vocabularies and experiences differ widely, which accounts for the various literary styles in the Biblical documents. Facts to be recorded are selected by the Spirit, who dictates the exact words He wishes preserved. Thus harmonizable differences in parallel accounts are easily explained. This view does not appear to most scholars, including conservative ones, adequately to explain the complex data that is Scripture.

Other Christian scholars of conservative convictions hold that inspiration by the Holy Spirit takes place in a thoroughly historical way. Paul wrestles with the problems of the church in Corinth in a way familiar to every faithful minister. Out of his concern, the Corinthian correspondence arises, a correspondence in which advice and counsel, rebuke and instruction, are given on a number of important matters. Some of Paul's words sound conventional and pedestrian. Some are erudite and intensely thought-provoking. All are *inspired* by the Holy Spirit, but none is dictated. Neither Paul nor any other inspired writer of Scripture was an automaton. This view is held by a large number of evangelical Christians in all denominations.

A third viewpoint stands somewhat in between the positions just described. It rejects the dictation theory but holds firmly to the conviction that inspiration insured the Biblical writers against error. Every statement in the Bible, whether of revelational import or of geographical, biological, historical, or any other matters, is true and accurate. The Scripture is without mistake. Whether this view is compatible with the facts is a question hotly debated in conservative Christian circles.

The opinions of equally devout persons may vary on the question of the nature of inspiration. Nevertheless, every Christian is happy to affirm with Paul that, "All Scripture is inspired by God and profitable for teaching, for reproof, for correction, and for training in righteousness, that the man of God may be adequate, equipped for every good work" (2 Timothy 3:16, 17).

The Authority of the Bible

Christians confess Jesus Christ as Lord, i.e., as the Sovereign Authority for their lives. The life and teaching of Jesus command us. All authority both in Heaven and on earth has been given to Him by God the Father (Matthew 28:18).

Scripture is the vehicle through which that authority is exercised in the church and in personal discipleship. We have no way of knowing the truth of Christ except as it is declared in the testimony of the apostles. Encounter theology (Brunner, Bultmann, et al) admirably stresses the importance of being confronted by the living Christ. What this theology does not make clear is how this may occur if we dispense with the witness of His words in the Gospels. Existentialist approaches to faith are notoriously fragile at the point of cognitive (meaningful) content. Unless God speaks and we understand the message, "encounter" is little more than numinous feeling.

Religious experience is an essential component of the life of faith. In fact, the entire Christian pilgrimage is a religious experience. But it is an informed experience, one in which intelligent obedience is offered to the Lord, whose will has been disclosed in the inspired literature of the New Testament. We are instructed by the Word, not merely warmed by glowing religious connotations.

If I have spoken in the above paragraphs of the importance of information in the New Testament writings (the apostolic witness), the same considerations prevail for the Old Testament records (the prophetic witness). The Scriptures of both covenants are inspired by the same Spirit and testify to the one salvation offered by God to the world through Jesus Christ. It is no more rational to reject the authority of the Old Testament as the word of God written than it is to reject the authority of the New Testament. In the unfolding of the divine drama of redemption, both Covenants play indispensable, authoritative roles.

Moses, Isaiah, and Paul all recognized their relationship to the Word as vehicular, not creative. The message they spoke and wrote was not invented in their remarkable intellects. God was the real source of their words. Canonical Scripture has been thought of in this way by both Jews (re. the Old Testament) and Christians (re. the entire Bible). Jesus himself referred often to Old Testament texts with the respect normally reserved for divine essentialities (Matthew 21:42; 22:29; 26:54; Luke 24:27; John 5:39). Paul established his claim to be heard on the ground that the gospel he proclaimed and the apostolate he received were authentic precisely because they did not issue from a human source, but from the Lord himself (Galatians 1:12-16).[28]

Paul's testimony, like that of every Biblical spokesman, is authoritative because it was inspired by the Holy Spirit. In the second epistles of Timothy and Peter, the reliability and edifying character of Scripture (authority) are ascribed to the inspiring Spirit (2 Timothy 3:16, 17; 2 Peter 1:20, 21). Thus, the inspiration and authority of Scripture are twin articles of doctrine in the Christian understanding of the Bible.

To affirm the authority of Scripture, however, is not to settle all theological problems. Every reader has the responsibility to interpret the text intelligently, appropriately, and in harmony with the writer's intention, so far as that may be discovered. The Bible is a kind of constitution for the church, authoritative and true, but subject to interpretations that often cause sharp controversy among those who acknowledge its authority. For this reason, it appears to be futile to call for unity among Christians on the basis of Scripture alone. Nearly every denominational group in Christendom holds the Bible to be its ground and guide. Some consensus on the indispensable elements of Biblical teaching in contrast to those matters on which opinions may harmlessly vary is needed (see chapter 3).

Nevertheless, the objective and changeless document, Holy Scripture, remains the authoritative source of Christian doctrine, the indefectible expression of the will of God for His creatures. It is an authoritative record of God's call of Israel. It is an authoritative presentation of the Law of God through Moses. It is an authoritative witness to the gospel of Jesus Christ. It is an authoritative history of the origins and development of the apostolic church. The Bible has no competition as the literary vehicle of divine grace and truth.

C. H. Dodd, the brilliant British New Testament scholar,

ended his work on *The Authority of the Bible* with the statement, "If the Bible is indeed 'the Word of God,' it is so not as the 'last word' on all religious questions, but as the 'seminal word' out of which fresh apprehension of truth springs in the mind of man."[29] This judgment is the logical deduction from reasoning based on the premise that revelation is a continuing phenomenon. I think that premise must be rejected, at least in the way Dodd conceived it. Revelation as the exhibit in history of God's deeds and will, confirmed in the faithful and true witness of Holy Scripture, is complete. God's last Word in time has been spoken. This is not to dispute, however, the contention that new light—new understanding—will continue to break forth from that Word as long as reverent and thoughtful persons attend diligently to it.

Hermeneutics—the Interpretation of Scripture
It is one thing to contend for the authoritative character of the Bible. It is something else to secure agreement on the meaning of disputed texts. How is this difficulty to be overcome? And how is the church to hear in its own time the word spoken in an ancient time and under very different circumstances? What is the relation between what Isaiah said and what God is now saying through Isaiah's words? These are hermeneutical questions with which every reader of Scripture deals in one way or another.

Obviously the "books" of the Bible come to us from a time and culture remote and foreign to modern eyes. Polygamous marriages, laws concerning the clean and unclean, distinctions between strange fire and holy fire, sanctuaries in which one section was off-limits to almost all worshipers—these sound strange and primitive to our ears. Yet they were familiar matters to the early Hebrews. In the context of such phenomena, God spoke to and through the prophets.

Historical context thus must be inquired into carefully if we are to apprehend the original meaning of Biblical texts to those for whose sake they were written in the first place. This kind of study is necessary if we are to come within an "understanding distance" of Scripture, to use Alexander Campbell's phrase.[30] Every possible piece of information on the political, social, economic, and religious ideas and conditions that obtained when the text under consideration was written is germane to the interpreter's task. Biblical literature arose at particular times and places, each segment having its own purpose and meaning. Historical and literary criticism of the relevant texts and backgrounds equip the contemporary student with invaluable aids for understanding the ancient documents. Language study and translation play their significant roles in providing access to the Bible for those who cannot read Hebrew, Aramaic, and Greek, since no part of Scripture was originally written in English.

All of the legitimate tools of Biblical scholarship must be employed in a serious effort to establish the text of Scripture and to determine its original meaning. We are indebted to a host of specialists who have worked for centuries to develop reliable data in the light of which sound hermeneutical study may proceed. Archaeological, linguistic, geological, anthropological, and a host of other scientific investigations have clarified the picture of the world of the Bible, which now lies before our eyes in sharper detail than in any previous time. All of this information greatly enhances the interpreter's art.

One problem that has perplexed many Protestants is the proper use of the Old Testament in the church. Is the Old Testament still the Word of God? Or are Protestants secret followers of Marcion, the second century heretic who rejected the Old Testament? Do we say nice things about Moses and the prophets but, in fact, ignore the Old Testament in our discipleship? Obviously, if one thinks all sixty-six books of the Bible equally authoritative and relevant for the Christian life, there is no theoretical problem. Practically, however, problems are piled upon problems in this view. No Christian group seriously tries to obey all the Old Testament laws. Most Protestants feel that the authority of the Old Testament was greatly diminished with the coming of Jesus and the production of the New Testament writings. They appeal selectively to portions of the Old Testament, such as the Ten Commandments, but do not feel irresistibly compelled to memorize Judges or Nehemiah.

Alexander Campbell's famous *Sermon on the Law* was influential beyond the restoration movement in elevating the New Covenant Scriptures over the Old as a present guide for the faith and practice of Christians. But some people in the restoration movement appear to think that the Old Testament has no authority at all for Christians who claim the New Testament to be their rule of faith and practice. That attitude cannot be justified in the light of Paul's teaching (Romans 15:4; 1 Corinthians 10:11; 2 Timothy 3:16, 17). Surely the Old Testament has some continuing usefulness as the Word of God in the Christian era. The law has been fulfilled in Jesus and is, therefore, no burden bound to our backs. But even Moses still speaks insightful and helpful words for our Christian pilgrimage—if we have ears to hear. And he that is not stirred, convicted, and challenged by Jeremiah and Amos needs the attention of a spiritual audiologist.

So heremeneutics depends first of all on intelligent listening to the testimony of Scripture. Much of the Bible can be readily understood by every sincere reader of the text. The Word concerning salvation from sin and death through Jesus Christ is eloquently simple. God calls us through the Word to faith in Jesus and submission to His Lordship. That is beyond dispute.

Texts that are less clear in meaning require further consideration. One hermeneutical approach that seems reasonable in these instances is to appeal to the "consensus fidelium," the common judgment of competent Biblical scholars in every period of history. This principle of interpretation was employed by Alexander Campbell in his plea to restore the one baptism of the apostolic church.[32] Men and women of scholarly competence and pious character, skillfully commanding the original languages of the Bible, reach remarkably similar conclusions in their understanding of difficult passages, irrespective of the religious traditions they embrace. This consensus has greatly reduced the number of texts over which debate continues. It has firmly established the central core of doctrine that is essential to the continuing life and work of the church.

No true perception of God's truth revealed through Scripture is possible without an appropriate approach to the material. Paul contends that "the unspiritual man does not receive the things of the Spirit of God, for they are foolishness to him, and he cannot understand them, because they are spiritually appraised" (1 Corinthians 2:14). Both Luther and Calvin thought this statement meant that an internal operation of the Holy Spirit on the reader was necessary before he could grasp the meaning of the Bible. It would be foolish to deny the sovereignty of the Spirit, who blows wherever and on whomever He pleases. But I seriously doubt that Paul intended to suggest that the Spirit serves as an inward (mystical?) interpreter of the Word.

What he certainly does mean, at least, is that spiritual truth can make no sense to the person who has opted for a purely sensual view of life. Unless we can discern the qualitative difference between "fleshly" (carnal) and "spiritual" realities, the gospel will elicit no response from us. Insofar as the Holy Spirit may properly be said to be at work wherever truth is exhibited (He is described as the Spirit of truth—John 16:13), we may say that He does assist us in understanding revelation. That assistance is neither mystical nor miraculous, however, and it is offered to every person who comes to the Bible in sincere faith. As Luther remarked, *"Spiritus Sanctus non est scepticus"* (the Holy Spirit is no skeptic)[32]

Conclusion

Samuel Taylor Coleridge paid tribute to the Scripture in his comment that "In the Bible there is more that *finds* me than I have experienced in all other books put together . . . and whatever finds me brings with it an irresistible evidence of its having proceeded from the Holy Spirit."[33] Coleridge's remark is eloquent testimony both of the Spirit-inspired character of Scripture and its function as God's address to humankind.

God speaks in order to be heard—understood and obeyed—by His human creatures.

His speech is not limited to verbal expression but takes the form of action, direct and indirect, in the arena of human affairs.

The Word of God is thus both the divine deed and the divinely inspired interpretation of that deed by prophet and apostle. Additionally, the Word of God is the expression of His *will* made known through appropriate human instruments for the instruction and guidance of His people.

Jesus the Christ is the incarnation of the Word, the perfect embodiment of grace and truth in human form. Christ is the Word made flesh, the Eternal Son of God become visible and temporal to effect the transformation of history by revealing the Father in His life, words, and crucifixion-and-resurrection. The Word apostolic is the inspired and infallible witness to Christ and the faithful record of His teaching (John 14:26; Ephesians 3:5).

The Bible is the deposit in literary form of the revelation of God and His will in the history of Israel and in Jesus, His Son. It is authentic, reliable, and authoritative. Christian faith rests squarely on the testimony of Scripture, which it properly regards as the written Word of God.That Word is most powerfully and consequentially communicated by the preaching of the gospel supported by the faithful witness of the Christian congregation.

We do not follow cunningly devised fables.

We do not base our faith on myths and legends.

We do trust the truthfulness and accuracy of the documents of the Old and New Testaments, a trust that Anglican scholar John A. T. Robinson assures us is not misplaced.[34] We are glad to be a part of that company for whom our Lord prayed, "Sanctify them in the truth; Thy word is truth" (John 17:17).

NOTES

[1]Owen Barfield, *Saving the Appearances, a Study in Idolatry* (New York: Harcourt, Brace, and World, 1965) p. 82.

[2]Ludwig Wittgenstein, *Philosophical Investigations* (New York: MacMillan, 1953).

[3]*Ibid.*, p. 20

[4]Gerhard Ebeling, *A Theological Theory of Language* (Philadelphia: Fortress Press, 1973), p. 102.

[5]See Ebeling, *Ibid.*, p. 130.

[6]Karl Rahner, *The Word, Readings in Theology* (New York: J. P. Kenedy and Sons, 1964).

[7]Cf. Otto Kaiser, *Introduction to Old Testament* (Augsburg, Minn., 1975), p. 210.

[8]Walter Ong, *The Presence of the Word* (New Haven: Yale University Press, 1967), pp. 32f.

[9]*Ibid.*, p. 115.

[10]G. Ernest Wright, *God Who Acts* (London: SCM Press, 1925), p. 18.

[11]*Ibid.*, p. 84.

[12]Eugene Nida, *God's Word in Man's Language* (New York: Harper and Brothers, 1952).

[13]Quoted in Jaroslav Pelikan, *The Christian Tradition, I, The Emergence of the Catholic Tradition* (Chicago: University of Chicago Press, 1971), p. 60.

[14]*Ibid.*

[15]*Ibid.*

[16]Origen, *De Principiis*, 4, 9, PG 11:360.

[17]Justin Martyr, *Apology*, 1, 36, PG 6.385, quoted in Bruce Vawter, *Biblical Inspiration* (Philadelphia: Westminster, 1972), p. 25.

[18]Ibid., p. 26.

[19]Vawter, *Biblical Inspiration*, pp. 53-57.

[20]Denz, 3006, quoted in Vawter, *Biblical Inspiration*, p. 70.

[21]*Luther's Works*, 1, p. 648; 54, p. 474.

[22]Calvin, *Institutes of the Christian Religion* IV, VIII, 9.

[23]Roland Bainton, "The Bible in the Reformation," in S. L. Greenslade, ed., *The Cambridge History of the Bible*, III (Binghampton, NY: Vail-Ballou Press, Inc., 1975), p. 12.

[24]*Ibid.*, p. 13.

[25]Hubert Cunliffe-Jones, *Christian Theology Since 1600* (London: Duckworth, 1970), p. 13.

[26]Alexander Campbell, *Millennial Harbinger* (1851), p. 483.

[27]*Millennial Harbinger* (1846), pp. 15-17; (1837), p. 397.

[28]Cf. Walter Schmithals, *Paul and the Gnostics* (Nashville: Abingdon, 1972), pp. 19ff.

[29]C. H. Dodd, *The Authority of the Bible* (London: Nisbet and Co., 1952), p. 300.

[30]Campbell, *Millennial Harbinger* (1846), p. 23.

[31]A. Campbell, *The Christian System* (Cincinnati: **Standard,** nd) pp. 171ff.

[32]Quoted in G. C. Berkouwer, *Holy Scripture* (Grand Rapids: Eerdmans, 1975), p. 138.

[33]Samuel Taylor Coleridge, *Aids to Reflection and Confessions of an Inquiring Spirit* (London: G. Bell and Sons, 1913), p. 296.

[34]John A. T. Robinson, *Can We Trust the New Testament?* (Grand Rapids: Eerdmans, 1977), p. 134.

PART ONE

THE PROCLAMATION

"The Word of faith which we preach" Romans 10:3

SECTION OUTLINE

3. APOSTOLIC PREACHING: ITS PURPOSE, POWER AND
   PREEMINENCE
   Introduction: The Importance of Recovering the Apostolic
   Proclamation
   A. The Biblical Evidence
   B. Verdict of Scholars
   C. Verdict of Restoration Pioneers
   Conclusion

4. THE NATURE OF BIBLICAL FAITH
   A. Perspectives on the Nature of Faith:
         Philosophers and Theologians
   B. Perspectives on the Nature of Faith:
         Reformers and Restorationists
   C. Biblical Conception of the Nature of Faith
   Conclusion

CHAPTER

3

APOSTOLIC PREACHING: ITS PURPOSE, POWER, AND PREEMINENCE

By Leroy Garrett

In thinking of Christian Doctrine today, it is important that we understand the nature of the message first proclaimed by the apostles. Since a renewal of the church is the concern of many believers, it is imperative that we realize that if this is to occur to any substantial degree, there must be a recovery in our day of the apostolic proclamation in its original purpose and power. The first task is to understand the *meaning* of that message, which in the apostolic documents is simply called *gospel* or *glad tidings (euangelion)* some seventy-six times, or, less simply, *preaching* or *proclamation (kerygma)* eight times. It may seem flagrant to suggest that the modern church may not even understand what the gospel is, but a case can be made for this conclusion, especially in view of the fact that the church appears to be both purposeless and powerless in the face of our secularistic, humanistic world. Part of our thesis in this study is that the church's purpose and power can be recovered only by a renewed appreciation of the apostolic gospel.

In spite of recent interpretations that contend that there was such plurality and diversity in the earliest church as to make for gospels many and kerygmas many, there is abundant evidence that the apostles knew what the gospel was, even if the modern church does not, and that they proclaimed it with persuasion, power, and purpose. This evidence comes from some surprising sources, such as the Jewish exorcists in Ephesus, who sought to control evil spirits through the name of the Lord Jesus. The text reveals that they understood something of the nature of the gospel that Paul preached, for their cant was, "I adjure you by Jesus whom Paul preaches" (Acts 19:13). Even those whom Paul considered enemies to his cause knew something of the nature of the gospel, for he wrote of those who proclaimed the message in envy and strife and out of selfish motives, "What then? Only that in every way, whether in pretense or in truth, Christ is proclaimed, and in this I rejoice, yes, and I will rejoice" (Philippians 1:18). One would not have expected such evidence: *the message had purpose and power even when proclaimed with impure motives.* That presupposes, of course, that the true gospel *was* proclaimed.

The Biblical Evidence

The context of the passage just quoted provides a suitable introduction to the study before us in that the key words for *preach* and *gospel* appear together.

Philippians 1:15: "Some, to be sure, are preaching [*kerusso*, verb form of *kerygma*] Christ even from envy and strife, but some also from good will."

Philippians 1:16: "The latter do it out of love, knowing that I am appointed for the defense of the *gospel (euangelion).*"

Philippians 1:17: "The former *proclaim (katangello)* Christ out of selfish ambition."

An understanding of these terms is important in determining the character of the apostolic proclamation. *Kerusso* means *to herald.* The noun derivation, *kerux*, meaning a *herald*, is translated *preacher* in the New Testament. In the ancient Greek world, he heralded messages for the prince or king, often on street corners, sometimes using a trumpet to gain attention. In Greek religion, the *kerux* brought a new message of salvation. Friedrich tells us that he was like the New Testament heralds in that the work of both consisted "in *kerrussein*, in the loud publication of the message entrusted to them."[1]

Unlike *kerygma*, which may be an evil message as well as a good one, *euangelion* is always good news or glad tidings. The Greeks saw it as "news of victory." The messenger would appear, raise his right hand in greeting, and cry with a loud voice, *Rejoice, victory is ours!*[2] Since his face shone with joy, his spear was decked with laurel, and his head was crowned, it was already known that he brought *gospel* (the English word derived from the Anglo-Saxon, meaning *God-story*, but better translated *good news*). The purpose of the gospel was clearly salvation. In Ephesians 1:13, Paul calls it "the good news of salvation"; and in Romans 1:16, 17, he refers to it as God's power to save, the revelation of God's righteousness.

Kindred terms are *euangelizo*, which means to preach glad tidings, and *euangelistes*, one who brings the glad tidings, translated *evangelist* in the New Testament. The terms are pregnant with purpose and power in that they call attention to what God has done in history, bringing peace, joy, grace, and salvation to man—in a new order of things, the kingdom of Heaven. The *euangelion* is a reality only because of what God has done through Christ.

Katangello, as Philippians 1:17 indicates, means to proclaim or announce. Like *kerusso* it needs an object, something to announce. In Acts 13:38, where forgiveness of sins is proclaimed, the verb is *katangello*. In 1 Corinthians 1:23, where the crucified Christ is proclaimed, the verb is *kerusso*. The objects of both *katangello* and *kerusso* range all the way from circumcision (Galatians 5:11) to oneself (2 Corinthians 4:5). But usually these verbs, expressive of vivid, urgent action, refer to preaching Christ, the grand object of the apostolic proclamation, such as in Mark 16:15, "Go into all the world and preach (*kerusso*) the gospel (*euangelion*) to all creation," and Acts 17:3, "This Jesus whom I am proclaiming (*katangello*) to you is the Christ."

These two verbs, which appear seventy-eight times in the New Testament, are more or less synonymous. They can be used interchangeably with no discernible difference, as we have seen in Paul's use of them in Philippians 1:15-17. *Euangelizo* is different. It needs no object, for the object is built into the verb, which means *preach glad tidings* or *preach the gospel*. Occasionally, however, an object will be used (e.g. Ephesians 2:17), but even so the verb maintains its "good news" quality. It is the most common verb for proclaiming the apostolic message, appearing almost as often as the other two verbs combined.

While a brief word study cannot yield final conclusions, we

already have some pointers as to the character of the apostolic proclamation. It was news or tidings; indeed, good news. It was a comparatively succinct message made up of facts, not unlike that of the king's crier, who bore the kerygma from corner to corner of ancient cities. The herald did not present long, learned discourses, but proclaimed an event.

Already we have seen that the event or fact proclaimed by the apostles and their associates centered in a Person, Jesus Christ, whom they believed to be the Son of God and the risen Lord.

That the proclamation was of an event or a body of facts is further supported by Paul's frequent use of kerygma (twenty-three times in both its noun and verb forms). First Corinthians 1:21b could be rendered: "God was well pleased through the foolishness of the thing preached (kerygma) to save those who believe." He does not mean that the act of preaching was deemed foolish to the Greeks, but the nature of the message, the content, or the thing proclaimed. This could not be what the Jews called midrash (commentary and explanation) or what the Greeks called didache (instructions and teaching), for it was a herald's message.

An equally impressive instance is 2 Timothy 1:11: "I was appointed a preacher (kerux) and an apostle and a teacher." Here, Paul distinguishes between the herald, who proclaims a message, and an instructor with a curriculum to teach. Indeed, the apostle says he was both a preacher and teacher, but the distinction he draws between them is clear. A preacher may, of course, teach, and a teacher may preach, but this text shows that the functions are distinct.

This is corroborated by 1 Corinthians 2:4: "My message (logos) and my preaching (kerygma) were not in persuasive words of wisdom, but in demonstration of the Spirit and of power," followed by "my ways which are in Christ, just as I teach (didasko) everywhere in every church" (1 Corinthians 4:17). The apostle states the essence of the message as "Jesus Christ and Him crucified" (1 Corinthians 2:2), the logos probably referring to an expanded statement of the kerygma, but all part of the proclamation that redeemed them. But the "ways in Christ" that he taught, not heralded, in every church must refer to the believer's behavior and ethics. The first reference points to the purpose and power that infused the proclamation, which no human wisdom could equal, for it was attended by the power of the Holy Spirit.

Thus far we have the basic content of the thing proclaimed, if not the detailed facts that made up the *kerygma.* "Jesus Christ is Lord" was the basis of the gospel, or "Jesus Christ and Him crucified." This message was, of course, placed within a larger context, and we may not be able to determine precisely what and how many facts made up the *kerygma.* Scholars have been debating this question for at least a half century. But this problem in no wise compromises what is amply evident: there was a distinct apostolic proclamation, the good news (gospel), the purpose and power of which was to redeem sinful humanity through the dynamic of the Holy Spirit, and that this mission had preeminence in the life of the earliest church.

As for the content of the proclamation, we are dependent almost entirely upon the book of Acts, especially the earlier chapters, and the letters of Paul. There is repeated reference to Jesus' being the fulfillment of Old Testament prophecies and promises, such as, "[David] looked ahead and spoke of the resurrection of the Christ, that He was neither abandoned to Hades, nor did His flesh suffer decay" (Acts 2:31), and, "The things which God announced beforehand by the mouth of all the prophets, that His Christ should suffer, He has thus fulfilled" (Acts 3:18).

There is also frequent mention of the apostolic witness to the facts proclaimed, as in Acts 2:32, "This Jesus God raised up again, to which we are all witnesses," and Acts 3:15, "[You] put to death the Prince of Life, the one whom God raised from the dead, a fact to which we are witnesses." Paul, both in Acts and in his letters, avows that he was a witness to the reality of the risen Christ, no less than the other apostles.

There is bare mention of Jesus' earthly life. Some such references include His miracles, wonders, and signs (Acts 2:22), and that He went about doing good and healing the oppressed (Acts 10:28). There is also reference to His being of the seed of David (Romans 1:3 and 2 Timothy 2:8). Sometimes the message also included references to Jesus' exaltation to the right hand of God (Acts 2:33), to His role as Judge of the world in the last day (Acts 17:31), and to His being the Savior of mankind (Acts 13:23).

At the heart of the proclamation, however, was the death, burial, and resurrection of Jesus Christ. "God raised Him from the dead!" was the evangelist's cry of victory, as in Acts 2:32; 3:15; 13:30. In 1 Corinthians 15:3-6, Paul spells out the content of the gospel (euangelion): 1. Christ died for our sins (v. 3); 2. He was buried (v. 4), a fact that is stressed perhaps because this was evidence that Jesus had, indeed, died (Acts 13:29 details that He was laid in a tomb); 3. He was raised on the third day (v. 4); 4. He appeared to the apostles, including Paul, and hundreds of other witnesses (vv. 5-8). That Christ "died for our sins" is emphatically a part of the kerygma in Paul's letters, but, oddly enough, it is not mentioned in Acts, not even in Paul's speeches, though there is the preaching of "remission of sins."

Throughout Acts and the epistles, the verbs for preaching have an array of objects. This variation suggests that the kerygma was given varying emphases, depending on the circumstance. There was always, of course, the preaching of Jesus, such as in 2 Corinthians 1:19: "The Son of God, Christ Jesus, who was preached among you by us—by me and Silvanus and Timothy," and the evangelist Philip to the Ethiopian: "Beginning from this Scripture he preached Jesus to him" (Acts 8:35).

But there was also the preaching of the kingdom of God (Acts 28:23) and the preaching of peace (Acts 10:36) and "the faith" (Galatians 1:23). Timothy is charged to preach the word (2 Timothy 4:2).There was the preaching of Jesus as Lord (2 Corinthians 4:5) and the preaching of the forgiveness of sins (Acts 13:38). In Romans 10:8, "the word of faith" is the object of preaching.

Acts 5:42 is especially informative in that it not only reveals the preeminence of the proclamation in the primitive church, but combines preach (euangelizo) and teach (didasko) in an interesting way: "Every day, in the temple and from house to house, they kept right on teaching and preaching Jesus as the Christ." This text shows the urgency with which the apostles viewed the proclamation. Even when restricted by the authorities who had punished them for their activity, they went right on with their ministry, not only in the temple area (in the sight of Sanhedrin police) but from house to house (not simply at home) as well. From center to circumference, they filled Jerusalem with the proclamation, both teaching and preaching Jesus as the Christ. This probably means that along with the proclamation of the message per se, the usual facts making up the euangelion (gospel), they enlarged upon the meaning and significance of the gospel by references to the Scriptures and things that Jesus did and taught.

J. W. McGarvey's treatment of the coupling of preaching and teaching may prove helpful. Commenting upon Acts 28:31, he says, "Preaching and teaching are here distinguished, as they are throughout the book of Acts, the former being addressed to the unbelievers, and the latter to the believers. That he did both shows that both believers and unbelievers were drawn to his lodging."[3] Allowing for some overlapping, since Paul probably both preached to and taught some of them, McGarvey's distinction will probably stand up. He was influenced by the apparent fact that the proclamation of good news was *generally* directed to a lost world, while teaching was for those who became disciples. This is the order of the commission given the apostles in Matthew 28:19, 20: "Go therefore and *make disciples* (*matheteuo*) of all the nations, baptizing them in the name of the Father and the Son and the Holy Spirit, *teaching (didasko)* them to observe all that I commanded you."

This indicates that one ministry, proclaiming the gospel, turned sinners into disciples and culminated in their being baptized, while another function, teaching the things that Jesus had commanded, was to educate those who had been enrolled in the school of Christ, an appropriate metaphor in view of the Greek word used, *make disciples*. There is surely a difference between matriculating students and instructing them in the curriculum. Even so, there may be some overlapping. This writer has enrolled many students in philosophy classes in both high school and college, but he has nonetheless taught some philosophy, by way of introduction, during the matriculation process. This is to suggest that the distinction drawn between preaching and teaching in the Scriptures is not to be too rigid, but neither is the distinction to be blurred or ignored.

In some instances, Paul gave great significance to this distinction. He reminded the Corinthians that while they might have countless teachers during their spiritual pilgrimage, they would never have but one father, "for in Christ Jesus I became your father through the *gospel (euangelion)*" (1 Corinthians 4:15). Doubling the metaphors, he insists that he was their only spiritual father because it was he who brought the gospel to them, but once they were enrolled as disciples, they had many tutors. In 1 Corinthians 3:6, he puts it another way with still a different metaphor: "I planted, Apollos watered, but God was causing the growth." Overlapping or not, we are unduly confused if we see no difference between planting and watering.

True, one may do *both*, even at the same time, but he should recognize the difference in the ministries.

Another crucial text in understanding the nature of the gospel is 1 Corinthians 1:17: "Christ did not send me to baptize, but to preach the gospel, not in cleverness of speech, that the cross of Christ should not be made void." It is noteworthy that the apostle believed the gospel would have its usual powerful effect even when preached out of envy and from impure motives (Philippians 1:15-18). But in this passage, he recognizes that "cleverness of speech," a form of projecting oneself, can destroy the gospel's effectiveness. This is a tribute to the power of the proclamation. If the facts are clearly set forth, if the message comes through as the good news that it is, it will have power, even if preached by a hypocrite. But when the gospel is made to serve the human ego and is couched in "persuasive words of wisdom," its power is lost. Paul seems to say that when the gospel is infused with intellectual conceit, it is still the gospel that is preached, but it loses its power. It is significant that intellectualism spoils the proclamation while evil motivation does not. It shows that what Paul wanted was a clearly articulated message, one not spoiled by prancing, clever words.

Moreover baptism is not *per se* part of the gospel proclamation, otherwise the apostle would never have written, "Christ sent me not to baptize but to preach the gospel." The glad tidings are facts to be believed about what God has done through Christ, while baptism is an act of obedience. Baptism, then, is the believer's response to the gospel, and Acts 2:38 shows that that response bears the promise of both the remission of sins and the gift of the Holy Spirit.

While Acts 10:37 refers to "the baptism which John preached" (KJV), which likely refers to the new age that he introduced, there is no indication that Christian baptism was ever preached or that it was part of the *kerygma*. We must assume that the apostle Peter had fully proclaimed the gospel on Pentecost in Acts 2 when his hearers were "cut to the heart" and in desperation cried out, "What shall we do?" It was then that the apostle charged them to repent and be baptized. In some instances, such as Acts 13:16-41, the gospel is proclaimed in all its resplendent glory, but there is no such response as there was in Acts 2, and, therefore, no reference to baptism. We may assume that if the Antiochians had responded to Paul as those on Pentecost did to Peter, Paul too would have pointed to baptism as the way to obey the gospel. Paul preached Christ, in season and out of season, for this is what God sent him to do. He commanded baptism (and even baptized) when it was appropriate to do so.

While almost certainly the speeches in Acts are Luke's summaries of what was said and not verbatim accounts, they nonetheless are reliable evidence as to the makeup of the apostolic proclamation. If one were limited to but one of these speeches in ascertaining the character of the gospel, Paul's speech in Acts 13, delivered while he was in Antioch, would provide sufficient evidence. It serves well in providing a summary of the character of the gospel preached by the apostles.

1. The prophets of Israel, from Samuel to David, promised that God would send a Savior to His people. Jesus is that Savior, being the offspring of David (vv. 17-23).

2. Jesus was condemned to death in fulfillment of the Scriptures (vv. 24-27).

3. He was executed under Pontius Pilate, even though innocent, and after He had died, He was laid in a tomb (vv. 28, 29).

4. God raised Him from the dead (v. 30). This, too, was in fulfillment of Scripture (v. 33).

5. There were many witnesses to the resurrection (v. 31).

6. Forgiveness of sins is promised to those who believe in Jesus, a deliverance not possible through the law of Moses (vv. 38, 39).

7. Judgment awaits those who do not respond to what God has done through Jesus (vv. 40, 41).

Even though the speeches in Acts differ in detail, as does the evidence in the epistles, this serves as an adequate description of "the thing preached." The bottom line is Jesus Christ: His death (for our sins), His burial, and His resurrection, which is testified to by many witnesses.

Verdict of Scholars

The most notable effort to identify the character of the apostolic message was made by C. H. Dodd, one-time renowned professor of New Testament at the University of Cambridge, in his *The Apostolic Preaching and Its Development* (1936), the conclusions of which were accepted almost without question by Biblical scholars generally for two decades or so. No less a scholar than A. M. Hunter described Dodd's thesis as "one of the most important and positive contributions to New Testament science in our generation." This book, in fact, made the word kerygma one of the most colorful terms in the church's vocabulary of the past generation, and Dodd's thesis has had an impact not only upon recent New Testament theology but upon the educational philosophy of the church as well.

Dodd charged the modern church with a failure to make an important distinction that is evident in the New Testament, between kerygma and didache, or preaching and teaching. What the church commonly calls preaching is not preaching in the New Testament sense at all, but teaching, exhortation, or moral and didactic instruction. Preaching is for unbelievers, teaching for believers, he contended, and the content of one is distinctly different from the other. "It was by kerygma, says Paul, not by didache, that it pleased God to save men," the professor wrote, referring to 1 Corinthians 1:21.[4]

For more than a generation, Dodd's influence in the church has been pervasive, especially upon educational philosophy, in that it has determined the content of much of the curricula in church schools. One educator, who credits Dodd for the basis of her conclusions, suggests that the church's primary mission is to proclaim the gospel, which in turn creates the church, which is "the context for Christian nurture." The content of teaching, she says, does not necessarily lead to faith, for this is the function of kerygma. Following Dodd, she insists that the early church preached the gospel as the way of faith, while teaching was the instruction that came later to strengthen faith and deepen knowledge.[5] Some of Dodd's critics, and in recent years there have been many, charge that the rigid distinction that he makes has led the Sunday Schools to abandon missionary effort and satisfy themselves with the teaching of ethics.

But for our purposes, it is enough to understand how Dodd defined the kerygma. Drawing primarily upon Acts and Paul's epistles, he found that the message consisted of seven facts, which he called saving facts.

1. The prophecies are fulfilled, and the new age is inaugurated by the coming of Christ.

2. He was born of the seed of David.

3. He died according to the Scriptures, to deliver us out of the present evil age.

4. He was buried.

5. He rose on the third day according to the Scriptures.

6. He is exalted at the right hand of God, as Son of God and Lord of the quick and the dead.

7. He will come again as Judge and Savior of Men.[6]

This arrangement is roughly equivalent to the one we prepared from Acts 13, and, as we shall presently see, similar to one formed by Alexander Campbell seven decades ahead of C. H. Dodd. Any list that draws upon the same sources will, of course, be similar. The most glaring omission in Dodd's list is the fact of many witnesses to the message proclaimed, such as in Acts 2:32: "This Jesus God raised up again, to which we are all witnesses," an ever-present element of the proclamation.

As we have already indicated, there was at first widespread acceptance of Dodd's thesis by Biblical scholars. While A. M. Hunter, C. T. Craig, Floyd V. Filson, F. F. Bruce, Bertil Gartner, T. F. Glasson all took some exception to Dodd's list, with some saying there were only five basic facts and others three, there was agreement on his overall thesis. Even Joachim Jeremias generally agreed, though he believed there was preaching inside the primitive community as well as to the world.

Dodd's thesis, however, finally came under severe attack, such as that by Robert C. Worley, professor at McCormick Seminary, in a book on the subject in 1968.[7] He charged that Dodd's distinction between kerygma and didache was not only too rigid, but that the evidence from the earliest church shows that there is no discernible difference in the content. While he granted that it cannot be proved that the terms were synonymous, he insisted that they were so similar in meaning that a new term, preaching-teaching, best represents the action in question. Worley was especially critical of Dodd's view of an evolutionary development of preaching and teaching, that the kerygma created the church, which expected an imminent return of Jesus, and when this was delayed, the didache gradually formed, providing the church with ethics and direction. Here Worley struck at the most vulnerable aspect of Dodd's theory, for there is evidence of the apostles' mingling ethical imperatives with the proclamation from the outset, drawn both from the Old Testament and the teaching of Jesus, such as in Acts 20:35: "Remember the words of the Lord Jesus, that He Himself said, 'It is more blessed to give than to receive,' " and Romans 2:21, "You who preach (kerygma) that one should not steal, do you not steal?" But a mingling of motifs does not necessarily make those motifs identical or synonymous.

An important difference between Dodd and such critics as Worley is that Dodd accepted the reliability of the speeches in Acts, admittedly the most important source for the *kerygma,* while Worley did not. The speeches are the creation of Luke, Worley contends. He goes on to brush aside this evidence with abandon: "It is certain that they do not represent the primitive central outline of preaching of the earliest Christian community."[8] It must be conceded that if Worley is correct about the unreliability of the kerygmatic sources in Acts, then Dodd's theory is in jeopardy. But even the demythologizing Rudolf Bultmann was not willing to go that far, for while he differed with Dodd in concluding that *kerygma* had more to do with the act of preaching than with content, he treated the speeches in Acts as reliable source material.

In more recent years, Dodd's thesis on the apostolic proclamation has been scrutinized by those who are emphasizing the diversities of earliest Christianity, particularly James D. G. Dunn of the University of Nottingham in his monumental study on the *Unity and Diversity in the New Testament,* (1977).[9] While Dodd had already recognized "an immense range of variety in the interpretation that is given the *kerygma,*" he nonetheless insisted that the essential elements of the gospel are always present. He stated it as if to anticipate the "diversity theologians" of this generation: "With all the diversity of the New Testament writings, they form a unity in their proclamation of the one Gospel."[10]

It is interesting in reading Dunn to notice that in spite of his apparent rejection of Dodd, he never allows himself to wander far from Dodd's conclusion that despite diversity, there is still the *kerygma,* the one gospel, for Dunn himself now and again refers to "the core kerygma" and concludes his study with, "There is a unifying strand which holds all the NT kerygmata together and enables us to grasp the distinctive character of the earliest Christian gospel."[11]

Dunn repeatedly refers to *kerygmata,* plural, and he writes of the *kerygmata* of Jesus, Acts, Paul, and John, as though repudiating Dodd's thesis. But in examining the evidence in Acts, he asks whether there is a single *kerygma* or many, and his answer is that there is but one. He proceeds to name its basic ingredients, and his list is in line with the list of everyone who treats the speeches in Acts as trustworthy. While he does find some incompatibilities in the messages proclaimed in the various New Testament sources, his overall conclusion is that "the core kerygma does give clear enough indication of the distinctive character of Christianity—a clear enough basis for common action, service and worship."[12]

Patrick Henry of Swarthmore College has done an interesting study of current trends of New Testament study. He describes one of these trends as the "waning of existentialism." Under this heading, he writes of kerygmatic varieties, which he sees as a new direction from the time when scholars like Dodd found kerygmatic unity. It is curious that he thinks of this as existentialism. Bultmann was an existentialist, but Patrick labels him thus not for the usual reasons, but because he thought he knew the basic message of the New Testament. Anyone is an existentialist, according to Patrick, if he has a definite answer to the question, "What is the Christian gospel?" He is adamant in his conclusion, therefore, that there are many gospels in the New Testament, and, unlike Dunn, he allows for no core kerygma.[13]

Conservative Roman Catholic scholars predictably disagree with Patrick in his comment on Romans 1:16, where Paul says he is not ashamed of the gospel (euangelion): "The kerygma proclaims that God raised Jesus from the dead, made him Kyrios, and through him offers life to all who believe in him."[14] Alan Richardson, representing the best of British scholarship, says the "content" of the gospel "is Christ himself." In Dodd-like terms, he goes on to say that the gospel is "the saving message which God has addressed to the world." And while Patrick sees the view of many gospels as the current trend of New Testament study, Richardson holds that "there can be no substitute for this one authentic gospel." Richardson, in fact, defines preaching as having nothing to do with the delivery of sermons to the converted, but "always concerns the proclamation of the 'good tidings of God' to the non-Christian world." This is to be distinguished from didache, which is instruction in the faith.[15]

We refer once more to the highly respected A. M. Hunter, of the University of Aberdeen in Scotland. Writing more than three decades after Dodd, he restates the Dodd position with a freshness that cannot easily be ignored, yet without any reference to Dodd. He reminds us that Jesus did not come simply to preach the gospel, but that there might be a gospel, and Hunter has no doubt as to the character of that gospel. Hailing kerygma as a rugged Greek word meaning proclamation, he proceeds to outline its ingredients as: (1) God's promises made through the prophets are now being fulfilled; (2) the long-expected Messiah, born of David's line has come; (3) He is Jesus of Nazareth, who went about doing good and performing miracles by God's power; was crucified according to divine purpose; was raised by God from the dead and exalted to His right hand; (4) He will come again in glory for judgment; (5) therefore, let all repent, be forgiven, and receive the Holy Spirit.

Hunter recognizes that there were differences in emphasis in the proclamation, but that "on its essentials the apostles were agreed," and it was the gospel that turned the world upside down. He was impressed with 1 Corinthians 15:11 as evidence of his conclusion, providing his own translation: "Whether then it be I or they (Peter, James, John, and the rest) it is in these terms we preach and in these terms you believed."[16]

But a summary for the verdict of scholars might best come from Hendrik Kraemer, one-time professor at Leiden University in the Netherlands, who was asked by the World Missionary Conference in 1938 to state "the fundamental position of the Christian Church as a witness-bearing body in the modern world." As a result, Kraemer wrote The Christian Message in a Non-Christian World, in which he concedes that there is no source for determining the message except the Bible, for the Christian faith is not a philosophy nor a system of ethics, but a story based upon divine acts and grounded in history. The heart of the message, he says, is found in Acts 2:38, where Peter responds to those who asked him, "What are we to do?" He replied, "Repent, let each of you be baptized in the name of Jesus Christ for the remission of your sins." So Jesus Christ and the remission of sins are the divine elements. The joyful news is the remission of sins, a never-ending wonder, a miracle of God's free and sovereign grace. This shows that God's love is radical as well as holy, Kraemer wrote, for He condemned man radically because He loved him radically. God's forgiveness reaches beyond all reason and reveals itself in the gospel of grace.[17]

Verdict of Restoration Pioneers

It is remarkable, if not uncanny, that Alexander Campbell as early as 1865 penned what he called "the seven Facts that constitute the whole gospel," a list strikingly similar to what

C. H. Dodd became famous for seventy years later. Rather than to suppose Dodd was influenced by Campbell, it is more likely that they were seeking an answer to the same question and were dependent upon the same sources, particularly the speeches in Acts. Campbell's list has the added drama of being part of the last essay he ever wrote, after forty-three years as an editor. Here is his list, which can be compared with Dodd's:

1. The birth of Christ, God being His Father and the Virgin Mary His mother.

2. The life of Christ as the oracle of God and the beau ideal of human perfection.

3. The death of Christ as a satisfactory sacrifice for the sin of the world.

4. The burial of Christ as a prisoner of the grave.

5. The resurrection of Christ, "O grave! I will be thy destruction."

6. The ascension of Christ, "He ascended up far above all heavens, that he might possess all things."

7. The coronation of Christ as Lord of the universe. God his Father constituted Him the absolute Sovereign of creation.[18]

Apart from Campbell's elaborations, five of the items are the same as Dodd's, the most notable difference being that Campbell did not include the fulfillment of prophecies as part of the original message, which is Dodd's first point.

But more important is the fact that a distinction between preaching and teaching was a vital part of Campbell's plea for reform from the outset. As early as 1824, he wrote in the *Christian Baptist*: "To make a fact known is to preach, and to explain the meaning of the fact is to teach."[19] And as late as 1853, he observed that preaching the gospel and teaching converts were as different as enlisting an army and training it, or matriculating students and teaching them. It is "a solid and important distinction," he urged, noting the dire consequence in the mission field when the distinction is not heeded.[20] Moreover, it is a general weakness of denominations generally to spend their time preaching regeneration to those who are supposed to be already saved, thus neglecting the teaching that confirms them in the faith. He expressed regret that the preachers in his own reformation did likewise by "preaching the gospel to churches as if their communities were still to be taught the rudimental elements of the Christian faith."[21]

It was Campbell's deep concern for the place of *didache* that distinguished him from Dodd, who gave to teaching not much more than ethical instruction. While "to preach is to proclaim the gospel facts," Campbell wrote, "teaching is the development of truth, the meaning of facts, precepts and promises for the comfort and edification of those who are converted by preaching."[22] To Campbell, then, teaching is far more than ethics in that its purpose is to ground one in the faith by expounding the deeper meanings and significance of the gospel.

If Campbell felt that his own people were remiss in making this distinction, there was at least one editor besides himself that saw this as a distinctive mark of the reformation. "The Disciples distinguish between preaching and teaching. The Baptists do not so distinguish," he wrote, noting that the Disciples labor to explain the Scriptures and to get their people to read and understand for themselves.[23]

Robert Richardson, Campbell's physician, associate editor, and alter ego, also filed this complaint against the denominational world. The root of partyism, the doctor insisted, was that "Luther and his coadjutors taught doctrines while the apostles preached the gospel," and so Protestantism has become one grand doctrinal controversy. "Even the gospel, which is for the world, can be contemplated only through the medium of doctrine," complained Richardson, noting that the "gospel" really becomes each party's peculiar doctrinal slant. He goes on to lament: "Thus doctrines are confounded with the gospel. Doctrines are preached for the conversion of both 'saints' and sinners."[24]

More than any of the pioneers, Richardson saw the practical value in a correct understanding of the nature of the gospel as it related to their unity plea. When he wrote, "That alone which saves men can unite them," he was saying that it is the gospel that unites believers, not unanimity in doctrine. "Men have lost sight of the obvious distinction which is made between the Bible and the Gospel," he wrote, noting that while the Bible contains the gospel, there is much instruction in the Bible that is not the gospel. He went on to draw a distinction that would go far in uniting the divided church of our day if heeded: "Let the Bible be our spiritual library, but let the Gospel be our standard of orthodoxy,"[25] an epigram that reveals what the pioneers sought to accomplish. The doctor went on to say that while the Bible generally is to be our test for Christian character and perfection, it is obedience to the gospel that is the basis for

THE APOSTOLIC PREACHING

adoption and unity. Or to put it another way, he added that the Bible should be everything that God intended for it, while "Christ crucified" should be the grounds of peace with God and peace with one another.

Campbell and Richardson were both influenced by the thinking of the aged Thomas Campbell, who at eighty-two wrote a letter that embodied in a practical form "the true principles of the reformation." In that letter he stressed the importance of distinguishing between preaching and teaching. Along with emphasizing baptism as the door into the church and unity as based upon the clear mandates of Scripture rather than opinions as hallmarks of the movement, he wrote: "We should carefully advert to the plain systematic distinction between preaching and teaching, the former being intended for the conversion of sinners, the latter for the comfort and edification of saints."[26]

Conclusion

In the light of the foregoing, it may be surprising to learn that in one group within the Restoration heritage, known as "conservative" or "non-cooperative" among the non-instrumental Churches of Christ, there is a vigorous rejection of any effort to distinguish between preaching and teaching or gospel and doctrine. The issue has become central in recent discussions of fellowship within the movement. The argument in the present chapter seeks to establish fellowship on the basis of the kerygma, on which most Bible believing people agree in general. The conservative objection is that fellowship must be based on doctrinal agreement.[27] But this position has provided the basis for tragic division among various segments of what was once a unity movement. As the Campbells realized, if such matters as instrumental music, societies, Sunday School, and cooperative endeavors are made part of the gospel, unity is impossible.

Furthermore, if the church cannot distinguish between kerygma and didache, it can only be confused as to what its proclamation is to be. In the Campbells' time, the tenets of Calvinism were treated as gospel. In Dodd's day, it was "sermonizing" on various themes, social and political as well as religious. Preaching can thus be made a hodge-podge of many forms of opinionizing and theorizing, both doctrinal and theological, with hardly a reference to the apostolic proclamation. Believers may hold different views on such controversial issues

85

as glossolalia, the nature of inspiration, divorce, abortion, and social drinking, but if these are made part of the gospel, it will place a serious strain on the fellowship of the church. Indeed, most of us will come up with diverse views as we interpret the Scriptures, especially such difficult portions as Daniel, Romans, and Revelation, but this does not mean that we differ as to the nature of the gospel, unless indeed "the thing preached" (kerygma) and "the apostles' teaching" (didache) are mere synonyms.

We conclude, therefore, that the apostolic proclamation was the preaching of Jesus Christ and Him crucified, with such attending facts as His dying for our sins, His burial, and His resurrection, all in fulfillment of the Scriptures, and that this was made credible by many witnesses. "Christ is preached, that He has been raised from the dead" (1 Corinthians 15:12), or, "We . . . preach . . . Christ Jesus as Lord" (2 Corinthians 4:5) is the gospel.

Any contention over precisely what facts make up the kerygma only begs the question, for the issue really is the nature of the gospel (euangelion), which by definition is glad tidings. It is evident that the message of good news was proclaimed in its power and fullness long before a body of Christian doctrine (didache) emerged. Paul could say, "I have fully preached the gospel of Christ" (Romans 15:19) long before there was what we call the New Testament. Once the didache began to form, there is no question but that it was in many instances closely related to the proclamation, and that their contents often intermingled and overlapped is also evident.

This is illustrated in the release of the American hostages in Iran on January 20, 1981. As with the kerygma, the various heralds did not announce the facts in exactly the same way, some announcing that the hostages were in flight to Wiesbaden, some that they were seen at the Tehran airport, some that all fifty-two hostages were alive and well, but they all had one message of power and purpose: The hostages are free! Even while a new President was taking the oath of office, the "good news" was imminent. The news of the event was one thing, and all that was to follow, its meaning, its effect upon U.S.-Iran relations, its impact upon the world, and the economic implications, which called for reams of interpretations, were something else. If we have no problem in distinguishing between the glad tidings of the release of the hostages and something like their debriefing in Wiesbaden, we should be able to see that the euangelion, which is "the power of God unto salvation," proclaimed by the apostles is one thing, and that the didache, the "sound doctrine" that builds one up in the holy faith, is something else.

The purpose of the proclamation was the redemption of sinful humanity, to reconcile man to God, to offer the forgiveness of sins and the gift of the Holy Spirit, thus creating a new humanity in a new community, which was to be the dwelling place of God on earth.

The power of the proclamation was the power that raised Jesus Christ from the dead, which proved stronger than all the might of Rome, for "the blood of martyrs became the seed of the church." The apostles were "full of the Holy Spirit," which gave them a dynamic never experienced before in human history, and their message was a love story of how God so loved the world that He gave His own Son. "This is how God loves!" was the essence of their message, one that proved foolish to the Greeks and a stumbling block to the Jews. But to those that believed it was the power and wisdom of God.

The preeminence of the proclamation was that it was vital, urgent, and absolute. Necessity was upon them to preach the gospel, whether it meant persecution, hardship, or even death. The earliest church "went everywhere preaching the word" and "turning the world upside down." It was their one imperative. Paul's mandate was, in effect, the mandate of earliest Christianity, "Woe is me if I do not preach the gospel" (1 Corinthians 9:16).

The mandate of the earliest church is our mandate. Their purpose and power must be our purpose and power. And when their gospel becomes our gospel, their victory will be our victory.

NOTES

[1]Gerhard Friedrich, "Kerux," Gerhard Kittell, Ed., *Theological Dictionary of the New Testament,* Vol. 2 (Grand Rapids: Eerdmans, 1964), pp. 693, 703.

[2]Gerhard Friedrich, "Euangelion," Kittell, *TDNT,* Vol. 2, p. 722.

[3]J. W. McGarvey, *New Commentary on Acts of Apostles* (Cincinnati: **Standard,** 1892), Vol. 2, p. 288.

[4]C. H. Dodd, *The Apostolic Preaching and Its Development* (Harper and Brothers, 1936), p. 8.

[5]Iris Cully, *The Dynamics of Christian Education* (Philadelphia: Westminster, 1958), p. 42.

[6]C. H. Dodd, *Apostolic Preaching, p. 17.*

[7]Robert C. Worley, *Preaching and Teaching in the Earliest Church* (Philadelphia: Westminster, 1968).

[8]*Ibid.,* p. 84.

[9]James D. G. Dunn, *Unity and Diversity in the New Testament* (Philadelphia: Westminster, 1977).

[10]C. H. Dodd, *Apostolic Preaching,* p. 74.

[11]James D. G. Dunn, *Unity and Diversity,* p. 32.

[12]*Ibid.,* pp. 21, 32.

[13]Patrick Henry, *New Directions in New Testament Study* (Philadelphia: Westminster, 1979), p. 258.

[14]*The Jerusalem Bible* (New York: Doubleday, 1966), p. 269.

[15]Alan Richardson, *A Theological Word Book of the Bible* (London: SCM Press, 1905), pp. 100, 171, 172.

[16]Archibald M. Hunter, *Bible and Gospel* (Philadelphia: Westminster, 1969), pp. 27, 28.

[17]"Notes on Recent Exposition," *Expository Times,* Vol. 50, No. 1, (1938), pp. 529f.

[18]Alexander Campbell, "The Gospel," *Millennial Harbinger*, Vol. 36 (1865), p. 516.

[19]Alexander Campbell, "A Familiar Dialogue," *Christian Baptist*, Vol. 1, No. 12 (1824), p. 233.

[20]Alexander Campbell, "Church Edification," *Millennial Harbinger*, Vol. 3 (1853), p. 541.

[21]*Ibid.*, pp. 544, 545.

[22]Alexander Campbell, "Acts of the Apostles," *Millennial Harbinger*, Vol. 17 (1846), p. 350.

[23]"Baptists and Disciples in Contrast," *Millennial Harbinger*, Vol. 26 (1855), p. 437.

[24]Robert Richardson, "Nature of Christian Faith," *Millennial Harbinger*, Vol. 27 (1856), p. 154.

[25]Robert Richardson, "Reformation," *Millennial Harbinger*, Vol. 18 (1847), pp. 508, 509.

[26]Thomas Campbell, "Mission to New England," *Millennial Harbinger*, Vol. 16 (1845), p. 230.

[27]A recent example of this position is Tom Roberts' *Neo-Calvinism in the Church of Christ* (Fairmont, IN: Cogdill Foundation, 1980). The author argues that any distinction between *kerygma* and *didache* is a myth, and that the "gospel" embraces all that is taught in the New Testament, including his own position against instrumental music and congregational cooperation. Other writers of this persuasion extend the list of essential doctrines on which fellowship is to be based to such issues as multiple communion cups, the Sunday School, premillennialism, *ad infinitum*.

CHAPTER

4

THE NATURE OF BIBLICAL FAITH

By Leroy Garrett

What may be called *general* faith has been variously described by poets and essayists through the centuries. It is the soul's venture and the inspiration of all endeavor. To Nathaniel Hawthorne, it is a grand cathedral with divinely pictured windows that reveal their unspeakable splendors only from within. Long before Christ, Heraclitus was persuaded that "much knowledge of divine things is lost to us through want of faith," while Emerson was persuaded that "all I have seen teaches me to trust the Creator for all that I have not seen."

Some have used quaint metaphors to get at the meaning of faith, such as Ghandi's, "That alone is true faith that stands the foulest weather," while Whittier ventured, "The steps of faith fall on the seeming void, but find the rock beneath." Schopenhauer saw faith as being like love in that it cannot be forced, and John Henry Newman saw it simply as an act of the will. Alexis de Tocqueville spoke politically when he observed that despotism may govern without faith but liberty cannot, and John Foster Dulles complained that while we are setting records in the production of material things, we lack a righteous and dynamic faith, without which all else fails.

Faith has been extolled not only as the root of all blessings but as a rock with roots. Some have been philosophical, such as

91

Unamuno, who insists that "faith which does not doubt is dead faith," and A. A. Hodge, who says that faith becomes mere superstition if it does not have adequate evidence. But it is Alexander Smith who wraps it all up with: "The saddest thing that can befall a soul is when it loses faith in God *and woman!"*

Before analyzing the Biblical concept of faith, which remains the final court of appeal on all questions of this sort, it may prove helpful to examine the insights of some modern philosophers and theologians, for they have a way of keeping us honest in the terms we use and the methods we employ. They also have a way of getting at the meaning of a thing, its "whatness," as they sometimes put it, stripped of the superficial. That is a large part of our task, to ascertain the whatness of faith.

Philosophers and Theologians

John Locke, who substantially influenced Thomas and Alexander Campbell, always related faith to revelation, which he identified as testimony made known only by God. Faith is assent to revelation, he observed, which may seem too simple; but like the Campbells after him, he understood that faith begins with assent to what is revealed, and then goes on to deepen into trust through experience. In fact, faith is "a settled and sure principle of assent and assurance, and leaves no manner of room for doubt or hesitation," though he warned that one must be sure that the principles he assents to are indeed a divine revelation and that he has the right understanding of them.

In distinguishing between faith and reason, Locke saw reason as that which judges the truth or falsity of propositions, while it is faith that assents to the propositions. The assent to the propositions is not due to reason, as such, but consists in confidence in the one who is responsible for them, such as in the proposition, *God is love.* Reason, drawing upon sensation and reflection, can go only so far in evaluating such a statement, while faith, looking beyond the proposition to Him who is responsible for it, gives assent to it. Concerning the nature of revelation as the basis of faith, Locke explained that it must always be in reference to the ideas that man already has; otherwise, there is no way for him to understand. When Paul was caught up into the third heaven, for instance, any revelation he received would have to be based on the ideas already in his mind. If something had been revealed to him in some kind of "sixth sense," it would not have been a revelation, for he could not have understood it.[1] This explains why the Scriptures speak of Heaven in terms of golden streets and jasper walls.

In the Lockean tradition, Karl Barth has seen faith and revelation as inseparable, and he defines faith as trust. "Faith means trust," he wrote, and trust is "the act in which a man may rely on the faithfulness of Another." *I believe* means *I trust*. To Barth, it is just that simple and that profound. Faith is the trust that we may hold to God, to His promise, and to His guidance. Faith comes in our meeting with God. Faith means that in our glory and misery we are not alone, for "I am in all circumstances in company with Him." But Barth makes it clear that this is not merely subjective, for it is rooted in revelation: "This meeting with God is the meeting with the word of grace which He has spoken in Jesus Christ."

To Barth, Jesus is the revelation of God. God is hidden from us outside His Word, but He is manifest in Jesus. If we look past Jesus, we will not find God. But Barth seems to say that God remains to some degree hidden even when we have Jesus, and it is this *hiddenness* of God that makes faith faith. The men in the Bible, he notes, did not come to faith by any kind of proofs, but when "they were so placed that they might believe," they then had to believe "in spite of everything." It is the hiddenness of God that reminds us of our brokenness, humbles us, and makes faith possible. Man does not really want to live by grace but by his own pride, and this is the greatest hindrance to faith. But when we meet God in Jesus, we accept the life of grace. Faith is therefore not a work of heroism, but an act of grace that we are to accept in the deepest humility.

Finally, to Barth, faith is a once for all decision, a final and lasting relationship. Its concern is not with "religion" but with real life in its totality. A temporary faith simply is not faith. This totality includes, of course, man's reason, which faith illuminates. By reason alone, untouched by illuminating faith, man may intuit or deduce that there is a supreme being or a "thing in itself," but he cannot know God until God makes Himself apprehensible through revelation. In this revelation, and particularly in Jesus Christ, God and man meet, and it is here that faith illumines the reason and deepens into trust. So to Barth, faith is also knowledge and is thoroughly logical in that it is grounded in *facts*, the basic fact being Jesus' resurrection from the dead. This doctrine of faith, which is eminently

93

Biblical, would please both John Locke and Alexander Campbell, both of whom defined a *fact* as something said or done. God has spoken and acted, especially through Jesus Christ, and because of these facts in history, faith is possible.[2]

Paul Tillich's view of faith is not radically different from Locke's and Barth's. Since "faith" needs much semantic purging, Tillich comes up with the term *ultimate concern*. By this, he means a state of being committed to something of supreme value over all other concerns. In this formal sense, everyone has faith, for it is impossible to live without being ultimately concerned about something. For Tillich, faith is a state of being "grasped by that toward which self-transcendence aspires, the ultimate in being and meaning." Faith is not belief in something intrinsically unbelievable, in contrast with Kierkegaard and others who have considered faith a leap into absurdity.

Beside this formal view of faith, Tillich has what he calls the material concept, which is Christian faith. This faith is "the state of being grasped by the New Being as it is manifest in Jesus as the Christ." It is the Spiritual Presence's (one of his substitutes for the term *God*) invasion into the conflicts and ambiguities of life. But it is here that he departs from Locke, Barth, and historic Christianity, and it is here that he shows his existentialism (by which he questions truth as ever being final or absolute), for he goes on to say that this faith is not a cognitive affirmation nor an assent to factual statements. For one to say, for instance, that he believes God exists (or that he does *not* believe it) is to Tillich absurd. Faith cannot be based on such "authority," whatever the source. Faith must be existential and subjective. It occurs within "the structure, functions, and dynamics of man's spirit." It is in man, not from man. In faith, the Spiritual Presence is conquering the ambiguities of life. This is done in three ways: the Spiritual Presence opens up one's being; one's being accepts this Presence in spite of the infinite gap between the human and the divine; he maintains the hope of a final participation with the divine in the transcendent unity and an unambiguous life. This is, to Tillich, the meaning of "regeneration" or "sanctification," which he prefers to describe by the term "the New Being."

Since he rejects faith as cognitive affirmation (such as saying the Apostles' Creed, or expressing belief in its statements), it may appear that Tillich is far removed from the biblical tradition, but such may not be the case. After all, one may believe the statement, "Jesus Christ is the Son of God," and still not have Biblical faith. When Tillich gets through with faith, which he does relate to Jesus as the Christ, he has the New Being. Man's spirit must open up to God's presence, which changes his life. He now has hope and an answer to his otherwise ambiguous and meaningless life. Tillich speaks to the church today in that it is filled with people who profess faith but have come nowhere near the changed life that he describes.[3]

Rudolf Bultmann, who is also regarded as a radical liberal, may likewise have more to say to the modern church about faith than we have been willing to acknowledge. Like Tillich, he relates faith to the future more than to the past. Once we have opened our hearts to the grace of God and our sins are forgiven, he says, we should forget the past and open ourselves freely to the future. This is what faith means: opening ourselves freely to the future. Faith also means obedience, he insists, and this means turning our backs on self and abandoning all security. It means giving up every attempt to carve out a niche in life for ourselves, surrendering all our self-confidence, and trusting in God alone, who raises the dead. And he quotes Scripture all the way, a device not always associated with Bultmann!

As other existentialists, Bultmann talks about the authentic life, which is to him the life of faith, which, in turn, is "life after the Spirit," and this means to abandon all self-contrived security. He insists that man must escape from the tangible realities of life and lay hold on the intangibles. This detachment from the world makes him capable of fellowship in a community of believers and delivers him from anxiety and frustration. It is here that he hears the fruit of the Spirit: love, joy, peace, patience, kindness, goodness, faithfulness, gentleness, and self-control (Galatians 5:22).

Bultmann ties faith irrevocably to the hearing of the word of God's grace, but not simply to a compendium of doctrines or a record of the faith of others. It is only when Scripture speaks directly to us as kerygma, and elicits an encounter and response, that true faith is cultivated. So Scripture becomes the word of God in the here and now, in the dynamic of our own personal encounter with it. He would call this existential faith.[4]

Reinhold Niebuhr was adept in debating the nature of faith with other theologians. He once responded to a criticism by Tillich to the effect that he did not give proper place to reason by his emphasis on "the mystery of grace," which reason has no way of discerning. When Tillich charged him with having a weak epistemology, Niebuhr replied by saying that there is no way to make a rational case for God's redeeming love as manifested in Jesus Christ. Faith is thus rooted in mystery. The faith of the Christian church, he says, is built upon the fact of Christ's resurrection, and while this faith may be validated by experience, it is hardly rational. In fact, faith is "the key which resolves the divine mystery into meaning and makes sense out of life," he writes, and then he adds, "But I know of no way of inducing this faith by purely rational arguments."

Niebuhr says he learned what faith was while sitting at the bedside of a dying woman during his days as a parish minister. In fact, there were two women in his church that were dying at the same time. While one was in constant hysteria of fear and resentment, the other faced death with utmost peace of soul. The pastor was at her side weekly, reading passages of her selection, most of which were expressions of praise and thanksgiving. Her heart was filled with gratitude for all God's mercies, even as cancer was taking it toll.

It was from this dying woman that Niebuhr "relearned" that faith holds out the hope that our fragmentary lives will be completed in a larger plan than any which we control or comprehend. In faith, we learn that even in our frantic efforts there is no way for us alone to complete our lives or to endow them with significance. From this dying woman, he learned the meaning of Jesus' prayer, "I thank Thee, Father, that Thou hast withheld these things from the wise and prudent and revealed them unto babes."

It is in this context that Niebuhr sees the church of today as "a curiously mixed body," made up of those, on the one hand, who have never been shaken in their self-esteem or self-righteousness and who use religion for purposes of self-aggrandizement, and, on the other hand, by those who live by "a broken spirit and a contrite heart." This is but one of the paradoxes that he points to in his theology, all of which are summed up by his favorite term for the exercise of the Christian faith in an immoral society, *the impossible possibility*. That is the mystery of faith. It somehow does what cannot be done.[5]

Edward John Carnell voices the position of orthodoxy as well as anyone, and his views on the nature of faith are most challenging. Defining faith as "the capacity of belief or trust," he sees the ground of faith as the *sufficiency* of evidence, and not only the source of the evidence. He is helpful in pointing out that there are two kinds of faith, general and vital. To believe a thing is a general faith; to trust a person is a vital faith. Vital faith calls for greater commitment than general faith. Geometry (and even much of the Bible) can be understood by the intellect alone, but really to know a person demands the intuitions of the heart.

General faith, he notes, is satisfied with the sufficiency of the evidence, and it is to be censured only when it pretends to be vital faith, such as in the case of demons who believed and shuddered (James 2:19). Theirs was only a general faith that called for no commitment. General faith assents to truth and believes in objects and propositions, but commits only part of self. Vital faith, which is required by the gospel, commits the whole self to Him who died for us and rose again.[6]

Carnell's view of two kinds of faith sits in judgment on what is claimed for Biblical faith today. Is it vital or only general?

Some philosopher-theologians who seem far removed from orthodox or traditional Christianity have shown deep insight into the nature of faith—as we have seen in Bultmann, Tillich, and Niebuhr. Their insights speak prophetically to the modern church. Even a humanist like John Dewey, in his *A Common Faith*, writes of faith with such keen perception that any professed believer would do well to read him, even though "God" is to him only a unification of ideal values. Perhaps God has called upon the children of this world to enlighten the children of light as to the true nature of faith.

Dewey, for instance, relates faith to the uniting of the actual and the ideal. Whether it be one's self, a home, an institution, or society in general, we are to face the reality of the way things are, believing that however decadent something may be, there is hope of amelioration. So he called himself a meliorist, a cross between being an optimist and a pessimist. By a creative imagination, man can contemplate the ideal, and thus commit himself to move both himself and society toward that ideal. This is faith. As he puts it, faith is the "unification of the self allegiance to inclusive ideal ends, which imagination presents to us and to which the human will responds as worthy of controlling our desires and choices."[7]

What is sometimes professed as Biblical faith often compromises at both ends of Dewey's spectrum by being blind to the real world around it and by being unimaginative as to ideal goals. Facing up to the actual and contemplating the ideal, and then working toward a unity of the two could be one way to express the church's faith, related of course to the grace of God through Jesus Christ. If Dewey did not know what Christian faith is, perhaps he knew what faith is, which may be a good place for any of us to start.

If we allow a humanist to tell us what faith is, we might let a process philosopher tell us what doubt is. Like Spinoza of the seventeenth century, a contemporary, Charles Hartshorne, has been called "a God-intoxicated man," though neither of their philosophies is anywhere near historical Christian faith, as is John Locke's. Still they lived and breathed the very idea of God. Hartshorne says, "Apart from God not only would this world not be conceivable, but no world, and no state of reality, or even of unreality, could be understood."[8] That is to say that one cannot think deeply and adequately about the world without thinking of God. One would hardly expect *any* modern day philosopher to say such as that.

And doubt? "Doubt of God," he says, "is doubt of any and all truth, renunciation of the essential categories of thinking."

Hartshorne gives us pause to look critically at our professed Christian faith. If it is other than vital, is it not actually only doubt? And if our faith fails here, what truths in this world do we really believe? Hartshorne is saying that it is God or nothing. Does not Christian faith say that it is Jesus or nothing?

These professional thinkers help us to realize that in seeking to understand the nature of faith, we are dealing with a difficult concept, one that moves deeply within human experience. They may be telling us that only the heart of a poet can really understand faith, for they speak of mystery, totality, and ultimate concern—terms that seem to be as poetic as they are philosophical. But they are also logical when they speak of faith as the principle of assent and assurance, and even pragmatic when they see it as that which opens up the future and unites the actual and the ideal. Most significant, however, is that they agree that faith reaches out into a dimension beyond man, that it is in some way a *given*, and not a matter of man's own creation. This gives us a handle to the problem and should enable us to look to the Scriptures with a better background. But the views of a set of men closer to us idealogically should also prove helpful.

Reformers and Restorationists

If the emphasis in this section is on the pioneers of the American Restoration Movement of the nineteenth century, it is not only because many of the readers of this volume are of that heritage, but also because these men are representative of the reformed tradition that began with Luther and Calvin. After all, the pioneers of Christian churches-churches of Christ were not restorationists in the tradition of the Anabaptists, who insisted that the true church no longer existed and that they alone had restored it; they were reformers in the tradition of Luther and Calvin, believing that the church has always existed and has always been in need of reformation. They, therefore, sought to reform the existing Christian church through a restoration of the ancient faith and order, and in this way to recover the church's hidden unity.

In their views on the nature of faith, these pioneers were Calvinists. If one reads Book 2 of Calvin's *Institutes of the Christian Religion*, he will not only be impressed with the depth and propriety with which the reformer treats the subject of faith, but it will be apparent that this is basically what Protestants have always believed about faith, including the leaders of the Stone-Campbell movement. It was the extremes of Calvinism, for which Calvin cannot be wholly blamed, that caused problems on the American frontier, especially when oppressively imposed in creedal form. What a man actually teaches and a sectarian application of that teaching are often different.

To Calvin, faith was "a firm and sure knowledge of the divine favour toward us, founded on the truth of a free promise in Christ, and revealed to our minds, and sealed on our hearts, by the Holy Spirit."[9] The anti-Calvinistic complaint has been that this gives the Spirit a regenerating role both before and apart from the hearing of the Word, but Calvin's definition does not imply this. He goes on, in fact, to say that faith is as dependent on the Word as a tree on its roots, and that "we must attend to the relation of faith to the word, and to salvation as its consequence."[10] Because of man's blindness and perverseness, the Word alone is not sufficient to produce faith, he states, and so "without the illumination of the Spirit the word has no effect."

While the pioneers were uneasy with this emphasis upon the Spirit's role in conversion, their position, when cautiously stated, was not all that different. When Alexander Campbell

99

was pressed to state his views on the Spirit's role in conversion during the controversy between his associate editor, Robert Richardson, and Tolbert Fanning, an editor in Nashville, he wrote as if he might have taken it right out of Calvin's *Institutes:* "It is the Spirit of God that *quickens*—and hence *the word* which is the garb—the clothing of the Spirit is to be preached to every man under heaven in order to his spiritual illumination, conversion, and regeneration." Calvin could not have said it better than when Campbell added: "The Christian ministry is to preach Christ to the world, and to pray for the Spirit to sanctify and comfort them that believe in and obey the Lord Jesus."[11] He emphasized that it is not by the Word alone or by the Spirit alone but by both.

Richardson, who did more than any of the pioneers in recovering the role of the Spirit in both conversion and in the life of the believer, wrote several extended series in Campbell's journal on the nature of faith, arguing that faith is personal, rather than doctrinal, and spiritual, rather than logical. It is not merely assent to historic testimony, he urged, but trust in a person; it is an assurance of the heart and not just a conviction of the head. He noted that nowhere in Scripture is faith spoken of as belief in facts, but it is belief on or into *(eis)* Christ. It is absurd, he insisted, to speak of trusting in facts, for we trust or believe only in persons.[12]

Dwight E. Stevenson, in a study of Richardson's view of faith, notes that he saw this as the crux of the Disciples' plea. While the parties around them saw faith as doctrinal and based on opinions, they taught faith as something personal, centered in the Lord Jesus Christ himself. "To believe in Christ," Richardson wrote, "is to receive him in all the glory of his character, personal and official; to trust in him in all the relations which he sustains to us." Faith in Christ means to be in fellowship with Him, to know Him as a person and to be known by Him, to speak to Him as one who hears, and to listen to Him as one who speaks. Such faith, according to Richardson, was the basis of unity. "The true basis of Christian union is the Christian faith," he said, stressing that Chirst himself is the basis of Christian union.

Stevenson concludes that Richardson was not as lonely a voice on the nature of faith among the pioneers as might appear, for both of the Campbells agreed with him, though they could not or did not state the case as well as he. Alexander

Campbell always stressed faith as a belief in testimony, the facts about Christ in history, but this initial faith was meant to lead to a personal trust and commitment. Actually, he seems to have had two views of faith, one barrenly intellectual, which was intended to combat the Protestant mysticism of his day; the other richly personal. He was compelled to choose between these two views, Stevenson observes, depending on the nature of the controversy at hand.[13]

Walter Scott, who was the greatest evangelist among the Disciples in the early period, came to have a more structured, if not legalistic, view of faith than the Campbells. He devised his famous five-step plan for a sinner's salvation, the first of which was faith. This faith was basically an assent to the facts of the gospel. But he placed such emphasis upon Jesus as the Christ as the Golden Oracle, which was his constant theme, that in his treatise of Christian unity he made Christ himself the basis of union. "It is not doctrine that Christ taught, nor any action that he performed, that forms the article of faith in the gospel. It is himself—as God's son."[14] He found other essentials in the ancient gospel and ancient order, a distinction important to him, but he seems always to have held that Christians unite only in the person of Christ Himself.

Barton W. Stone's ministry was turned toward reformation in part by a rediscovery of the nature of faith. John 20:30, 31 had particular influence on him, especially the line "these are written that ye might believe." He had supposed that faith was some mysterious spiritual substance that was given of God miraculously quite apart from any human effort. The sinner was to "pray through" at the altar or mourners' bench until the Spirit operated in this special way, filling his soul with this substance called faith. But later Stone concluded that in some sense and to some degree, faith is the act of the human will, which was adamantly denied by the Calvinistic preachers on the frontier. When a fresh look at John 20:31 caused him to see that the Gospel was written that man might read and believe, it changed his whole outlook on the nature of regeneration.

Twenty-five years later, when Stone wrote his history of the Christian church, he was ready to conclude that it is the Word of God that is the foundation of faith. Again quoting John 20:31, he argued that the Scriptures themselves produce faith in that they provide sufficient evidence for the facts set forth. And it is "the strength of the testimony" that makes faith possible, not some special disposition upon the sinner's heart. He states it rather simply: "No Christian will deny that there is sufficient evidence in the *word* to produce faith. For if there is not, God cannot require us to believe it, nor condemn us for not believing, when it is impossible to be believed."[15]

But Stone, like Campbell and Richardson, realized that it is not the Scriptures alone that produce faith, but the illuminating power of the Spirit as well. Quoting another editor with approval, he ventured that "God through grace *inclines* man, by his Spirit,—man when *thus persuaded* believes the gospel. The instrument by which the spirit accomplishes his work is the *truth*."[16]

All this would suggest that the pioneers stood moderately within the tradition of the Protestant Reformation as to the nature of faith. If they emphasized the role of the spoken or written word, even to the point of overstatement, it was because of the irresponsible positions taken on the work of the Spirit in a frontier country that had become brutally creedal and sectarian. Campbell's maxim, "No testimony, no faith," was suitable for controversy in the new world, and it would, properly interpreted, gain even Calvin's approval. But he may overstate his case when he says, "Where testimony begins, faith begins; and where testimony ends, faith ends."[17]

This kind of reductionism continued to pervade the thinking of the second-generation Disciples. Moses E. Lard, seeking a workable definition of faith in an extended treatment, concluded that faith is the conviction that a thing is true. It is not strong or weak conviction, or shallow or deep conviction, he allowed, but "simply and precisely conviction."[18]

In their better moments, the pioneers conceded that this was to oversimplify. Faith is conviction, to be sure, but it is more than that. On those occasions when they considered the role of the Spirit in faith, they recognized that the end of faith is a changed heart and a changed life, focused upon trust in a person.

Biblical Conception of the Nature of Faith

If one approaches the Scriptures with a view of what faith is, he can only conclude that it is not at all simple. The Bible does not define faith any more than it defines God. It is common to refer to Hebrews 11:1 to the effect that "faith is the assurance of things hoped for, the conviction of things not seen," but it is doubtful that the writer intended this as a definition. It was but his introduction to a statement on what faith does in the lives of believing people, to which he devotes the rest of that long chapter. We learn best what faith is by what faith does, and this seems to be the way the Scriptures treat the subject. If there is a pivotal passage, it might be Romans 4:20, 21, where it is explained why Abraham is the father of the faithful. Even though Abraham's aged body was "now as good as dead," he did not stagger in the face of the promise that he would beget a son who would become the father of many nations. He was fully assured that God was able to perform what He had promised. When the apostle says that he did not waver in unbelief, "but grew strong in faith," he confirms the verdict of philosophers and theologians that faith is implicit trust in a person. In Paul's use of Abraham, we may conclude that the apostle sees faith as "extravagant" trust.

This extravagance is dramatized in the offering of his son on the altar. Even though young Isaac was the heir of the cherished promises, Abraham never doubted that his son should be sacrificed. There could be no wavering, for God had spoken. It was extravagant but not absurd, for Abraham never divorced his faith from reason. Hebrews 11:19 reveals that Abraham figured that God would still make good His promise by raising Isaac from the dead. Sarah, whose role in the story is usually depicted as merely laughing at the idea of her conceiving (Genesis 18:12) is also honored in this passage. But when Yahweh as a "guest" made the promise to Abraham, Sarah, who was back in the family tent, did not know who the "guest" was. She laughed at the idea that she, at ninety, would become pregnant. When she learned who had made the promise, she took back the laughter. Hebrews 11:11 makes it clear that it was by her faith that she conceived, "since she considered Him faithful who had promised."

So Sarah's faith, like Abraham's, was in a person whom she considered faithful. This was what motivated Abraham, moving him all the way to Moriah, where he bound his own son, the son of promise, to the altar as a sacrificial offering. God did not stop him until the ugly knife loomed above the victim. God called to him to do the boy no harm. "Now I know you fear God," the Lord said to him. "You have not refused me your son, your only son." God assured him that because of what he had done, "I will shower blessings on you." This is the reward of faith, and what is faith in this story except *implicit trust?* Faith is thus unwavering assurance that God will do what He says He will do.

Abraham's faith, which is the *beau ideal* of Scripture, was neither credulity nor optimism. To be credulous is to be gullible, uncritical, and undiscerning. To be optimistic is to draw upon the power of positive thinking. Biblical faith is not simply believing, irrespective of what power this exercise may conjure up. It is not faith in faith or faith in oneself. It always has an object, and that object is divine. Thus, John R. W. Stott says, "Faith is a reasoning trust, a trust which reckons thoughtfully and confidently upon the trustworthiness of God."[19] He properly distinguishes between faith and sight, which oppose each other in Scripture, and faith and reason, which do not. Biblical faith does not close its eyes to the facts, but it sees God behind the facts and in control. That Biblical faith is reasonable does not mean that the thing believed can be proved. *Believing what cannot be proved* is at the heart of faith.

Alan Richardson observes that in both the Old and New Testaments, faith may be seen as an "act of utter reliance on God," and that obedience is its inevitable concomitant.[20] Some Scriptures treat faith and obedience as if they were synonyms, such as John 3:36: "He who believes in the Son has eternal life; but he who does not obey the Son shall not see life, but the wrath of God abides on him." The story of Abraham also shows this, for while Paul refers to his having believed God (Romans 4:3), Genesis 22:18 has God saying that he *"obeyed* my voice." That is why baptism, an act of obedience, can be viewed as the response of faith.

While everywhere in Scripture faith is trust and obedience, the emphasis is different with the various writers. In the synoptic Gospels, faith is the confident conviction that God has done through the Messiah what He promised through the prophets. In Hebrews, the emphasis is on believing in the unseeen reality of God's present help. In Paul and John, faith becomes a relationship to God in trust and self-abnegation. In Revelation, faith is related to the perseverance of the saints.

In an attempt to get inside the teaching of Jesus on the nature of faith, D. Martyn Lloyd-Jones refers to a statement he once heard that affected him deeply. Although offered in criticism of current attitudes, it served to point to what having Christian faith really means: "We believe on the Lord Jesus Christ, but we do not believe Him." This meant to him that while many, if not most, Christians believe on Jesus for their salvation, they do not really believe Him when He says things like God is going to take care of your food and drink and even your clothing. So he draws a distinction that seems to be made in Scripture—saving faith and a larger, growing faith. When Jesus says, "Oh, ye men of little faith" (Matthew 6:30), He is addressing people who are saved but who have not gone beyond that.

To understand what Jesus meant by "little faith" is to understand what He meant by a larger faith, Lloyd-Jones surmises. Little faith selects the promises it wants to believe and the times it desires to be religious, a practice that invites worry and anxiety. A larger faith embraces the whole of life and the fullness of Jesus' promises. Little faith is manipulated by life and victimized by circumstances, especially by hardship and persecution, while true faith rejoices in persecution and never gives way to whimper. So little faith allows things to master it and to get it down, while a larger faith is victorious amidst life's difficulties.

Lloyd-Jones suggests that the basic difference between little faith and real faith is that *little faith does not think*. He sees Jesus as teaching that faith is thinking. We are to be right in our whole conception of what the Christian life is about, and if we are wrong here, the world will cut us down. The way to keep the world from defeating us is *to think*, think about the promises Jesus has given, look at the birds and flowers and think about what Jesus said about them. Instead of thinking, people sit down and ask what is going to happen to them, and it is here that the world batters them. Hence, little faith is the failure to think seriously about what Jesus says and to take His promises at face value.

Lloyd-Jones thus ventures this definition of faith: "It is a man insisting upon thinking when everyone seems determined to bludgeon and knock him down in an intellectual sense."[21] When the Christian fails or refuses to think upon the claims of Christ, he is letting some other influence control his mind. If we really thought about what it means to be children of the Father, we would never worry and fret again. So Lloyd-Jones sees faith as a realization of what it means to be a Christian. Faith is, thus, to think about what Jesus really means.

But of all Scripture, it is in Romans that the doctrine of faith reaches its culmination. Paul states what no son of Judaism would ever be expected to say: "One is justified by faith in the Messsiah apart from works of the law." The book is replete with what faith is and what it does. A summary of some of the points is appropriate for this study.

1. Paul's mission as an apostle was for "the obedience of faith" among all the Gentiles. This shows that the apostle viewed faith as obedience to the gospel, not merely intellectual assent to its facts (1:5).

2. God's power to save is in the gospel, not in the law or anywhere else, and that salvation is for every one who believes, to the Jew first, but also to Gentiles (1:16).

3. The righteousness of God is revealed "from faith to faith," even as it is written, "The righteous man shall live by faith." The quote from Habakkuk 2:4 is Paul's way of showing that the principle of justification by faith has always been the will of God, and the "faith to faith" expression must mean that it is only by faith that this revelation has been given (1:17).

4. In 3:22, Paul uses faith and belief together in an interesting way. The righteousness (justice) of God has been revealed through faith to everyone that believes, he says. This shows that Paul's view of all that God has done is saturated with faith. The new order is given through, and appropriated by, faith.

5. Faith is reliance on God and not on self. The "law of faith" excludes all other law, even a law of works (3:27).

6. Justification by faith is a free gift from God (3:24).

7. Faith relates to the promise made to Abraham, whose faith is an example of Christian faith (chapter 4).

8. Faith is inseparably related to baptism, which symbolizes the gospel as death, burial, and resurrection (6:4).

Roman Catholic scholars, in their notes on this passage in the Jerusalem Bible, comment as follows: "Baptism is not separated from faith but goes with it, and gives it outward expression by the operative symbolism of the baptismal ceremonial. For this reason, Paul ascribes to faith and to baptism the same effects. The sinner is immersed in water (the etymological meaning of 'baptise' is 'dip') and thus 'buried' with Christ, with whom also he emerges to resurrection, as a 'new creature,' a 'new man,' a member of the one Body animated by the one spirit."

9. Salvation is promised to those who believe in their hearts that God raised Christ from the dead (10:9).

10. Faith comes by hearing the gospel (10:17).

11. While the Jews were cut off from God by their unbelief, the Gentiles must fearfully keep in mind that their standing with God is only by faith (11:20).

12. In chapter 14, Paul uses faith in a different way, referring to good conscience or personal scruples, such as, "Whatsoever is not of faith is sin," and, "Accept the one who is weak in faith," referring to one with a conscience more likely to be offended.

Conclusion

After all is said about faith, a measure of obscurity enshrouds it, and so we find Paul saying, "We walk by faith and not by sight" (2 Corinthians 5:7), which gives it a touch of mystery. If Hebrews 11:1 is to be seen as a definition of faith, it is noteworthy that it relates faith to the "unseen" and to what is "hoped for." There is no surprise, therefore, that the Scriptures speak of "the mystery of the faith" (1 Timothy 3:9), which must mean not only that it is something that had to be revealed for us to be able to experience it—for that seems to be the force of the term *mystery* in Scripture—but also that it has infinite depths and defies definition.

Perhaps it is this element of mystery that intrigues philosophers and theologians. Their insights into the nature of faith are found to be impressive. They find faith to be many things, but their diverse views are complementary rather than contradictory, for faith is all these things: assent to revelation, belief in testimony, ultimate concern, opening ourselves freely to the future, the unity of the actual and the ideal, and even the impossible possibility.

The reformers and restorationists are, of course, less philosophical and more Biblical. Faith is knowledge, assurance, conviction, and obedience. Some tie it inseparably to all the Christian virtues. And they are more concerned with both the source and the object of faith than the philosophers seem to be.

A bottom line does emerge from all these thinkers, the one essential ingredient that pinpoints the essence of faith, and that is *trust*. We conclude with all these men that faith is multifaceted, but that the crucial characteristic is trust. This makes faith *vital*, and it implies implicit confidence, assurance, and commitment. If faith begins with the conviction that the facts of the gospel are true, it is to grow into a quiet trust in the person of Christ. This may be what Paul meant by "the spirit of faith" (2 Corinthians 4:13), which suggests that even faith has a soul, which is trust.

Add to this the touch of mystery, which is evident all the way from Abraham to Paul, and we get close to the nature of Biblical faith. If love believes all things, hopes all things, and endures all things, which points up its mystery and power, does not faith also believe all things, hope all things, and endure all things? And this because it is eminently personal, centered in the wonderful Person of the Bible.

NOTES

[1]John Locke, *Essay Concerning Human Understanding*, Chap. 18 (Great Books of the Western Word, Vol. 35, Chicago: Encyclopedia Britannica, 1952).

[2]See Karl Barth, *Dogmatics in Outline* (New York: Harper's, 1959), pp. 15-27.

[3]Paul Tillich, *Systematic Theology*, Vol. 3, (Chicago: University of Chicago Press, 1963), pp. 130f.

[4]Rudolf Bultmann, *Kerugma and Myth: A Theological Debate*, Edited by Hans Warner Bartsch (New York: Harper's, 1961), pp. 19f, 201.

[5]Charles W. Kegley, and Robert W. Bretall, *Reinhold Niebuhr: His Religious, Social, and Political Thought* (New York: Macmillan, 1961), pp. 7, 432.

[6]Edward John Carnell, *The Case for Orthodox Theology* (Philadelphia: Westminster, 1959), pp. 23-30.

[7]John Dewey, *A Common Faith*, (New Haven: Yale University Press, 1960), p. 33.

[8]Alan Grag, *Charles Hartshorne*, Bob E. Patterson, ed. (Waco: Word, 1973), p. 102.

[9]John Calvin, *Institutes of the Christian Religion*, Vol. 1 (Grand Rapids: Eerdmans, 1953), p. 475.

[10]*Ibid.*, p. 495.

[11]Alexander Campbell, "Spiritual Influence," *Millennial Harbinger* (1857), pp. 545, 546.

[12]Robert Richardson, "Faith versus Philosophy," No. 5, *Millennial Harbinger* (1857), pp. 395-406.

[13]Dwight E. Stevenson, "Faith Versus Philosophy," Ronald E. Osborn, ed., *The Reformation of Tradition* (St. Louis: Bethany Press, 1963), pp. 33f.

[14]*Ibid.*, p. 49.

[15]Barton W. Stone, "History of the Christian Church in the West," No. 7, in *Christian Messenger*, Vol. 1 (1826), p. 218.

[16]*Christian Messenger*, Vol. 5 (1831), p. 199.

[17]Alexander Campbell, *Christian System* (Cincinnati: **Standard,** n.d.), p. 93.

[18]Moses E. Lard, "Faith: Its Definition," in *Lard's Quarterly*, Vol. 4 (1867), p. 238.

[19]John R. W. Stott, *Your Mind Matters* (Downers Grove, Ill.: Inter-Varsity, 1973), p. 36.

[20]Alan Richardson, *A Theological Wordbook of the Bible* (London: SCM Press, 1962), p. 76.

[21]D. Martyn Lloyd-Jones, *Studies in the Sermon on the Mount*, Vol. 2 (Grand Rapids: Eerdmans, 1960), p. 130.

PART TWO

THE WORD MADE FLESH

"God, after He spoke long ago to the fathers in the prophets in many portions and in many ways, in these last days has spoken to us in His Son. . . ." Hebrews 1:1, 2

SECTION OUTLINE

5. GOD SPOKE LONG AGO: THE RELATION OF THE NEW
   COVENANT TO THE OLD
   A. Continuity and Discontinuity in the Purpose of God
      Continuity
         The story of salvation
         Between the testaments
         The preaching of Jesus
         Early Christian preaching
         The New Testament writings
         Moral-ethical teachings
      Discontinuity
         The story of salvation
         Ethical-moral limitations of the Old Testament
   B. How the Old Testament Is Understood in the New
      Testament
   C. The Old Testament in the Church Today

6. GOD HAS SPOKEN IN HIS SON: THE LIFE OF JESUS
   A. The Nature of Our Sources About the Life of Jesus
         The relationship between the Gospels
         The Gospel writers as evangelists
         The threefold basis of interpreting Jesus' life
   B. The Contours of Concern About the Life of Jesus in the
      Gospels
         The infancy narratives
         The ministry of Jesus
         The passion narrative
         Accounts of the resurrection
   C. The Continuity Between Jesus and the History of Israel
         A theology of history
         Jesus the link between the past and the future

CHAPTER

5

GOD SPOKE LONG AGO: THE RELATION OF THE NEW COVENANT TO THE OLD

by Robert Hull

God spoke long ago . . . God spoke in these last days;
God spoke to the fathers . . . God spoke to us;
God spoke by the prophets . . . God spoke in a Son.
(See Hebrews 1:1, 2.)

By this series of contrasts, the author of Hebrews raises, implicitly, the question of the relationship between God's revelation given in the Old Covenant Scriptures and His revelation in Christ. For the present-day reader, the issue may be focused in terms of the problem of the relationship between the Old Testament and the New Testament.[1] That the Old Testament continues to be a problem for many Christians is demonstrated by the neglect of the Old Testament in much contemporary preaching and worship, and by a fundamental ignorance in the church of the contents of the Old Testament, aside from the Bible stories remembered from childhood.

Any work on Christian doctrine must take seriously the implications of God's revelation in the Old Testament as well as in the New. It is misleading to speak of "New Testament Christianity" in such a way as to imply that the study of the New

Testament alone is adequate for Christian discipleship. As paradoxical as it may seem, those who are most concerned with the character of earliest Christianity ought to be most seriously engaged in the study of the Old Testament.

The major reason for this is well known, but its implications are not sufficiently appreciated. What we today refer to as the "Old Testament" was the only Bible of the first Christians. In these Scriptures, they heard, not the dead accents of the ancient past, but the living and active Word of God. A more comprehensive statement of the place of the Old Testament in the life of the church cannot be found than in 2 Timothy 3:16, 17: "All Scripture is inspired by God and profitable for teaching, for reproof, for correction, for training in righteousness, that the man of God may be adequate, equipped for every good work." Something important is contributed to one's Christian perspective when it is understood that for a first-century reader of these words, "all Scripture" consisted of "the Law and the Prophets," or "Moses, and the Prophets, and the Psalms."[2] These were "the sacred writings which are able to give you the wisdom that leads to salvation through faith which is in Christ Jesus" (2 Timothy 3:15).

It is the purpose of this essay to explore some of the implications of a Christian Bible with both an "Old" and a "New" Testament. Specifically, we want to know how the earliest Christian communities heard and responded to the Word of God spoken of old to the fathers and how the church found in that ancient Word the presence and activity of "the God and Father of our Lord Jesus Christ" (Romans 15:6; 2 Corinthians 1:3; Ephesians 1:3; 1 Peter 1:3). Implicit in these issues is a concern to understand how the church of today ought to read the Old Testament.

Continuity and Discontinuity in the Purpose of God

Nothing is more likely than that the New Testament (N.T.) should reflect a great many influences from the Old Testament (O. T.) writings. Its message centered upon one who was himself a son of Abraham, and all but one of the writers were Jews. The influence of the O.T. on the N.T. is more pervasive than is often realized. The marginal references in the Greek N.T. texts of Westcott-Hort, Nestle-Aland, and the United Bible Societies indicate something of the debt the reader of the N.T. owes to the O.T. in regard to textual content alone.[3] Henry M. Shires has calculated that there are some 1604 N.T. citations of the O.T., in which 1276 different O.T. passages are employed. In addtion to these are thousands of other N.T. passages bearing some reasonably certain relationship to O.T. texts.[4] Moreover, the N.T. gives abundant evidence that the conceptions and thought-forms of its authors are heavily dependent on the O.T.

How did the O.T. function in the early church? To what end was it read and quoted by the N.T. writers? The answer is somewhat complex, but for our purposes, two categories that are convenient and widely-used may be helpful: "continuity" and "discontinuity." On the one hand, God's revelation in Jesus is the continuation of a divine purpose that began with Abraham, or even creation. To this end, the O.T. is cited, the events within it expounded, and its promises quoted with reference to the church. The word spoken by means of the Son is thus seen to be in direct continuity with the word spoken by means of the prophets. On the other hand, Jesus and His followers criticize, re-interpret, and even set aside parts of the O.T. The word spoken by means of the Son is a new and better word, going beyond and to some extent challenging the word spoken by means of the prophets. It is likely that both approaches to the O.T. may be traced back to Jesus himself.

Continuity

There is much to suggest that Jesus reflected upon His mission and message in light of the Scriptures He knew so well.[5] In the Gospels, thirty-nine quotations from the O.T. are attributed to Jesus, as well as dozens of allusions.[6] According to the Gospel of Mark, Jesus began His public ministry with the announcement, "The time is fulfillod, and the kingdom of God is at hand; repent, and believe in the gospel" (Mark 1:15). The expression, "the time is fulfilled," refers to an expectation that surely must have been shared by those who listened to Jesus. His mission is not seen as inaugurating a totally new and unexpected scheme of things but as related to ancient hopes and expectations.[7] We may recall the words of the author of Hebrews that God spoke in His Son "in these last days." The O.T. is generally perceived in the N.T. as having the character of expectancy or anticipation.

This "forward-looking" character of much of the O.T. derives from the conviction that the presence and the actions of God in the world are not random, but purposive, and that God, humankind, and the world are bound up together in the unfolding of these purposes.[8] Although the concerns of God are sometimes expressed in the O.T. in universalistic terms (Isaiah 2:1-4; Zephaniah 3:9, 10), for the most part, the purposes of God are conveyed to the people of Israel and worked out in their experiences.

It will be helpful first to give attention to some of the events, motifs, and themes that appear to be central to the story of the people of Israel and that reappear in the N.T. as evidences of the continuity in God's saving purposes.

The Story of Salvation. Genesis 1-11 presents the creation of the world and humankind and shows the disruption of God's good creation as a result of human disobedience and rebellion. Genesis 12 discloses the intention of God to bless "all the families of the earth" through Abraham. To Abraham, God makes a threefold promise of land, descendants, and a covenant relationship (Genesis 12:1-3; 15:1-6; 17:1-8). In one way or another, most of Genesis 12 through the book of Joshua is concerned with God's confirmation of these promises in the midst of, and sometimes in spite of, the changing experiences of the patriarchs and their descendants. Thus, we see the promise endangered by the childlessness of Abraham in his old age (Genesis 15:1-6), the famine that threatens Jacob and his family (Genesis 45:4-8), the enslaving of the Hebrews in Egypt (Exodus 2:23, 24), the wilderness rebellions (Numbers 14:1-35), and the temptations of Canaanite culture (Judges 2:1-5). Through all these exigencies, God sustains His promises so that we read in Joshua 21:45, "Not one of the good promises which the Lord had made to the house of Israel had failed; all came to pass" (cf. Joshua 23:14). At the same time, it is made clear that the relationship between God and Israel symbolized especially by the covenant made at Sinai (Exodus 19:1—24:8) would be severely tested in the new land, and that judgment would replace blessing if Israel proved unfaithful.[9]

In the recounting of the story of Israel in the books of Judges, Samuel, and Kings, it is shown that, in spite of Israel's repeated unfaithfulness to God, the purposes of God go forward. Even the institution of the monarchy, which appears at first to be a rejection of the rule of God (Judges 8:23; 1 Samuel 8:6-8) becomes a way in which the promises of God to His people may be sustained. Through the prophet Nathan, God establishes with King David a covenant containing three significant promises: (1) that the king of Israel will be a descendant of David; (2) that God will be a "father" to the king, and the king a "son" to God; and (3) that the Davidic kingship will be everlasting (2 Samuel 7:12-17). The added promise of a secure dwelling place for Israel (2 Samuel 7:10) provides a link with the earlier promises to Abraham of posterity, land, and an everlasting covenant. Implicit in the Davidic covenant is the expectation that Israel's kings will be faithful, so that God may be said to rule through them. With few exceptions, however, Israel's monarchs were not faithful to God. The O.T., especially in Kings and Chronicles, candidly records the unflattering picture of the divided kingdom and the eventual decline of each realm.

The great prophetic literature of the eighth/seventh centuries sounds the note of God's judgment on His people for their failure to remain faithful to the relationship He had established with them. The pathetic record of failure is rehearsed in Hosea, where nothing less than the very death of God's people is threatened: "I will destroy you, O Israel; who can help you?" (Hosea 13:9, RSV). Through the political events in which Israel and Judah are caught up, God intends to make an end of His people: "She has fallen, she will not rise again—the virgin Israel. She lies neglected on her land, there is none to raise her up" (Amos 5:2). All the benefits of Israel's previous history with God appear to be nullified. Israel is to be removed from the land, her posterity cut off, her blessings replaced by the curses attending war and captivity. Here is the verdict of God: "You are not my people and I am not your God" (Hosea 1:9). The Davidic king, with whom God had made an "everlasting covenant," will be taken away (Jeremiah 22:28-30), the holy city destroyed, and the temple demolished (Jeremiah 7:14).

In spite of the bleak prospects set forth, these and later prophets make clear that God has not abandoned His purposes nor forgotten His promises. The story of God's dealings with Israel indicates that God is not a victim of history, but its Lord, and He has a program for the future. This future is a radical break with the past. "Do not call to mind the former things, or ponder the things of the past. Behold, I will do something new . . ." (Isaiah 43:18, 19; cf. 48:6-8). On the other hand, God's new act of salvation is set forth in the familiar language of His past deeds. After Israel has been thoroughly chastized for her sins, God will again "choose Israel" (Isaiah 14:1) as He chose Abraham of old. Her journey back from exile to the homeland is seen as a new exodus (Isaiah 11:16; 51:9-11; 52:11, 12; Jeremiah 23:7, 8). There will be a new wilderness wandering (Isaiah 43:19-21; Hosea 2:14, 15), a new covenant (Hosea 2:23; Jeremiah 23:7; 31:31-34; Ezekiel 36:27, 28), a new gift of land (Zephaniah 3:20; Jeremiah 24:4-6; 29:10; 32:37), a large posterity (Isaiah 49:19, 20; 54:1-3; Jeremiah 23:3; Ezekiel 36:37, 38), and a renewed temple and ceremonial arrangements (Ezekiel 20:40; 40—48; Nahum 1:15; Malachi 3:3, 4).

The promises to the Patriarchs are thus not forgotten, but enlarged and understood as being appropriate to a new situation. Morever, to those who feared that the promises to David had been nullified, Jeremiah delivered this message from God: "If you can break my covenant for the day, and my covenant for the night, so that day and night will not be at their appointed time, then my covenant may also be broken with David my servant that he shall not have a son to reign on his throne . . ." (Jeremiah 33:20, 21).[10] A great many O.T. texts referring to an ideal future ruler find their most likely context of meaning in the Davidic covenant of 2 Samuel 7. Thus the prophets speak of a descendant of David who will rule righteously and wisely (Isaiah 9:7; 11:1-5; Jeremiah 23:5; 33:15). His origin will be "from of old" and will be related to Bethlehem, where David had once kept sheep (Micah 5:2). He will, in fact, be the ideal shepherd of God's people, not like the corrupt "shepherds" of old (Micah 5:4; Ezekiel 34; 37:24; Jeremiah 23:1-6).[11]

The texts are vague concerning when the new ruler should arise. Operative terms are "in that day" (Amos 9:11), or "the days are coming" (Jeremiah 23:5), or other similarly indefinite but forward-looking expressions. There is some indication that the post-exilic community of Israel attempted to find the fulfillment of some of these expectations in the events and persons connected with the return from exile, to identify their own times with those of which the prophets had spoken, to believe that the kingdom of God was to be set up among the remnant. These hopes appear to have rested particularly on Zerubbabel, grandson of king Jehoiachin, and therefore a descendant of David.[12]

The restored community was far from being the golden age so longed for; its governors hardly sufficed to fulfill the expectations of a "righteous branch" to be raised up for David. Yet the faith in the ancient covenant promises did not die. The hopes were thrust farther into the future and were increasingly expressed in terminology suggesting far more than a simple political event. The salvation and exaltation of Israel are often portrayed, especially in the post-exilic prophets, in terms of a great conflict in the end-times, when God will defeat all the enemies of His people and set up a kingdom over the faithful (Ezekiel 38—39; Zechariah 14:1-21). The book of Daniel describes a vision in which God, referred to as "the Ancient of Days," delivers over "dominion, glory, and a kingdom" to "one like a Son of Man" (Daniel 7:13, 14).

Between the Testaments. Although our primary concern is with the Old and New Testaments, it is of some importance to know how the issues discussed above were treated in Jewish literature outside the canon, particularly in the two centuries before the Christian era.[13] These writings are characterized by great diversity in their understandings of the Old Covenant promises and in the shape of their expectations for fulfillment.[14] Of greatest interest for students of the N.T. are the strong indications that the hope for a restoration of the Davidic monarchy continued, as witnessed by a host of references in the Qumran texts, many of which cite the classical prophetic passages in Amos, Isaiah, and Jeremiah alluded to above.[15] In the Eighteen Benedictions, recited by pious Jews three times a day, the fifteenth includes a prayer for God to "speedily cause the Shoot of David, Thy servant, to shoot up, and raise up his horn through thy salvation."

It is particularly intriguing to note that some of this literature brings together the promises made to Abraham and those made to David. The Targum to Psalm 39:4 reads "I made a covenant for Abraham my chosen one, I swore to David my servant."[16] It can also be shown that the term "seed" (i.e. offspring) used in both the Abrahamic and Davidic passages, is interpreted in some targumic and midrashic[17] literature to refer collectively to Israel and singularly to a coming ruler.[18]

The Preaching of Jesus. When Jesus appeared in Galilee and announced, "The time is fulfilled, and the kingdom of God is at hand" (Mark 1:15), His hearers would likely have been quite alert to the O.T. contents of the key terms. They knew that the announcement that "good news" was to be proclaimed indicated that the time had indeed been fulfilled, "the year of the Lord's favor" had come, as the speaker in Isaiah 61:1, 2 had said. How fitting that in His sermon in the synagogue at Nazareth, Jesus applied to His own ministry this ancient text

(Luke 4:17-19). Thus, Jesus presented His own program as one of continuity with the divine plan begun centuries before.

The Gospels represent Jesus as having explicated His mission again and again as unfolding "according to the Scriptures."[19] Particularly was this true with respect to His suffering and death (see Mark 9:12; cf. Mark 8:31; 9:31; 14:21). Perhaps the most noteworthy development is seen in the linking of the Danielic Son of Man figure with the Suffering Servant of Isaiah in Jesus' understanding of His mission as expressed in Mark 10:45: "The Son of Man did not come to be served, but to serve, and to give His life a ransom for many."[20] In the Gospels, all the major components of the ministry of Jesus are related to the O.T.—His work of preaching and healing, His suffering, His death, and His exaltation.

Early Christian Preaching. The pattern identified above continues in early Christian preaching. Paul affirms that the essential elements of the gospel are all "according to the Scriptures" (1 Corinthians 15:3, 4). The sermons in the Book of Acts confirm Paul's statement; almost all of the O.T. quotations in Acts occur in public addresses. When Peter stood up to explain the significance of the strange phenomena that occurred at Pentecost, he told his audience, "This is what was spoken of through the prophet Joel . . ." (Acts 2:16; cf. Joel 2:28-32). The sermons of Peter (2:14-36; 3:12-26; 10:34-43), Stephen (7:2-53), Philip (8:26-40), and Paul (13:16-41; 17:22-31) contain copious quotations from and references to the O.T. Scriptures. R. N. Longenecker lists twenty-seven explicit O.T. quotations in the sermons and speeches of early Christian leaders in Acts.[21]

The New Testament Writings. As later Christian writers reflected upon the implications of the gospel, they went beyond even the teachings of Jesus and early Christian preaching in their use of the O.T. The N.T. authors do not all make the same emphases or mine the same texts in order to show the deep significance of the person and work of Jesus. For example, Jesus, in declaring His mission, made almost no use of those texts that refer to a restoration of David's kingdom, but some N.T. writers make much use of the Davidic covenant promises.[22] The first two chapters of Luke are reminiscent, in both style and content, of hymns and Psalms of the O.T., especially those Psalms that express the hopes of Israel in terms of a prince of David's line (Luke 1:32, 33, 67-79). It is particularly important to see in Zechariah's *Benedictus* how the promises to

David are allied with those to Abraham and how both are related to the deliverer soon to be born: "[God] has raised up a horn of salvation for us in the house of David His servant . . . to remember His holy covenant, the oath which He swore to Abraham our father . . ." (Luke 1:69-73). In another canticle in Luke, there are allusions to Isaiah's "Servant of the Lord" (cf. Luke 2:29-32; Isaiah 49:6).

The purpose of the brief survey above is to demonstrate that, by their use of the O.T., the writers of the N.T. express a conviction that the story of God and His people is one story, and that God's dealings with, and promises to, Israel are important for the church. In the N.T., many of the ancient designations of the people of God are taken up and applied to the followers of Jesus. These include such descriptive terms as "sons of Abraham" (Galatians 3:29; Romans 4:16), "a chosen race, a royal priesthood, a holy nation, God's own people," (1 Peter 2:9) and the more formal designation "the Israel of God" (Galatians 6:16).[23] The most astonishing development is the extension of language long associated with Jews alone to Gentiles, who can be called "sons of Abraham" (Galatians 3:29; cf. Colossians 2:11, 12; Romans 2:25-29; 4:16) without hesitation or any sense of awkwardness. The enlarging of Old Covenant concepts to embrace all members of the new community constitutes one of the clearest evidences of the continuity between the O.T. and the N.T.

Moral-Ethical Teachings. The continuity between the Old and New Testaments applies to some extent also to ethical and moral teachings. In part, this is true because there is a sizable overlap in the moral teachings in antiquity, whether from Jewish, Christian, or pagan sources.[24] To the extent that "sources" and parallels to the moral teachings of the N.T. may be discerned, the O.T. provides the most fertile background. The Ten Commandments, the heart of the moral code of the O.T., reappear in the N.T. with positive connotations. Five of them are quoted in Matthew 19:17-19 (Mark 10:19; Luke 18:20), and four are cited in Romans 13:9. The two commandments under which Jesus summed up the whole law (Deuteronomy 6:5 and Leviticus 19:18) appear several times in the N.T.[25] In the teaching of Jesus, the grounding of one's moral responsibilities to others on one's relationship to God "stands in the direct line of succession to all the prophets and psalmists and sages of Israel."[26] The N.T. writings in general stand within this same framework. Jesus' statements that He did not come to abolish the law and the prophets, but to fulfill them (Matthew 5:17) accords with Paul's acknowledgement that the law is holy, righteous, good, and spiritual (Romans 7:12, 14). As we shall see below, this notion that Jesus comes to "fulfill" the law implies that the continuity between O.T. and N.T. is not a static relationship in which the N.T. simply mirrors the Old, but is a dynamic one in which the N.T. has its own emphases to make.

Discontinuity

The Story of Salvation. Although the author of Hebrews is concerned to show that the speaking of God has taken place within the unfolding of one continuous story, he also recognizes that God's speaking in His Son is a decisive event that is not to be understood as simply continuous with past revelation.

The O.T. can be read as a record of failure. So understood, it proves to be a remarkably candid account of the breakdown of law, sacrifice, and monarchy as channels to God. The prophetic word concerning these institutions was frequently one of complete destruction rather than reform.[27] There is an element of discontinuity between God's speaking in His Son and His previous forms of address.[28] The history of Israel is a history of a covenant repeatedly broken, whereas the new possibility in Christ is a covenant that will not be broken (Hebrews 8:7-13).

This sense of discontinuity is radically Christ-centered. It has its beginnings in His teachings. The new and disturbing act of Jesus was to set His own words on a par with, or even above, God's revelation in the Scripture of old. All of the Gospels, in one way or another, take note of the newness of Jesus in this regard: "And they were amazed at His teaching; for He was teaching them as one having authority, and not as the scribes" (Mark 2:22; cf. Matthew 7:28, 29).

In the presentation of Jesus alongside O.T. persons and institutions, the N.T. indicates the unique status of Jesus: He is "greater than the temple" (Matthew 12:6); "greater than Jonah" (Matthew 12:41; Luke 11:32); "greater than Solomon" (Matthew 12:42; Luke 11:31) greater even "than our father Jacob" (John 4:12) and "our father Abraham" (cf. John 8:33). Whereas Moses is the mediator of God's revelation, by means of the law, Jesus is himself God's revelation (John 1:17). In John's thought, Jesus, as Word of God, was with God before there was any other word of revelation at all (John 1:1). Although the Gospel of John most systematically identifies Jesus the Son as God incarnate, all of the Gospels make it clear that Jesus claims prerogatives and receives honor that are due to God alone (Matthew 16:16; Mark 3:11; Luke 8:28; John 5:18). In one extraordinary statement (Matthew 11:27; Luke 10:22), "Jesus claims not only that he alone stands in a special relation to God, but also that he is the only one through whom others can be brought into a similar relation."[29]

The radical newness symbolized by Jesus probably has its sharpest focus in regard to the law of the O.T. In the so-called antitheses in the Sermon on the Mount, Jesus sets a pattern that must result in conflict between himself and the custodians of the law. The distinction implied in "You have heard that it was said . . . but I say . . ." (Matthew 5:21-48) is not simply that between the inner and the outer, the deed and the motive, or the written code and the spirit. Had such been the case, Jesus might be understood as illustrating the conflict between the prophetic spirit and the legal, for the prophets of old also called into question the understanding of the will of God as minimal compliance with written codes. What was at issue here was the role of the law itself in one's relationship to God.

Recent studies have pointed out that Judaism in the first century was characterized by great diversity, so that one hesitates any longer to speak of "normative" Judaism.[30] Nevertheless, Judaism during the time of Jesus was one in its appreciation of the centrality of the Torah for all of life. However, Torah, meaning *instruction*, is not to be understood only as *law*; the heart of the Torah was considered to be the revelation, both written and oral, given to Moses by God. "As the gift of Yahweh and the ground plan of the universe it could not but be perfect and unchangeable; it was impossible that it should ever be forgotten; no prophet could ever arise who would change it, and no new Moses should ever appear to introduce another Law to replace it."[31] The Hebrew Scriptures as a whole could be referred to as "Torah."[32] Jewish expectation of sharing in the kingdom of God, of participation in God's salvation, was, to a great extent, contingent on obedience to the law. The N.T. establishes the basis for the eventual break between church and synagogue and, from one point of view, between the O.T. and the N.T. in the conviction that the kingdom of God has become a reality with the appearance of Jesus and that participation in the life of the kingdom is dependent upon a faithful relationship to Him. Jesus himself forced the issue by calling to repentance those who most zealously guarded the law (Matthew 5:20; 23:13-15; Luke 11:39-51). When Jesus made participation in salvation dependent on one's relationship with His own person, He effectively undercut the validity of the Pharisaic understanding of the law.[33]

The history of early Christianity, as presented in the Acts of the Apostles, shows that the place of the law in Christian faith and practice was the subject of much controversy. The story of Stephen's sermon and subsequent martyrdom (Acts 7) illustrates the breach between church and synagogue over the approach to the O.T. in general and the law in particular. The issue became particularly critical as the gospel was extended to Gentiles (Acts 10:1—11:26), for it eventually became obvious that, if Gentiles could have salvation in Christ apart from the law, then Jews could also come to Christ apart from the law. Paul drew out the implications of this conviction most strongly, holding that "Christ is the end of the law, that everyone who has faith may be justified" (Romans 10:4, RSV).[34]

If the O.T. no longer pointed the way to salvation by means of the law, how was it to function in the life of the church? The solution was not, of course, to abandon the Scriptures. Rather, the N.T. reveals a serious process of rethinking with regard to the redemptive story unfolded in the O.T. so that the O.T. is understood as having prepared the way for salvation apart from law. From the vantage point of the present-day reader of the Bible, it becomes clear that the discontinuity is not so much between O.T. and N.T. as between the understanding of the O.T. in rabbinic Judaism and the understanding of the O.T. in early Christianity in the light of the gospel. Paul did not preach a gospel discontinuous with the O.T. Indeed, he insisted that both the law and the prophets bear witness to the righteousness of God manifested apart from the law (Romans 3:21). Nevertheless, to the extent that historical Judaism represented itself as continuous with the ancient revelation of God in Moses and the prophets, the N.T. is clearly moving in a different direction.

Moral-Ethical Limitations of the Old Testament. There is also discontinuity between the O.T. and the N.T. with regard to moral and ethical concerns, although it may be preferable to speak of the limitations of the O.T. rather than simple discontinuity. That is to say, the revelation given to Israel in the O.T.

was perceived and acted upon within a cultural context that could have but limited application to later ages. It is well-known, for example, that the O.T. laws make a sharp distinction between the duties of an Israelite toward another Israelite (or a "sojourner") and toward one outside the covenant.[35]

The whole ethos of war in the O.T. may be deeply disturbing to contemporary readers. This applies particularly to the so-called Holy War (or "Yahweh War") ideology, which portrays God as leading Israel in battle and commanding wholesale slaughter of complete cities (Deuteronomy 20:16-18; Joshua 6:17, 21; 8:24-29; 1 Samuel 27:8-11).[36] In this connection, the "imprecatory Psalms," in which the worshiper curses his enemies, are also problematic for the Christian (cf. Psalm 109:6-20, 28, 29; 137:7-9; 139:19-22; 143:12). The moral teaching of the N.T. is a marked advance over these attitudes. The same is true with regard to sexual relationships. Although the law has powerful strictures against adultery, prostitution, homosexuality, and the like, polygamy and a "double standard" are implicitly sanctioned. The ethics of social relationships in the N.T. are, in some cases, also discontinuous with those of the O.T. The N.T. elevates the status of slaves, foreigners, and women relative to the prevailing social practices.[37]

The true uniqueness of the moral teaching of the N.T. is its locus in the person of Jesus Christ.[38] Jesus both taught and exemplified a pattern of behavior that went beyond the ethical traditions of the O.T. and of His own people. He taught that the will of God was embodied not only in the O.T. written code, but also in himself. His freedom to move beyond the written code was consistent with His announcement that in His ministry, the kingdom of God was at work. That the person of Jesus Christ remained central to the ethical concerns of the early church is supported by the many injunctions, explicit and implicit, to "imitate Christ," or, in Paul, to "imitate me, as I imiatate Christ" (1 Corinthians 10:33—11:1; Galatians 2:20; Ephesians 5:1, 2; Philippians 1:27; 2:5-8; Colossians 3:1-11; 1 Thessalonians 1:6; 2 Timothy 1:13; Hebrews 12:1, 2; 1 Peter 2:21).

How the Old Testament Is Understood in the New Testament

How did the authors of the N.T. show the relationship between God's speaking in the O.T. and His speaking in the events expressed by the gospel? They did so by reflecting on the Scriptures in the light thrown upon them by the career of Jesus. By means of this light thrown backward, shapes and patterns previously hidden in God's ancient revelation were exposed.

The broad framework in which the relationship between God's Word of old and God's Word in Christ is developed is frequently referred to as promise/fulfillment. It may be illustrated by Paul's sermon in Antioch of Pisidia, in which he said, "We preach to you the good news of the promise made to the fathers, that God has fulfilled this promise . . ." (Acts 13:32, 33). It must be emphasized that promise/fulfillment does not imply a mechanical process in which the O.T. is evacuated of any meaning and validity in its own historical setting and is simply a mine of "proof texts" for Jesus.[39] We have to do, rather, with the way in which the authors of the N.T. read the O.T. and discovered that the unfinished story therein found its continuation in Christ. The forward-looking thrust of the Scriptures in light of the life, death, and resurrection of Jesus was not confined to a search through the prophets for messianic prophecies; rather, "the Law of Moses and the Prophets and the Psalms" were all understood as fulfilled in Jesus Christ (Luke 24:44).

The church did not need to develop a set of new interpretative techniques in order to enlist the O.T. in the service of the gospel. Christians simply made use of some of the methods of Scripture exegesis already in practice in the Judaism of the first century.[40] By means of the mechanics of quotation, several techniques could be used to derive meanings not at first obvious from the Scriptures. A few examples may be given:

(1) "Chain" quotations, in which a number of O.T. texts are cited serially, ideally from the law, the prophets, and the writings, because they all bear on a common idea or are all related to a catchword in which the author is interested. In Romans 15:9-12, texts from Psalm 18:49; Deuteronomy 32:43; Psalm 117:1; and Isaiah 11:10 are all joined because they have something to do with the Gentiles' rejoicing or glorifying God.

(2) "Testimony" collections, the use of O.T. texts that have been gathered together early in the life of the church for use in instruction and preaching, with a view to supporting various Christological emphases. For example, a number of O.T. passages referring to a "stone" (Psalm 118:22; Isaiah 8:14; 28:16;

Daniel 2:34, 35) appear in various combinations in Mark 12:10; Luke 20:17; Acts 4:11; Romans 9:33; and 1 Peter 2:6-8.[41]

(3) Paraphrasing, or quoting and interpreting the text simultaneously. In Galatians 4:30, Paul quotes Genesis 21:10, but substitutes the words "the son of a free woman" for the phrase "my son Isaac" in order better to relate the text to his argument.

(4) Choosing from different forms of the O.T. text the one that best accords with the purpose of the N.T. author. Most often, this involves the use of the Septuagint, the Greek translation of the O.T., in place of the Hebrew text. In Hebrews 10:5, in place of the Hebrew phrase in Psalm 40:6, translated, "My ears thou hast opened" (the Masoretic Hebrew text translates literally, "Ears thou hast dug for me"), the author loosely quotes the Septuagint, which reads, "A body thou hast prepared for me." A more startling example is the quotation of Psalm 68:18 in Ephesians 4:8. Whereas both the Hebrew and Septuagint texts read, "Thou hast led captive Thy captives; Thou hast *received* gifts among men . . ." Ephesians 4:8 reads, "He led captive a host of captives and He *gave* gifts to men . . . ," in keeping with the text of the Peshitta (Syriac) and the Targum (Aramaic paraphrase).

All of these techniques may be paralleled in the Jewish exposition of Scripture broadly designated as "midrash," the purpose of which was to show the contemporary significance of ancient texts in quite specific ways.

The circumstance that permits the N.T. authors to find current significance in O.T. texts is that both they and their earliest readers shared the belief that in the record of God's saving history, there are certain patterns of agreement, significant correspondences that furnish clues to the events summarized in the gospel.

The identification of these correspondences is usually referred to as "typology." Typological interpretation is one of the most characteristic ways in which the N.T. writers "see" the O.T.[42] This understanding is based on a historical view of revelation in which (a) the past is prophetic of the future and (b) there are resemblances between God's activity in the past and God's activity in the present.[43] These writers see O.T. history as a history of salvation, leading up to Christ and leading on to a future hope. Thus, the events that are central to the history of Israel ultimately relate to the church. Paul, in summarizing the exodus/wilderness events, can write that all these things "were written down for our instruction, upon whom the ends of the ages have come" (1 Corinthians 10:11). "Typological exegesis is the search for linkages between events, persons, or things *within the historical framework of* revelation. . . ."[44]

A somewhat similar approach to Scripture is found already in the O.T. as, for example, when the prophet presents the return from Babylonian captivity as recapitulation of the exodus from Egypt (Isaiah 43:14-21). We have seen how the prophets used the old motifs of creation, election, exodus, and others to speak to their own generation about God's saving acts to follow.

The typological patterns applied most vigorously in the N.T. include the following:

(1) Creation typology. In Romans 5:14 Paul can speak of "Adam, who is a type of Him who was to come" (cf. 2 Corinthians 4:4; Colossians 1:15; Hebrews 1:3). Included in this typological framework are such passages as Romans 8:18-25, which speaks of the creation as waiting for its redemption, 2 Corinthians 5:17, which speaks of the new creation in Christ, and Revelation 21, 22, with its description of "a new heaven and a new earth." (See also Ephesians 4:24 and Colossians 3:10.)

(2) Patriarchal typology. Not many parallels are drawn between the patriarchal period and the church. The most obvious one is the continuity between the faith of Abraham and the faith of those who follow Christ (Romans 4; Galatians 3:6-9). In the "allegory of the two covenants" (Galatians 4:22-31), Sarah and Hagar foreshadow the later relationship between Judaism and the church.[45]

(3) Covenant typology. Included within this framework is a whole complex of themes, including release from bondage, wilderness wandering, the Sinai agreement, inheritance of the land, and the monarchy. In 1 Corinthians 10:11, Paul speaks of the wilderness rebellion and the judgment of God with the comment that "these things happened to them as an *example*" (Gk. *typikos,* "typically," "as a type"). Covenant motifs furnish by far the greatest stock of material for typological use in the N.T., perhaps because of "the Jewish conviction that God's redemptive acts are always patterned after the Exodus."[46] The key figures and institutions of the covenant of Israel are drawn upon by the author of Hebrews in an intricately-developed typology that finds relationships between Jesus and Moses

(3:1-19), Jesus and Joshua (4:1-10), Jesus and the high priests (5:1-7), and the Old Covenant and the New Covenant, including institutions and rituals of worship (8:8—10:25). The Moses/Jesus typology is widespread in the N.T. (compare the following: Deuteronomy 18:15 and Acts 3:22, 23; Exodus 4:19 and Matthew 2:20, 21; Exodus 19 and Matthew 5; Exodus 16:4, 15 and John 6:31-51; Exodus 15:1-18 and Revelation 14:3, 4; 15:3, 4). Within the larger "covenant" typology may be included the David/Jesus relationship as richly developed in the N.T. (Mark 12:35-37; Luke 1:32, 33; Acts 2:29-32; Revelation 3:7; 5:5).

The correspondences between persons, events, or things may be developed very explicitly, as in most of the examples given above, or only suggestively, implicitly. For example, it seems more than likely that Matthew intends for the reader to perceive Jesus, giving His new "Torah" in the Sermon on the Mount, as superseding Moses, who delivered another law on another mount.[47]

The relationship between the O.T. type and the new-age reality may be both synthetic and antithetic, that is, it may witness to both similarity and dissimilarity. Jesus is like Adam in that He is the head of a new creation; but unlike Adam, who introduced death, Jesus brings life (Romans 5:12, 15; 1 Corinthians 15:22). Although "the law is holy, and the commandment is holy, and just, and good" (as is the "law of Christ"), dependence on "works of the law" for salvation makes the law a means of condemnation (Galatians 3:10-13). Similarly, the O.T. type may function in unexpectedly different ways in different N.T. contexts. Thus Abraham is a type of faith in Romans 4:1 5 and of "works" in James 2:21-24.

Although the typological perspective is prominent in N.T. interpretation of the O.T., it is by no means the only way in which prophecy and fulfillment are related. Frequently, the N.T. writers assert that an event in the career of Jesus, rather than corresponding to an O.T. parallel, is simply the occurrence of that which was predicted long ago with reference to the new age. The triumphal entry of Jesus into Jerusalem is understood, not as the recapitulation of a former occurrence, but as the fulfillment of a prediction that a long-expected prince of David's line would come to Zion "humble and mounted on an ass" (Zechariah 9:9/Matthew 21:4, 5; John 12:14, 15). Similarly, when Jesus announced in Nazareth the program for

His ministry by quoting from Isaiah 61:1, 2, He was asserting that "the favorable year of the Lord," long expected, had finally arrived.

The progression from the Old to the New Covenant is not based simply on analogy, "as if two isolated facts belonging to different historical contexts would have some intrinsic right to be combined."[48] Nor is it based on a view of Scripture that made it necessary to ignore the original contexts of the Old Covenant passages or to evacuate them of all meaning except in relation to Christ. Rather, the N.T. writers bear witness to a dynamic process in which God's purposes are worked out in the order of history in such a way as to unite past, present, and future in a broad range of relationships.

Although an impressive list can be made showing N.T. fulfillment of O.T. promises, such examples do not function very well as rationalistic "proofs" of Scripture. This is because the N.T. writers do not treat the O.T. promise as an exact programmatic description of what later occurred in the career of Jesus and the birth of the church. The relationships between promise and fulfillment are not so precise that, if a person had only one part of the equation, the rest could be constructed. In other words, when one reads Hosea 11:1, "When Israel was a youth I loved him, and out of Egypt I called My son," one cannot immediately deduce that this text requires that Mary and Joseph will one day take the infant Jesus to Egypt. Conversely, if one had only the record of the flight to Egypt, there would be no reason for the reader to make a connection with the passage in Hosea 11:1. When the connection is made in Matthew 2:15, it represents the culmination of a complex process of reasoning and reflection.[49] The unity between promise and fulfillment is found in the continuing divine activity of revelation that finds its consummation in Jesus Christ.[50] The range of themes caught up in this consummation is astonishingly comprehensive, as may be seen in this summary by F. F. Bruce:

> In Jesus the promise is confirmed, the covenant is renewed, the prophecies are fulfilled, the law is vindicated, salvation is brought near, sacred history has reached its climax, the perfect sacrifice has been offered and accepted, the great priest over the household of God has taken his seat at God's right hand, the Prophet like Moses has been raised up, the Son of David reigns, the kingdom of God has been inaugurated, the Son of Man has received dominion from the Ancient of Days, the Servant of the Lord, having been smitten to

death for his people's transgression and borne the sin of many, has accomplished the divine purpose, has seen light after the travail of his soul and is now exalted and extolled and made very high.[51]

The Old Testament in the Church Today

The writer of Hebrews wrestles with the issue of how God still speaks to His people in the ancient Scriptures, now that He has spoken in Jesus. This question is, if anything, more relevant to the twentieth-century reader of the O.T. than it was to the first-century reader. How do we read the O.T. so as still to hear the Word of God as "living and active" (Hebrews 4:12)? It is not realistic to expect the Christian to read the O.T. without considering the perspective of the N.T. At the same time, it is not legitimate simply to "read back" the N.T. into the Old, without regard to the various contexts to which the O.T. has spoken in the course of history.

The revelation of God in the O.T. is not confined to the function of the O.T. as promise. The O.T. has significance in its own right, and needs to be heard by the church in every age. It makes contributions to the Christian life and world view that the N.T. touches upon only briefly or indirectly.

The O.T. stands as a strong defense against all types of natural or cultural religion, helping the church to guard against the tendency to slip into various forms of paganism. The O.T. doctrine of creation portrays the one God as both Creator and Redeemer. Nature is seen in its proper perspective as a creature of God, not as a creator bringing forth all sorts of spirits and powers that influence human life. The O.T. insistence on the objectivity, majesty, and grandeur of God serves as a check against the contemporary tendency to sentimentalize and patronize God or to reduce the knowledge of God to a feeling or an experience.[52]

The O.T. also serves to help the Christian guard against the practice of focusing all Christian worship and reflection on Jesus Christ alone, without reference to the God of Jesus, who was the God of Abraham, Isaac, and Jacob. The tendency to focus all attention in hymns, prayers, and Christian instruction sharply on the person of Jesus can lead to a one-sided doctrinal emphasis, what has been called a "unitarianism of the Second Person."[53]

The O.T. plays an even more creative and important role for Christian faith than these examples suggest. For the writers of the N.T., a major function of the O.T. is exhortation, and it is

needed precisely because of the dual character of Christian
existence. On the one hand, the N.T. testifies to the reality and
presence of the new age in Jesus Christ, insisting that the powers of death and sin have been defeated and that those in Christ
have been "delivered . . . from the dominion of darkness and
transferred . . . to the kingdom of His beloved Son" (Colossians
1:13). On the other hand, the N.T. frankly recognizes that we
still struggle against the problems of our historical existence in
this world, but it is the O.T. that gives the most potent description of what it means to seek the will of God amid all the
ambiguities of historical existence. The language of protest,
tears, and doubts reflected in the books of Job and Lamenta-
tions and in some of the Psalms is not robbed of its relevance by
the assurances of victory in Christ.[54] When the Jew reflects on
the contemporary realities of life and asks, "In what sense is the
world redeemed?" the Christian dare not give a flippant answer. One may find in the N.T. some guiding principles for the
exercising of one's social and political duties, but it is the O.T.
that more often confronts us with the awful and continual
necessity of discerning the will of God in the political and
social crises of this world.

The author of Hebrews wrestles with the ambiguity of Christian existence by moving from the realized goals of
salvation—all that "we have" in Christ—to the historical
realities of our struggle to remain faithful in the present moment ("Let us hold fast").[55] We are reminded by the hortatory
language of much of the N.T. that we have not yet arrived. To
the extent that this is so, much of the Scripture, O.T. and N.T.,
retains the character of promise for us. Are the O.T. texts about
the "last days" fully realized even in Jesus, or do we await yet
another coming, a second coming, when "the kingdom of the
world has become the kingdom of our Lord, and of His Christ;
and He will reign forever and ever" (Revelation 11:15)? Mean-
while, we of the church are still a pilgrim people, like Israel in
the wilderness or Abraham in search of "a city which has foundations, whose architect and builder is God" (Hebrews 11:10).
This is the reason that the human career of Jesus is so often held
before the reader of Hebrews. He stands before us in His human
existence in this world as an exemplar, the "pioneer of faith."[56]

The O.T. remains an essential witness, on more than one
level, to the revelation of God. The God who "spoke long ago to
the fathers in the prophets" still speaks in these ancient texts,

even to those who have heard "in these last days" the word spoken in His Son.

NOTES

[1]For a short, popular account of various proposals for dealing with the problem of the Old Testament in the church, see John Bright, The Authority of the Old Testament (Nashville: Abingdon, 1967).

[2]In the N.T. writings, several terms are used to refer to the O.T. Scriptures. It is still a matter of dispute whether the precise limits of the Jewish canon of Scripture had been recognized during the first Christian century. That there were two well-known divisions, most often designated as "the Law and the Prophets" is certain (see, e.g., Matthew 7:12; Luke 16:16; John 1:45; Acts 24:14). A threefold division was known as early as 130 B.C. (see the Prologue to Ecclesiasticus, or The Wisdom of Jesus ben Sirach) and may be implied in the words of Jesus in Luke 24:44 (cf. 24:27). It is known, however, that the status of some books in the third division of the canon, the Writings, continued to be debated by some of the rabbis up into the first century, A.D. See Sid Z. Leiman, The Canonization of Hebrew Scripture: The Talmudic and Midrashic Evidence (Hamden, Connecticut: Anchor, 1976); Neil R. Lightfoot, "The Canon and Text of the Old Testament," The World and Literature of the Old Testament, John T. Willis, ed. (Austin: Sweet, 1979), pp. 41-70; Albert C. Sundberg, Jr., The Old Testament of the Early Church (Cambridge, Mass.: Harvard University Press, 1964).

[3]The most convenient recent listing of N.T. quotations of and allusions to O.T. literature is found in Novum Testamentum Graece, Eberhard Nestle, Erwin Nestle, Kurt Aland, and others, eds. 26th new revised ed. (Stuttgart: Deutsche Biblestiftung, 1975), Appendix 3.

[4]Henry M. Shires, Finding the Old Testament in the New (Philadelphia: Westminster, 1974), p. 15.

[5]There is no consensus of scholars with reference to the possiblity of recovering the actual words of Jesus in the Gospels. Various problems arise when parallel accounts of the teachings in the Gospels are compared; in addition, our knowledge of how these teachings were transmitted in both oral and written states is quite limited. Despite these obstacles, there is widespread agreement (1) that Jesus used the O.T. authoritatively, (2) interpreted it freely, and (3) reflected upon His own mission in light of its contents. See D. Moody Smith, Jr., "The Use of the Old Testament in the New," The Use of the Old Testament in the New and Other Essays: Studies in Honor of William Franklin Stinespring, James M. Efird, ed. (Durham: Duke University Press, 1972), pp. 20-25. A good treatment of the use of the O.T. in the teachings of Jesus appears in Richard Longenecker, Biblical Exegesis in the Apostolic Period (Grand Rapids: Eerdmans, 1975), pp. 51-78.

[6]Longenecker, op. cit., pp. 57-62; cf. Shires, op. cit., pp. 190-196, 205-206.

[7]See F. F. Bruce, The Time is Fulfilled (Grand Rapids: Eerdmans, 1978), pp. 15-19.

[8]See Elizabeth Achtemeire, The Old Testament and the Proclamation of the Gospel (Philadelphia: Westminster, 1973), pp. 37, 38.

[9]See especially Deuteronomy 17—30, where this theme appears almost as a key for the book.

[10]Jeremiah 33:17-21 also makes reference to the perpetuity of the priesthood through the house of Levi, but this promise does not have the place in Israel's hopes that the Davidic covenant occupied.

[11]See F. F. Bruce, New Testament Development of Old Testament Themes (Grand Rapids: Eerdmans, 1969), pp. 72, 73; 100, 101; also The Time is Fulfilled, pp. 49, 50.

[12]Haggai 2:33; cf. Zechariah 6:12, 13.

[13]This literature includes not only most of the so-called "Apocrypha," but also many of the writings from Qumran (the "Dead Sea Scrolls") and a variety of other material. It is likely that rabbinic writings such as the Mishnah, Toscphta, the Talmud, and the Midrashim also contain much pre-Christian material, although in their present form all date from Christian times. Study of the development of ideas and understandings during the interim period is, then, vital to this essay.

[14]For example, under the Hamoneans (142-63 B.C.), when the kingship was united with the priesthood, "the expectation of a deliverer from David's line was overshadowed by one from the tribe of Levi . . ." (Bruce, New Testament Development, p. 76).

[15]Bruce, New Testament Development, p. 76.

[16]Targums (or Targumim) are free translations of the Hebrew O.T. into Aramaic for the benefit of Jews who had little or no knowledge of Hebrew. The evidence of Targums must be used with caution because all of the texts extant date A.D. 600 or later. There is no doubt, however, that much ancient, and some pre-Christian, material is contained in them. See Martin McNamara, Targum and Testament (Grand Rapids: Eerdmans, 1972), pp. 79-89.

[17]A midrash is an ancient Jewish commentary on Scripture, whether a random comment in the Talmud or a discrete literary work devoted to a particular book or section of the Hebrew canon.

[18]See Max Wilcox, "The Promise of the 'Seed' in the New Testament and the Targumim," Journal for the Study of the New Testament, 5 (1979), pp. 2-20.

[19]Some argue that it is impossible to recover from the text Jesus' own interpretation of Scripture; cf. Norman Perrin, Rediscovering the Teaching of Jesus (New York: Harper & Row, 1976). It must be acknowledged that, in view of the special interests and perspectives exhibited by each of the Gospel writers, we do not have simply four "biographies" of Jesus out of which we may confidently reconstruct one life story. This does not mean, however, that the Gospels reflect only the theology of the early church and not the actual life and ministry of Jesus. Clearly, both fact and interpretation are there.

[20]For "Son of Man," see Daniel 7:13-22. Some scholars believe that this "Son of Man" terminology owes something to Psalm 8:4 as well. The four "Servant Songs" of Isaiah occur at 42:1-4 (some include 5-9); 49:1-6 (7-13); 50:4-9 (10, 11); and 52:13—53:12. The notion that the mission of the Servant involves suffering is explicit in the second and third passages.

[21]Biblical Exegesis in the Apostolic Period, pp. 85-87.

[22]Although Jesus did not deny the title "Son of David" when others used it of Him (Mark 10:47, 48; Matthew 15:22), His only explicit reference to Davidic sonship is in the engimatic encounter in Mark 12:35-37. On the problems regarding that passage, see W. L. Lane, The Gospel According to Mark (Grand Rapids: Eerdmans, 1974), pp. 435-438.

[23]See Paul Minear, Images of the Church in the New Testament (Philadelphia: Westminster, 1960), pp. 66-104.

[24]C. S. Lewis reminds us that both Jesus and the apostles "came demanding repentance and offering forgiveness, a demand and an offer both meaningless except on the assumption of a moral law already known and already broken" (Christian Reflections [Grand Rapids: Eerdmans, 1967], p. 46; cf. Mere Christianity [New York: Macmillan, 1958], p. 64).

[25]See Shires, Finding the Old Testament in the New, pp. 118-121, for these and other examples from both Gospels and Epistles.

[26]T. W. Manson, The Teachings of Jesus, 2nd. ed. (Cambridge: Cambridge University Press, 1945), p. 286.

[27]See John L. McKenzie, "The Values of the Old Testament," How Does the Christian Confront the Old Testament? Pierre Benoit et al., eds., vol. 30, Concilium: Theology in the Age of Renewal (New York: Paulist Press, 1967), pp. 28-29.

[28]Carried to its limits, this discontinuity virtually excludes the possibility of the Christian's finding the revelation of God in the O.T. Rudolf Bultmann is probably the best-known contemporary representative of this view. For him, the O.T. represents largely an "inner contradiction" and a "miscarriage." See his "Prophecy and Fulfillment, Essays on Old Testament Hermeneutics, Claus Westermann, ed., trans. James L. Mays (Richmond: John Knox Press, 1963), p. 72; cf. Bultmann, "The Significance of the Old Testament for the Christian Faith," The Old Testament and Christian Faith, Bernhard W. Anderson, ed. (New York; Herder & Herder, 1969), pp. 8-35.

[29]Bruce M. Metzger, The New Testament: Its Background, Growth, and Content (Nashville: Abingdon, 1965), p. 155.

[30]See David Daube, The New Testament and Rabbinic Judaism (London: The Athlone Press, 1956); W. D. Davies, The Setting of the Sermon on the Mount (Cambridge: Cambridge University Press, 1964); Paul and Rabbinic Judaism (New York: Harper & Row, 1967), pp. 1-17.

[31]Davies, The Setting of the Sermon on the Mount, p. 158.

[32]For references, see Daniel Patte, Early Jewish Hermeneutics in Palestine, S. B. L. Dissertation Series 22 (Missoula, Mont.: Scholars Press, 1975), p. 22

[33]This is expressed most forcibly in Leonhard Goppelt, Jesus, Paul, and Judaism, trans. and ed. Edward Schroeder (New York: Thomas Nelson & Sons, 1964), p. 94.

[34]The issue between "law" and "gospel" must not be oversimplified into a conflict between "works" and "grace," for the N.T. commands "works" and the O.T. expresses grace. This issue is treated in great detail in E. P. Sanders, Paul and Palestinian Judaism (Philadelphia: Fortress Press, 1977), pp. 446-523; cf. Eldon J. Epp, "Paul's Diverse Imageries of the Human Situation and His Unifying Theme of Freedom," Unity and Diversity in New Testament Theology, Robert A. Guelich, ed. [Grand Rapids: Eerdmans Publishing, 1978], pp. 100-116).

[35]It should be pointed out, however, that the quotation in Matthew 5:43, "You have heard that it was said, 'You shall . . . hate your enemy,' " is not in the O.T., and reflects the spirit of the O.T. only when "enemy" is understood not as a private individual, but as a member of a community outside of the covenant of Israel.

[36]Peter C. Craigie deals with this issue soberly and with fine insight in his book, The Problem of War in the Old Testament (Grand Rapids: Eerdmans, 1978).

[37]The difficulty of extrapolating a general ethical norm from teachings related to particular cultural settings remains extremely problematic. Perhaps adherence to a culture places limits on the extent to which God can transform a people. See the suggestive comments of John McKenzie, "The Value of the Old Testament," How Does the Christian Confront the Old Testament? Concilium: Theology in the Age of Renewal, vol. 30 (New York: Paulist Press, 1968), pp. 19-24. Writes McKenzie: "The limits of revelation are not the limits of God, but the limits of man."

[38]"The early church reinterpreted the moral tradition of the Old Testament and Judaism in the light of Christ; and it is the Person of Christ that is normative for the understanding of morality, as of all other aspects of life, in the New Testament." W. D. Davies, "The Moral Teaching of the Early Church," The Use of the Old Testament in the New and Other Essays, ed. Efird, p. 314.

[39]Nils A. Dahl points out that the N.T. does not often speak of a fulfillment of promises, but more often of God's confirming His promises or simply doing what He has promised, and that fulfillment is used more often in other contexts, such as a fulfillment of the law and fulfillment of Scriptures. See "Promise and Fulfillment, Studies in Paul (Minneapolis: Augsburg, 1977), p. 121. Although Dahl is correct in the semantic distinction he draws, in fact, this distinction is not consistently made either in the N.T. or in present-day usage.

[40]See Longenecker, Biblical Exegesis in the Apostolic Period, pp. 19-50. A more technical analysis is provided in E. Earle Ellis, "How the New Testament Uses the Old," Prophecy and Hermeneutic in Early Christianity (Grand Rapids: Eerdmans, 1978), pp. 147-172. I have relied on Ellis for some of the examples used in the present section.

[41]C. H. Dodd's book, According to the Scriptures, (New York: Scribner's, 1953) is the classic expression of the theory that selected blocks of O.T. material were combined in early Christian preaching

and teaching into a "sub-structure of Christian theology." A discussion of the subsequent development of the hypothesis is found in D. Moody Smith, Jr. "The Use of the Old Testament in the New," pp. 25-30. Support for the idea of a formal collection of "testimonies" has been found by way of some fragmentary "testimony collections" at Qumran.

[42]See Ellis, "How the New Testament Uses the Old," p. 165.

[43]G. W. H. Lampe and K. J. Woolcombe, *Essays on Typology*. Studies in Biblical Theology, No. 22 (London: SCM Press, 1957), p. 40.

[44]*Ibid.*

[45]As Ellis points out, the passage, although labeled an allegory (Galatians 4:24), functions more like a typology than like the classical types of allegory in Philo and Origen. See Ellis, *Paul's Use of the Old Testament* (Grand Rapids: Eerdmans, 1957), p. 140.

[46]E. Earle Ellis, "How the New Testament Uses the Old," p. 166; cf. David Daube, *The Exodus Pattern in the Bible* (London: Faber & Faber, 1963).

[47]But see the cautionary remarks of W. D. Davies, *The Setting of the Sermon on the Mount*, pp. 25-93.

[48]Bo Reicke, "The God of Abraham, Isaac, and Jacob in New Testament Theology," *Unity and Diversity in New Testament Theology*, Guelich, ed., p. 187.

[49]It is likely that Matthew intends to draw a correspondence between God's preservation of His people in Egypt and in their release from that land, and the preservation of Jesus, the representative Israelite, in Egypt, and His subsequent return to His homeland. See Robert H. Gundry, *The Use of the Old Testament in St. Matthew's Gospel* (Leiden: E. J. Brill, 1967), pp. 93, 211.

[50]"There is no claim that without the New Testament one could deduce it from the Old, or that a process of natural evolution could carry us from the Old to the New. There is the claim that God was speaking through the Israelite voices that announced these hopes and that he was active in the fulfillment, which gave a fullness to the meaning of the Old that it could not otherwise have had, and provided firm ground for the belief that the Old Testament not alone did lead to Christ in fact, but was intended by the God whose partial revelation it contained to lead to Christ." H. H. Rowley, "The Authority of the

Bible," *From Moses to Qumran* (New York: Association Press, 1963), pp. 20, 21.

[51]Bruce, *New Testament Development,* p. 21.

[52]See the forcible remarks of George Ernest Wright in the chapter "The Church's Need of the Old Testament," *God Who Acts.* Studies in Biblical Theology (London: SCM, 1952), pp. 15-32; cf. Kornelis H. Miskotte, *When the Gods Are Silent,* trans. with an introduction by John W. Doberstein (New York: Harper & Row, 1967), p. 135.

[53]The expression is attributed to Elton Trueblood, who derives it from H. Richard Niebuhr, who speaks also of a "practical monotheism of the Son." See his "The Doctrine of the Trinity and the Unity of the Church," *Theology Today,* 3 (1946/47), pp. 371-384, esp. pp. 374-376. George Ernest Wright protests strongly against this "Christomonism" in his essay "Theology and Christomonism," *The Old Testament and Theology* (New York: Harper & Row, 1969), pp. 13-38.

[54]See Miskotte, *When the Gods Are Silent,* pp. 246-248.

[55]See Graham Hughes, *Hebrews and Hermeneutics* (Cambridge: Cambridge University Press, 1979).

[56]". . . When the Christian community is forced to reckon with its own unfinality, as being still very much enmeshed in the process of history, it then discovers a real and existential continuity between itself and the community of the old covenant" (Hughes, *Hebrews and Hermeneutics,* p. 108). It is this conception that lies behind Dietrich Bonhoeffer's sometimes misunderstood statement written in a letter in 1945: "In my opinion it is not Christian to want to take our thoughts and feelings too quickly and too directly from the New Testament." He went on to explain that Christians are always engaged in the struggle to appropriate the realities introduced by the gospel. "One cannot and must not speak the ultimate word before the penultimate. We live in the penultimate and believe the ultimate, don't we?" Martin Kuske, *The Old Testament as the Book of Christ: An Appraisal of Bonhoeffer's Interpretations,* trans. S. T. Kimbrough, Jr. (Philadelphia: Westminster, 1976), pp. 124-127.

CHAPTER

6

GOD HAS SPOKEN IN HIS SON: THE LIFE OF JESUS

by Ronald E. Heine

The purpose of this essay is to survey the life of Jesus of Nazareth, the ultimate Word from God. It may seem strange at first glance to see a chapter dealing with the life of Jesus in a treatment of doctrine. It is, however, of crucial importance to include such a study, for all of our doctrines about Christ's person and work must maintain contact, as Ralph Martin has said, "with a Jesus whose feet touched the ground in Galilee and Jerusalem."[1] Any theology that loses that vital contact with the Word made flesh is drifting dangerously toward the ancient heresy of docetism.

The Nature of our Sources

Our knowledge of Jesus' life is drawn from the four Gospels. New information about Jesus in the remainder of the New Testament is negligible. In the secular literature of the first century, mention of Jesus is almost totally lacking. The only reference of any consequence in this literature is Tacitus' statement (Annals XV. 44) that Christ, from whom Christians were named, had been executed by the Roman procurator Pontius Pilate in Judea. It is the Gospels, therefore, that concern us in this section. What is the nature of these four documents from which we derive our knowledge of Jesus?

The Relationship Between the Gospels

The most obvious factor to be taken into account about the nature of the Gospels as source material for knowledge about Jesus is the close relationship between Matthew, Mark, and Luke—the Synoptic Gospels—and the somewhat different treatment of Jesus in the Gospel of John.

A careful comparative reading of the first three Gospels in Greek reveals that there are large blocks of material in Matthew and Luke that are the same as in Mark. The similarity often extends even to the order of the words. There are, in addition, several blocks of material consisting mostly of sayings of Jesus that are common to Matthew and Luke but absent from Mark. There is also some material in each of the first three Gospels that is peculiar to each.[2]

The close similarities between the Greek text of the Synoptic Gospels, involving even the same words and order of words, is most remarkable when one considers that the mother tongue of Jesus and His disciples was Aramaic, and that it was in this language that He would have addressed the common people in Galilee. Anyone who has worked at translating material from one language to another knows how unlikely it is that three different people could translate the same passage in exactly the same way, choosing the same words and grammatical constructions to express the ideas, and arranging these words, sometimes at least, in the same order. These and other similar factors led many New Testament scholars to the conclusion that there were some common sources, written already in the Greek language, available for use by Matthew and Luke in composing their Gospels.[3]

A considerable period of time—in some estimates as many as thirty-five years—separated the death of Jesus and the writing of the first Gospel. It is obvious that throughout this period, the followers of Jesus were continually telling the deeds and words of the Master and being guided by them. Various statements in Acts make it clear that the apostles and others in the church preached and taught about Jesus (see Acts 5:42; 8:35; 11:20; 17:18).

In Luke's abbreviated report of Peter's sermon to Cornelius, he tells us that Peter related "how God anointed [Jesus of Nazareth] with the Holy Spirit and with power, and how He went about doing good, and healing all who were oppressed by the devil; for God was with Him. And we are witnesses of all the things He did both in the land of the Jews and in Jerusalem. And they also put Him to death by hanging Him on a cross. God raised Him on the third day, and granted that He should become visible" (Acts 10:38-40). This passage helps us understand two things about the handing on of the story of Jesus before there were written Gospels. First, it shows us that the material about Jesus was related orally in sermons.[4] Note that there is a reference to Jesus' good deeds and especially His healings, and to His crucifixion and resurrection. We may assume that in the actual sermon, Peter gave examples of Jesus' deeds and healings, narrated details of the crucifixion, and related some of the events clustered around the resurrection of Jesus. Second, this text shows us why no need for written Gospels was felt at this early period. The preacher was an eyewitness of the events he was relating (v. 39).

Given the situation outlined in the preceding paragraphs, we can theorize that there were four stages in the transmission of the material about Jesus from the time of His life to the composition of our Gospels.

1. There were the events themselves in Jesus' life, witnessed by the apostles and sometimes by large crowds of other people.

2. There was the very early period following Jesus' death and resurrection. In this time, His various teachings and deeds were told orally, first by those who had been eyewitnesses themselves (as Peter in Acts 10), and then by those who had heard the eyewitnesses (as the scattered believers in Acts 8:4).[5]

3. This period was followed by a time in which various stories about Jesus were written down while they continued to be circulated orally. Luke prefaces his Gospel by saying that "many have undertaken to compile an account of the things accomplished among us, just as those who from the beginning were eyewitnesses and servants of the word have handed them down to us" (Luke 1:1, 2). Furthermore, it seems implicit, if not explicit, that Luke made use of some, at least, of these earlier written documents as sources for his own Gospel: he proceeds to say that he has "investigated everything carefully from the beginning" (Luke 1:3). This last quoted statement from Luke seems to suggest also that he has consulted some eyewitnesses and hence has oral, as well as written, sources for his Gospel. These first three verses of Luke's Gospel, then, (1) make it certain that he knows of accounts of Jesus preceding his own, (2) strongly suggest that he has carefully studied some of these

preceding accounts, and (3) suggest that he has himself consulted eyewitnesses for some of the material contained in his Gospel.[6]

4. The final stage in the transmission of the material about the life of Jesus was the composition of our written Gospels.

Two factors probably prompted the decision to put the material about Jesus in a definitive written form. One was the awareness that the eyewitnesses who could authenticate the traditions were beginning to pass from the scene. The time was coming when no eyewitnesses would be present. The second reason is closely related to the first. The rise of various heresies within the church made it necessary for the church to be able to say that its account of Jesus was correct in opposition to that of the heretics. This demanded a definitive, authentic account of Jesus. The best way to guarantee the continuance of such an account was to preserve it in writing.

We are able thus to trace what may be called the human factors in the preservation and composition of the Gospels. It is important also to emphasize the role of the Holy Spirit in this process. For example, the Gospel of John records Jesus' promise to the apostles in the upper room that the "Helper, the Holy Spirit," would "bring to their remembrance" what He had said to them (John 14:26). In addition, we may affirm that however much a writer such as Luke had to do research (Luke 1:3), he was guided in the process by the Spirit of God.

The Gospel of John differs in several respects from the first three Gospels. At some points, the chronology of events in Jesus' life seems different. Perhaps most noticeable is the fact that although in the Synoptics, Jesus teaches with parables and short proverbial type statements, in John's Gospel, He teaches in lengthy discourses.[7] Johannine scholars continue to devote much study and debate to these and other aspects of the relation of John to the Synoptics.[8] While we cannot resolve the issue here, it is important that we take note of them.

From very early times the church was aware of differences between John and the Synoptics.[9] Yet it deliberately received the four individual accounts rather than one account made by blending them together. The latter was attempted by Tatian in the second century. His *Diatesseron* (i.e. one Gospel made from the four) was widely used in Syria for a time but was rejected by the church in general and is now a curio known only to scholars.

The Gospel Writers as Evangelists

A second factor to be noted about the nature of the four Gospels is that the writers were not annalists recording chronicles. They were not antiquaries interested in relics of history. Nor were they biographers, in the modern sense of that term, interested in writing a life of Jesus. *Each Gospel writer was a proclaimer of faith in Jesus.*[10] Each writer wrote to produce, confirm, or defend that faith. Three statements from the Gospels make this clear.

1. John says near the end of his Gospel, "Many other signs therefore Jesus also performed in the presence of the disciples, which are not written in this book; but these have been written that you may believe that Jesus is the Christ, the Son of God; and that believing you may have life in His name" (John 20:30). This statement shows clearly that John has not attempted to write a comprehensive life of Jesus, but has been selective in what he has included in his Gospel, and that his purpose has been to select material that will convince the reader "that Jesus is the Christ, the Son of God." His goal in writing is to produce faith in Jesus.

2. Luke, in the preface to his Gospel, relates his purpose in this way: "Inasmuch as many have undertaken to compile a narrative of the things which have been accomplished among us . . . , it seemed good to me also . . . to write an orderly account for you, most excellent Theophilus, that you may know the truth concerning the things of which you have been informed (Luke 1:1-4, RSV). We have already considered the meaning of some of Luke's statements in that tightly compacted paragraph. It is sufficient for our present purposes to note Luke's explicit statement of intention for writing his Gospel. He wants to confirm Theophilus' faith.

3. Mark begins by calling his work "the gospel *(euangelion)* of Jesus Christ" (Mark 1:1). Elsewhere in Mark, the noun *gospel* is used to indicate the content of preaching (Mark 1:14, 15; 8:35; 10:29; 13:10; 14:9). The verb derived from this noun *(euangelizesthai)* is used throughout the New Testament for the preaching of the gospel (see Acts 8:4, 12, 35, 40; Romans 1:15; 1 Corinthians 1:17; 15:1). By his use of the phrase "the beginning of the gospel of Jesus Christ" as the title of his work, Mark is signaling that what we should expect to find therein is a record of "how the good news about Jesus Christ the Son of God began."[11]

This recognition about the nature of the Gospels should not be taken to suggest that the authors fabricated the events they recorded. This would have been counter-productive. The faith they were seeking to produce or defend was that God had visited the world and fulfilled the promises He had made to Israel. This He had done in the historical person, Jesus of Nazareth. While they were not writing history qua history, they were definitely interested in historical events and in keeping their accounts anchored in real history. The moment any hint of historical fabrication could have been shown, the edifice they had constructed for the defense of the faith would have become a death trap, collapsing on that very faith.

It must be remembered, as we have stated earlier, that when the Gospels were first written and circulated, there were still people alive, both within and without the church, who had been eyewitnesses to the events in Jesus' life. F. F. Bruce related an anecdote from a radio broadcast by C. H. Dodd in which Dodd said that in his younger days he had considered the gap of thirty-five years between the writing of the Gospel of Mark and the events recorded in that Gospel to be a very serious matter. Later he realized that thirty-five years did not seem such a long time, for he and his contemporaries in 1949, the year in which he was broadcasting, had a vivid memory of the events of the summer of 1914, thirty-five years earlier. The events of that summer had led to the outbreak of World War I.

> When Mark was writing there must have been many people about, who were in their prime under Pontius Pilate and they must have remembered the stirring and tragic events of that time at least as vividly as we remember 1914. If anyone had tried to put over an entirely imaginary or fictitious account of them there would have been middle-aged or elderly people who would have said, as you or I might say, "You are wasting your breath. I remember it as if it were yesterday."[12]

The Threefold Basis of Interpreting Jesus' Life

One last factor remains to be noted about the nature of the Gospels in their presentation of Jesus. We must note that the Gospels present an interpreted Jesus. The authors of the Gospels are looking at Jesus (1) in the light of His resurrection, (2) in the light of Old Testament prophecies, and (3) in the light of His continued presence with them through the Spirit in the church.

The Gospels do not contain a dispassionate, objective list of facts, like a lab report describing an experiment. They are written by people who have looked at the facts of Jesus' life, who have set that life in the context of the Old Testament and seen the correspondences between what happened to Jesus and what the prophets had predicted, and who have seen and been a part of what has been happening in the church since Jesus' ascension. John 12:16 makes this especially clear. There, in relation to the events of the triumphal entry and the application of Old Testament prophecy to those events, John says, "These things His disciples did not understand at the first; but when Jesus was glorified, then they remembered that these things were written of Him, and that they had done these things to Him." John thus indicates his Gospel is setting forth his post-resurrection reflections on Jesus in the light of the Old Testament (cf. John 2:22; 13:7). The Gospels were written by men who had drawn conclusions about Jesus and had committed their lives to those conclusions. The authors were evangelists proclaiming their faith.

The Gospels give us Jesus as known to those who believed in Him. They do this in order to produce the same kind of faith response in those who had no direct experience of the earthly Jesus. They have been functioning in precisely this way for the past twenty centuries. If we ask more of them than this, our demands are illegitimate and force them into areas where the information they convey is inadequate, as a thoroughbred is inadequate if forced to compete with a Clydesdale in dragging a weighted sled. Some, perhaps, would prefer to have a lab-report type of presentation. But the wisdom of God has given us something better. It has given us Jesus as seen by His followers after all the information on Him was available: His resurrection, His fulfillment of Old Testament prophecy, and the power of His continued presence in the church.

It is helpful to compare the makeup of the Gospels to orchestral scores. The Gospels contain various kinds of material: words of Jesus, events in Jesus' life narrated by the evangelists, statements and images drawn from the Old Testament to interpret Jesus, and interpretative statements made by the evangelists. To concentrate on the identification and isolation of these various strands of material is like isolating the part for the French horn or trombone in a symphony. The parts were not intended to stand alone. But when all the parts are played together, the result is meaning communicated through music. In the Gospels, we have historical information about Jesus mixed with the lingering impressions Jesus made on people. We have history and symbolism; the prose of facts mingled with the poetry of the Spirit of Jesus in the life of the church. Perhaps there is no other way to communicate the mystique of that sum total of deity and humanity called Jesus of Nazareth, the Christ, the Son of God, the Way, the Truth, and the Life. Our purpose in the pages that follow is to listen attentively to the music of the Gospels as they communicate their message of Jesus that speaks to the needs of everyone, whether he be scholar or novice in the literature of the Bible.

The Contours of Concern
About the Life of Jesus in the Gospels

When we look at the Gospels as a whole, as one might look at a relief map that indicates the general contours of a region, we can see that the material about Jesus in them falls into four general blocks. These are (1) infancy narratives, (2) stories from Jesus' ministry, (3) the passion narrative, and (4) stories about the resurrection. It can be said in general that these represent the areas the early Christians considered to be necessary in order for one to be informed about Jesus. These same areas of concern, with the exception of the infancy narratives, can be paralleled with the emphases made about Jesus in the sermons in Acts.[13] We shall look at the life of Jesus in relation to these four general areas of material in the Gospels, noting especially how the evangelists interpret the events of the life of Jesus they record in light of the Old Testament.[14]

The Infancy Narratives[15]

Only Matthew and Luke discuss the birth of Jesus in the New Testament. Outside of these two Gospels, brief references to Jesus' birth or genealogy can be found only at Romans 1:3 and Galatians 4:4. Nor do Matthew and Luke present parallel accounts at this point in their Gospels. While the essential information about Jesus' genealogy, the manner of His conception, the place and time of His birth, and the town of His childhood agree in the two Gospels, it is quite apparent that they are relating separate accounts with different emphases for their own particular Gospels. What do Matthew and Luke teach us about Jesus in these narratives?

Both Matthew and Luke trace Jesus' ancestry through extended genealogies (Matthew 1:1-17; Luke 3:23-38). The primary intention of these genealogies seems to be to show that Jesus is in the direct line of descent from David and Abraham, both of whom were the recipients of special covenants with God, which contained promises with Messianic implications (see Genesis 12:1-3 and 2 Samuel 7:12-16). This intention is especially obvious in Matthew, where the Gospel begins with the words: "The book of the genealogy of Jesus Christ, the son of David, the son of Abraham" (Matthew 1:1). In the annunciation, Joseph is again referred to by Matthew as a "son of David" (Matthew 1:20).

Luke makes several references to the linkage between Jesus and David in the various stories he includes in his infancy narrative. Joseph is "of the descendants of David" (Luke 1:27). In the annunciation to Mary, it is stated that the child she will bear will be given "the throne of His father David" (Luke 1:32). Bethlehem is twice referred to as "the city of David" (Luke 2:4, 11) and Jesus is born there because Joseph belongs to "the house and family of David" (Luke 2:4).

There are no additional allusions to Abraham in Matthew's infancy narrative outside of the genealogy proper and the opening statement of the Gospel quoted above.[16] Luke twice mentions the previous promises made to Abraham in his infancy narrative (Luke 1:55, 72, 73), and quotes the angel's reponse to Sarah's laughter (Genesis 18:14) as Gabriel's answer to Mary's question about herself, a virgin, having a son (Luke 1:37). It seems quite clear that both Matthew and Luke want to link Jesus with these two key figures in Israel's history by means of their genealogies.

The unique manner of Jesus' conception is made explicit by both Matthew and Luke. Luke, in his annunciation story, twice refers to Mary as a virgin (Luke 1:27). The angel's announcement that Mary would bear a son is couched in the language of Isaiah 7:14, though without the terms "virgin" and "Immanuel." Mary's response to this announcement is, "How can this be, since I am a virgin?" (Luke 1:34), to which the angel replies that it will be brought about by "the Holy Spirit" (Luke 1:35).

Matthew, who concentrates on Joseph's reaction to Mary's pregnancy, does not use the term "virgin" of Mary in his description, but says the pregnancy was discovered "before they came together" (Matthew 1:18) and was "of the Holy Spirit" (Matthew 1:18, 20). The angel's statement to Joseph of the birth of Jesus is, as in Luke's account, couched in the language of Isaiah 7:14 (Matthew 1:21). Matthew then proceeds to interpret the whole account by an explicit quotation of Isaiah 7:14: "All this took place that what was spoken by the Lord through the prophet might be fulfilled, saying, 'Behold, the virgin shall be with child, and shall bear a Son, and they shall call His name Immanuel,' which translated means, 'God with us' " (Matthew 1:22, 23).

There is also close agreement between Matthew and Luke on the place of Jesus' birth. Matthew's consideration of the place of Jesus' birth is set in the context of his discussion of the visit of the magi (Matthew 2:1-12). The magi enter Jerusalem seeking the birthplace of the "King of the Jews" (Matthew 2:1, 2). The chief priests and scribes announce that the Messiah is to be born "in Bethlehem of Judea" (Matthew 2:4, 5). This is ascertained from Micah 5:2, which Matthew quotes in full, having introduced it with the formula: "for so it has been written by the prophet" (Matthew 2:5, 6). The magi then proceed to Bethlehem and discover the child (Matthew 2:8, 9). Later, Herod, in his attempt to destroy what he fears may be a claimant for his throne, kills all the infants in Bethlehem (Matthew 2:16). This led to the fulfillment of two Old Testament prophecies. First, Joseph, having been warned by God, had fled to Egypt with Mary and Jesus. This brought about the fulfillment of Hosea 11:1, "Out of Egypt did I call My Son" (Matthew 2:15). Second, the outcry at Bethlehem when the infants were slaughtered fulfilled Jeremiah's word (Jeremiah 31:15) about Rachel weeping for her children at Ramah (Matthew 2:17, 18).

Luke has no explicit Old Testament quotations in connection with his account of Jesus' birth in Bethlehem (Luke 2:1-20). His references to the birthplace of Jesus are set first in the context of the enrollment ordered by Augustus (Luke 2:1), which explained why Joseph and Mary, who lived in Nazareth of Galilee, were in Bethlehem of Judea when Jesus was born. Joseph, who "was of the house and family of David," had to go to "the city of David, which is called Bethlehem" (Luke 2:4), because each had to be enrolled in "his own city" (Luke 2:3). While there are no explicit Old Testament quotations in this passage, it should be noted again that Luke intended to show by this account that Jesus was, indeed, the son of David.

The other reference to Jesus' birthplace in Luke's account is in the context of the angelic announcement of His birth to the shepherds (Luke 2:8-20). Here, again, Jesus is explicitly linked with David when the angels say He is born "in the city of David" (Luke 2:11). The shepherds then go at once to Bethlehem, where they find the infant lying in a manger (Luke 2:15, 16).

Matthew and Luke each make reference also to the time of Jesus' birth. Luke is quite specific. It occurred when Augustus, who ruled the Roman empire, published a decree requiring a census of the empire (Luke 2:1). Luke further states that Quirinius was governor of Syria at this time (Luke 2:2). Syria was the larger province of which Judea and Galilee were two of the subsections. Luke's only reference to Herod, the local king of Judea, is in his dating of the annunciation to Zechariah (Luke 1:5).

Matthew's references, on the other hand, are more vague than Luke's and are limited solely to the references to Herod's being king of Judea (Matthew 2:1, 3, 7, 12, 13, 16). He dates the end of the sojourn in Egypt by the death of Herod (Matthew 2:15, 19) and the reign of his successor Archelaus (Matthew 2:22).

Despite the points of agreement between Matthew and Luke in the infancy stories, neither of them makes any apparent attempt to relate *the time of Jesus' birth* to the Old Testament. It is, of course, quite apparent that there were no time references given in the Old Testament concerning the advent of the Messiah, just as the New Testament refuses to be specific about the second advent (cf. Luke 12:39, 40, 46). These references to rulers in relation to the birth of Jesus represent primarily each evangelist's attempt, in his own way, to set his account of the birth of Jesus in the larger context of world history.

Some other extraordinary phenomena related in the birth narratives. Matthew records that a star indicated the place of Jesus' birth to the magi from the East, who appear in the Gospel account, elicit the connection between Micah 5:1 and the birthplace of the Messiah, offer their worship and gifts to the Christ child, and disappear from history (Matthew 2:1-12). Luke tells us that an angelic host spoke to shepherds in the fields outside Bethlehem on the night of Jesus' birth and directed them to the birthplace of "Christ the Lord" (Luke 2:8-14).

What do the evangelists intend to teach about Jesus through these stories about His birth? The various extraordinary phenomena connected with Jesus' conception and birth set this birth apart from all other births and show that this child is unique. They seem intended to show what the angel said to Mary: "The child to be born will be called holy, the Son of God" (Luke 1:35, RSV). There is, however, another very important side that the evangelists want to convey through the infancy narratives that is in tension with this uniqueness. They do not want to present Jesus as an alien visitor in the world with no connections with human history and life. He is born in the world of Caesar Augustus, Quirinius, and Herod. He has a human ancestry that is very diligently traced by each evangelist. His family has deep historical roots in ancient Bethlehem, the city of His birth. And we must not overlook what is most obvious in both Gospels: He is born a human baby of a human mother. While there are unique aspects about His birth, even in this birth He is tied to the history and hopes of Israel, and beyond that to the history and hopes of the world (note Luke 2:30-32). He is the child of promise! The songs of Mary (Luke 1:46-55) and Zechariah (Luke 1:67-79), and the prayer of Simeon (Luke 2:29-35) along with the several connections each evangelist shows between the circumstances of Jesus' birth and the Old Testament make this transparently clear.

The Ministry of Jesus

Our treatment of Jesus' ministry will be limited to an abbreviated survey showing (1) the significance of the events immediately preceding the ministry of Jesus, (2) the kingdom of God to be the major theme of Jesus' ministry, (3) Jesus' relation to the kingdom of God, and (4) the importance of the Old Testament for the evangelists' interpretation of Jesus' ministry.

Three significant events preceded the beginning of Jesus' ministry and set the stage for it. First, as all four Gospels record, Jesus' ministry was preceded by the preaching of John the Baptist (Matthew 3:1-6; Mark 1:2-6; Luke 3:1-6; John 1:19-23). Each evangelist relates the Baptist's ministry to Isaiah 40:3 to show that he is the one who is to "prepare the way of the Lord." John called the people to repentance and pointed them to the one who was to come after him (Matthew 3:2, 11, 12). His preaching and baptizing stirred Messianic anticipations and debate (John 1:19-27).

John the Baptist's ministry reached its climax in the baptism of Jesus, for after this the attention of the evangelists moves from John to Jesus. Alan Richardson has stated that the significance of Jesus' baptism for the Synoptic evangelists is "that it represents the anointing of Jesus with the Holy Spirit to the office and work of the Messianic servant of the Lord." Jesus was thus identified with the Old Testament kingship (1 Samuel 16:13; Psalm 89:20; 2 Kings 9:3), the priesthood (Exodus 29:7; 40:13-15; Leviticus 8:12; Psalm 133:2) and the "Isaianic Prophet" (Isaiah 11:2; 42:1; 44:3; 61:1).[17]

That the Synoptic Gospels see the significance of Jesus' baptism primarily as the time of anointing with the Spirit for His ministry can be implied also from the Heavenly voice following the baptism, which blends Psalm 2:7 and Isaiah 42:1 (Matthew 3:17; Mark 1:11; Luke 3:22). Recent studies of the Psalms have suggested that Psalm 2 was one of the Psalms sung by Israel at the enthronement of her kings.[18] Anointing was a part of the enthronement process. By alluding to this psalm, therefore, the statement points implicitly to the anointment of Jesus with the Spirit of God. Isaiah 42:1, to which the second half of the statement made by the Heavenly voice alludes, says explicitly: "I have put my Spirit upon him." It appears, therefore, that the function of this statement following Jesus' baptism is to call attention to His anointment with the Spirit by pointing back to these two well-known passages in the Old Testament.

The third preparatory event preceding Jesus' ministry was His temptation. The Synoptic Gospels record that immediately after His baptism, Jesus went into the wilderness for a period of forty days to be tempted by the devil (Matthew 4:1-11; Mark 1:12, 13; Luke 4:1-13). Matthew and Luke seem to intend that their readers see this experience, in some senses, as parallel to Israel's forty years in the wilderness. It is significant that each of the temptations is answered by Jesus with a quotation from Deuteronomy. The temptation to turn stones into bread is answered by Deuteronomy 8:3 (Matthew 4:4; Luke 4:4). The attempt to get Jesus to cast himself from the pinnacle of the temple and force a divine rescue is countered by Deuteronomy 6:16 (Matthew 4:7; Luke 4:12). Finally, the appeal of power over the kingdoms of men is rejected by a quotation from Deuteronomy 6:13 (Matthew 4:10; Luke 4:8). Thus, Jesus, at the end of His forty days in the wilderness, emerges victorious over the devil through the words Moses had addressed to Israel in the wilderness. The period of preparation had come to an end, and Jesus was ready to set forth on His ministry.

We have noted in these three events in the preparation for Jesus' ministry what we also saw in our study of the infancy narratives. Each event is set in the context not only of Jesus' earthly life, but, what was perhaps even more important for the evangelists because of its tremendous implications, in the context of the Old Testament.

When Jesus returned from His period of temptation in the wilderness, He went to Galilee and began proclaiming the dawn of the kingdom of God (Mark 1:15; cf. Matthew 4:17). This theme was to be the pivot around which His entire ministry moved. Norman Perrin, for example asserts that Jesus' teaching centered in the kingdom of God. "Of this there can be no doubt. . . . All else in his message and ministry serves a function in relation to that proclamation and derives its meaning from it."[19]

Luke 4:43 records a statement of Jesus in which He says explicitly that the purpose of His mission is to "preach the good news of the kingdom of God" (NIV). It is not difficult, when one is alert to this issue, to see the importance this theme has in the teachings of Jesus. The phrase "kingdom of God" and its equivalent expression "kingdom of Heaven" occur over one hundred times in the Gospels. It is a prevalent theme in the Sermon on the Mount (see Matthew 5:3, 10, 19, 20; 6:10, 13, 33; 7:21). Numerous parables are about the kingdom (Matthew 13:24, 31, 33, 44, 45, 47; 18:23; 20:1; 22:2; 25:1). When Jesus commissioned the twelve to go forth, their message was to be: "The kingdom of heaven is at hand" (Matthew 10:7; Luke 9:1, 2). The seventy were later commissioned to preach the same message (Luke 10:9). Acts 1:3 states that the teaching of the risen Christ to His followers in the days before the ascension still concerned the kingdom of God. The proclamation of the kingdom of God is obviously the central theme of Jesus' teaching.

It is not quite so obvious how the miracles of Jesus are related to His proclamation of the kingdom. Luke 11:14-22 provides some essential clues.

And He was casting out a demon, and it was dumb; and it came about that when the demon had gone out, the dumb man spoke; and the multitudes marveled. But some of them said, "He casts out demons by Beelzebul, the ruler of the demons." And others, to test Him, were demanding of Him a sign from heaven. But He knew their thoughts, and said to them, "Any kingdom divided against itself is laid waste; and a house divided against itself falls. And if Satan also is divided against himself, how shall his kingdom stand? For you say that I cast out demons by Beelzebul. And if I by Beelzebul cast out demons, by whom do your sons cast them out? Consequently they shall be your judges. *But if I cast out demons by the finger of God, then the kingdom of God has come upon you.* When a strong man, fully armed, guards his own homestead, his possessions are undisturbed; but when someone stronger than he attacks him and overpowers him, he takes away from him all his armor on which he had relied, and distributes his plunder" (italics mine).

Here Jesus explicitly interprets his exorcisms as a sign of the presence of the kingdom of God (11:20). His assertion that He performs His exorcisms "by the finger of God" points back to Exodus 8:19, where the Egyptian magicians, unable to bring forth gnats from dust as Aaron had done, said to Pharaoh, "This is the finger of God."[20] The rabbis said of this verse in Exodus, "When the magicians saw that they could not produce the lice, they recognized immediately that the happenings (the plagues) were the work of God and not the work of demons."[21] Jesus must have assumed some such understanding of this saying among His hearers. We can, therefore, see that Jesus is doing even more in this saying than relating His exorcisms to the presence of the kingdom of God. He is also showing that He, as the messenger of the kingdom, is engaged in battle with the demonic kingdom of Satan (cf. Luke 11:17, 18) and that His exorcisms show that He is the stronger and that victory is going to the kingdom of God. This is confirmed by His statement that a strong man preserves his own goods until he is overcome by one who is stronger (Luke 11:21, 22). Jesus is the One who is stronger than Satan, who has overcome him, and is now, by His exorcisms, plundering his house.

This conflict between Jesus and the demonic kingdom of Satan is brought out by Luke also in his account of the mission of the seventy. They are sent out to heal the sick and preach that the kingdom of God has come near (Luke 10:9). They return from this mission joyful, saying, "Lord, even the demons are subject to us in your name!" Jesus replies: "I was watching Satan fall from heaven like lightening" (Luke 10:17, 18). There are several important points to notice here. First, there is no disjuncture between healings and exorcisms. The seventy are sent out to heal the sick and they return talking about the demons being subject to them. They evidently saw their ability to heal the sick as implying power over the demons (cf. Luke 13:11; Acts 10:38). Second, this activity of healing is done in conjunction with the proclamation that the kingdom of God has come near. The two appear to be seen as a natural part of one another, even as Jesus' exorcisms in Luke 11:20 are placed in the context of the kingdom of God. Finally, Jesus' response about Satan falling from Heaven implies that Satan has been overcome and cast forth from the Heavenly realm. This, of course, implies a struggle, as that mentioned in Luke 11:21, 22. This victory has been accomplished by Jesus' disciples in their mission for the kingdom of God, and shows that the kingdom of God has overcome the demonic kingdom.

Matthew's account of the mission of the twelve also joins the proclamation that the kingdom of Heaven is at hand with healing the sick, raising the dead, cleansing the lepers, and casting out demons (Matthew 10:7, 8). Here, raising the dead and cleansing lepers are specified in addition to what we have already noted as part of the work connected with the proclamation of the kingdom of God.

How do these various elements fit together into a harmonious whole in relation to Jesus' proclamation of the kingdom? Jesus' miracles can be categorized as healings, exorcisms,[22] raising the dead, and nature miracles. They all involve the world over which Satan was regarded to have control. Note John's ominous references to "the ruler of this world," who is in conflict with Jesus (John 12:31; 14:30; 16:11). Jesus' miracles were the visible manifestation of the invisible spiritual struggle being waged between himself and Satan at this critical point in history. When Jesus' ministry is viewed in this light, the temptation narrative that precedes His ministry takes on strong symbolic overtones. Here is a picture in miniature of what is really happening in the ministry of Jesus. He is locked in a battle to death with the ruler of evil. His victory in the temptation narrative is also symbolic of the final victory that He will gain in the end.

Joachim Jeremias, who treats the miracles as "the vanquishing of Satan," says:

Jesus enters this world enslaved by Satan with the authority of God, not only to exercise mercy, but above all to join battle with evil. . . . [His] victories over the power of evil are not just isolated invasions of Satan's realm. They are more. They are manifestations of the dawn of the time of salvation and of the beginning of the annihilation of Satan.[23]

When Jesus' miracles are viewed in this way, it becomes clear that both in word and deed, His ministry was centered in the kingdom of God.

However, Jesus was more than simply a proclaimer of the kingdom of God. John the Baptist had also been a proclaimer of the kingdom (Matthew 3:1, 2), as were all the messengers whom Jesus commissioned (Luke 9:2; 10:1, 9). Jesus' relationship to the kingdom was essentially different from all these. He *was himself its king.* Peter's confession, "Thou art the Christ" (Mark 8:29), was equivalent to saying, "You are God's anointed king."

Two questions arise at this point: (1) What is the basis for linking the title Christ with king? and (2) Why did Jesus never use this title (Christ) of himself as part of His public announcement concerning the kingdom?

The title *Christ*[24] is the Greek equivalent of the Hebrew title *Messiah. Messiah,* in Hebrew, means one who has been anointed. The Hebrew people anointed kings and priests. The Old Testament refers to the anointing of Saul (1 Samuel 9:16; 10:1), David (1 Samuel 16:3, 12, 13; 2 Samuel 2:4, 7; 5:3, 17), and Solomon (1 Kings 1:34, 39, 45). Several Psalms also refer to the king as one who has been anointed (Psalm 18:50; 45:1, 6, 7; 89:20). Joined with this background of the title was the fact that God had made a covenant with David in which He had promised, "Your house and your kingdom shall endure before Me forever; your throne shall be established for ever" (2 Samuel 7:16). After the fall of the Davidic kingdom to the Babylonians, the Hebrew people began to anticipate the raising up of a new king of David's line. This new anointed one, or Messiah (Christ), they thought, would restore Israel as a political kingdom much as it had been in David's day. These hopes can be seen arising abortively around Zerubbabel, who was a descendant of David (1 Chronicles 3:1, 19; Matthew 1:12; Luke 3:27), after the return from exile (Haggai 2:20-23). Gamaliel's comments in Acts 5:36, 37, along with the numerous nervous discussions that took place about Jesus among the people (see, for example, John 7:26, 27, 31, 41, 42) show that such hopes were still alive in the time of Jesus.

The identification of the title Christ with an anticipated king is explicit in a few passages in the New Testament. When, for example, the magi ask, "Where is He who has been born King of the Jews?" (Matthew 2:2), Herod inquires of the chief priests and scribes "where the Christ was to be born" (Matthew 2:4), thus identifying the two concepts. In Mark 15:32, the mockers at the cross refer to Jesus as "the Christ, the king of Israel," again showing what the title Christ meant in the popular mind. Likewise, before Pilate, Jesus' accusers say that He claimed to be "Christ, a king" (Luke 23:2).

Given this background of the meaning and implications of the title Christ, it becomes apparent why Jesus did not openly use this term of himself nor permit His followers to do so (Matthew 16:20). His mission would have been aborted by the revolutionary zeal that would have burst forth among the people. Direct military encounter with the Romans would likely have been inevitable. John tells us that there was at least one occasion when Jesus had to dampen the enthusiasm of a crowd that wanted to make Him king (John 6:15).

Jesus did, however, permit His closest followers on a few occasions to use the title Christ of himself. Martha used it of Him privately when her brother Lazarus had died (John 11: 27). Peter used the title in his confession (Matthew 16:16; Mark 8:29; Luke 9:20). Matthew tells us that Jesus approved Peter's insight (16:17), but then strictly "warned the disciples that they should tell no one that He was the Christ" (16:20). Mark and Luke record only the prohibition (Mark 8:30; Luke 9:21). In accepting this title, although it was not to be used for the reasons discussed above, Jesus does acknowledge that He is the long awaited king of the house of David. Jesus' refusal to deny that He was "king of the Jews" before Pilate should also be mentioned here (Mark 15:2; Matthew 27:11; Luke 23:3; John 18:33-37). C. H. Dodd says of this conversation with Pilate: "At this juncture a refusal to disown the title would have the same effect as an avowal, and it was a matter of life and death. Jesus . . . allowed himself to be condemned to death for claiming to be (in Jewish terms) Messiah."[25]

It is significant that each of the Synoptic Gospels records that immediately after Peter's confession, Jesus "began to show His disciples that He must go to Jerusalem, and suffer many things from the elders and chief priests and scribes, and be killed, and be raised up on the third day" (Matthew 16:21; cf. Mark 9:31; Luke 9:22). This represents a major modification of the popular Messianic expectations. Jesus is interpreting messiahship in terms of Isaiah's suffering servant (Isaiah 42—53). Rather than being the invincible military leader whom the people, including the twelve, expected, He was going to suffer and be killed by His own people. Peter, who shortly before had identified Jesus as the Messiah, could not accept this interpretation (Mark 8:32). It was not until after the resurrection that the disciples began to understand what Jesus had been saying here.

The importance of the Old Testament in the evangelists' interpretation of Jesus' ministry. We have already noted some of the connections made between Jesus' ministry and the Old Testament. We shall now take one example from Luke to show how Luke looks at Jesus' ministry in its entirety in the light of the Old Testament.

The first event that Luke describes in detail in Jesus' ministry is His sermon in the synagogue at Nazareth.

> And He came to Nazareth, where He had been brought up; and as was His custom, He entered the synagogue on the Sabbath, and stood up to read. And the book of the prophet Isaiah was handed to Him. And He opened the book, and found the place where it was written, "The Spirit of the Lord is upon Me, because He anointed Me to preach the gospel to the poor. He has sent Me to proclaim release to the captives, and recovery of sight to the blind, to set free those who are downtrodden, to proclaim the favorable year of the Lord." And he closed the book and gave it back to the attendant, and sat down; and the eyes of all in the synagogue were fixed upon Him. And He began to say to them, "Today this Scripture has been fulfilled in your hearing" (Luke 4:16-21).

The passage is Isaiah 61:1, 2. It is no accident that this Scripture is set at the beginning of Jesus' ministry. This incident in the synagogue at Nazareth was not Jesus' first activity; Luke refers to an earlier activity in Luke 4:14, 15. However, he passes over this previous activity with a brief general statement in order that Isaiah 61:1, 2 may be placed at the head of his description of Jesus' ministry. Luke wants to establish at the very beginning that Jesus' ministry should be seen as the fulfillment of this Old Testament Scripture. Both Jesus' preaching and His mighty works are covered in this prophecy.

The importance of Isaiah 61:1, 2 for the understanding of Jesus' ministry can be seen also from its use later as an interpretation of Jesus' ministry to John the Baptist's question, "Are You the Expected One, or do we look for someone else?" (Luke 7:18-23). This passage answers the ultimate question about the identity of Jesus. By setting Isaiah 61:1, 2 at the beginning of his account of the ministry, Luke is asking the reader to look at the entire ministry as the activity of "the Expected One."

The Passion Narrative

It is obvious from the amount of space devoted by each Gospel to the events of the final week of Jesus' life that what happened during this period was considered to be of major importance in the life of Jesus. It is also noteworthy that there is more similarity among all four Gospels in the passion narrative than anywhere else,[26] which also suggests the intense concern for the details of these events in Jesus' life. Günther Bornkamm calls attention also to the fact that the passion narrative is permeated with sayings from the prophets and Psalms, "not only as explicit quotations but also suggested in many individual features and allusions."[27]

We shall focus our attention on the following events in the passion narrative (the first two precede the passion narrative proper) and notice especially how the evangelists set these events in the context of the Old Testament: (1) the entry into Jerusalem, (2) the cleansing of the temple, (3) the last supper with the disciples, and (4) the crucifixion and burial.

Jesus' entry into Jerusalem was greeted by a large crowd of people who were in Jerusalem for the Passover (John 12:12). They lined His way, strewing the road with their garments and palm branches and shouting the words of Psalm 118:26: "Blessed is He who comes in the name of the Lord" (Mark 11:9).

It is clear that the evangelists understood the triumphal entry to be a Messianic sign. Their reports of the shouts of the multitude contain references to the kingship of Jesus in connection with the quotation from Psalm 118. In Mark, the quotation is followed by, "Blessed is the coming kingdom of our father David" (Mark 11:10). In Matthew, the quotation is prefaced by, "Hosanna to the Son of David" (Matthew 21:9). In Luke's account, the title, "the King," is part of the saying: "Blessed is the King who comes in the name of the Lord" (Luke 19:38). In John, the quotation from Psalm 118 is followed by, "even the King of Israel" (John 12:13).

Matthew and John also apply Zechariah 9:9, which speaks of kingship, to the manner of Jesus' entry: "Behold, your King is coming to you, gentle, and mounted on a donkey, even on a colt, the foal of a beast of burden" (Matthew 21:5, cf. John 12:15). Otto Michel calls attention to the fact that Zechariah 9:9 and Genesis 49:11 describe the eschatological king as appearing on an ass and cites passages from the rabbinic literature that show that Zechariah 9:9 was understood as a Messianic prophecy among the Jews.[28] Matthew and John, by the quotation of this verse, make the Messianic implications of the entry into Jerusalem unmistakable.

The cleansing of the temple is recorded by Matthew and Luke soon after the triumphal entry (Matthew 21:12, 13; Luke 19:45, 46).[29] The outer court of the temple was filled with those selling the animals to be used for sacrifice and exchanging the foreign currency of the numerous visitors in the city for the proper Hebrew coinage for the temple tax. Jesus pushed His way through this crowd of merchants and buyers, overturning their tables and driving out their animals. In support of His action, He quoted a combination of Isaiah 56:7 and Jeremiah 7:11: "Is it not written, 'My house shall be called a house of prayer for all the nations'? But you have made it a robbers' den" (Mark 11:17; cf. Matthew 21:13; Luke 19:46).

A part, at least, of the significance of this act lies in the words from Isaiah 56:7, "for all nations," included by Mark, but omitted by Matthew and Luke in the quotation. The area of the temple cleansed by Jesus was the outer court or court of the Gentiles, the one area in the temple into which a non-Jew could enter to worship God. This area had been taken over by the temple merchants, and consequently, the Gentiles had no access to worship in the temple. Isaiah 56 has several things to say about God's acceptance of Gentiles.

> Let not the foreigner who has joined himself to the Lord say, "The Lord will surely separate me from His people." . . . Also the foreigners who join themselves to the Lord, to minister to Him, and to love the name of the Lord, to be His servants, every one who keeps from profaning the sabbath, and holds fast My covenant; even those I will bring to My holy mountain, and make them joyful in My house of prayer. Their burnt offerings and their sacrifices will be ac-

163

cepted on My altar; for My house shall be called a house of prayer for all the peoples (Isaiah 56:3a, 6, 7).

Jesus' quotation of the closing statement in this passage was probably intended to bring the whole passage to the minds of His hearers. Matthew and Luke, in another context (Matthew 4:12-16; Luke 2:32) apply the references about a light for the Gentiles in Isaiah (9:1, 2; 42:6; 49:6) to Jesus, thus showing their understanding that His mission reached beyond the Jews, even as this quotation from Isaiah 56 suggests. Jeremiah 7 is the prophet's indictment of the temple services. The people live corruptly, he says; "then come and stand before Me in this house, which is called by My name, and say, 'We are delivered!'—that you may do all these abominations" (Jeremiah 7:10). He threatens that the Jerusalem temple will be destroyed as Shiloh was if the people do not change (Jeremiah 7:12-15). Jesus fuses these two Old Testament passages, which show (1) God's concern for the Gentiles and (2) His condemnation of corruption covered by a deceptive confidence in the external structures of religion. In quoting these two passages as an explanation for His action, Jesus shows the leaders of the temple to be in opposition to the will of God for the Gentiles. At the same time, in a veiled way, He threatens the destruction of the temple, which has become corrupt. It comes as no surprise, then, that this encounter between Jesus and the rulers of the temple is soon followed by the question about His authority for such actions (Matthew 21:23-27; Mark 11:27-33; Luke 20:1-7; cf. John 2:18).

Jesus ate His final meal with His disciples in an upper room in Jerusalem on the night of His betrayal. This took place during the week of the Passover celebration, and each of the Synoptic Gospels refers to the meal as the Passover meal (Matthew 26:17-20; Mark 14:12-27; Luke 22:7-14).[30] In the course of this last meal with the disciples, Jesus instituted the memorial meal that the church continues to celebrate as the Lord' supper. Mark's account of the institution is as follows:

> And while they were eating, He took some bread, and after a blessing He broke it, and gave it to them, and said, 'Take it; this is My body.' And when He had taken a cup, and given thanks, He gave it to them, and they all drank from it. And He said to them, 'This is My blood of the covenant, which is poured out for many. Truly, I say to you, I shall never again drink of the fruit of the vine until that day when I drink it new in the kingdom of God' (Mark 14:22-25).

There are some differences in wording and in the order of presentation between the Synoptics in their accounts of the institution, but they agree in the following points: (1) each makes an allusion to Jesus' forthcoming death and links the supper with that death, (2) each indicates that His death is for others in a sacrificial way, and (3) each links the allusion to His death with a reference to a covenant.

The first two of these points, which refer to the pouring out of Jesus' blood for many, should be seen as alluding to Isaiah 53:12, where the servant of the Lord is said to have "*poured out* Himself to death" and to have borne "the sin *of many*," thus setting what is about to happen to Jesus in the context of the suffering servant passages of Isaiah.

Matthew and Mark set the saying about the covenant in the context of Exodus 24:8. There, after Moses had read the book of the covenant to the people and the people had agreed to obey it, he threw the blood from the sacrifices on the people and said, "Behold *the blood of the covenant,* which the Lord has made with you. . . ." Luke (as Paul in 1 Corinthians 11:25) sets the covenant saying in the context of Jeremiah 31:31 when he writes, "This cup . . . is the *new covenant* in my blood" (Luke 22:20). Jeremiah contrasted the covenant made at Sinai, which had been broken, with a new covenant to be made in the future, which would be internal.

Whether Jesus stated it exactly as Matthew and Mark have the saying or as Luke has it, the meaning is the same. The shedding of His blood is going to inaugurate a new relationship between God and man, which is parallel to, but distinct from, the covenant ratified by Moses. While the term "covenant" occurs on the lips of Jesus only in the account of the last supper,[31] it is, nevertheless, of pivotal significance. The concept is taken over from the Old Testament and used by Jesus to interpret the significance of His death. It is tied, moreover, to the cup of the last supper, thus binding the participant in that cup to the obedient acceptance of the new covenant as the Israelites were bound to the covenant at Sinai by being participants in the blood.

The story of Jesus' crucifixion, more than any other event in His life, is set in the context of Old Testament prophecy. Paul states that a basic part of the message he preached was that "Christ died for our sins *according to the Scriptures*" (1 Corinthians 15:3). This same concern can be demonstrated in the sermons in Acts. Peter argued at Pentecost that Jesus was "delivered up by the predetermined plan and foreknowledge of God" (Acts 2:23) and on another occasion said, "The things which God announced beforehand by the mouth of all the prophets, that His Christ should suffer, He has thus fulfilled" (Acts 3:18). Philip preached Jesus to the eunuch on the basis of Isaiah 53, which describes the suffering servant of the Lord (Acts 8:30-35). The closing chapter of Luke's Gospel has Jesus instructing His disciples after the resurrection to show them how the suffering of the Messiah had been predicted in the Old Testament (Luke 24:25-27, 44-46).

The reason for this careful and extensive relating of the crucifixion to the Old Testament is not difficult to discover. The crucifixion of Jesus was the great stumbling block in the Christian message (see 1 Corinthians 1:23). The disciples themselves had stumbled over it, as the mournful reply of the two on the road to Emmaus shows: "We were hoping that it was He who was going to redeem Israel" (Luke 24:21). That hope had died with Jesus on the cross!

The Jews found the crucifixion especially offensive because of Deuteronomy 21:23, "He who is hanged is accursed of God." The Jew in Justin's *Dialogue with Trypho* illustrates this difficulty clearly when he says, "This so-called Christ of yours was dishonorable and inglorious, so much so that the last curse contained in the law of God fell on him, for he was crucified." In another passage he remarks, "Whether Christ should be so shamefully crucified, this we are in doubt about. For whosoever is crucified is said in the law to be accursed."[32] Justin also shows, in his *First Apology*, the way the Gentile world responded to the Christian message of the crucifixion: "They proclaim our madness to consist in this, that we give to a crucified man a place second to the unchangeable and eternal God, the Creator of all."[33] The pagan Lucian, writing in the third century A.D., said that Christians abandoned the cults transmitted by the preceding generations and worshiped that impaled sophist.[34]

Because of the offense of the cross, it was especially important to be able to demonstrate that the crucifixion was a part of God's predetermined plan. We shall consider some of the more important Old Testament quotations and allusions incorporated into the narrative of the crucifixion.

When Jesus arrived at Golgotha, the soldiers offered Him a drink. This drink, the wording of the texts suggests, was foretold in Psalm 69:21, "And for my thirst they gave me vinegar to drink" (cf. Matthew 27:34, 48; Mark 15:23, 36; Luke 23:36; John 19:29). Jesus' prayer on the cross, "Father forgive them; for they do not know what they are doing" (Luke 23:34) may allude to Isaiah 53:12, where the servant of the Lord "interceded for the transgressors." The dividing of Jesus' clothes by the soldiers is related by each of the Synoptics to Psalm 22:18, "They divide my garments among them, and for my clothing they cast lots" (cf. Matthew 27:35; Mark 15:24; Luke 23:34). The fact that Jesus was crucified between two thieves (Matthew 27:38; Mark 15:27) may have been seen as a fulfillment of Isaiah 53:12, where the servant is "numbered with the transgressors." The description of the blasphemers around the cross (Matthew 27:39; Mark 15:29) echoes Psalm 22:7, "All who see me sneer at me, they separate with the lip, they wag the head" (cf. Psalm 109:25). Likewise, the words of the mockers in Matthew 27:43 are a reflection of Psalm 22:8, "Commit yourself to the Lord; let Him deliver him, let Him rescue him, because he delights in him!" Jesus' cry of dereliction is a quotation of Psalm 22:1, "My God, my God, why hast thou forsaken me?" (cf. Matthew 27:46; Mark 15:34). Jesus' final words in Luke (23:46) are a quotation from Psalm 31:5, "Into thy hand I commit my spirit." The statement that Jesus' followers watched the crucifixion from afar (Matthew 27:55; Mark 15:40; Luke 23:49) may have been regarded as a fulfillment of Psalm 38:11, "My loved ones and my friends stand aloof from my plague." John says that the fact that Jesus' bones were not broken was in fulfillment of Scripture (John 19:36). His words are drawn from the instructions given to the Israelites that they should not break any bones of the Passover lamb (Exodus 12:46). They may also allude to Psalm 34:20, "He keeps all his bones; not one of them is broken." He further takes the piercing of Jesus' side to be a fulfillment of Zechariah 12:10, "They will look on Me whom they have pierced" (cf. John 19:37).

Three observations need to be made about this list of Old Testament passages incorporated into the narrative of the crucifixion. First, it is apparent that the Psalms were especially important to the early Christians in understanding the death of Jesus. Second, it is interesting that in Luke 24:44 "the Psalms" are mentioned as one of the parts of the Old Testament to which Jesus directed the attention of His disciples to help them understand His suffering. Finally, it is clear that a primary concern of the evangelists in their narratives of the crucifixion is to show that the suffering and death of Jesus took place in accordance with God's foreordained plan and that, consequently, the crucifixion confirms rather than negates Jesus' Messiahship.

Accounts of the Resurrection

There are two kinds of resurrection narratives in the Gospels. There are, first, those that relate the discovery that the tomb of Jesus was empty and the disciples' reaction to this discovery. Second, there are the narratives of the several appearances of Jesus to various of His disciples. There are, in addition, hints in the Gospel accounts that a new understanding of certain Old Testament passages played a major role in convincing the disciples that Jesus had actually been resurrected.

The discovery of the empty tomb the day after the Sabbath is reported in all four Gospels. The Synoptics all relate the visit of a group of women to the tomb about dawn (Matthew 28:1-8; Mark 16:1-8; Luke 24:1-12).[35] They discover that the stone has been removed and that the body of Jesus is gone (Luke 24:3). Matthew says an angel dressed in white announced to the women that Jesus had risen from the dead (Matthew 28:2-6). Mark says a young man dressed in white made the announcement to the women (Mark 16:5, 6), while Luke says it was two men dressed in "dazzling apparel" (Luke 24:4-7). Both Mark and Luke probably intend these men to be understood as angelic messengers also because of the description of their apparel and the reaction produced in the women. Matthew and Mark both relate that the women fled in fear (Matthew 28:8; Mark 16:8). Luke does not mention their fear, but says that when they reported what they had seen and heard to the apostles, "these words seemed to them as nonsense, and they would not believe them" (Luke 24:11).

In the Gospel of John, Mary Magdalene goes to the tomb, but when she sees that the stone has been removed, she runs and tells Peter and another disciple. These two then run to the tomb and discover that it is empty (John 20:1-8). While there are two angels at the tomb in John's account (20:12, 13) they do not announce that Jesus is risen. John says that the other disciple "believed" when he saw the empty tomb (John 20:8). The implication is that Peter did not yet believe, for John goes on to say, as if in explanation for disbelief at this point, "For as yet they did not understand the Scripture, that He must rise from the dead" (John 20:9). John then relates that the disciples returned home, leaving Mary at the tomb. When Mary looks into the tomb, she sees the two angels, who ask her why she is crying, and she replies, "Because they have taken away my Lord, and I do not know where they have laid Him'" (John 20:10-13).

Despite their varied details, two things emerge clearly from these accounts: (1) The tomb in which Jesus' body was placed after His crucifixion was empty the morning after the Sabbath when various of His followers went to visit it; (2) the disciples, with the exception of the unnamed disciple mentioned by John (John 20:8), did not immediately conclude from learning that the tomb was empty that Jesus had arisen from the dead. Luke says they did not believe the women's report, but that their "words seemed to them as nonsense." (Luke 24:11). The first conclusion drawn by most of the disciples was probably the same that Mary Magadalene concluded: someone had removed the body (John 20:2, 13, 15).

Appearances of Jesus to His followers are the thrust of the other stories of the resurrection. He appeared to various women (Matthew 28:9, 10; John 20:14-18), and to two disciples on the road to Emmaus (Luke 24:13-35). He appeared to the disciples in Jerusalem when Thomas was absent (Luke 24:36-43; John 20:19-24) and again when he was present (John 20:26-29). He appeared to the disciples by the sea of Tiberias (John 21:1-14), on a mountain in Galilee (Matthew 28:16-20), and in the vicinity of Bethany (Luke 24:44-53). In each of these last three mentioned appearances, Jesus gave instructions about the mission of the apostles. Finally, Paul, in 1 Corinthians 15:5-8, gives a list of appearances of the risen Christ, most of which have no parallels in the Gospels, and concludes with the appearance to himself.

There is a rich diversity in these stories of the appearances of Jesus to His disciples after the resurrection. None of the accounts has an exact parallel. Some of them seem intended to show what we observed above in the stories of the empty tomb, that the disciples were very slow and cautious in coming to accept that Jesus was alive again. They seem at first to have been more disturbed than comforted by the appearances, as Luke indicates when he says that when Jesus suddenly appeared in their midst, "they were startled and frightened, and thought that they were seeing a spirit" (Luke 24:36, 37). John clearly wants to show this in his story about Thomas, who, when the other apostles reported that they had seen the Lord, replied, "Unless I see in His hands the imprint of the nails, and put my finger into the place of the nails, and put my hand into His side, I will not believe" (John 20:25). The appearance stories all go ahead to show, however, that the disciples advanced beyond this initial disbelief and became thoroughly convinced that the Jesus whom they had known in Galilee and Judea as their Master had indeed been raised from the dead.

A new understanding of the Old Testament contributed to the disciples' acceptance of the resurrection of Jesus as a fact. There is only a hint of this in John, when he comments on the reaction of Peter and the other disciple at the empty tomb, "For as yet they did not understand the Scripture, that He must rise again from the dead" (John 20:9). Luke twice portrays the resurrected Christ instructing the disciples in how the Old Testament had predicted the things they were witnessing (Luke 24:25-27; 44-46). While these passages refer to the importance of the Old Testament in convincing the disciples of the reality of the resurrection of Jesus, it is noteworthy that no Gospel writer quotes or alludes to any Old Testament Scripture in connection with any aspect of the resurrection of Jesus. The only connection given in the Gospels between the resurrection of Jesus and a specific Old Testament passage is Matthew's account of Jesus' reference to the sign of Jonah: "For just as Jonah was three days and three nights in the belly of the sea monster, so shall the Son of man be three days and three nights in the heart of the earth" (Matthew 12:40; cf. Jonah 1:17).

It is only in Luke's record of the preaching of the early church in Acts that we discover what some of these Old Testament Scriptures were. There we find the following Psalms related to the resurrection: Psalm 16:8-11 (Acts 2:24-31); Psalm 110:1 (Acts 2:34, 35); and Psalm 118:22 (Acts 4:10, 11). Acts 8:30-35 may imply that Isaiah 53:10-12, which speaks of the victorious vindication of the suffering servant after his death, was also one of the Old Testament Scriptures related to the resurrection. Acts 8:30-35 does not mention these verses, but if we are to assume from verse 35 that Philip related the whole story of Jesus to Isaiah 53, he would have surely connected these verses with the resurrection, as Justin does later in the second century (First Apology 50, 51).

We have noted a great divergence in details in the stories both of the empty tomb and in those of the appearances of the risen Christ. There is no divergence, however, in the one message that comes through all of these stories: Jesus of Nazareth, crucified under Pontius Pilate, was raised from the dead three days after He was placed in the tomb. This was the foundation on which the faith of the earliest Christians rested. It was the guarantee of everything they preached. Paul sums it up clearly and concisely: "If Christ has not been raised, then our preaching is vain, your faith also is vain" (1 Corinthians 15:14).

Continuity Between Jesus and the History of Israel

In our brief survey of the life of Jesus, we have seen ample evidence of the deep concern of the evangelists to link Jesus with the promises of God in the Old Testament. Luke, as we have already noted, tells us it was Jesus himself who taught His disciples to view the events of His life in relation to the Old Testament Scriptures (Luke 24:25-27).

A Theology of History

This perspective involves more than simply the accumulation of proof texts to prove that Jesus was the Messiah, as the early apologists sometimes used the Old Testament against their Jewish opponents and as the church continues to use it when it loses sight of the essential continuity between the message of the Old Testament and of the New Testament. What we are dealing with is rather a theology of history. This perspective assumes that God is an active participant in the processes of history. It is the theology of history expressed by Isaiah:

> I am God, and there is none like Me, declaring the end from the beginning and from ancient times things which have not been done, saying, 'My purpose will be established, and I will accomplish all My good pleasure';
> . . . .
> Truly I have spoken, truly I will bring it to pass.
> I have planned it, surely I will do it (Isaiah 46:9-11).

This perspective on Jesus and the Old Testament stresses the continuity between what God began to do for the salvation of mankind in Abraham and brought to its climax in Jesus of Nazareth.

Jesus the Link Between the Past and the Future

The evangelists, by their constant references to the Old Testament, show that Jesus of Nazareth forms the link between what God has done in the past and what He will do in the future. He is the link between Israel and the new people of God. What the evangelists show to be taking place in Jesus is something both new and old. It is new in that God is coming to man in a new way (cf. John 1:1-18; Hebrews 1:1, 2) and is ordaining a new access to himself (cf. John 14:6). But at the same time, it is very old. The evangelists do not present Jesus as an alien visitor from outer space. He is, instead, a member of the royal family whose ancestry stems from the golden era of Israel's national life (Luke 1:32; 3:31), and beyond that from the first father of the Hebrew people (Matthew 1:1).

The Jesus presented by the four evangelists emerged from the history of Israel "like a root out of parched ground" (Isaiah 53:2) in the last days of Israel's vassalage, when her days of glory and power were far behind her. He was deeply entwined in Israel's past life and her future hope. There had not been a ruler of David's line since the brief activities of Zerubbabel had stirred Messianic hopes among the paltry remnant recently returned from Persia (Haggai 2:20-23). Jesus of Nazareth came forth as "a shoot from the stem of Jesse," a "branch" from Jesse's "roots" (Isaiah 11:1), to be given "the throne of His father David" to "reign over the house of Jacob for ever" (Luke 1:32, 33). When Israel rejected Him, she rejected the culmination of her own history.

The evangelists set Jesus in the context of the fulfillment of Israel's history, while at the same time they showed Israel's rejection of Jesus (cf. Matthew 27:39-43; Mark 15:29-32; Luke 23:35-38). The people of God would no longer be constituted solely by the physical descendants of Abraham. The proclamation about God's saving activity in Jesus of Nazareth would reach out "to all the nations" as Luke and Matthew state in their report of Jesus' final commission to His disciples (Luke 24:47; Matthew 28:19). Jesus of Nazareth thus becomes the hinge on which swings the hope of all the peoples of the world.

NOTES

[1]Ralph Martin, *Mark, Evangelist and Theologian* (Grand Rapids: Zondervan, 1972), p. 161.

[2]This peculiar material is smallest in Mark, amounting to only about 50 verses that have no parallels in Matthew or Luke. John C. Hawkins, *Horae Synopticae* (Grand Rapids: Baker, 1898/1967), p. 11.

[3]It is usually assumed that there were two such sources: (1) the Gospel of Mark or something like it, and (2) a source containing primarily sayings of Jesus, which is referred to by the cipher Q. To these two common sources, each author in addition added the special material in his Gospel that is not present in the other two. This is only a working hypothesis, and not fact. Most scholars think that such a hypothesis best accounts for the evidence in the Gospels themselves. For other views on the problem of the relationship between the Synoptics and a list of literature on the subject, see Paul Feine, Johannes Behm, and Werner G. Kümmel, *Introduction to the New Testament* (Nashville: Abingdon, 1966), pp. 33-60, and Donald Guthrie, *New Testament Introduction*, 3rd ed. (Downers Grove, IL: InterVarsity Press, 1976), pp. 121-187. Helpful material for understanding the issues can also be found in Ralph P. Martin, *New Testament Foundations*, (Vol. 1 (Grand Rapids: Eerdmans, 1975), pp. 139-160, and R. C. Briggs, *Interpreting the New Testament Today* (Nashville: Abingdon, 1973), pp. 59-86.

[4]It is interesting that Papias, who provides our earliest extant account of the writing of the Gospels (mid-second century, A.D.), says that the Gospel of Mark consists of Mark's recording of the oral teaching of Peter as he remembered it *(Eusebius, Ecclesiastical History, III. xxxix. 15).*

[5]This period of oral transmission should not be considered to be a degenerative time for the accuracy of the material. We know how hard it is for ourselves to remember things exactly. But ours is a culture of the printing press, tape recorder, and computer, which store and retrieve information for us so that we do not have to rely on memory. Theirs was a culture of few books (and those handwritten) and no machines to store and retrieve information. All the important events in their lives were remembered and passed on orally from generation to generation. See the important study by Birger Gerhardsson, *Memory and Manuscript: Oral Tradition and Written Transmission in Rabbinic Judaism and Early Christianity* (Uppsala, 1961).

[6]R.C. Foster disagrees at this point, holding that Luke's prologue

"offers absolutely no support to the supposition that he [Luke] copies his narrative from preceding ones." *Studies in the Life of Christ; Introduction and Early Ministry* (Grand Rapids: Baker, 1966), pp. 87, 88.

[7]See D. Moody Smith, "The Presentation of Jesus in the Fourth Gospel," *Interpretation* (31, 1977), pp. 367-372 for a more complete listing and discussion of the differences between John's picture of Jesus and that in the Synoptics.

[8]For a survey of debates about the Gospel of John, see Robert Kysar, *The Fourth Evangelist and His Gospel* (Minneapolis: Augsburg Publishing House, 1975), and an updated survey by the same author, "Community and Gospel: Vectors in Fourth Gospel Criticism," *Interpretation* (31, 1977), pp. 335-366.

[9]See *The Cambridge History of the Bible*, Vol. 1, ed. by P. R. Achroyd and C. F. Evans (Cambridge: Cambridge University Press, 1970), p. 426 for a brief account of the acceptance of the Gospel of John in the early church. See also M. F. Wiles, *The Spiritual Gospel* (Cambridge: Cambridge University Press, 1960), pp. 13-21 for various ways the differences between John and the Synoptics were treated by the early Fathers.

[10]For an excellent survey of contemporary research on Jesus, see Gustaf Aulen, *Jesus in Contemporary Historical Research* (Philadelphia: Fortress, 1976).

[11]See Vincent Taylor, *The Gospel According to Mark*, second ed. (New York: St. Martin's Press, 1966), pp. 151, 152. For a discussion of Mark's use of the term *gospel*, see Ralph Martin, *Mark*, pp. 17-28 and Willi Marxsen, *Mark the Evangelist* (Nashville: Abingdon, 1969), pp. 117-150.

[12]Taken from a taped lecture by F. F. Bruce given at Regent College in 1977, entitled "Tradition and Redaction."

[13]Cf. our discussion above regarding Peter's sermon recorded in Acts 10.

[14]Our study of the use of the Old Testament must necessarily be limited. There have been numerous studies on this subject. C. H. Dodd's seminal study, *According to the Scriptures* (Fontana Books, 1965/1952), is worthy of special attention.

[15]The most complete study of the infancy narratives available is that by Raymond E. Brown, *The Birth of the Messiah* (Garden City:

Doubleday, 1977). This work should be consulted for bibliography as well as Brown's own extensive discussion.

[16]Brown, (Birth of the Messiah, pp. 180, 181) thinks Matthew 2:1-12 contains an implicit reference to Jesus' relation to Abraham.

[17]Alan Richardson, An Introduction to the Theology of the New Testament (New York: Harper & Row, 1958), pp. 178, 179.

[18]See Herman Gunkel, The Psalms (Philadelphia: Fortress, 1967), pp. 23-24, and Sigmund Mowinckel, He That Cometh (Nashville: Abingdon, 1954), pp. 62-69, passim.

[19]Norman Perrin, Rediscovering the Teaching of Jesus (New York: Harper & Row, 1967), p. 54.

[20]This allusion is noted by Perrin (Rediscovering, p. 66) who credits it to T. W. Manson. E. E. Ellis (The Gospel of Luke [Greenwood, SC: Attic Press, 1974], p. 167) also notes it.

[21]Quoted in Perrin (ibid.) from Midrash Exodus Rabbah 10.7.

[22]These first two are not always distinct.

[23]New Testament Theology (New York: Scribner's, 1971), p. 94.

[24]This title is sometimes used by the evangelists and by Paul as a proper name.

[25]C. H. Dodd, The Founder of Christianity (New York: Macmillan, 1970), p. 102.

[26]See C. H. Dodd, Historical Tradition in the Fourth Gospel (Cambridge: Cambridge University Press, 1963), pp. 21, 22.

[27]Jesus of Nazareth (New York: Harper & Row, 1975/1956), p. 156.

[28]"Onos, onarion," TDNT, 5, p. 284, 285.

[29]Mark places the cleansing a day later (Mark 11:11, 17). John's Gospel records a cleansing early in Jesus' ministry (John 2:13-17). See Taylor, Mark, pp. 461, 462 and C. K. Barrett, The Gospel According to St. John, second ed. (Philadelphia: Westminster, 1978), pp. 194-197.

[30]John indicates that the meal took place before the Passover (John 13:1-4; 18:28). For a discussion of this problem and some proposed

solutions see Joachim Jeremias, *The Eucharistic Words of Jesus* (Philadelphia: Fortress, 1966), pp. 15-26.

[31]The term *covenant* appears only one other time in the Gospels (Luke 1:72). It is not especially frequent in Acts or the Epistles, except for Hebrews, where it occurs seventeen times.

[32]Chapters 32 and 89. Quoted from *The Ante-Nicene Fathers* I, pp. 210, 244.

[33]Chapter 53. Quoted from *The Ante-Nicene Fathers*, I, p. 1967. For an excellent discussion of crucifixion in antiquity see Martin Hengel, *Crucifixion* (Philadelphia: Fortress, 1977).

[34]*De morte Peregrini*, p. 13.

[35]Not all of these are identified in each of the Synoptics (cf. Matthew 28:1; Mark 16:1; Luke 24:10). Mary Magdalene and another woman named Mary, identified as the mother of James in Mark and Luke, are constant in all three lists. Only Mary Magdalene is mentioned by all four Gospels (cf. John 20:1).

PART THREE

THE WORD OF TEACHING

"What you have heard entrust to faithful men." 2 Timothy 2:2

SECTION OUTLINE

7. GOD THE FATHER
   Introduction: Should God Be Addressed As Father?
   A. The Example and Teaching of Jesus
   B. The Apostolic Testimony
   Conclusion

8. THE SON: JESUS ACCORDING TO THE NEW TESTA-MENT
   Introduction: The Importance of Christology
   A. The Word
   B. Son of Man
   C. Son of God
   D. Christ
   E. Lord

9. THE HOLY SPIRIT
   A. The Identity of the Holy Spirit
      Extended earthly presence of God
      A part of the Trinity
   B. The Work of the Holy Spirit
      A Two-dimensional purpose
      Initiate the new age
      Regeneration in man
      Unity in the church
      The Holy Spirit and freedom
      Spiritual maturity in Christians

C. Manifestations of the Holy Spirit
   Baptism of the Holy Spirit
   Indwelling presence of the Holy Spirit
   Miraculous signs
D. Gifts From the Holy Spirit
   Foundational
   Universal
   Service
Conclusion

10. THE IMAGE OF GOD
   A. People: Noble and Cruel, Individual and Social
   B. God: Majestic and Moral, One and More
   Conclusion

11. THE DOCTRINE OF SALVATION
   Introduction
   A. The Scheme of Redemption
      The people of God
      Captivity and deliverance
      Deliverers and the Deliverer
      Salvation in the New Covenant
   B. The Nature of Salvation
      Justification
      Sanctification
      Reconciliation
      Eternal Life

12. THE WAY OF SALVATION
   Introduction: Primal Focus
   A. God's Initiative
   B. Man's Decision
   C. Receiving the Word
   D. Baptism
   E. Salvation as Eschatological and Historical
   F. Salvation and the Community of Faith
   Conclusion

13. THE CHRISTIAN LIFE
   Introduction: Pictures and Paradoxes
   A. The Primary Christian Ideal—Christlikeness
   B. Characteristic Features of Christian Living

Worship
Service
Meditation
C. Aids to Christian Devotion and Dedication
D. The Mutual Ministry of Christians

14. THE CHRISTIAN HOPE
Introduction: Confusion and Apathy Regarding Prophetic Hope
A. The Historic Premillennial View
B. The Amillennial View
C. The Postmillennial View
D. The Dispensational Premillennial View
Conclusion

CHAPTER

7

GOD THE FATHER

By David Root

Should God Be Addressed As Father?

I believe in God, the Father, Almighty. These words, echoing those of Paul in 1 Corinthians 8:6, formed the entire first article of the earliest western creed. They are very simple, acknowledging, as B. F. Westcott says, "God's dealings with the individual soul and with the world, as Father and Ruler."[1] One must take care, however, not to allow the simplicity of the words to mask the complexity and significance of the ideas that they contain. Everyone knows what a father is from his own experience; but which, if any, of those experiences corresponds to the reality of God? Is He the stern disciplinarian whose word is law, or the pal who takes his children (especially the boys) hunting and fishing? Is He the commuting breadwinner who works long hours to guarantee his children's security, or the ghetto father who lives away from his family so that they can receive welfare? Is He, as Freud argued, the authority figure who is first admired, then envied and displaced, only to reappear as the superego or conscience?[2]

Culture and experience combine to produce many different ideas of fatherhood and expose the believer to danger. He may affirm his belief in God the Father more to demonstrate his orthodoxy than to express an understanding. In such a case, his creed says more about himself than about God, and he may fall prey to what Westcott calls "a practical atheism, orthodox in language and reverent in bearing, which can enter a Christian Church and charm the conscience to rest with shadowy traditions."[3] On the other hand, he may contend earnestly for his belief in terms drawn from his own experience and provoke a hostile reaction from those whose experience is different or who think that his ideas have intolerable implications. Mary Daly, for example, sees the idea of God as Father as expressive and productive of a society where rape, genocide, and war predominate. She therefore calls for an understanding of God as "the Verb who transcends anthropomorphic symbolization."[4] The believer, of course, may be called graciously to suffer such hostility for the sake of Christ; but he ought at least to ask whether the hostility results from a misrepresentation of God. To communicate error about God is at least as grave a sin as to communicate nothing.

Such diversity of understanding and potential for error tempt one to silence, to the holding of his belief between himself and God alone. Wiser heads than his have wrestled with the problem for centuries, and it appears arrogant to dispute with them. Yet the Scriptures say, "I believed, therefore I spoke" (Psalm 116:10; 2 Corinthians 4:13); and they themselves testify to God's self-disclosure and are profitable for teaching (2 Timothy 3:16). They, therefore, summon all believers to consider God's revelation of himself so that they might think His thoughts after Him and speak intelligently of His character and reconciling love. Response to such a summons certainly includes consideration of the Biblical symbol of God the Father.

The Example and Teaching of Jesus

To say that Jesus addressed God as Father is to say what virtually the whole world knows. The entire gospel tradition substantiates such a usage. Early Christian worship evidently echoed the usage of its Lord, crying "*Abba*" in the Aramaic tongue even when Greek was the predominant language of the congregation. This echo was heard both in churches established by Paul (Galatians 4:6) and in congregations he did not establish (Romans 8:15). Such persistent and widespread usage, even across a linguistic barrier, only serves to emphasize the importance of this symbol.

That importance has at least two foundations. The first is the distinctiveness of such an address to God in the Judaism of the first century. The Hebrew Scriptures, though they provide a most important background for understanding the symbol, nowhere record individuals addressing God as Father. Furthermore, as Joachim Jeremias has shown, although early Judaism developed many forms of address to God, "in the literature of Palestinian Judaism *no evidence has yet been found* of 'my Father' being used by an individual as an address to God."[5] The second foundation is the fact that the Gospels indicate that Jesus always used this form of address in His prayers to God, with the single exception of His cry from the cross (Mark 15:34), which is a quotation of Psalm 22:1. Jesus, therefore, not only addressed God as Father, but did so uniformly, and so introduced a new usage to His followers by which they could express the character of their relationship to God.

That relationship, as has been suggested, has its roots deep in the Hebrew Scriptures. According to the record of Exodus, God told Moses:

> Then you shall say to Pharaoh, "Thus says the Lord: 'Israel is My son, My first-born. So I said to you, "Let My son go, that he may serve Me"; but you have refused to let him go. Behold, I will kill your son, your first-born' " (Exodus 4:22, 23).

This text, however, does not speak of a "natural" relationship, as if Israel and Israel alone (or Israel first) were the offspring of God. Many nations of antiquity, indeed, thought themselves to be descended from their god or gods; but Israel knew better (or should have known better). For Israel, relationship with Yahweh did not depend upon the fate of descent, but upon Yahweh's own gracious call of Abraham and especially upon His mighty acts of deliverance.

> Say, therefore, to the sons of Israel, "I am the Lord, and I will bring you out from under the burdens of the Egyptians, and I will deliver you from their bondage. I will also redeem you with an outstretched arm and with great judgments. Then I will take you for My people, and I will be your God; and you shall know that I am the Lord your God, who brought you out from under the burdens of the Egyptians. And I will bring you to the land which I swore to give to Abraham, Isaac, and Jacob, and I will give it to you for a possession; I am the Lord" (Exodus 6:6-8).

Using language like that of adoption ("I will take you"), this text clearly emphasizes Yahweh's gracious and powerful activ-

GOD THE FATHER

ity in making Israel His first-born. In Deuteronomy, Moses
strengthens this emphasis when he reminds the poeple:

> The Lord did not set His love on you nor choose you because you
> were more in number than any of the peoples, for you were the
> fewest of all peoples, but because the Lord loved you and kept the
> oath which He swore to your forefathers, the Lord brought you out
> by a mighty hand, and redeemed you from the house of slavery,
> from the hand of Pharaoh king of Egypt (Deuteronomy 7:7, 8).

The fatherhood of God, then, is first of all a symbol of God's
liberation of His people from bondage, of His gracious calling
and their free response.

Given such a symbol, prophets and poets naturally develop it
to enhance the effectiveness of their messages. Deuteronomy
32:10 and Hosea 9:10 describe Israel as a foundling whom
Yahweh adopts; but each develops the image in its own way.
The Deuteronomy text continues:

> He encircled him, he cared for him,
> He guarded him as the pupil of His eye.
> Like an eagle that stirs up its nest,
> That hovers over its young,
> He spread His wings and caught them,
> He carried them on His pinions (Deuteronomy 32:10, 11).

This introduces an element of tender care into the metaphor,
an element that many cultures associate with the idea of
motherhood.[6] Numerous other texts (e.g., Psalm 103:13; Isaiah
49:15; 66:10-13) also present this element. They sometimes associate such tender care or compassion with fatherhood and
sometimes with motherhood, all with the effect of emphasizing
this dimension of God's character. On the other hand, the
Hosea text uses the idea of God's gracious adoption of the
foundling Israel as a foil to emphasize the seriousness of Israel's apostasy. In Hosea, Yahweh says:

> I found Israel like grapes in the wilderness;
> I saw your forefathers as the earliest fruit on the fig tree in its first
> season.
> But they came to Baal-peor
> And devoted themselves to shame,
> And they became as detestable as that which they loved
> (Hosea 9:10).

This element in the development of the metaphor emphasizes, from a negative standpoint, the fact that Israel must freely choose to live as Yahweh's first-born. To refuse is to risk provoking His wrath. Hosea 11, however, presents an eloquent and touching picture of the ironic and ultimately creative tension that exists in the loving, compassionate Yahweh when He is confronted by the rebellion of His first-born. In that situation, neither the stern, just "Father" nor the soft, loving "Mother" prevails. Instead, Yahweh announces a creative judgment that maintains both dimensions of the divine character and shatters the dichotomy between mercy and justice. Yahweh, in His great love, has a right to forgive His first-born. He also has the right to require the first-born to bear the consequences of his free choice to rebel. What is more, both of these rights derive from God's decision to adopt this wilderness foundling. In short, Hosea 11 combines with other texts of the Hebrew Scriptures to present "a symbol of free relationship and divine kindness in 'father' as used of God."[7]

Early Judaism, though it does not use the symbol extensively, also emphasizes divine kindness when it refers to God as Father. Jeremias cites the following story about Hanin ha-Nehba, who was famous for his prayers for rain. School children would come to him crying, "abba, abba," and ask him to give them rain. Hanin would then pray, "Master of the world, grant it for the sake of those who are not yet able to distinguish beween an *Abba* who has the power to give rain and an *abba* who has not." "Hanin appeals to the mercy of God by using the trustful *'abba, abba'* which the school children cry out to him and describes God—in contrast to himself—as the *'Abba'* who has the power to give rain."[8] Such a story illustrates that it was not totally inappropriate for one to think of God as Father and that to think about Him in such a way was to think about His kindness. Hanin's words nevertheless imply that such thinking is somewhat childish (or childlike). After all, "*abba* was a children's word, used in everyday talk, an expression of courtesy."[9] Hanin may condescend to use it to help teach children a lesson, but when he prays, he addresses God as "Master of the world."

Jesus, however, consistently addresses God as Father, and the content of His prayers indicates that His understanding of the Father symbol was consistent with that of the Hebrew Scriptures. For example, in Matthew 11, Jesus says:

> I praise Thee, O Father, Lord of heaven and earth, that thou didst hide these things from the wise and intelligent and didst reveal them to babes. Yes, Father, for thus it was well-pleasing in Thy sight (Matthew 11:25, 26; cf. Luke 10:21).

Addressing God as Father, Jesus here describes Him as one who freely chooses to disclose himself, to reveal His character. Like ancient Israel, the recipients of this revelation have no significant power or wealth by which to earn or even force such a revelation. It comes from God's good pleasure (eudokia) and brings to any who will receive it the opportunity to enter into an intimate relationship with God. Of course, this revelation takes place in and through the Son, who both knows and is known by the Father. The Matthew text continues:

> All things have been handed over to Me by My Father; and no one knows the Son, except the Father; nor does anyone know the Father, except the Son, and anyone to whom the Son wills to reveal Him (Matthew 11:27).

This saying, though it opens the door for profound theological speculation about the essential deity of Jesus and the relationship of the divine Son to the divine Father, is proverbial and gives expression to an insight. As a rule, fathers and sons do have a special relationship. That relationship has many dimensions and varies from case to case, but Jesus' saying stresses its intimacy and openness and the privilege granted to the Son to receive from the Father whatever the Father has and knows. John 5 presents a similar saying of Jesus (John 5:19, 20), which C. H. Dodd describes as "a simple picture of a son apprenticed to his father's trade."[10] Because the Father loves the Son, He shows Him what He is doing. In both of the sayings, then, Jesus suggests that one comes to know God as Father inasmuch as he responds positively to God's free and loving self-disclosure.[11] In fact, the existence of such love and kindness that prompt God to disclose himself in Jesus is one of the realities to which the father symbol points.

Because Jesus knows God as a kind and loving Father, He trusts God with life itself, as the accounts of the Gethsemane episode show.[12] Hamerton-Kelly remarks:

> The Gethsemane pericope does not give the impression that Jesus is being coerced into the Crucifixion by an arrogant will; rather, he is

being asked to cooperate. His struggle is not that of a rebel against unreasonable authority, but rather that of human weakness against the inability to trust and the fear of death. He does not accept God's will with doomed resignation, but with free confidence. "Yet not what I will but what thou wilt," are words of triumph not defeat, of serenity not resignation. God's will is true, therefore death by it is life, despite the shrinking of the flesh. The Resurrection reveals the content of God's Gethsemane will, the nature of an "Abba" to be trusted.[13]

Jesus calls His disciples to this trust when He asks them to give up family and occupational ties and other means of acquiring power to secure one's existence and to take up their crosses and follow Him.

The Hebrew Scriptures' ideas of free relationship and divine kindness also underlie the use of Father in the Lord's Prayer.[14] In the Matthew text of the Prayer, Jesus introduces it with a warning against continuous babbling like that of the Gentiles. He assures them that God, *their Father*, knows what they need before they ask. Such an assurance assumes that God is involved in the lives of the disciples and that His involvement is benevolent. Jesus, therefore, instructs them to pray in terms that show their believing acknowledgement of God's kindness and that express their desire to participate in the free relationship that they see in Jesus. They show their belief by accepting Jesus' understanding of God as Father. Given such an understanding, they can pray without qualification that His rule become a reality and His decision be accomplished on earth. They do not require a huge stockpile of food supplies as a hedge against drought or inflation; instead, they can rely on God to supply the bread of tomorrow [15] They can believe that God forgives and that He will sustain and strengthen them in the face of temptation. On the other hand, they express their desire to participate in the relationship that God offers inasmuch as they recognize, as E. Schweizer says "that God's will is carried out all the time by the action of his people."[16] They, therefore, know that the benefits of forgiveness come to those who forgive and that they must not shrink back from oppression and hardship but must follow where God leads, believing that He will sustain them. It follows, then, that when they pray the Prayer in belief, they are already beginning to fulfill their destiny as God's children,[17] not by procreation but by gracious election and believing response. As Hamerton-Kelly notes:

The Lord's Prayer reveals God the Father to be the one who moves history towards true humanity. He gives us a foretaste of that humanity in the experience of forgiveness and reconciliation, and in the sustenance that comes in times of temptation. Most of all, however, the prayer reveals Jesus to be the human face of God, for "Abba" is an address of deepest intimacy which only the son could use. In giving his disciples this prayer Jesus admitted them to the privilege of divine sonship and daughterhood, the right to call God "Abba" (cf. Romans 8:15, 16), and thereby bestowed on them the true humanity of the Kingdom of God.[18]

John's gospel presents some of the same ideas, primarily through its stress on Jesus' activities as the true Son of God. On the one hand, John strongly emphasizes Jesus' function of revealing God. He is the Word become flesh (John 1:14); the unique One, himself God, who dwells in the Father's bosom and has made God known (John 1:18);[19] the One who says, "He who has seen Me has seen the Father" (John 14:9). On the other hand, John points out that Jesus' revelation of God depends upon His acting always as a true Son, as one who relies totally upon the Father. He does what He sees the Father doing, including giving life and judging (John 5:19-24). He speaks only what the Father commands (John 12:49, 50). He even refers to His death as the cup that the Father has given Him (John 18:11). In fact, it is His suffering and resurrection (His being "lifted up") that reveal most clearly His dependence on the Father and His effective, functional unity with the Father. He says to His opponents in John 8:28, 29,

> When you lift up the Son of Man, then you will know that I am He, and I do nothing on My own initiative, but I speak these things as the Father taught Me. And He who sent Me is with Me; He has not left Me alone, for I always do the things that are pleasing to Him.

Nevertheless, John also emphasizes Jesus' extension of such a relationship with God from himself to His disciples. Already in the prologue, He speaks of Jesus' giving people authority to become children of God (John 1:12, 13). Since receiving such authority depends upon believing in His name, one assumes that the character of these children of God—their ideas, words, and actions—will be like that of the true son that John describes in the body of the narrative. Jesus, however, makes that explicit in the prayer of chapter 17:

> I do not ask in behalf of these alone, but for those also who believe in Me through their word; that they may all be one; even as Thou, Father, are in Me, and I in Thee, that they also may be in Us; that the world may believe that Thou didst send Me.
>
> And the glory which Thou hast given Me I have given to them; that they may be one, just as We are one; I in them, and Thou in Me, that they may be perfected in unity, that the world may know that Thou didst send Me, and didst love them, even as Thou didst love Me (John 17:20-23).

This is bold language, especially from a writer who stresses Jesus' uniqueness as John does. It is no isolated phenomenon, however,[20] and it conveys the same basic ideas as those that adhere to the father symbol elsewhere, namely, the ideas of a God whose love and kindness can be counted upon and who summons people to a free relationship characterized by reconciliation and wholeness.

The Apostolic Testimony

Any consideration of the father symbol in the New Testament must, of course, take Paul into account. His writings are extensive and early, and he frequently employs father-child imagery to describe both the relationship between God and Christians and the relationship between himself and certain other people. Moreover, given his rabbinic training, one may assume that Paul was familiar with the development of the father symbol and its application to God in the Hebrew Scriptures. This familiarity, along with certain ideas that were present in the Hellenistic culture of his day, provided a background for his usage. It did not, however, serve as the primary focus of Paul's thinking about the fatherhood of God. That focus came from his conviction that God is preeminently "the Father of our Lord Jesus Chrsit." He thus describes the gospel of God to the Roman Christians as the gospel

> concerning His Son, who was born a descendant of David according to flesh, who was delcared the Son of God with power by the resurrection from the dead, according to the spirit of holiness, Jesus Christ our Lord (Romans 1:3, 4).

In this description, he cites what many exegetes think to be a primitive Christian liturgical formulation.[21] Yet he evidently feels free to adopt it as an expression of his own thinking with, at most, minor modifications. In so doing, he expresses his essential agreement with the primitive gospel, which viewed the resurrection as proof that Jesus' relationship with God was that of a true Son and as the decisive demonstration of the character of God as a Father who could be trusted.[22] Such a gospel is indeed good news, because it offers all the nations the opportunity to become Christ's called saints, that is, to respond to the gracious and loving call of God in the obedience of belief and so come to know Him as Father.[23] It is no wonder, then, that Paul so frequently associates the father symbol with the Lord Jesus Christ.[24]

Nevertheless, like the prophets and poets of old, Paul does not hesitate to develop the metaphor with reference to his own experience and insight. He takes the ideas that are implicit in Jesus' giving His disciples the Lord's Prayer and the privilege of calling God "Abba" and makes them explicit. For example, in Galatians 3 he says:

> For you are all sons of God through faith in Christ Jesus. For all of you who were baptized into Christ have clothed yourselves with Christ. There is neither Jew nor Greek, there is neither slave nor free man, there is neither male nor female; for you are all one in Christ Jesus. And if you belong to Christ, then you are Abraham's offspring, heirs according to promise (Galatians 3:26-29).

Here he stresses both the reality of the Christian's sonship to God and its dependence upon the true sonship of Jesus. Such ideas are not new,[25] but Paul gives them particular emphasis, especially when he goes on to say:

> And because you are sons, God has sent forth the Spirit of His Son into our hearts, crying, "Abba! Father!" Therefore you are no longer a slave, but a son; and if a son, then an heir through God (Galatians 4:6, 7).[26]

Furthermore, in the context of his discussion, Paul adds at least two elements to the father-child imagery. First, by reference to the promise made to Abraham, he links the Christians' sonship to God with the ancient motif of the election of the fathers, with all its stress on the divine initiative and kindness.[27] Second, by introducing the contrast between a slave and a son, he emphasizes the responsibility inherent in the privilege of sonship. A slave does not enjoy his master's confidence; he simply does what he is ordered to do. The same thing is true of a minor child, as Paul points out (Galatians 4:1, 2). The adult child, by contrast, enjoys a different relationship. Hamerton-Kelly describes this relationship as follows:

> The legal bonds dissolve and he is free to enter into a responsible relationship with his father based on mutual recognition and taking the form of adult reciprocity.[28]

Paul uses this development as the basis of his encouragement of the Galatians to act like true sons rather than slaves, who depend on the letter of the law.

In the same context, Paul introduces still another development of the metaphor—the idea of adoption (Galatians 4:5). H. D. Betz notes: "The term 'adoption' . . . is originally a legal term referring to adoption as sons of those who are not kin by birth."[29] Paul, however, probably uses the term to bring to mind the experience of the exodus, as presented in Exodus 6 and Deuteronomy 7. In both Galatians 4:5 and the parallel text in Romans 8:15, he contrasts the state of sonship with the state of slavery, just as Yahweh does in Exodus 6:6-8. Furthermore, in Romans 8, he describes Christians both as "sons" (huioi, suggesting legal privilege) and as "children" (tekna, born children) of God.[30] Finally, as if to guard against the idea that God makes people His children by means of a unilateral judicial fiat, Paul says that Christians are God's heirs and Christ's fellow-heirs, "if indeed we suffer with Him in order that we may also be glorified with Him" (Romans 8:17). He further reminds the Romans that they are saved in hope (Romans 8:24) and warns them against presumptuous exclusivism, just as Moses had warned the Israelites (Romans 9—11, especially, 11:17ff). For Paul, then, adoption means liberation through God's gracious calling, making it possible for people to respond freely to His love, live holy lives in reliance upon Him even in the face of suffering), and so fulfill their human destiny.[31]

In Romans 8:32, Paul hints at another dimension of the father-child imagery: "He who did not spare His own Son, but delivered Him up for us all, how will He not also with Him freely give us all things?" This rhetorical question takes its force from the underlying assumption that the father greatly cherishes the son. The idea also stands behind such texts as Romans 5:8 and John 3:16, and is explicit in such expressions as "the Son of His love" (Colossians 1:13)[32] and "the beloved."[33] Although Paul certainly did not originate this idea, his usage of it provides insight into his referring to his congregations and such people as Onesimus as his children.[34] For although he uses the analogy of natural generation, Paul certainly does not mean that he takes God's place as the one who generates life. He is simply the one through whom the gospel, God's power for salvation, comes to these people. Nevertheless, they are as dear to him as any children could be to their fathers, and he tries to nourish and care for them just as God cared for Israel in the wilderness. His relationship with them, therefore, provides an example of how a proper understanding of the father symbol as it applies to God can transform relationships among people. Elsewhere, as Hamerton-Kelly says:

> Paul emphasizes the themes of adoption and freedom; we enter the family as mature adults, by the free choice of faith, and live in adult responsibility, not in infantile obedience.[35]

In this usage, Paul shows his understanding that at least one dimension of that adult responsibility is the imitation of the Father's kindness and concern for reconciliation. He thus agrees with Jesus, who does only what He sees the Father doing and who urges His disciples: "Therefore, you are to be perfect, as your heavenly Father is perfect."[36]

The rest of the New Testament writings generally use the father symbol in similar ways, though the epistles of John and Peter present some interesting twists. 1 John 3, for example, reminds the readers that it is the love of the Father that has made it possible for them to be God's children (1 John 3:1). That, of course, is not new, but the text goes on to say, "No one who is born of God practices sin, because His seed abides in him; and he cannot sin, because he is born of God" (1 John 3:9).

Such language pushes the biological metaphor to its limits, that is, to the very edge of the Gnostic heresy. John, however, is a sensitive and gifted literary artist, and he knows just how far the metaphor can take him. He immediately guards against any attempt to ride it too far by saying, "By this the children of God and the children of the devil are obvious: anyone who does not practice righteousness is not of God, nor the one who does not love his brother" (1 John 3:10).

To be sure, one might insist still on understanding this idea in the literal, biological way; but to do so, he would have to step outside the Biblical tradition within which John is writing. He would also have to ignore John's later statement, "We love, because He first loved us" (1 John 4:19), where the metaphor is dropped in favor of an explicit idea of imitation. Such an idea agrees with ideas presented in the Gospels and Paul, as noted above.

The blessing of 1 Peter 1:3-5 presents another interesting combination of ideas, remarkable for its consistency with the thought of Paul. There God is identified as the Father of our Lord Jesus Christ. Having made that identification, Peter qualifies God's Fatherhood both by the biological metaphor of begetting and by explicit mention of God's great mercy and mighty action in raising Jesus from the dead. Like John, Peter protects the metaphor by linking it to specific, non-biological realities. He also guards the idea of a free relationship by emphasizing both hope and belief. In the next four verses, he develops the emphasis on belief still further and also brings in love. All of these ideas appear elsewhere in the New Testament.

In 2 Peter 1:4, however, the phrase "partakers of the divine nature" appears. This phrase, together with its immediate context, has led some scholars to assign a late date and a syncretistic milieu to 2 Peter. Ernest Käsemann, for example, remarks that this sentence "in its expression, its individual motifs and its whole trend . . . clearly marks the relapse of Christianity into Hellenistic dualism."[37] In response, we note that the familiar themes of election, promise, and obedient response also appear in the context, opening the way for an understanding that is consistent with the Biblical tradition.[38] Once again, Peter protects his metaphor.

Conclusion

This survey of Biblical data concerning the symbol of God as Father reveals a remarkable consistency. The ideas of divine kindness and free relationship persistently adhere to the symbol, despite various embellishments and extensions of the metaphor. Not surprisingly, Jesus provides the focus of it all. Hamerton-Kelly declares that the term "father" was the "appropriate symbol" of Jesus' "intimate relationship with God." In turn, when Jesus encouraged His disciples to address God as "Abba," He was opening to them the possibility of their participating in the same experience, expressed as "the spirit of sonship." The difference lay in the fact that Jesus' sonship was "natural" while that of the disciples was "adoptive." "Withal, however, fatherhood and sonship symbolized the new relationship of adult freedom in union with Christ, and constituted the new family of God which was united by bonds of faith."[39]

In all of this, the Biblical tradition shows a remarkable sensitivity to the power and limitations of metaphor. Unfortunately, exegets and theologians have not always shown the same sensitivity. Robert Frost warns,

> Unless you are at home in the metaphor, unless you have had your proper poetical education in the metaphor, you are not safe anywhere. Because you are not at ease with figurative values: you don't know the metaphor in its strength and its weakness. You don't know how far you may expect to ride it and when it may break down with you. . . . All metaphor breaks down somewhere. That is the beauty of it. It is touch and go with the metaphor, and until you have lived with it long enough you don't know where it is going. You don't know how much you can get out of it and when it will cease to yield. It is a very living thing. It is as life itself.[40]

One may hope that such a study as this, limited as it is, will prompt more living with the Biblical metaphor of God as Father to protect it from cultural encroachment and so make the world of theology a safer place.

NOTES

[1]Cf. B. F. Westcott, The Historic Faith: Short Lectures on the Apostolic Creed (London: Macmillan, 1913), pp. 37, 38.

[2]Cf. Freud's use of this idea to explain the development of religion and morals in S. Freud, Moses and Monotheism. The Standard Edition of the Complete Psychological Works of Sigmund Freud, ed. by J. Strachey and others, vol. 23 (London: Hogarth, 1964).

[3]Westcott, Historic Faith, p. 41.

[4]Mary Daly, Beyond God the Father, Toward a Philosophy of Women's Liberation (London: Beacon Press, 1973), p. 97.

[5]Joachim Jeremias, The Prayers of Jesus ("Studies in Biblical Theology," II, 6; London: SCM Press, Ltd., 1967), pp. 66-81; New Testament Theology: the Proclamation of Jesus (New York: Charles Scribner's Sons, 1971), p. 64.

[6]I do not argue here for a change in the language of the symbol. I am quite content with the father metaphor, but I should like to insist that it be understood and applied on its own terms instead of having to bear a meaning derived from any particular culture. In fact, the metaphor, properly understood and applied, has the power to transform the idea of fatherhood, at least in the "culture" of the Christian community. Such a transformation, however, will not take place if we insist on calling God Mother instead of Father and so confirm the culturally generated idea that tenderness is gender related. On the other hand, we certainly should not shy away from the Scriptures' use of maternal metaphors with reference to God.

[7]R. Hamerton-Kelly, God the Father: Theology and Patriarchy in the Teaching of Jesus ("Overtures to Biblical Theology"; Philadelphia: Fortress Press, 1979), p. 51. This fine work is very stimulating and helpful. I freely acknowledge my debt to Stanford's Dean of the Chapel for helping me crystallize a number of ideas.

[8]Jeremias, New Testament Theology, pp. 65, 66.

[9]Ibid., p. 67.

[10]C. H. Dodd, "A Hidden Parable in the Fourth Gospel," More New Testament Studies (Grand Rapids: Eerdmans, 1968), p. 31.

GOD THE FATHER

[11]Compare John 1:12, 13, where the genetic metaphor is developed even more strongly.

[12]Matthew 26:36-46; Mark 14:32-42; Luke 22:39-46. Notice especially Mark 14:36, where "Abba" again appears in Jesus' prayer.

[13]Hamerton-Kelly, God the Father, pp. 72, 73.

[14]Matthew 6:7-15; Luke 11:1-4.

[15]This translation of epiousios is defended by Jeremias in New Testament Theology, p. 199. W. Forester, however, disagrees and favors the sense of "necessary," cf. his article on the word in G. Kittel, ed., Theological Dictionary of the New Testament, trans. by G. W. Bromily (Grand Rapids: Eerdmans, 1964), vol. 2, pp. 590-599. Jeremias agrees with Jerome and others in regarding the petition as "a petition for the bread of the time of salvation, the bread of life." He nevertheless cautions that this does not mean that the prayer for bread has been spiritualized. There is no antithesis "between earthly bread and the bread of life." The bread used in the Upper Room was "earthly bread" but was at the same time "bread of life." Hence every meal for the followers of Jesus took on "eschatological significance . . . an anticipation of the heavenly feast" (New Testament Theology, pp. 200-201).

[16]E. Schweizer, The Good News According to Matthew, trans. by D. E. Green (Atlanta: John Knox Press, 1975), p. 152.

[17]Compare Ephesians 1:5 with Schweizer's comment: "To be human means to accept responsibility under God's mandate and according to his will (Genesis 1:26-28); and we are praying here simply that man will become human." The Good News According to Matthew, p. 153.

[18]Hamerton-Kelly, God the Father, p. 77.

[19]Cf. J. H. Bernard, A Critical and Exegetical Commentary on the Gospel According to St. John (2 vols.; Edinburgh: T. & T. Clark, 1928, repr. 1962) vol. 1, pp. 31, 32.

[20]Compare, especially, the development of such ideas in 1 John and 2 Peter, on which see below.

[21]Cf., for example, E. Käsemann, Commentary on Romans, trans. and ed. by G. W. Bromily (Grand Rapids: Eerdmans, 1980), pp. 10ff.; C. K. Barrett, The Epistle to the Romans ("Harper's New Testament Commentaries"; New York: Harper & Row, 1957), pp. 18ff.

²²Compare Peter's Pentecost citation of Psalm 16: "Thou wilt not abandon my soul to Hades, nor allow Thy Holy One to undergo decay," along with the rest of the sermon, with its themes of kingship/sonship.

²³All of these ideas appear in Romans 1:5-7. Thus, Christians, even in far-off Rome, are Christ's called ones (1:6), saints, i.e., holy ones (1:7; compare "spirit of holiness" in 1:4), who are loved by God (1:7), who know Him as "our Father" (1:7), and whom Paul is commissioned to bring to the obedience of belief (1:5).

²⁴For example, Paul's standard salutation like that of Romans 1:7: "Grace to you and peace from God our Father and the Lord Jesus Christ"; blessings like those of 2 Corinthians 1:3 and Ephesians 1:3. Check any standard concordance for a complete list.

²⁵Consider, especially, Jesus' statements to His disciples concerning "your heavenly Father" (Matthew 5:7; 7:11 and so forth) and His prayer that the disciples be one in himself and in the Father (John 17:20-23).

²⁶Note the clear sense of dependence in the statement that the *Spirit of God's Son* is sent to the heart crying, "Abba."

²⁷Paul develops this idea still further in Romans 4, where he shows that the proper response to God's gracious election is belief, and that all who believe Christ therefore participate in a relationship with God like that of Abraham.

²⁸Hamerton-Kelly, *God the Father*, p. 85.

²⁹H. D. Betz, *Galatians: a Commentary on Paul's Letter to the Churches in Galatia* ("Hermenela"; Philadelphia: Fortress Press, 1979), p. 208.

³⁰"Sons" in Romans 8:14; "children" in Romans 8:16, 17. Käsemann also comments that the two are interchangeable. *Commentary on Romans*, p. 229.

³¹Cf. Ephesians 1:5 (where the term "adoption" is also used) along with M. Barth's comments in *Ephesians: Introduction, Translation, and Commentary on Chapters 1—3* ("Anchor Bible"; Garden City, New York: Doubleday and Company, 1974), pp. 105-109. Cf. also Romans 8:29.

³²Author's translation: *tou huio tes agapes autou.*

GOD THE FATHER

[33]Matthew 3:17 and parallels. Cf. also John 17:23, among many
Johannine texts.

[34]For example, 1 Corinthians 4:14, 15; Philemon 10; and 2 Timothy
2:1.

[35]Hamerton-Kelly, God the Father, p. 99.

[36]Matthew 5:48. Cf. also such texts as Matthew 5:16 and the series of
"father-sayings" in Matthew 18.

[37]E. Käsemann, "An Apologia for Primitive Christian Eschatology,"
Essays on New Testament Themes (London: SCM Press, Ltd., 1964),
pp. 179, 180.

[38]Cf. G. E. Ladd, A Theology of the New Testament (Grand Rapids:
Eerdmans, 1974), p. 604, where he suggests that Peter uses "becoming
partakers of the divine nature" to mean what Paul means by union
with Christ.

[39]Hamerton-Kelly, God the Father, p. 103.

[40]R. Frost, "Education by Poetry," Robert Frost: Poetry and Prose,
ed. by E. C. Lathem and L. Thompson (New York: Holt, Rinehart and
Winston, Inc., 1972), pp. 334, 335.

Suggestions for Further Reading

Barth, Karl. *Dogmatics in Outline*. New York: Harper and Row, Publishers.

Hamerton-Kelly, Robert. *God the Father: Theology and Patriarchy in the Teaching of Jesus*. ("Overtures to Biblical Theology") Philadelphia: Fortress Press, 1979.

Jeremias, Joachim. *New Testament Theology: the Proclamation of Jesus:* New York: Scribner's, 1971.

Kümmel, Werner Georg. *The Theology of the New Testament*. trans. by J. E. Steely. Nashville: Abingdon Press, 1973.

Ladd, George Eldon. *A Theology of the New Testament*. Grand Rapids: Eerdmans, 1974.

Moltmann, Jürgen. "The Crucified God and the Apathetic Man" in *The Experiment Hope*. Trans. and with a foreword by M. D. Meeks. Philadelphia: Fortress Press, 1975.

Trible, Phyllis. *God and the Rhetoric of Sexuality* ("Overtures to Biblical Theology"). Philadelphia: Fortress Press, 1978.

Wainwright, Arthur W. *The Trinity in the New Testament*. London: S.P.C.K., 1975.

8

THE SON: JESUS ACCORDING TO THE NEW TESTAMENT

By Burton B. Thurston

The Importance of Christology

The personal companions of Jesus were at times astounded, confused, and even bewildered by His teaching and acts. What they wrote about Him and the use of their testimony by others reflect these attitudes. The passage in Mark 4:41 is a striking illustration of their internal reaction to Jesus on different occasions. "They became very much afraid and said to one another, 'Who then is this . . . ?' " Their close association with Him and the force of His teaching and acts only served to heighten the tension between their attraction to Him and the hesitancy they felt toward Him because they did not understand Him.

As John has indicated (John 20:30, 31), Jesus did many things that were never recorded. Shortly after the apostolic period, the imaginations of some people went wild with suggestions to fill in the biographical gaps in the New Testament records. From a scholarly standpoint, we might wish that many more things were recorded than are contained in the rather abbreviated writings the apostolic community thought adequate for the propagation of the faith. But Robert Richardson reminds us, in his *Memoirs of Alexander Campbell,* that the silences of the Scriptures should be respected as strongly as the clear statements.[1] We must rely upon these recorded events.

Before we can develop the meaning of the titles that were used to express the faith of the early disciples, it is important to emphasize that for us, as for them, all of the experiences they had with Him must be taken into account in coming to an understanding of our relationship to Him. Yet by using the model of the account in Mark 4, which ended with such a bewilderment, we can delineate some guidelines that will control other exegetical and historical definitions.

In Mark 4, we have an experience on the sea immediately following a long period of teaching in which crowds had pressed in upon Jesus. He was exhausted with the strain and tension of the day. The crowds had gathered about Him, and He had poured himself into teaching them as well as giving private teaching to His disciples following His public activities.

The boat had gone away from the land in the quiet and calm of the evening, and then there came almost immediately a furious storm, setting the whole sea in turmoil. The wind forced water in great quantities into the boat. Although sudden storms were characteristic of the Sea of Galilee, Mark indicates that this furious tempest was more than the usual storm. In the midst of it all, Jesus was in the vessel fast asleep. But even the fishermen, who had been accustomed to the fury of the sea on other occasions, were disturbed by it and finally, at their wits end, came and awakened Him with the query, "Teacher, do You not care that we are perishing?" When He awakened, the attitude of the disciples disturbed Him more than the threat of the storm. He rebuked the sea very sternly, saying, "Be still!" (literally, muzzled). Then He turned to the disciples and said, "Why are you so timid? How is it that you have no faith?"

We can see several things going on in this pericope. The situation in the original event has been preserved not only for its own intrinsic value in portraying the power of Jesus as a worker of miracles, but it is also being used at the time that Mark wrote his Gospel to deal with some very real problems in the life of that infant Christian community. We could only guess at the great number of times that new Christians as well as those seasoned in the faith would ask the question "Who is this person?" Long after the problem of drowning was forgotten, the word apollymi was carried over into the vocabulary of the church as "perishing" or "lostness." In the Shepherd of Hermas and Clement, it was "future damnation."

Thus, two questions are tied together as a means of relating the person of Jesus to deliverance from eternal spiritual loss. The first has to do with His nature, "Who then is this?" The early disciples must have thought that they knew who Jesus was; yet just at the moment they felt secure, something would happen to shake their well-organized picture and present a new feeling of uncertainty. As they looked upon Him asleep, they must have wondered about Him. He needed sleep, and He was able to sleep. That was possibly a sign of perfect physical and mental health. But the fact remains—he needed sleep. This was a factor the later generations began to forget, namely, that there was in Jesus a true and perfect humanity as well as the divine toward which they moved so readily in their tendency to become monophysite (one-nature) in their understanding of Him.

This was not the only event preserved in Scripture that presented the dual hypostatic union in the person of Jesus. It was present at the baptism, where He comes to respond to the call of John for a baptism of repentance and hears the voice from Heaven saying that He is the Son of God. He stands weeping at the grave of Lazarus and then raises him from the dead. The final heart of the gospel proclamation has Jesus crucified as a common criminal and then raised from the dead in vindication.

The second question is the opening of the door to the whole purpose of the mission of Jesus, "Do You not care . . . ?" If God did not care what happened to us, Jesus would never have come in the first place. Where the disciples originally asked this question in relation to a specific event, the question itself expresses a universal concern. At some point in life, every thoughtful person who has been overcome with suffering and anguish or confronted with the destructive force of the tide of evil may cry out to God, "Do You not care?" The crucifixion of Jesus is the ultimate answer to that question. Hence, our understanding of the person of Jesus is dependent not only upon the record of the experiences of Jesus by His first disciples, but also upon the factors in the life of the early church that led to the preservation of the records of those experiences. While attempting to avoid the pitfalls of historical reductionism, we will follow this model in presenting the New Testament portraits of Jesus.

Living several centuries and several councils following the writing of the New Testament, we may feel a little too secure in our belief that we know all there is to know about Jesus. We may have used the Nicean formulas so many times in our discussions about Jesus and become so familiar with that vocabulary that we assume that no problem still remains.

It is impossible to explain the incarnation or any other miracle to someone whose world view excludes a God who acts or a God who in any way is involved in the human dilemma. Such a person can by the utilization of a subjective world view eliminate any item from Scripture, tradition, or faith upon which a believing person might depend heavily. Our purpose here is to understand, first of all, the world view of the writers of the New Testament. The overall impression one gets from reading the Gospels is that there is an almost dogmatic faith that makes up the infrastructure of those records. At the same time, the periods of question in the direct encounter with Jesus are also preserved. They appear to be saying to us, "Look what we went through before we arrived at the conclusions that make up the central proclamation of the event of Jesus."

The last of the Gospel statements in the New Testament records show where all of these underlying factors finally lead. The Gospel of John, as an apologetic for Jesus as a universal figure, opens with the conclusion! Jesus is the Word of God. This is a "confessional" title and is understood under the rubric of the faith expressions of the early Christians.[2]

From the standpoint of faith, the Christian community has always had a problem when Christology—or the study of the person of Jesus Christ—was made a subdivision under theological studies. Unfortunately, there has often been a lack of awareness of the results of this approach. Essentially, Jesus is the center of the meaning of all theology and cannot be isolated from any other aspect of Christian teaching. The writers of the New Testament clearly found that Christ was the center of a theology of history: their understanding of the world (God was in Christ reconciling the world to himself), the Church (the body of Christ), world religions (for us there is one Lord), and the pattern of life (Christ liveth in me); so that all aspects of theological concern receive their focus in the person of Jesus. A failure to understand Him may put everything else into a distorted or erroneous position.

The method followed in this chapter is to treat "the Son," as designated in the trilogy of Father, Son, and Holy Spirit, as a historical person, as the one who bridges the Jewish-Christian divergences, and as the object of the Christian faith. It will not be possible to draw hard and unmoveable lines between these three concepts, but each should have its own peculiar focus and support the final conclusions. In writing from the standpoint of faith, we assume the responsibility to move from the historical and dispensational views of Jesus to a concentration upon Him as the object of personal faith in a way commensurate with the faith of early Christians and the writers of the New Testament. We should be grateful that the writers of the New Testament were friends of Jesus. Their descriptions are preferable to what might have been written by those who clamored for His execution. An example of that style of writing can be found today in Marxist attacks on Jesus and His followers.

From the perspective of salvation-history, Jesus was "the Coming One" or "the Expected One." John sent word from prison, "Are you the Expected One, or shall we look for someone else?" (Matthew 11:3). This obviously is not a title but the description of one who would fulfill some expectation.[3] The answer Jesus sent back to John was that "the blind receive sight and the lame walk, the lepers are cleansed and the deaf hear, and the dead are raised up, and the poor have the gospel preached to them" (Matthew 11:5, 6). We assume that this evidence satisfied John that Jesus was "the Coming One." The Jews lived in expectation of a Coming One who may have been their God rather than a messianic figure.[4] It was not only the Jews who looked for a deliverer who would bring in a new age; the Fourth Ecologue of Virgil spoke of one who was coming and would usher in a golden age. Whether this prediction was to confirm the people in their appreciation of Augustus or someone else, it was understood by the early Christian fathers to be a prophecy concerning Jesus.

It is possible on an ex-post-facto basis to identify many of the references in the Old Testament to the coming of Jesus. While this is not to be discouraged, it is better to stress the passages in the New Testament that identify Him with the fulfillment of Scripture. A theological interpretation of Old Testament passages would open the door to a wider assortment of references of this nature; and using "salvation-history" as a point of departure, one could feel comfortable with this method. In the limitations we have placed upon this essay, however, New Testament references and titles will be used exclusively. This should not be construed to mean that a Christian interpretation of the Old Testament is without value in seeking to understand the person of Jesus. One of the most fruitful areas of study for a deeper appreciation of Jesus, considering Him as the Old Testament's "suffering servant," takes this very approach (cf. Acts 3:13; 4:27-30; Philippians 2:7). In Acts, the use of *pais* may be a double entendre with child/servant possibilities in translation. But the "servant" motif never developed into a full-blown Christological concept in the New Testament or early Christian literature.

Arising out of the experiences the disciples had with Jesus, there are five prominent titles that must be explored in connection with any study of His person. One of them, the Son of Man, was used by Jesus rather regularly in relation to himself. In the New Testament and the early church, the titles Word (*logos*) of God, Son of Man, Son of God, Lord, and Christ stand out from the other titles by which He was designated. Each title is drawn from a specific background and represents one facet of the early Christian convictions about Jesus or portrays the faith that they shared in regard to His person. By limiting the study to five titles, there is no intention of minimizing the importance of any other designation.

The Word (Logos)

The use of *Logos* in the Johannine writings is unique in the New Testament (John 1:1, 14; 1 John 1:1; Revelation 19:13). The ideas implied in the doctrine of the *Logos* serve several purposes.

By the end of the first century, the Synoptic Gospels were being used by the churches throughout the Roman Empire. Mark gave no information about the birth of Jesus, but Matthew and Luke dealt directly with the problem. There are no parallel accounts in Matthew and Luke in their infancy narratives, but they both clearly establish the fact of His being virgin born.

Where Mark left the door open for the later doctrine of adoptionism, Matthew and Luke still did not resolve the problem of the nature of the person born. This is the special concern of the prologue of John's gospel.[5] Generally speaking, the use of *logos* by philosophers sheds little light on the use of the term in the prologue of John's gospel. It is much easier to see the relationship between later Jewish wisdom literature, where the wisdom of God was present at creation (Wisdom 9:9), and through His word (*davar*) all things were made, and wisdom formed man (Wisdom 9:1, 2). The Stoics saw in *logos* the seminal reason that gave life to all things, but it was Philo who was able to bridge the difference between Judaism and the Hellenistic developments and thus open the door for the acceptance of Christianity in the Hellenistic world on the intellectual level.[6]

Even where there are points of contact such as the above, what the prologue of John affirms is really something else. It is not that all wisdom is summed up in the law (Sirach 24:23), nor some intermediary being (Philo, *Who Is The Heir?* 205). What John here affirms is that the Creator of the world is the God of Christian faith. The Son is certainly more than *logos* in John. He is not only Creator but Revealer, Redeemer, and the One who returns an alienated world to a reconciled state with God. In the Semitic mind, the prophetic word brings events to pass by the power of the word. Jesus, as the Word, reveals God and restores men as children of God (John 1:12). He is the true Word of God because what he does is the revelation of God. On this basis, the integrity of the message of the Gospel of John fits in directly with the prologue. Even if we were to recognize that it was originally a hymn to Wisdom,[7] which is still an open question, the signs, acts, and passion, which follow the prologue, are those things that show Jesus as the Word. We will present this relationship between the prologue and the Gospel with one illustration. The Gospel prologue introduces to its readers the uniqueness of Jesus as the Word. His vocation is built upon His role as that Word. It is a clear attempt to give an explanation to the great mystery of God appearing in the person of Jesus.

The next account is almost as strange as the prologue is mysterious. No other Gospel records the account of the marriage feast and the reference to changing gallons of water into the best wine of the celebration. This scene from Jesus has been a source of wonderment, questioning, and even embarrassment. Did John intend to record a historical event that on a rather commonplace occasion saw one hundred twenty gallons of water become choice wine in a moment? There was no problem about the miracle with the writer, who records also the giving of sight to the blind and raising Lazarus from the dead. Appearing as it does at the very outset of the Gospel, is it not rather intended to portray something more significant than the account of a wedding at an unknown village called Cana?

The true meaning of this account is found in the prologue, where the Word reconciles men to God and makes them His children. The wedding celebration is an ideal metaphor used to convey the total impact of this Gospel that is now about to be written. The marriage feast is a religious symbol of ancient vintage. We do not question that there was a wedding feast or that a miracle was performed. These items are both outside of the main question, which has to do with the place it appears in the Gospel and the fact it is given such a prominent place in John while absent from the Synoptics. John is here characterizing the impact of the unique Word of God, whom he has just introduced. The changing of water into wine could have been presented as an act of God without reference to anything that went before or came afterward. However, he is talking about the significance of Jesus as the incarnate Word, who is inseparably involved in the totality of human existence. The whole scene becomes a metaphor of transformation. ("Whatever He says to you, do it.") It serves as a framework for the narrative, which leads ultimately to the "glory" of Jesus. Just as there is a link with Philo in the prologue, there is also a link with the Jewish allegorist in this scene where water becomes wine. "Let Melchizedek instead of water offer wine . . . seized by a divine intoxication more sober than sobriety itself."[8]

This transformation, called the "wine of God," takes place through the Word, who by the revelation of His acts brings men into relationship with the Father (John 17:3). The coming of the Word has its fulfillment in the realization of the presence of God in man more than in some ineffable experience. The Logos apprehended in Jesus finally reveals the nature of God, giving meaning to life and granting to man through sonship the realization of that meaning.

The designation of Jesus as the Word of God is in keeping with the purpose of the Gospel of John, which presents Jesus as a universal Savior. In order to accomplish this goal, the Gospel writer does not hesitate to use Hellenistic thought forms that are then defined more precisely by the acts that reveal the nature of God and His purpose.

Son of Man

As in the case of *logos*, much scholarly attention has been devoted to the "Son of Man" title—with conclusions ranging from the suggestion that Jesus never used it at all to the view that all the authentic categories of the meaning of this expression are found to have been used during the ministry of Jesus.[9] Our purpose here is to show as clearly as possible what the title meant to the writers of the New Testament and to the early Christians.

The term is used eighty-one times in the Gospels and is also found in the New Testament outside of the Gospels (Acts 7:56; Revelation 1:13; 14:14; Hebrews 2:6). Those who are familiar with Semitic idiom are aware that the expressions "son of . . ." prefixed to a noun simply means the noun that follows the expression. Thus, *Ben adam* means "man" and not "son of man." *Ibn Arab* means "Arab," not "son of an Arab." In parallelism, it appears in Psalm 8, where the first phrase in verse 4 has "man" and its parallel has "son of man." This, however, is only one use of the expression; it can also refer to "I," that is, to the speaker himself. The third use of the term has to do with the presence of the definite article in the Greek *ho huios tou anthropou,* which would mean not just "son of man," but "the son of man."

In the Gospels, this expression occurs in passages in which Jesus is represented as speaking of himself. In most occurrences, then, it designates Jesus. (In Mark 3:28, it is in the plural and means man in general.) It would be in keeping with the nature and purpose of the Gospels to utilize the apocalyptic figure in Daniel 7:13, 14, where dominion, glory, and a kingdom were given to Him by God. By adopting the title "Son of Man" for himself, Jesus was using a description the people of His time would understand. It portrayed the mystery of His own personality as the representative man who could forgive sins and even countermand the authority of Sabbath regulations. "The Son of Man is Lord even of the Sabbath" (Mark 2:28). It gave Him a specific identity when He asked His disciples what people were saying about Him (Matthew 16:13).

If the reference in Daniel 7:13, 14 is construed to mean that He is the representative man standing for the saints, it can be noted that there is no question about the individual nature of "the Son of Man" in the forty-sixth chapter of Ethiopic Enoch. Here the face of the Heavenly man is compared with the face of an angel. The Enoch literature is entirely taken up with the individual nature of "the Son of man." His relationship to the people of God is clearly brought out in the Enoch literature. In the end time, He will share with the people of God in a great banquet (62:13ff). The whole future of mankind rests upon the son of Man (48:8).

The pattern of the ministry of Jesus is different from the "Son of Man" in Enoch. In the Gospels, He is not a ruler but a servant. "The Son of Man did not come to be served but to serve" (Mark 10:45). In the Gospels, the glorification of Jesus is preceded by His suffering and death (John 6:62). In addition, He will return in judgment (John 5:27-29). The similarity between the "Son of Man" sayings in the Gospels and Daniel 7 and Ethiopic Enoch is clear enough to conclude that the latter form the background for the use of the title; however, the term is given new meaning in the Gospels.

In the New Testament, Jesus is "the Man" standing apart from all other men as the special representative for the saints of God. He is the judge of the last days. His work was accomplished not with kingly power, but with suffering and divine compassion. As the author of the new creation, He has not brought to us an escape from the world of men but has revealed to us our responsibilities to others (Matthew 25:31-46). The fact that Jesus had to suffer is the direct consequence of mankind's rebellion against true humanity. Having found man on a sub-human level, it was divine love that took upon itself the consequence of our sin and failure. The apocalyptic "Son of Man," who was portrayed as a king, became on account of our rebellion a crucified redeemer—with a cross instead of a throne.

Son of God

The title "Son of God" was a common designation in the East for the king. It was present in Egyptian kingship, where Horus was the son of Osiris. Alexander the Great believed in his double paternity, and after he was proclaimed the son of Amon Re at Siwah, he was referred to as the son of Zeus by his followers. When "Son of God" is applied to Jesus, however, it is in a very different way.

Klausner says directly that Jesus did not regard himself as the Son of God in the later trinitarian sense.[10] Klausner bases this assertion not on the Gospel records, but on the contention that no Jew during this period of history could have believed that about a human being. The writers of the New Testament were not so restricted in their belief. Matthew quotes a saying of Jesus, "All things have been handed over to me by my Father; and no one knows the Son, except the Father; nor does ayone know the Father, except the Son" (Matthew 11:27). While Jesus does not call himself the Son of God in this passage, the words and the thought are clearly present. If Jesus is not the Son to which He referred, then He would have made some move to establish relationship with the Son mentioned in the passage. His sonship was central to His message.

In each of the four Gospels, the claim that Jesus is God's Son is considered to be the highest designation possible for the object of their faith and devotion. In Mark, the voice from Heaven at the time of baptism declares the sonship of Jesus (Mark 1:11). The reference to the Son in the parable of the wicked husbandmen implies the divine sonship of Jesus (Mark 12:6). At the crucifixion, the statement of the centurion is taken to be a reference to the fact that he had recognized Jesus as "Son of God" (15:39). The absence of the article in the Greek text may imply something quite different from the English. The anarthrous noun in Greek does not always imply an indefinite article (cf. RSV or NIV footnote), but rather it may speak of the nature of a thing. What the centurion is probably saying by this usage is that Jesus is a divine person. Just what that might mean to a Roman soldier is not clear, but Mark understands it as a declaration of what he and the early Christians affirmed about Jesus.

The Gospel of Luke is just as clear in its assertion that Jesus is the Son of God and affirms in the birth narrative that the child will be called the Son of God (Luke 1:35).

In Matthew, a further development of the idea of the sonship of Jesus is found in the confession of Peter (Matthew 16:16). The title is introduced twice in the passion narrative (Matthew 27:40, 43), and is then included in the charge that Jesus made to the disciples when He sent them out to make disciples and baptize in the name of the Father, Son, and Holy Spirit (Matthew 28:19).

In the Gospel of John, the title "Son of God" is used frequently, and the author takes the trouble to give a clearer definition of what is meant by it. Several people in the Gospel of John call Jesus the Son of God. Since John has indicated that all who believe on Jesus may become "children of God" (John 1:12), he makes the distinction between these children of God and Jesus by use of the word monogenes, which is translated variously as "only begotten," "only" and other such synonyms. It has the force of our word "unique" or "one of a kind." While we all may become the children of God, Jesus is the unique Son of God. In this position, He has life and authority (John 5:21, 22), He is in the bosom of the Father (John 1:18), and anyone who sees Him sees the Father (John 14:9). In this way, John can keep the integrity of the uniqueness of Jesus and still open the door for the concept of people's becoming the children of God.

The sonship of Jesus presented problems to the Semitic world, but the Christology of the "good man" in the Jewish-Christian sects was rejected by the church. The fact that the Greco-Roman world was familiar with this vocabulary presented different kinds of problems for the evangelists. The Greek gods had sons; they had dying and rising gods as did the Mesopotamians in an earlier period. The mystery religions had the new birth and salvation, while the Stoics had a surrender to the will of God. Hence, these terms as well as "son of God" had to be filled with a new and dynamic content to avoid a takeover by the older religious structures. The history of the councils and the Christological controversies is adequate proof of the great struggle to maintain the integrity of this new faith. The task of clarification has never been finished because there can never be a satisfactory answer to the question of how there is one God if Christ is divine and in the fullest sense God. Unfortunately we experience the limits of human language when trying to explain things that are not human. Karl Barth may not be any clearer, but he says, "The New Testament statement about the divinity of Christ means something only as witnessing to God's revelation."[11] He explains this to mean that God is found in Jesus. In the view of P. T. Forsyth, "The Godhead of Christ can only be proved religiously."[12]

I quote these two significant theologians because they, too, have been forced to recognize the inadequacy of human language to explain or clarify this understanding of Jesus. Because of the power of faith, however, it can never be set aside or ruled out.

In spite of the limitations of language, we are certain from the New Testament writers that the Sonship of Jesus was absolute in a sense in which ours is not. We are sons only through the possibility being made open to us through the unique Sonship of Jesus. Whether we understand all that it means, it was certainly the fact of the early Christians as witnessed in their confession that Jesus was the Son of God.

Christ

There is both a very technical, limited definition of the title "Christ" as well as a broad, more general definition. In the technical sense, Christ means, first, the ointment or oil that is placed on a person to set him apart and, second, the person thus anointed. The broad definition includes all of the ideas that have to do with the Jews' "coming" Messiah (the Hebrew form of *Christ*). In this latter definition, all that has been said above falls under the title "Christ." We are concerned here with the development from the proposition that "Jesus is the Christ" to the title that came to be used of Him—Jesus Christ.

When the evangelists were trying to convince the people that Jesus was the Christ, they also had to explain the reason for His suffering and death, which were a "stumbling block" to the Jews. There was a tradition in the time of Jesus that a prophet would be persecuted and killed. If this tradition is related to Isaiah 53, then the prophet suffers for the sins of others. The Son of Man passage in Mark 10:45 closes with the idea that He will die for the cleansing, healing, and forgiving of others. It would only be possible to apply the title of Messiah or Christ to Jesus if this view of the Messiah was established in place of the deliverer-King concept, which was popular with the people and also with the disciples. Even after the resurrection, they looked for the restoration of the kingdom to Israel (Acts 1:6).

Once the concept of Christ as one who would give himself a ransom for many was established, then many ideas from the Old Testament, such as Psalm 22, Isaiah 53, and even the Passover sacrifice could be introduced to develop this picture of the Christ. This is what happened in the New Testament descriptions of the Christ. The opposition of the religious leaders and their attacks on Him become a part of the mosaic (cf. Luke 1:67-75) Jesus is no longer a prophet, mighty in word and deed, but He is the anointed Messiah with a divine destiny to deliver His people. He has come to save His people (Luke 2:11). Since suffering was a problem in the concept of Messiah, it became the ultimate revelation of the mercy and character of God. It was the Messiah who would suffer for the guilty even though He was guiltless, and He would bring light to the Gentiles and glory to Israel (Luke 2:29-32).

Lord

The use of this title for Jesus in the Roman empire had certain political overtones. Legally, only the emperor was lord in the full sense of the word. But to the Christians, Jesus was Lord, and this confession placed them on a collision course with the Roman Empire. They did not refer to Jesus as "the Lord" simply as a polite term such as "sir" or "mister," but with the full understanding of the meaning of one who has ultimate and absolute authority. For centuries, God's name, expressed in the tetragram *JHVH* had been pronounced *Adonai*, "Lord," and this sacred name of God was now applied to Jesus. Not only the Gospels, but the letters of Paul are filled with this emphasis upon the Lordship of Jesus. There is no clearer statement about the meaning of this Lordship than that given in Philippians 2:9-11, where He is exalted above everything and all shall bow before Him and confess that He is Lord. If one is to be saved, he will call upon the name of the Lord (Romans 10:13). Even the day of the Lord becomes the day of Christ (1 Corinthians 1:8).

In what sense then did the early Christians and the New Testament writers think of Christ as Lord? In addition to the respect and reverence they would give to God, they were ready to recognize the power He had demonstrated in both the material and spiritual worlds. As a result of this faith and trust, they were willing to place their lives at His disposal. The deeper meaning of His Lordship was shown in the way they gave their lives as martyrs for their new-found faith. They were devoted to Him as a person, and nothing could break their relationship with the Lord of the universe who was also their Lord. The presence of the Aramaic *Maranatha* in 1 Corinthians 16:22 indicates that the title of Lord appeared in the spoken language and became a fixed expression, at least in this form, before the New Testament was written in Greek.

NOTES

[1]Robert Richardson, *Memoirs of Alexander Campbell*, Vol. 1 (Philadelphia, 1868), p. 237.

[2]It is difficult for me to see how Professor C.F.D. Moule in his latest book, *The Origin of Christology*, which rejects the evolutionary theory of Christology in favor of a developmental view, can eliminate the Johannine "Word of God" title completely from his treatment of the subject. But his second chapter on the corporate Christ is a very useful contribution to the study of Christology.

[3]It is natural to find this treatment in Matthew's Gospel, since one of the concerns in Antioch (where it was written) was the relation between the Jewish and Hellenistic Christians. There are several expressions in Matthew that seek to clarify the relationship between the Christian faith and its Jewish matrix.

[4]We cannot overlook the fact that messianism in the time of Jesus was greatly colored in popular belief derived from the Hasmonean rule, which had ended just about thirty years before Jesus was born. The conflict between the Hasmoneans and the Pharisees could not erase from the minds of the people a firm conviction that a political deliverer would appear.

[5]The amount of work done on *Logos* and the prologue of John's Gospel by the scholarly world is a library in its own right. The scholarly debates are fruitful and rewarding, but even a brief summary would be large volume. A good summary of *Logos* can be found in chapter 9 of Cullmann's *Christology of the New Testament* (Philadelphia: Westminster, 1980).

[6]Cf. Foakes Jackson and Lake, *The Beginnings of Christianity*, Vol. 1, p. 155.

[7]For example, see A. T. Robertson, *Word Pictures in the New Testament*, Vol. 5 (Nashville: Broadman, 1932), pp. 3, 4.

[8]Philo, *Allegorical* Interpretation, III. 82.

[9]A summary of the various points of view on "Son of Man" can be read in I. H. Marshall's article "The Synoptic Son of Man Sayings in Recent Discussion," *New Testament Studies*, Vol. 12, pp. 327-351. A briefer summary will be found in Moule, *The Origin of Christology* (New York: Cambridge University Press, 1977), pp. 11-22.

[10]J. Klausner, *Jesus of Nazareth* (New York: Menorah, 1978), p. 377 (A Jewish biography).

[11]Karl Barth, *Church Dogmatics*, Vol. 1, Part 1 (Greenwood, SC: Attic Press, 1977), p. 460.

[12]P. T. Forsyth, *The Person and Place of Jesus Christ*, p. 243.

CHAPTER

9

THE HOLY SPIRIT

By Knofel Staton

There are many differences between a Christian and a non-Christian, but what is the *essential* difference? What does a Christian have that a non-Christian does not have? "Essential" refers to that without which something does not exist; it is necessary for life—vital. My arm is important to me, but not vital. Without it, I can continue to exist. However, my heart is essential as well as important. Without it (or some workable substitute), I cease to exist in my earthly, bodily form.

What is the *essential* difference between a Christian and a non-Christian? Attending the church assemblies? No, non-Christians may attend regularly. A total refraining from smoking, drinking, or immoral practices? No, non-Christians may refrain from these habits. The ingredient that is absolutely essential to the life of a Christian is the indwelling of the Holy Spirit. Without the Holy Spirit, a Christian ceases to exist: "But if anyone does not have the Spirit of Christ, he does not belong to Him" (Romans 8:9).

The Identity of the Holy Spirit

It is popular to identify the Holy Spirit as a "person." The approach to substantiate that theory goes like this: "A person prays, can be jealous, and can be grieved—as can the Holy Spirit (Romans 8:26; James 4:5; Ephesians 4:30); thus the Holy Spirit is a person."

This approach tends to humanize the Holy Spirit in the minds of many. The truth is that we humans pray, can be jealous, and can be grieved because we were created in the image of God. It is better to try to understand man's identity and potential from the characteristics of the Holy Spirit than to try to understand the Holy Spirit's identity and potential from the characteristics of man.

Extended Earthly Presence of God
The Holy Spirit is a person in one sense; but in another sense, He is much more than a person. A person (as we normally use the word) is finite; the Holy Spirit is infinite. A person is mortal; the Holy Spirit is immortal. A person was created; the Holy Spirit participated in the creative act. The Holy Spirit is not what a person is, but rather what God is. The Holy Spirit is the extended earthly presence of deity.

God is both transcendent (there) and immanent (here). He is above and beyond the limitations of the time and space dimensions of the earth. He created this existence and cannot be trapped by it. He is Lord of it all. He masters the universe; He is not mastered by it. But God is not just "out there" somewhere as Lord. He is also "here" as a Servant. He is the eternal Providential One as well as the Ever-present One.

The Holy Spirit is God himself acting in the created realm of time and space. Any time God manifests himself, He does it through the Holy Spirit—His extended self. In the creation, "the Spirit of God was moving over the surface of the waters" (Genesis 1:2). When God extended himself by creating a being in His own image, He did so by breathing into man the breath of life (Genesis 2:7). What was that breath of life that resulted in man's being in the likeness of God? God breathed into man His own life—His Spirit (Note: *neshamah* is used in Genesis 2:7 instead of *ruach*, but *neshamah* also refers to God's Spirit elsewhere—Job 27:3; 33:4; 34:14; 37:10; Isaiah 30:33).

It is true that every living creature has breath or spirit of life, but the distinction is that man has God's kind of breath of life, while each animal has its own kind.

When God wrote the commandments on the tablets of stone, He did so through His Spirit (compare Exodus 31:18 with Luke 11:20 and Matthew 12:28). Through His Spirit, God spoke through the prophets (2 Peter 1:20, 21). Through His Spirit, He spoke through angels (see Acts 8:26, 29, where "angel" and "spirit" are used interchangeably). Through His Spirit, He came in Jesus (Matthew 1:20); so much so that the Spirit enfleshed in Jesus was declared to be "God with us."

The psalmist understood the Holy Spirit to be the extended earthly presence of God. The Hebrew parallelism in Psalm 139:7 expresses this idea: "Where can I go from Thy Spirit? Or where can I flee from Thy presence?" Notice how Spirit and presence parallel. (Note: a Hebrew parallelism is an often-used literary device that expresses a thought and then expresses the same thought using different words.)

In Acts 5:3, 4, Peter used Spirit and God interchangeably. When the Holy Spirit lives in us, God's presence is within us (1 Corinthians 6:19; Ephesians 2:21, 22). Paul could say, "Christ lives in me" (Galatians 2:20) because the Holy Spirit resides within the Christian (Galatians 3:2). Paul also spoke about God's being at work in us (Philippians 2:13) and about Christians' having "fellowship of the Spirit" (Philippians 2:1).

Jesus also identified the Holy Spirit as the extended presence of God. Notice the interchanging of terms in John 14:

"He will give you another Helper . . . that is the Spirit of truth"—vv. 16, 17.

"I will come to you"—v. 18.

"In that day . . . I in you"—v. 20.

"If anyone loves Me, he will keep My word; and My Father will love him, and We will come to him, and make Our abode with him"—v. 23.

The word "another" in verse 16 (allos) means another of the same kind, meaning a helper of the same kind as Jesus. The word helper further amplifies the thought. The Greek word (parkaletos) is used in the New Testament to refer to only two realities—the Holy Spirit on earth (John 14:16, 26; 15:26; 16:7) and Jesus in Heaven (1 John 2:1). It is clear that the Jesus in Heaven is also on earth via the Spirit.

Some of the designations for Jesus and God are also designations for the Spirit. Jesus was called the Word, and His words were called spirit and life (John 6:63). Life is in God and Jesus (John 5:26; 11:25; 14:6), and the Spirit is called the Spirit of life (Romans 8:2).

A Part of the Trinity
The idea of identifying the Holy Spirit as the extended earthly presence of God does not eliminate the distinction between the Father, the Son, and the Holy Spirit. Rather than to try to make a clear-cut distinction between the three (a task that has plagued theology throughout history and has caused schism within Christianity), it would be better to acknowledge that Biblically all three individually and collectively give us the full expression of God. Where the Father is, there is God in His fullness. Where the Spirit is, there is God (John 4:24). Where Jesus is, there is God (John 1:1, 14; Colossians 1:15, 19; Hebrews 1:3; John 10:30). The three are so united in cooperation and coordination that the character and conduct of one are the character and conduct of all, which is fellowship perfected to the final degree. That is the reason we can read about the Spirit of Christ and the Spirit of God in the same context (Romans 8:9).
The unity between the three is seen in the fact that not one of them acted or spoke independently from the others. The Father created, but not apart from the Spirit or the Son (Colossians 1:16). Jesus sent the Spirit, but not independently from the Father (Acts 2:33; John 14:16). Jesus was submitted to the Father (John 5:30; 8:28), and so is the Holy Spirit (John 16:13, 14).

The Work of the Holy Spirit

A Two-dimensional Purpose
The work of the Holy Spirit is basically to undo what man did in Genesis 3, to restore what man shattered—the unity with God and with fellowman. Such unity could be called both vertical (with God) and horizontal (with man). Included in this work is giving man the character to maintain this vertical and horizontal unity. All the satellite activities of the Holy Spirit feed into this main artery of restoring and maintaining unity, which is accomplished by pointing man to Christ (John 16:14; Galatians 3:28).
The activity of the Holy Spirit in the Old Testament was for the purpose of unity and had the Christ as the target. The Holy Spirit came upon man to equip him for particular historical functions in preparation for the coming Redeemer and Restorer, Jesus. The prophets spoke about the New Age of Restoration that was to come—God's last days.

222

The incarnation of the Word in Jesus was the work of the Holy Spirit (Matthew 1:18), in order to communicate to man a clear understanding of God (John 1:18) and to equip Jesus to become the ransom (Matthew 20:28) that would restore men to God and to each other (Ephesians 2:11-22). God's written Word was also supplied for this purpose (2 Timothy 3:16, 17). It is through the action of the Holy Spirit in the spoken and written Word, in the person of Jesus, and in the hearts of men, that men are convicted of sin, righteousness, and judgment (Romans 1:16; Hebrews 4:12; John 16:8) and are "made complete in Christ" (2 Timothy 3:19).

Initiate the New Age

The coming of the Holy Spirit is God's objective demonstration that the last days have begun. The Holy Spirit is God's eschatological gift to man, for the day of victory is that to which all of history is aimed.

The prophets spoke of a new era that would be accompanied by the coming of the Holy Spirit: "Moreover I will give you a new heart and put a new spirit within you . . ." (Ezekiel 36:26). (See also Jeremiah 31:31ff; Ezekiel 11:19; 37:14; Joel 2:28ff; Zechariah 4:6.) That day did not come until after the death, resurrection, and ascension of Jesus: "for the Spirit was not yet given, because Jesus was not yet glorified" (John 7:39).

Some think the Holy Spirit initiated the new age on the day Jesus was raised from the dead. "And when He had said this, He breathed on them, and said to them, 'Receive the Holy Spirit' " (John 20:22). However, the apostles did not see this as the beginning point. If any reception of the Spirit took place in John 20, it must have been an interim manifestation of the Holy Spirit until the fuller promise would be fulfilled. We do not know that anything happened in John 20, more than a visual aid accompanying a command for them to receive. Jesus later instructed them to go to Jerusalem (after His ascension) and wait for the coming of the Holy Spirit (Acts 1:4-11).

Peter understood that the coming of the Spirit on the day of Pentecost was the fulfillment of the promise of the Old Testament prophets: "But this is what was spoken of through the prophet Joel: 'And it shall be in the last days . . .' " (Acts 2:16, 17). Later, Peter referred to this event as being the "beginning" (11:15). Note how Peter connected Joel's prophecy with Jesus' promise of the Holy Spirit baptism (cf. Acts 1:5 and Acts 11:16).

Regeneration in Man

The last days are here, and the Holy Spirit is here. But how can man appropriate the Holy Spirit? Peter gave the answer in Acts 2:38, "Repent, and let each of you be baptized in the name of Jesus Christ for the forgiveness of your sins; and you shall receive the gift of the Holy Spirit."

The Holy Spirit cannot be separated from baptism, for both spotlight new beginnings. While the Holy Spirit emphasizes the beginning of the new age and the power of the age to come (Hebrews 6:4, 5), baptism is that transition point where we die and are buried to the old life and arise to walk in a newness of life (Romans 6:4). We rise to newness because we are raised with Jesus (Romans 6:4-8; Colossians 2:12, 13).

The newness takes on the character of a regeneration (Titus 3:5). This regeneration (new birth) is the result of the Holy Spirit's bringing renewal (John 3:3-8). This renewal re-creates us in God's image, and we become new persons (Ephesians 4:23, 24). In Christ, we become new creatures, and the old things pass away (2 Corinthians 5:17). The word creature in this verse should really be translated "creation." The point is that the original creation is restored in us: "For we are His workmanship, created in Christ Jesus" (Ephesians 2:10).

Baptism is not a magical rite that automatically sends the Holy Spirit into our bodies. The Holy Spirit does not come to dwell within a person at baptism unless faith and repentance precede the baptism. To take baptism out of the context of faith and repentance is to separate it from the Holy Spirit; but to neglect baptism because there is faith and repentance is to stop short of the Holy Spirit's entrance into the life of the repentant believer. The New Testament is clear that faith, repentance, and baptism are a trinity that should not be pulled apart.

Unity in the Church

God's plan in history has been to unite all things in Christ (Ephesians 1:9, 10; Colossians 1:20). Sin began the alienation process in every area of life on earth (man with God, man with man, man with nature, and nature with nature). God's strategy was to make cosmic unity and balance possible once again, but that unity and peace will not be fully consummated until the second coming (Romans 8:19-25). Yet redemption and salvation have begun that peace process, for man can be reunited with God and his fellowmen.

Sinful man is alienated in two dimensions—vertically and horizontally. Vertically, he is alienated from God; horizontally, he is alienated from his fellowman. "Remember that you were at that time separate from Christ, excluded from the commonwealth of Israel" (Ephesians 2:12). Jesus died and rose so that He might "reconcile them both in one body to God" (Ephesians 2:16). To be reconciled "in one body" is to be united in the horizontal dimension. Through Christ, we all have access in one Spirit to the Father, meaning we are no longer strangers and aliens, but fellow citizens and of God's household (Ephesians 2:18, 19).

If we are united with God, then it follows that we will be united with His people, regardless of cultural or racial differences. To put on Christ is to be united with all others who have also put on Christ, whether they are Jews, Greeks, male, female, rich, or poor (Galatians 3:27, 28). By the Spirit we are baptized into one body (1 Corinthians 12:13). There is only one body because there is only one Spirit of God (Ephesians 4:4). His Spirit is God's *sperma* (seed, 1 John 3:9, 24) that resides within us and allows us to call Him "Abba, Father" (Romans 8:15), and our fellow Christians, brothers and sisters.

Sometimes we use the terms "brother and sister" in a formally religious way, but these terms should also describe how we function with each other. All those who have God's Spirit residing within them are related and are in the same family. God is indeed our Father, for we share His eternal seed.

Jesus emphasized the unity between himself and His people when He said that whatever was done to the least of the brethren was being done to Him (Matthew 25:31-46). The early Christians demonstrated this unity brought about by the action of the Holy Spirit when they held all things in common (Acts 2:44) and continued in the apostles' teaching, fellowship, breaking of bread, and in prayers (Acts 2:42). All of these responses encompass both the vertical and horizontal dimensions of unity. They received truth from God and related it to others; they received fellowship and material blessings from God and shared with others. They remembered Christ's death and declared it to others (breaking of bread); and they spoke to God on others' behalf (prayers).

The first truth Jesus revealed to Paul was the inseparable unit between Christ and His people. Paul was persecuting the church, but Jesus asked, "Why are you persecuting me?" (Acts

9:4). It is no wonder that Paul wrote more about unity than any other Biblical writer. In Ephesians, Paul tightened up the reality of this unity when he spoke about the church's being connected to Christ—the church being the body with Christ as the head (Ephesians 1:22, 23).

The Holy Spirit not only unites us to God and each other, but also equips us with the character to maintain that unity. We Christians have a mandate to maintain the unity (Ephesians 4:3). The Christian who acts or reacts in a way that would destroy the unified body of Christ ultimately will be destroyed (1 Corinthians 3:16, 17; the temple of God referred to in these verses is the corporate church). We do not live just for the head of the body; we also must live for the body (2 Corinthians 12:15). God has given us His Spirit so that we can care for each other the way the Father would care for us if He were here. In this way, He is here—living in us (see the discussion on ministry below, in Chapter 18).

The fruit of the Spirit (Galatians 5:22, 23) is the moral character of God that dwells within us and enables us to maintain the unity. The life-style portrayed in these verses is the only lifestyle that can promote and maintain that unity. After Paul discussed the unity of the Spirit in the first three chapters of Ephesians, he told the readers to live a life worthy of that unity (4:1) by putting on the new self (4:24), which will be demonstrated by new attitudes and actions in relationships with others (4:25—6:9). Not to live with each other as Paul described is to grieve the Holy Spirit (4:30); it gives the devil an opportunity to undo what Christ died to do (4:27). To live with each other in the fruit of the Spirit is to "be imitators of God as beloved children" (5:1).

The Holy Spirit and Freedom

The Holy Spirit frees us to be what we were created to be. Some think freedom means to be liberated from any type of dependence, but that is not true. Biblical freedom is not the right to do what we please, but to please to do what is right. It is to act and react as a person made in God's image. Sin had enslaved and fettered us so that we could not behave as God intended when He created us.

The Holy Spirit also frees us from the law, which could only expose sin. The Spirit joins us to Another, who empowers us to live out the intentions of the law with the power of God

(Romans 7:4; 8:3, 4). The law could not give us the power to live out God's character (Galatians 3:21), the "life" we need to live righteously. The Holy Spirit, however, does indeed give us this *life* (Romans 8:2).

The Old Testament law was given by God and dealt with love in its content. The law outlined the way people were to show love to one another. If a man found a lost ox, he was to return it to his neighbor—an expression of love. If he had no love, he would barbeque the ox in his own backyard for the benefit of his own family. But the people did not have the inner presence of God to enable them to live out the love that God desired to be between men; thus, the law was given for their guidance.

The fruit of the indwelling Holy Spirit is love, and love lived out in our daily lives will fulfill the intent of God's law (Matthew 22:36-40; Romans 13:8-10). Love from the Holy Spirit's presence within us is always other-oriented; thus, the Spirit frees us from living for ourselves and frees us for living for others (Galatians 5:13). The Holy Spirit frees us from the loneliness of our own egos for the fellowship of the community of believers (1 Corinthians 12:18).

The Holy Spirit frees us from being the pawns of Satan; we are now the property of God (1 Corinthians 6:19, 20). In fact, the Spirit is God's identification mark of His ownership of us. That is what Paul meant when he said, "You were sealed in Him with the Holy Spirit of promise" (Ephesians 1:13; the "seal" referred to the king's method of labeling what belonged to him). In the Spirit, we are not "nobodies" looking for a place to land; we are royalty—related to the King!

Because of the Holy Spirit, we are also freed from condemnation (Romans 8:1) and have an eternal inheritance (Romans 8:17). The Spirit is God's pledge of our inheritance (Ephesians 1:14). A pledge is the same as a down payment, or what we would call earnest money. God has given us His Spirit as the first installment of our rich inheritance. A pledge in the first century was also used to verify the promise of marriage—the engagement-ring concept. God has given to us the Spirit as evidence that He intends to go through with the wedding of the bride of Christ (the church) and the Bridegroom (Christ) for all eternity. The Spirit is God's guarantee that the eternity outlined in Revelation 21 will come to be.

The Holy Spirit is also God's primary provision for keeping the bride (the church) a pure and faithful virgin until the wedding ceremony takes place (Ephesians 5:26, 27; 2 Corinthians 11:2). As we walk in the Spirit, we walk with Christ and in Christ (Colossians 2:6; Galatians 5:16-25). However, the Holy Spirit does not operate independently from God's Word and God's people in keeping us faithful and pure (Ephesians 6:17; 1 Peter 2:2; Ephesians 4:16; Hebrews 10:23-25; 2 Corinthians 3).

Spiritual Maturity

We come into the family of God by being "adopted" by God (Romans 8:15). But we are more than adopted by God; we are also born of God (John 3). God gives to us His own life, seed, or nature—the Holy Spirit (1 John 3:9, 24). And it is His Spirit that enables us to mature into the likeness of Christ rather than staying as babes.

His Spirit lives within us yet never ceases to be His. But the Spirit does seek daily to transform our minds and spirits to become like His. He wants our characteristics to be like His; when they become so, we are mature as Christians (2 Corinthians 3:18; Romans 8:29; Luke 6:40; Colossians 1:28, 29; Ephesians 4:13, 15).

But that maturity does not come in a moment. It comes by daily transformation. While in the process of growing up, Christians move in and out of both mature and immature actions and attitudes. One action may be mature while another may be immature. A mature action or attitude is one that squares with the character and conduct of the indwelling Holy Spirit. But when a person acts or thinks immaturely, it does not mean the Spirit has left him. Only if every characteristic of our lives squares with that of the Holy Spirit could we say that we have reached full maturity and the full potential that God has given to us. In any other condition, we are growing, seeking to reach that goal. And that growing process goes on continuously as the Holy Spirit resides within us.

But how can we ever reach that full maturity? Total commitment is called for: commitment to study the Word, commitment to die to self and live for God, commitment to fellowship with God's people, commitment to pray, and commitment to use our abilities in service.

Each Christian is in the body of Christ in the same manner that cells are in our physical bodies. Detached from the body, a cell dies. But involved in the body and its functions, the cell grows healthily and abundantly. The cell feeds other cells and is fed by the surrounding cells. Thus, the whole body grows and develops. The church functions in the same manner (Ephesians 4:8-16; 1 Corinthians 12). Each Christian is joined to the head (Christ), but we are held together in this world by other Christians, who supply our needs. When every part works for the other parts, the body builds itself up in love (Ephesians 4:16; Colossians 2:19). The cells in Christ's body are not functionally alike (Romans 12:4; 1 Corinthians 12:4-7), but they are functionally connected (Romans 12:5; 1 Corinthians 12:14-27). Each cell needs the unselfish service of every other cell.

God has given Christians gifts from the Holy Spirit so they can serve others unselfishly (1 Corinthians 12: ; Romans 12:4-8; 1 Peter 4:10; Ephesians 4:11-16). God's church is interconnected, much like a spider web. If any part of it is weakened, the whole is weakened. The failure of any one Christian anywhere in the world to function unselfishly hinders every other Christian from reaching full maturity. Believers we may not even know may thus be hindered.

What does the New Testament mean by such expressions as walk "in the Spirit," love "in the Spirit," and pray "in the Spirit"? It does not mean that we have some kind of ecstatic, mystical experience. The meaning is very simple. If I am in a gymnasium, whatever I do, I do in the gymnasium. If I sing, I sing in the gymnasium. I can rejoice there; I can pray there; I can walk there. If I am in the Spirit, then whatever I do, I do in the Spirit. Paul explained it this way: "However, you are not in the flesh but in the Spirit, if indeed the Spirit of God dwells in you" (Romans 8:9). If God's Spirit lives within us, then we are "in the Spirit" in whatever we do and say. To say, "Do something in the Spirit," is to say, "Do it as a Christian," or "Do it as you are in Christ" (a phrase that Paul uses 164 times). To be "in the Spirit" is not to be in a different dimension or environment, but it is to be in God and Christ.

Manifestations of the Holy Spirit

Three different manifestations of the Holy Spirit are recorded in the book of Acts. It would be improper to treat the subject of the Holy Spirit with a straight-line method, that is, to teach that every mention of the Holy Spirit is referring to the same function or manifestation as any other mention of Him does. Failure to differentiate between them has created a great amount of confusion.

Perhaps an analogy will help to illustrate the point. There are many different kinds of functions in an airport control tower—such things as ground control, departure ˙control, approach control, and clearance delivery. However, the same controllers work all the different positions at different times. A person could say about any of those functions, "The control tower did such and so," and be correct.

The Holy Spirit is also diverse in function. The Holy Spirit is always doing the functioning, but at times performs differently for different reasons. When speaking about the Spirit, it is important to determine by context and a holistic study which function is being discussed. The chart and comments on the next page will clarify the point.

Much confusion centers around *when* a person receives the Holy Spirit. Acts 2:38 speaks about receiving the Spirit after repentance and baptism. However, after just such a baptism, the Holy Spirit had not "fallen upon any of them" in Samaria; thus, two apostles arrived so "that they might receive the Holy Spirit" (Acts 8:14-16). Many commentators conclude from this that baptism is not a prerequisite for receiving the Holy Spirit. But the event in Acts 8 does not erase the truth of Act 2:38, for Luke was discussing different manifestations of the Holy Spirit. The Samaritans had received the manifestation that follows baptism that was promised by God. To say "they had *simply* been baptized in the name of the Lord Jesus" does not mean baptism was not effective. "Simply" is from a Greek word *(monos)* that means "only" or "alone." Luke was saying that baptism was the *only* action performed; thus they did not have *another* kind of manifestation of the Holy Spirit.

The expression *fall upon* (8:16) is never used to refer to the manifestation of the indwelling presence of the Holy Spirit, but refers only to those manifestations that empowered persons to work signs and wonders (Acts 10:44; 11:15). Obviously the laying on of hands was the action needed to impart the power to do miracles apart from the direct action of God, as in the baptism of the Holy Spirit (Acts 2 and 10). Only the events in Acts 2 and 10 were related to the prophecy about a Holy Spirit baptism (Matthew 3:11; Acts 1:5; 11:16). To identify every other activity of the Spirit as fulfilling this prophecy steps outside of Biblical evidence. This prophecy was related to the historical beginning of a new age that began in the first century.

Three Manifestations of the Holy Spirit				
What	**Action**	**For Whom**	**When**	**Purpose and Result**
1. Baptism of the Holy Spirit	No action by man; direct act of God	Apostles, Acts 1:5; 2; House of Cornelius, Acts 10, 11	Before water baptism	Signs and wonders to show God's new age had begun Acts 1:4, 5; 2:17ff; 11:15-18
2. Indwelling of the Holy Spirit	Faith, repentance, baptism	Anyone who obeys; Promise of God Acts 2:30-39; 5:32; 2 Corinthians 1:20; 2 Peter 1:4; Samaritans received this prior to laying on of hands	At water baptism	Salvation, Forgiveness, Added to church, Raised with Christ, New Life, Temple of Holy Spirit, Put on Christ, Restore unity, Equip us
3. Impartation of miraculous activity	Laying on of hands; only done by apostles	Hellenistic leaders, Samaritans, John's disciples Acts 6; 8; 19; 1 Corinthians 12—14	After water baptism	Miracles to certify the inspired preaching and teaching Hebrews 2:1-4; 1 Corinthians 12:12; Acts 2:22; 14:3

NOTE: (1) It is possible to have manifestation number 1 without having number 2 (Acts 10). It is possible to have manifestation number 2 without having numbers 1 or 3. It is possible to have manifestation number 3 without having number 1.

(2) To have the indwelling Spirit for salvation does not mean that one has miraculous powers (Acts 4:33; 6:6, 8; 1 Corinthians 12:8-11, 29ff).

(3) To receive miraculous powers required a different action from faith, repentance, and baptism (Acts 2, 8, 10, 19).

231

Gifts From the Holy Spirit

Not only are there distinctly different manifestations of the Holy Spirit, but there are also three kinds of gifts from the Holy Spirit: foundational, universal, and service gifts.

Foundational (sign) Gifts

Foundational gifts were not given to all people, but were given to specific people for specific reasons in certain periods of history. They were given at times both when God had new revelation for man and when there was reason for people not to believe the message of God or those who brought His message.

These gifts were given to authenticate or to verify either the message or the messenger as being from God so people would build their lives upon the foundation of the truth spoken by God's messengers. If the people did not know who was God's real messenger, they would build upon a counterfeit foundation.

These gifts were often referred to as "signs and wonders," and were given to Moses, the Old Testament prophets, Jesus, the apostles, and the New Testament prophets. Each of these persons had a new revelation from God; each spoke at a time in history when people did not believe that the message was from God or that the messenger was from God.

Moses was a fugitive—a murderer; yet God wanted him to return to Egypt and lead Israel out of slavery. Moses was rightly concerned that the people would not believe him (Exodus 4:1). Because of this situation, God gave Moses a sign-gift—turning the staff into a snake and back again (Exodus 4:2, 3). This gift certified that Moses was a messenger of God. The people observed the sign and believed Moses' words; they did not themselves ask that they be able to duplicate that gift. Later, Moses put into writing the Word of God (Exodus 24:4), and the people accepted his writings without asking for special signs.

God also communicated His Word through the Old Testament prophets, but because of the presence of so many false prophets, the people did not know whom to believe. So God guaranteed both His messengers and His message by foundational sign-gifts. The Jews who believed these prophets did not seek these gifts for themselves. The message of these prophets was written down, and the Jews read them and considered them the Word of God.

Jesus himself had foundational sign-gifts. He came with a

new revelation, and many people did not believe Him. God vouched for Him partly by signs and wonders. Peter emphasized this point: "Men of Israel, listen to these words: Jesus the Nazarene, a man attested to you by God with miracles and wonders and signs which God performed through Him in your midst, just as you yourselves know" (Acts 2:22).

The apostles also had sign-gifts. They had a new revelation from God, but there were many false teachers around. So God pointed out His messengers by the signs and wonders that they performed. The writer of Hebrews attests to this fact: "By signs and wonders and by various miracles and by gifts of the Holy Spirit" (2:3, 4), God confirmed His message and messengers (see also Acts 14:3 and 2 Corinthians 12:12). There were also New Testament prophets who were validated by sign-gifts (Acts 6:8-13; 8:6).

Consistency demands that for sign-gifts to be used today, we would have to have a new revelation from God. The New Testament affirms that a full revelation of God's nature and will has been made in space and time through Jesus. We have all the truth as Jesus promised (John 16:13). Since God has affirmed His message and His spokesmen, we ought to build our lives upon the foundation of their teachings. We ought to accept their writings as the Word of God without asking that we receive the same signs and wonders that the writers received. These gifts of the Spirit were foundational and are no longer being dispensed by God.

Universal Gifts

All Christians have the universal gifts from the Holy Spirit. The following gifts are specifically mentioned in the New Testament: (1) eternal life—Romans 6:23; (2) encouragement—Romans 1:11, 12; 12:6-8 (same word as for "exhortation"); (3) justification and righteousness—Romans 5:15-18, 21; (4) either to marry or remain single—1 Corinthians 7:7; and (5) answered prayer—2 Corinthians 1:11 ("favor" is the same word as "gift").

Service Gifts

The Holy Spirit has also given each Christian a type of service gift. Each has an ability or abilities that can be used to help others; these abilities are gifts from God. In fact, our entire lives are a gift from God. As we grow after conversion to Christ, we begin to use our abilities unselfishly in service of others.

In Romans 12:6-8, Paul mentioned seven categories under which all service-gifts fall: (1) prophecy, (2) service, (3) teaching, (4) exhorting (ability to encourage people), (5) giving in liberality, (6) leading, (7) showing acts of mercy (benevolence). Every ability will fall under one of these categories. For instance, a mechanic who helps a poor widow fix her car is exercising the gift of service; a person who gives money to help a needy family get food is practicing benevolence; a Bible School teacher exercises the gift of teaching; an elder exercises the gift of leadership.

It is not enough to know that we have these gifts for service. It is not enough to volunteer our abilities to serve others. It is also important that we grow up in the character of God as we use our abilities. When we share our lives together in Christ, we can become the kind of maturing children God wants us to be.

Conclusion

The Holy Spirit is the extended earthly presence of God. Although the Holy Spirit has different manifestations and gives different gifts, His primary purpose is to unite man both to God and to his fellowmen and to equip him with the moral character to keep the unity of the Spirit in the bond of peace. In this way, the Spirit is God's life living in believers to fulfill the requirement of the law, which is that they love one another, doing no wrong to each other, and serving to meet each other's needs. The fruit of the Spirit shows their participation in the character of God.

We grieve the Holy Spirit when we do not act or think with the character of our Father. Instead of grieving Him, let us rejoice in Him by daily becoming more like the Christ who lives within us—through the Holy Spirit. And let us live in the Spirit by treating other Christians as brothers and sisters— serving them and building them up.

Suggestions for Further Reading

Barrett, C. K. *The Holy Spirit and the Gospel Tradition*. Out of print.

Berkhof, Hendrikus. *The Doctrine of the Holy Spirit*. Philadelphia: John Knox, 1976.

Bruner, Frederick D. *A Theology of the Holy Spirit*. Grand Rapids: Eerdmans, 1970.

Crawford, C. C. *The Eternal Spirit* (2 Volumes). Joplin: College Press, 1973.

DeWelt, Don. *The Power of the Holy Spirit* (4 Volumes). Joplin: College Press, 1976.

Dunn, James D. *Baptism in the Holy Spirit*. Philadelphia: Westminster, 1977.

Green, Michael. *I Believe in the Holy Spirit*. Grand Rapids: Eerdmans, 1975.

Hamilton, N.Q. *The Holy Spirit and Eschatology in Paul*. Out of print.

Hendry, G. S. *The Holy Spirit in Christian Theology*. Out of print.

Hull, J. H. E. *The Holy Spirit in the Acts of the Apostles*. Out of print.

Kuyper, Abraham. *The Work of the Holy Spirit*. Grand Rapids: Eerdmans, 1956.

Moody, D. *Spirit of the Living God*. Out of print.

Moltmann, Juergen. *The Church in the Power of the Spirit*. New York: Harper and Row, 1977.

Rahner, K. *The Dynamic Element in the Church*. Out of print.

Stagg, Frank. *The Holy Spirit Today*. Nashville: Broadman, 1974.

Staton, Knofel. *Spiritual Gifts for Christians Today*. Out of print.

Swete, Henry B. *The Holy Spirit in the Ancient Church*. Out of print.

_____. *The Holy Spirit in the New Testament*. Grand Rapids: Baker, 1976.

THE HOLY SPIRIT

Taylor, John V. *The Go-Between God*. Oxford: Oxford University Press, 1979.

Vonier, A. *The Spirit and the Bride*. Out of print.

CHAPTER

10

THE IMAGE OF GOD

By Frederick W. Norris

There are few if any agnostics when it comes to beliefs about human nature. More than any other doctrine, the Christian understanding of humanity immediately confronts opposing views, positively stated, in the surrounding cultures. Some may not believe in God or gods, but all have a view of what it means to be human. Although wise Christians will want to turn to the Bible as the norm and to the considered judgments of Christian saints and scholars through the centuries as guides,[1] they will also find it quite enlightening to take some cues from the non-Christian world. Those cues not only allow us to gain perspective on what people outside the church think, but they also offer insights into important questions that Christians should address and discuss among themselves. There is a great mass of materials, but perhaps one of the most pointed comparisons comes from Edmund Wilson, the noted American literary critic. In writing about the Marquis de Sade, Wilson suggested that de Sade and Jean Jacque Rousseau represent opposite extremes in Western theories of human nature. Rousseau insisted that humans were noble savages, while de Sade demonstrated that at least one man was a cruel beast.[2]

Those poles have often become the gallows upon which various Christian teachers have been hanged. If these teachers emphasize the abilities and talents of humans and insist upon free will, they are accused of accepting the noble savage view.

Since no human community seems to be without its sadists, such a progressive, optimistic picture of people suggests that those who propound these doctrines resemble Miss Muffett before she saw the spider. On the other hand, those who have pointed out the depravity of human beings and the inability of people to choose freely have been attacked for seeing only the cruel beast. Since every human society appears to have within it individuals so noble that savagery seems to be an absurd epithet, such a regressive, pessimistic picture implies that those who teach these views resemble a Miss Muffet who sees only spiders.

Yet Rousseau and de Sade did agree on at least one point. Both depicted society and its institutions as a threat to the individual. Rousseau declared that the noble savage was corrupted by a decadent society. De Sade insisted that society was basically at fault since it restrained the freedom of the individual. Christians have long debated their relationship to groups and nations. Most have appreciated the corporate nature of the church, sensing that all Christians are incomplete until they know themselves to be in, and to act as parts of, the body of Christ. Yet some emphasize the individual character of salvation to the point that societal relationships are basically outside the scope of the gospel. For them, the plight of Humpty Dumpty consists of his own fall, and is unrelated to the fact that "all the King's horses and all the king's men, couldn't put Humpty together again." Others stress the social character of grace so much that the needs of individual persons are submerged in the masses. For them, the retraining of the king's horses and men is the issue, not the tumble of Humpty.

Similar problems also arise concerning God's own nature and His relationship to human beings. Any number of people outside the church react in sincere horror to the present age. They find it difficult, if not impossible, to conceive of a loving and just God who created and controls such a world. This is certainly one of the most important questions that faces both non-Christians and Christians. Furthermore, this issue affects any Christian discussion of the nature of humanity. Some believers, who view the freedom of humanity as a significant indication of the nature of God, continue to see the Creator as restricting His own powers by giving people the power to choose. From their vantage point, God so desired the possibility of personal response rather than marionette reaction that He allowed for the probability of rebellion and enormous suffering. To the world, such an explanation at times appears to resemble the confused mutterings of the Mad Hatter's tea party.

Other Christians, however, have insisted that the human will is not free. They have elevated the majesty of God so as to put His nature and activity completely beyond the questions humans ask. God alone has decided who will or will not be saved. His judgments are not open to rebuttal. To the world such remarks resemble the shouts of the Queen of Hearts: loud, capricious, and final. "Off with their heads."

Each of the above views apparently has strong Biblical and traditional support, both in the Christian faith and in influential representations in the non-Christian world. Together, they offer opposing opinions about the image of God within humanity: whether it has been retained, distorted, or lost.

People: Noble and Cruel, Individual and Social

Both Rousseau and de Sade made two errors. First, careful observation of those around us, as well as reference to Biblical and later Christian texts, makes us aware that people are neither entirely good nor entirely evil. We may, indeed, be overwhelmed by the power of the saint and the sadist. But the masochism of certain saints and the compassion of certain sadists should warn us not to create systematic theories of humanity.[3] Nobility and cruelty tend to mark every human being. Second, neither societal pressures nor individual strength alone determines who persons are. It is not difficult to document the ways in which the environment of home, school, and neighborhood affect growing children. But individuals react differently to the same environments. In the midst of concentration camps, some remained rational, moral, and religious.[4] The views of Rousseau and de Sade on these two points were too simplistic and, thus, are of little assistance in formulating a solution, except that their writings do alert us to the danger of broad generalizations about humanity.

Psychology is one area in which to search for clues about human beings. It is not as new a field as it occasionally appears; but its form has changed radically since the work of Sigmund Freud. Prior to his efforts, most insights about the inner workings of the human soul were to be found among poets, novelists, and historians. From the earliest writings available to us, perceptive individuals have offered descriptions of human motivation and action. Such resources, plus those in the contemporary period, should be consulted when one considers human nature. Certainly knowledge of Homer, Dostoyevsky, or Thucydides increases anyone's understanding of human beings. Freud himself, in spite of his active imagination and originality, found many of his observations explained through terms and concepts borrowed from his classical, European education. Much of his writing is filled with allusions to Graeco-Roman culture: terms such as ego, id, superego, and narcissism, for example. This use of earlier insight does not detract from, but indeed enhances, the depth and value of Freud's work.

His views must not be rejected out of hand because he was critical of belief in God. To his mind, much of religion was based on uncritical thinking and was accepted precisely because it was absurd. When he moved to a fuller explication of religion, he saw it in terms of what he called the Oedipus complex: the desire of sons to kill and eat their fathers. Later, Freud described religion as being involved in the sense of childlike helplessness, and viewed it as an illusion to be avoided. Only a scientific world would provide the way forward.[5]

In spite of such an attack, his observations and those of other psychologists should be given attention. One can reject such atheistic views while still paying heed to their insights. Freud was not the only leader in that field. As is often the case with such genius, his life brought him into conflict with his peers, including some of his own students. Jung, Alder, and others were in some ways forced out of the circle because of Freud's rigidity and their own inventiveness. Jung in particular has continued to draw the attention of theologians.[6] The healthy disagreements within psychology are part of what led to its acceptance as a legitimate tool for investigating human understanding. Some still have reservations about its rigor. Psychology remains a lesser field in European universities, surprisingly so in the German speaking areas, which have first-hand access to the literature of its nineteenth century giants. But it is quite likely that psychology eventually will establish itself as firmly as most other disciplines, even in spite of the popular quackery so often seen in the United States.

Among the various observations that experts within psychology have offered, two stand out as directly related to our theme. One is the depth of human brokenness and cruelty. Freud's imaginative investigations of the unconscious led to the opening of a dark cavern inhabited by "creatures" worthy of Pandora's box. Various studies have indicated the enormity of human distortion and have related it not only to childhood experiences but to a myriad of other possibilities for sickness and death. No worthy student of psychology can be unaware of the depth of human depravity.

But human beings are quite complex and indeed must be seen as both cruel and noble. Since many psychological studies have been concerned with those who have the most problems, it has been difficult for a researcher to make a reputation by concentrating on the more healthy. Thus the preponderance of studies deals with the so-called abnormal. Yet in spite of this emphasis, a second basic point remains. The psychologists, psychiatrists, or counselors who limit their concern to humanity and who avoid any questions concerning divinity have learned that each person has creative, healing potential within. Whether the therapy be individual or group, the expert depends on the fact that persons have inner powers for healing. Much of the discipline is now concerned with finding ways to release such powers, rather than discussing the question of whether or not such healing forces exist within the individual.

Presently, psychology offers a number of explanatory theories about human health, many of which are in direct conflict. But the two fundamental principles mentioned above are found in every school. Even those who work with autistic children or catatonics are aware of more than just the severe disruption. They often sense also that the problems lie in their own inability to get through to the patient rather than in the fact that a particular individual has no reservoirs of health. The deepest psychosis may itself be a creative attempt to preserve some semblance of life in the midst of whatever excruciating pain led to the imbalance. Therefore, from the discipline of psychology, one should learn to underestimate neither the capacity of human beings for deep distress and evil nor their capacity for relief and good. Even without any invocation of religion, some recover. For the Christian, such psychological evidence would suggest that the image of God, while horribly distorted, is still retained. All have sinned and fall short, but each can respond to grace.

At least one weakness of large proportion remains within the discipline of psychology, however. In spite of the growing sub-area of social psychology, much energy is devoted to the treatment of individual patients. Group therapies have grown in prominence within this century and presently are burgeoning as part of the popular fads. Those within the discipline show greater sensitivity to social concerns; but the need for more emphasis on an overview of humankind has led to the rapid growth of sociology.

We must again turn to the nineteenth century in the West to find the great leaders of sociology. Of course, insights into the social relationships of men and women did not wait until that era to arrive. The seers of earlier times—poets, literary figures, and historians, as well as others—have offered keen observations. Yet rigorous study of these relationships found a new level within the nineteenth century. Perhaps the key person in social theory then was Karl Marx. For many Christians, especially those living in the United States, the introduction of Marx calls forth immediate negative reactions. Resistance is justified, not merely because Marx rejected religion as the opiate of the people, but just as importantly because he does not describe the human condition adequately. His influence, however, has been so remarkable that attention must be given to his views.

For Marx, the hope of assistance from somewhere outside the observable human scene was not merely senseless; it was addictive, creating a stupor that kept human beings from recognizing the problems and organizing their energies to create solutions. Marx agreed with Feuerbach that religion was a projection of human need. But he criticized Feuerbach and certain socialists for not seeing that the root difficulties of the human race were social and economic. For Marx, the only reality that had ultimate importance was social. And within that reality, it was the economic forces that had to be taken over by the proletariat if any changes for the good were to occur. From his pen came reams devoted to both social and economic theories.[7]

Marx's work must be taken seriously even in terms of clearly positive gains. Much of the discipline of sociology owes its beginnings at least to the turmoil of discussion Marx created. Durkheim, Weber, and others were caught by the insights Marx expressed, even when they did not accept either the singular focus of his work on economics or the political structures he suggested. After the efforts of Marx, it was no longer possible to ignore social reality and its bearing on the human condition. Now, in the twentieth century, people commonly talk about the social environment, the way in which large groups and structures in society influence the lives of individuals. But not all concern with social issues is communist inspired. Even the strongest anti-communists must recognize how significant social forces are in forging the character of human beings. To ignore such forces would be to make anti-communism impotent, if not irrelevant.[8]

Yet such insights should not be linked merely to Marx. Robert Owen, whom Alexander Campbell debated before Marx finished high school, also had recognized the importance of social conditions for the life of human beings. He had looked after the welfare of those within his British factories and had implemented remarkable changes in their pay, hours, and housing. In his view, social reform could eradicate evil. The pain of humankind resided in the environment.[9] Even in the present era, a noted psychologist such as B. F. Skinner can insist that modifying the environment to mold behavior can effect the changes in human beings that are necessary for the creation of the good life.[10]

Before such notions are rejected, it is important again to note their helpful insights. There is a deep-seated individualism in the images of American culture. The heroic figure is not by any means an American invention, nor is individual effort to be denied its place. But the lonesome cowboy who perhaps needs his horse and gun but no other, and the James Bond who can trust no man or woman, are basically mutants and not persons to be imitated. People need people. The family and neighborhood environment of a child have an enormous effect on who that child becomes. There is not one shred of fairness in equating the chances of ghetto children and those of "wealthy" middle or upper class families. The American conscience must be informed by social concerns that dictate a more equitable distribution of chances for survival and growth.

Yet accepting the role of the social environment does not mean that those who have emphasized it as the ultimate foundation of human nature should be followed in every respect. The most telling criticism of Marxism is that its conception of evil is not worthy of the reality that can be observed in humans and their societies.[11] Not all the harm that befalls the human community stems from social and economic relationships. One of the deepest problems for the avowed Marxists is the attempt to integrate the early writings of their leader with the later ones. The earliest pieces, only recently gathered and published, are much more concerned with individual rights and freedom and the importance of their protection. That view has been defended as quite "Marxist" by certain dissidents in the eastern bloc, particularly in Poland, Czechoslovakia, and Yugoslavia.[12] The Leninist-Stalinist line of total sacrifice for the emergence of the final society raises enormous questions. Of first-rate importance outside the academic discussions of Marxist theory is the clear inability of communist systems to create the human situation that they promise. Most recently, the peaceful strikes in Poland and the slow erosion of the hard-line Maoists in China have suggested that concern only with social reality, with group structure, is not sufficient to provide the good life for people.

Robert Owen's reforms were of great value to those working within his factories. But his attempt to create a utopian community of long duration at New Harmony, Indiana, was a failure. The observations of B. F. Skinner concerning behavior modification through environmental change are pragmatically true and effective. They have helped change human beings and not merely rats. But it is not clear what a Skinnerian society would be like, nor which types of behavior would be kept and which abandoned. The spector of Orwell's 1984 casts a dark shadow over any plan to adopt the proposals of Owen or Skinner. Such views fail to grasp the depths of human brokenness, just as was the case with that of Marx.

Yet in spite of criticisms of both psychological and sociological approaches to human nature, no serious attempt to describe or deal with human beings can afford to ignore the insights these disciplines have gleaned. We should not be surprised that Biblical materials reflect the descriptions and theories of humankind that psychology and sociology have presented. If, indeed, God is the creator of humanity and His truth is revealed in Jesus Christ through the report of Scripture (as we believe), then there should be a positive correlation between the truth of these disciplines and Scripture. What we find in the Bible, however, is not only a positive relationship, but a deepening of such insights and their unity within a more comprehensive and elegant view. The Biblical doctrine of sin and evil is much stronger than that to be found either in psychology or sociology. As noted above, the almost baffling complexity of the unconscious and the wealth of psychological literature concerning it has certainly deepened our knowledge concerning the intricacies of evil. But in many ways, the Biblical narratives of intrigue and injustice have made an even deeper impression down through the centuries. Experiences of ill will, lust, despair, greed, and all manner of evil abound. One of the most telling accounts in the Old Testament depicts God's chosen, David, desirous of another's wife to the point of arranging the death of her husband, even though that husband was faithful to the king and to his own vows of battle (2 Samuel 11). The despondency of the prophets clearly describes the despair of any human being (Jeremiah 20; 1 Kings 19). Psalm 22 uses ancient language, but the message is plain even to a twentieth century human. It is not merely physical injury that leaves one "poured out like water," with a wax heart melted within the breast, strength "dried up like a potsherd," and a tongue stuck to one's jaws.

Probably the most obvious Old Testament reference is the account of Adam and Eve. Although much has been written about that incident, some of it highly informed by later writers such as Milton, the inner tensions within the narrative catch our attention. Humans were intended to live in paradisial bliss, but they found it impossible to use their freedom for fulfillment. Their desires overrode their judgment. They knew the right, but did the wrong. Then each refused to accept the blame, and both were punished. They were expelled from the garden to live in a world where even the gathering of food would be difficult and the woman's pain in childbirth would be increased (Genesis 2—3).

Present day psychological descriptions of the human condition may seem to be preferable, but the depth of insight carried in these Biblical texts remains impressive. Even those outside the church might well admit the forceful way these accounts portray the problems of humanity. The story form itself is one that for most people evokes a deeper response than other forms of prose. Thus, neither in content nor form can such attempts be faulted as inferior.[13]

When we turn to the New Testament, the situation is no different. The accounts of the life of Jesus are marked by His dealings with the "sinful." His demeanor and sensitivity attracted the broken and maimed. So many of the helpless come to Him that He is accused of avoiding the righteous and eating only with publicans and sinners (Mark 2:15-17). Once he responded that those who thought themselves to be the righteous were whitewashed tombs (Matthew 23:27-29). But perhaps the strangest narratives concern His confrontation with demons. We moderns have suffered from a style of Biblical criticism that has presupposed that such events could not possibly be true. The issues involved in these interpretations are more complex than can be adequately treated here, but through research in depth psychology, the reality of such accounts has been treated with increased seriousness. Yet that awareness of the unexpected pressures within the unconscious has only begun to uncover the importance of the Biblical points.

In the Gospels, people control much of their own lives, but they are influenced by powers outside. Jesus forgave the adulterous woman and told her to go and sin no more (John 8:1-11); yet he freed the Gadarene demoniac by confronting demons (Mark 5:1-20). There is no Biblical theory that would make all people puppets, but neither is the enormous power outside denied. In such cases, we await the broadening of the reductionistic outlook of modern Western culture so that it may include phenomena that can be found in many cultures outside our own, with its technologically oriented worldview. Mission among the nations would be impossible if the Bible were written in the language and concepts of twentieth century Western man. On the other hand, the Enlightenment period of Western culture should be welcomed by Christians since it put an end to the burning of "witches," began the abolishment of slavery, and encouraged the development of modern medicine. Belief in demons can be demeaning and even deadly. Yet the advances of the Enlightenment were not so overpowering that all religion, including Christianity, should be rethought in its categories alone. There is a certain elegance as well as danger in Scriptural concern with powers and principalities.

Paul's comments on people are quite similar to those of Jesus. He was also aware that all humans have fallen short—have missed the mark. Their need is overwhelming. And he was furthermore sensitive to the problems of motivation and action that plague the Christian. He saw within himself warring powers that not only kept him from doing what he intended, but also influenced him to do what he did not desire. At times, his explanations speak of his own responsibility for such actions; at other times they talk about the "law of sin," which is part of what moves people to action (Romans 1—3 and 7—8).

Such a description of the inner psyche of persons and the outer forces that make their way into the human personality serves to explain certain phrases often heard in daily life. "I just don't know what got into him," may be highly metaphorical, but it indicates the way in which certain odd behavior is viewed. The Bible contains both a recognition of the internal plight of humans and a deeper sensitivity to the uncontrollable. From the Christian point of view, the problem of evil cannot be resolved merely by correctly relating all the internal tensions to be found within an individual. Evil is much more serious than it is often seen by many contemporary psychologists. For them, problems are seldom seen as rooted anywhere but in the single psyche and its relationships.

That same kind of observation is in order when one deals with either social psychology or sociology. There is no lack of Biblical support for the fact that human beings are conditioned by their social environment. Communal consciousness is basic to the Old Testament. The prophets spoke to Israel as a nation. Identity was finally found within the group. One belonged to a tribe, then to a nation, and finally to the people of God, which transcended national boundaries and included even proven enemies (Deuteronomy 26:5-11; Isaiah 19:18-25). The legal and moral codes of the Pentateuch indicate clearly how important peer group influence and codified restraints can be (especially Leviticus). The story of Babel shows how definitive language is for group identity and how capable it is of creating confusion and enmity (Genesis 11:1-9). The individualism that has so often occupied the American consciousness is totally absent from the Old Testament. Heroes dominate the stories, but they do not find find their destiny by keeping their own counsel and relying on themselves alone. The sense of the community is so deep that the sins of the fathers are said to be visited upon the sons down through the generations (Exodus 20:5).

Jesus also attacked groups and customs. He was not unaware of the conditioning power of institutions. He answered the Pharisees and scribes not merely by giving a response to individuals and single questions, but by attacking the system itself, the traditions that created a climate in which individuals had great difficulty doing the right (Matthew 5—7; Luke 19:45-48).

He opposed some of the very laws given within the Old Testament codes because they had become oppressive. And yet he also insisted that not one jot or tittle would be abolished (Matthew 5:18).

Paul appears to be an opponent of all law, when in reality it is ultra-legalism against which he contends. In the same letter in which he warned the Galatians about returning to the Jewish law, its customs and practices—and perhaps also a return to similar pagan situations—he introduced lists of virtues as fruits of the Spirit "against which there is no law" (Galatians 5:16-24). Those fruits have close resemblances to certain Stoic lists and can also be found in Jewish literature. Furthermore, he offered practical pieces of advice and called the basic response of the Christian "faith working through love" (Galatians 5:6). And if the pastoral epistles are genuinely Pauline—and cogent arguments have been offered in favor of that position—then Paul himself was quite concerned with the particular structure of specific Christian communities.

One of the most fascinating aspects of a Biblical description of individual human nature and human community, then, is that the two are not seen in isolation from each other. In fact, a third element, the cosmic principalities and powers, is added to the picture. From a Christian point of view, it would be impossible to understand the human condition without seeing all these aspects as part of the whole. Each has its own existence. One person can resist both societal and demonic powers. Yet this person cannot be understood without reference to the other two. Throughout the Bible, sin is viewed as rebellion in each of these three areas. Lists of vices and virtues occur, but they are seldom if ever given valuation as lesser or worse. It is revolt against God that is the basic problem. Vices tend to be symptoms, not the disease itself.

This multiplex and elegant explanation is broadened further. Neither of the three realms—individual, social, cosmic—is without its good aspects. The same David who had Uriah killed becomes with Bathsheba the parent of Solomon, the builder of the temple. David was evil but not totally depraved (2 Samuel 12:24; 1 Kings 6-9). God drove Adam and Eve from the garden but did not destroy them. Even Cain, who killed his brother, was protected by the mark of the Lord (Genesis 3—4). Indeed, the Old Testament does not know of any situation in which the image of God in man is completely destroyed. Psalm 8 can speak of man as being made a bit lower than the angels, and thus as being the object of special affection and attention from God. Jesus saw not only the deficiencies in people, but also their positive attributes. He did not deny that Zaccheus was a "little" man in that he had used his position to bilk the needy (Luke 19:1-10). Nor did He condone the adulterous activity of the Samaritan woman (John 4:7-42). But from both He evoked responses that led to repentance and changed lives. Paul also saw himself in this kind of tension. His understanding of revelation and his own observations of people led him to assert that all sin and come short, both by acts committed and those omitted. Yet in the same epistle to the Romans, he also mentioned that Gentiles could be a law unto themselves with "good' results if they followed what they knew (Romans 1—3, especially 2:14, 15). He showed great appreciation for the Jewish tradition from which he had come, although he was also sometimes critical of it (Philippians 3; Romans 9—11). And on the basis of Jewish and Gentile precepts—as well as revelation—he preached to and argued his case among people whom he expected to have the intellect to understand and the will to respond.

Neither is there in Scripture a sense that all institutions are evil and without hope. The necessity of such groups and structures is recognized in the Old Testament even though it also sees the ways in which they can deteriorate and become a source of evil. The call, then, is for the reform of the structures, not their abandonment. Even the most harsh of the prophets did not call for the abolishment of worship and the law but for putting both on a basis other than a reliance on fossilized customs (Micah 6:8 and 4:1-13).

The same pattern is true within the New Testament. Some have criticized early Christian literature for not being more concerned with social problems.[14] That criticism is ill formed for two reasons. First, Jesus must be seen in the role of a social prophet, a critic of the structures that kept the poor and the needy in despair. Whenever Christians insist upon an individual gospel that has no social concern, they must again hear at least Jesus' conception of His purpose for life in Luke 4.[15] The beatitudes in Luke also have a sharper ring of social justice than those in Matthew (Luke 6:20-31; Matthew 5:3-12). Even if one does not see ultimate conflict between the two accounts, the more spiritual interpretation of Matthew should not be allowed to dilute the social one in Luke. Both are true, and each must receive its due.

Second, the language used in the New Testament goes to the heart of social reality. Exact plans for social change are not found in the books of the New Covenant. But when people from various strata of society—rich and poor, Greek and Jew, male and female—find themselves as part of one body, then relationships begin to change (Galatians 3:28; 1 Corinthians 12). Neither 1 Corinthians 7 nor Philemon demonstrates that Paul supported slavery. What he emphasized was Christian calling and relationship as in a large family. When Erastus, the Corinthian city treasurer; Gaius, who owned a house large enough to accommodate the congregation (Romans 16:23); and their rich cultured friends were called upon to view slaves as brothers and sisters, then social change had already occurred (1 Corinthians 11). Such an altered consciousness is basic for any type of plan or program. In fact, the very calling of assemblies, the creation of the church as the continuing people of God, indicates continuity with the Old Testament social ideals and a positive judgment on social institutions. The existence of the church as a social unit, as a family and a body, emphasizes the social character of human reality while at the same time indicating the importance of each individual.

Neither is the realm of principalities and powers left without its good aspects. The Old Testament shows awareness of pluralistic claims for divinities throughout the cultures in which the Israelites lived, but it also gives witness to the one true God (Exodus 20:2, 3; 1 Kings 18). It warned against worshiping idols made by human hands, but also recognized forces that worked against God. The New Testament speaks of the evil powers, but also of God, Christ Jesus His Son, and the Holy Spirit. There is indeed a prince of this age, but not one who will never be vanquished (John 12:30-32). One of the most striking aspects of Christian revelation is the claim that this third realm beyond the individual and the community belongs ultimately to God himself (Colossians 1:11-20).

Within the history of the church, the same kinds of tensions can be seen. Among the most significant debates of the early church was that between Pelagius and Augustine concerning the nature of grace and free will. The Augustinian position has tended to triumph, primarily because of his own genius and his emphasis upon grace. Few, if any, Christians would explicitly claim that they can find hope in this life without God's love. To see the majesty of God as primary, and His grace as the creative force that brought humankind into existence and lifts it from its plight, is truly the only vision of Christian faith that can claim to be faithful.[16] Yet the position of Pelgaius is not without its own merits. It is not clear that he limited God's grace to creation alone. His concern was the immorality of his age and the need for repentance. If, indeed, all persons were depraved to the point that faith must be a gift of God, then how could immoral humans be held responsible for their own actions? Moral reform would be impossible without human responsibility.[17] Only through the inclusion of points from both Augustine and Pelagius would it be possible to represent the holistic position of Scripture. While Augustine erred on the side of determinism, Pelagius' followers—if not Pelagius himself—erred through the limitation of grace. Only grace and free will together could do justice to the Christian faith and human observation. When such debates were resumed during the Reformation, it was Erasmus and the Left Wing Reformers who tended to develop the holistic position, daring to argue for the ellipse rather than denying the pole of free will as Luther and Calvin usually did.[18]

Within the history of the church, there have been few who did not see the communal character of the faith as a primary emphasis. But the way Christendom confronted its society has caused a number of difficulties. The demand that political and economic power support the church has brought with it enormous dangers. Eusebius praised Constantine as God's bishop to the outside world, even though the emperor apparently had more than one member of his family killed.[19] Evidently, in Eusebius' view, if the structure of political power could be supportive, then charges of murder had to be absurd. We may understand the sense of relief that he and others felt with the end of persecutions, but the price was a great one. During the Middle Ages and continuing into the Reformation, some felt that church and state should act in tandem. Often the church was not shy in accepting privileged positions within the state and was angry if its place of prominence was questioned.[20] Even Calvin's Geneva indicated how impossible it was for the ideal of theocracy to create a pluralistic, free state. Those who did not agree were either banned or burned, all in the name of the gospel.[21] The apparent solution of Luther, two kingdoms basically separated, is also suspect. If the gospel deals with individual acts and virtues, but not with social relationships, then where is the prophetic voice that challenges the social realities? Were Luther correct, few sensible people would opt for Christianity in the present age.[22] Here the continued witness of certain Left Wing Reformers calls us to account. They struggled with the gospel and for a social climate in which free choice and association were necessary. For them the gospel spoke to every relationship in life, including those deeply individual and those broadly social.[23]

And for most Christian theologians until the Western Enlightenment, the gospel's definition in terms of principalities and powers has been descriptive and true rather than figurative and false. They saw the appeal of the good news in its ability to speak forcefully of all three aspects of human relationships: individual, social, and supra-human. This comprehensiveness and elegance should continue to be marks of Christian doctrine.

God: Majestic and Moral, One and More

At least one other question is essential to any discussion of the image of God in mankind. What sort of God lies behind that image? In order to answer such an inquiry, it is worthwhile to turn to philosophical discussions for some cues. In the modern period, no single figure in philosophy has dominated the field like Freud in psychology and Marx in sociology, particularly in reference to the question of determinism. On the contemporary scene, however, a series of positions have been staked out on that issue. Some have argued for what might be termed a hard determinism, which denies the possibility of uncaused action either within the world of nature or the world of humanity. Everything has some prior cause and thus must be seen as determined by that cause. Free will is only an illusion. Heredity and environment determine choices.[24]

Others have suggested what might be called a soft determinism. To them, all morality fails if it is impossible to hold humans responsible for making choices. No one coerced into actions is punished by the law. Yet it would also be foolish to suggest that all human effort is uncaused, or that determinism is incompatible with moral responsibility. In fact, parental punishment of children does change behavior and is itself deterministic in the sense that it is a cause for altered patterns of action. Without such discipline for children or adults, there would be no morality. According to such an understanding, causality is emphasized without moving into fatalism.[25]

Still others have recognized the strength of the case for determinism but have suggested that self-determinism must be a part of any explanation for human life. Even though choices are quite limited, and prior causes are definitely in evidence, there is no theory that does justice either to the actions or words of humans unless it recognizes the individual choice of the agent. This position still emphasizes causality, but insists that human agents in themselves are causes.[26]

A fourth position suggests itself on the basis of symmetry, even though it is not widely held by contemporary philosophers. That would be a complete indeterminism in which no causes are recognized as determinative. David Hume argued strongly concerning the difficulty of specifying causes, an argument which still has merit.[27] But there are few who would find ultimate validity in total free will or indeterminism.

These discussions can form a creative context in which the Christian problem of predestination and free will can be encountered. Yet even as a context for discussion, these contemporary views must be handled with care. Scripture does not appear to be particularly interested in the full explication of such issues. What it expresses looks like an antimony in which the predetermining power of God and the free choice of humans seem to be enclosed within an ellipse. Both the Old and New Testaments view God as the Creator and Sustainer of all we know and of that which we do not fully know. Genesis begins with an account that views God as making all that is, but which also emphasizes that He made the so-called gods that others worship. That total claim is a mark of monotheism, one of the core concepts that form Judaism and Christianity. Throughout both Testaments, appeals are made to the absolutely predominant power of the one God. Indeed, some texts tend to shake, if not destroy, any platform from which humans might interrogate divinity. Both Isaiah and Jeremiah warn that God treats His creation as a potter would handle his clay (Isaiah 29:16; Jeremiah 18:5-11), doing with it what He wills. It is said that the Lord hardened Pharaoh's heart, while a similar point is made when He uses Cyrus to punish His people (Exodus 9:12-16; Isaiah 45:1). The latter parts of Job ridicule any haughty claims of humans against God (Job 38—41).

Such statements offer proper perspective, but they neither demand nor imply that humans cannot question the judgments of God. The list of those within Scripture who raised questions concerning the wisdom of His actions is impressive. Abraham, who had the faith to follow God's leading away from his homeland into unknown territories, bartered with God. How many righteous persons had to be found in Sodom and Gomorrah for the cities to be saved? (Genesis 18:16-33). In Psalm 22 the poet cried out in anguish and perhaps even anger, wondering why God has forsaken him. Job questioned (Job 29—31; 42). Jesus felt free to pray that the cup might be avoided, and himself uttered Psalm 22:1 from the cross (Matthew 26:36-46; 27:46). Paul prayed repeatedly for release from his thorn in the flesh even though it did not go away (2 Corinthians 12:7-10). Neither Abraham, the Psalmist, Job, Jesus, nor Paul were unfaithful in asking these questions. They all submitted their wills to God's will. But they did not believe because it was absurd, or because God coerced them into faith. They believed as a free response.

In this regard, it must not be overlooked that both Testaments make claims for the morality of God as well as for His majesty. And it is precisely the questioning of His goodness that is indicated as legitimate inquiry. To such questions God not only replies with defenses of His majesty and the belittling of human knowledge—an important and necessary point—but He also speaks of His justice and righteousness. One continuing theme throughout the Old Testament is God's steadfast love for His people in spite of their rebellious actions. He is depicted as having the power to destroy all Israel, as being justified in His actions against their whoring after false deities. But particularly in the prophets, God refuses to annihilate His people because, unlike men, He does not react on the basis of His might or righteous rage (Hosea 11:9). His main characteristic is a compassion that limits His power even when reprisals would be justified. In the New Testament, Jesus is clearly portrayed as One who could still the waves and drive out the demons. Yet in contrast to the Gnostic accounts,[28] the canonical Gospels tell of His limiting such power. He did not destroy His enemies, nor did He employ such potency to enhance His own position. Once more, the steadfast love of God, which limits His power, is clearly in evidence.

Perhaps the most enigmatic passages in the New Testament that deal with these themes are to be found in Paul's apistle to the Romans. After a confession in which Paul praises God for His saving grace and emphasizes His majesty, chapter nine opens with a defense of that royalty. God can have mercy on whom He will and harden the heart of whom He will. The clay does not ask the potter about the shape it is given. Here there is no doubt that Paul views God as the majestic ruler of all. Yet the tenth chapter states the importance of preaching and the responsibility of persons deciding for or against God's grace. If one is to take Scripture seriously, the ellipse formed by the themes of these two chapters must be accepted as normative for Christian faith. God is in charge; humans must decide. Here as elsewhere in the Bible, there is no release from that tension.

Particularly in passages that deal with the concept of predestination, it is important to recognize the context in which early Christians were preaching. They were combatting Graeco-Roman polytheism and other cults, the conduct of whose powerful deities would have been considered immoral for humans.[29] Many of the most sensitive minds and spirits of the ancient world had been sickened by the contention that the gods of Olympus played with people as if they were personal puppets.[30] In such stories, the destinies of humans were determined by the jealousy, anger, and lust of the Olympians. Some of the more exotic cults of the East, which had begun to penetrate the whole of the Mediterranean by the time of the appearance of Christ, had even more bizarre pictures of their powerful divinities.[31]

Thus, it is not outlandish to insist that Paul's references to predestination are linked to the claims of the Old Testament for the steadfast love of God as opposed to the fickleness of the fatalistic religions that saturated the region. To know that God would pursue His purpose was a relief. And to know that His purpose was the loving salvation of humankind created ecstacy. Many, some even within Judaism, had turned to magic because of this devastating fickleness of the deities (Acts 19:11-20).[32] If God knew beforehand, and forcefully enacted His own designs, then that terrible dread would be eliminated. Yet it is a distortion of Paul's words to insist that God so determined the destiny of individuals that nothing they willed could change it. Such a view reintroduces the fatalism of the pagan religions as if it were a Christian doctrine.

The similarity of these positions to the philosophical discussions of the present era is interesting and enlightening. In spite of the strong language about predestining, foreknowing, and calling in Romans 9, chapter 10 insists on decision and moral responsibility. The weaknesses of a hard deterministic position in philosophy should alert us to the weaknesses of the theological position of double predestination. The brilliant early Christian theologian, Augustine of Hippo, clearly saw the problems of determinism in his younger years. He became disenchanted with Manichaean dualism because it did not appear to be true to observations in life or particularly to the Scriptural description of God. If God did determine beforehand whether each person could be saved or damned, then because they could not choose, they could not be held responsible for their deeds. In that case, the problem of evil would be thrown directly into God's lap. Evil certainly exists. If humans are not responsible for it, and God determines all, then God himself is the source of evil. Augustine found that view to be utterly abhorrent, as have a number of Western and Eastern teachers before and after him.[33]

But with the advent of the so-called Pelagian controversy, Augustine reversed his ground and systematically moved toward a full deterministic position, double predestination. He emphasized God's total majesty and man's inability to ask questions concerning God's morality.[34] There are indications that Pelagius may not have stressed the grace of God as clearly as Scripture would demand. A few of his students became almost indeterminists in their views. But the orthodoxy of Augustine in his double predestinarian position has been questioned with some frequency in recent years, precisely in the climate after two world wars in which the morality of a majestic God is such a biting question.[35]

One may, indeed, applaud the efforts of Luther and Calvin to break the back of a works-righteousness system that had developed in medieval Roman Catholicism. Both of them found freedom in the sovereign grace of God. Furthermore, Calvin's concept of total depravity involves the totality of each human being as coming under the effects of sin; he did not mean each aspect of mankind is itself totally without worth. Both men hammered away on the "heretical" doctrine of free will when they made more general statements. In their commentaries, however, they were not as rigid.[36] But it was still Erasmus and the Left Wing Reformers who most clearly saw the problem of the ellipse and insisted on the second pole of free will, in order to state what Scripture and observation taught about man and to protect the morality of God.[37]

In philosophical circles, there will continue to be some who view hard determinism as the only responsible view of human life. And a few indeterminists will continue to bring forward their arguments. But the positions most likely to gain adherents are those that see the necessity of free choice as the basis of all morality and yet recognize the fact that causes such as heredity and environment affect behavior. Even though such discussions do not determine the nature of God, they do square with the Scriptural depiction of Him as sovereign and yet as limiting himself to the point that both He and His creatures may be moral. God is majestic, but to be God, He must also be good. The fact that He has restricted His own sovereignty by His love is the essence of grace. Christ did not count equality with God something to be grasped, but emptied himself, took on our humanity, and died the death of a cross (Philippians 2:5-11). Such limitation of absolute power for the sake of another is the only possible solution to our world's problems. Having such a mind within ourselves can create individuals and communities capable of making earthly life worth living.

When the problem of evil is discussed in terms of the majesty and morality of God, one further point must be stressed. No philosophy offers the promise of life after death, or of retribution and forgiveness, as does the Christian doctrine of resurrection. In fact, some of the early strata of the Old Testament do not evidence concerns with a resurrection. Yet one thing is certain. There is no possibility of talking about a moral God unless there is a possibility of justice and mercy in a life hereafter. All attempts to defend God's goodness and power (theodicy) that would forego discussions of immortality are doomed to failure by the weight of evidence for evil and suffering in this present age. No deity could be considered moral on the basis of observations concerning the lives of the innocent and loving humans on this planet. Both the Old and New Testaments have portions that insist on resurrection. The logic of the situation demands that such a doctrine be held if the theodicy question is to be answered affirmatively.

Finally, God has revealed himself not only as the God of majesty and morality, but as a God of fellowship. Certainly, reservations must be placed against a fully circumscribed doctrine of the Trinity as expressed within the ancient creeds of

Christendom.[38] But many Biblical references militate against a view of God as being alone within himself. He is one and more. Fellowship with His Son and with His Spirit is evidently a part of His very nature. Therefore, His image in humans will be social, since His own being is not wholly singular. Persons seek fellowship with each other because they are made in His image.

Conclusion

The image of God in humankind is still present but greatly distorted. Human beings stand in nature as supreme examples of creativity, whether they produce great culture through art, architecture, music, or literature, or whether they make weapons of war and torture that far outstrip the possibility for cruelty in animals. Sin is rebellion against God, the distortion of His image. When we look at mankind, individually and communally, we find the beauty of Miss Muffet, but also the spider. Whether Humpty Dumpty fell of his own accord or had been influenced by his background is important; but more significant is the fact that neither he nor the king's cavalry and infantry could save him. Salvation has to come from the outside, because temptation to rebellion comes partially from outside the human realm. And this salvation comes not from a capricious Queen of Hearts who treats all as she pleases, but from a loving Father who limits His majesty through His morality and, indeed, His mercy. Therefore, humans, to be what they were meant to be, must resemble God, in whose image they were created. They can limit their power for the sake of others.

NOTES

[1]William Robinson, *The Biblical Doctrine of the Church*, Revised Edition (St. Louis: The Bethany Press, 1966), pp. 148-151.

[2]Edmund Wilson, *The Bit Between My Teeth* (New York: Farrar, Straus and Giroux, 1965), pp. 169, 170.

[3]Paul Holmer, *C. S. Lewis: The Shape of His Faith and Thought* (New York: Harper & Row, 1976), particularly chapter 4, which gathers a number of insights giving fair warning against constructing a theory of humanness.

[4]Victor Frankl, *Man's Search for Meaning,* trans. by Ilse Lasch (Boston: Beacon Press, 1963).

[5]Sigmund Freud, *Standard Edition of the Complete Psychological Works of Sigmund Freud* (London: Hogarth Press); *Totem and Taboo* Vol. 13, 1957, pp. 1-161; *Moses and Monotheism,* Vol. 23, 1964, pp. 3-137; *The Future of an Illusion,* Vol. 21, 1961, pp. 5-56; *New Introductory Lectures on Psycho-Analysis,* Vol. 22, 1964, pp. 7-182. For a Christian response to Freud, see Hans Kueng, *Freud and the Problem of God* (New Haven: Yale University Press, 1979).

[6]As one example, see Louis Dupré, *Transcedent Selfhood* (New York: Seabury Press, 1976), esp. chapter 8.

[7]Karl Marx and Friedrich Engels, *Basic Writings on Politics and Philosophy,* ed. by Lewis S. Feuer (Garden City: Doubleday, 1959). Karl Marx, *Capital: A Critique of Political Economy,* ed. by Friedrich Engels (New York: International Publishers, 1967).

[8]A fellow student from India once told me a proverb from his early days. "He who is not a Marxist by thirty has no heart. He who is a Marxist after thirty has no head."

[9]Robert Owen and Alexander Campbell, *A Debate on the Evidences of Christianity, Etc.* (Nashville: Mcquiddy Printing Company, 1957 reprint). Note specifically his second address, points 1-12, pp. 16, 17, which emphasize environmental conditioning.

[10]B. F. Skinner, *Beyond Freedom and Dignity* (New York: Alfred E. Knopf, 1971).

[11]John Bowker, *Problems of Suffering in Religions of the World* (Cambridge: University Press, 1970) esp. chapter 4.

[12]Karl Marx, *Writings of the Young Marx on Philosophy and Society*, ed. and trans. by Lloyd D. Easton and Kurt H. Guddat (Garden City: Doubleday, 1967). Among the many dissidents, Milan Machovec is one of the most interesting. A Czech, critical of both Christianity and the Lenin-Stalin tradition of Marxism, he has written *A Marxist Looks at Jesus* (Philadelphia: Fortress Press, 1976). The introduction to Machovec's book by Peter Hebblethwaite mentions others who hold similar views.

[13]For example, see Hans Frei, *Eclipse of Biblical Narrative* (New Haven: Yale University Press, 1974) and Frans Joseph Van Beec, *Christ Proclaimed: Christology as Rhetoric* (New York: Paulist Press, 1979).

[14]Ernst Troeltsch, *The Social Teachings of the Christian Church*, trans. by Olive Wyon (Chicago: University of Chicago, Press, 1976 reprint), Vol. 1, chapter 1 insists that earliest Christianity had no real social consciousness.

[15]Edward Schillebeeckx, *Jesus: An Experiment in Christology*, trans. by Hubert Hoskins (New York: Seabury Press, 1979), pp. 105-271.

[16]Augustine, *On Nature and Grace.*

[17]Pelagius, *Commentary on Romans.*

[18]Erasmus, "De Libero Arbitrio," LCC, Vol. 17, trans. by E. Gordon Rupp with A. N. Marlow (Philadelphia: Westminster Press, 1969), pp. 35-97. Kenneth Davis, *Anabaptism and Asceticim* (Scottsdale, Penn: Herald Press, 1974), pp. 266-292 shows similarities between Erasmus and the Anabaptists and particularly Erasmus' influence on the Left Wing. John Calvin, *Institutes of the Christian Religion*, LCC, Vol. 20, trans. by Ford Lewis Battles, particularly sections II. i. 8 and II. iv. 1. Martin Luther, "De Servo Arbitrio," LCC, Vol. 17, trans. and ed. by Philip S. Watson with Benjamin Drewery (Philadelphia: Westminster Press, 1969), pp. 101-334.

[19]Eusebius, *Life of Constantine.* A.H.M. Jones, *Constantine and the Conversion of Europe* (New York: Collier Books, 1962), esp. chapter 15.

[20]See the documents and comments in Brian Tierney, *The Crisis of Church and State* (Englewood Cliffs: Prentice Hall, 1964).

[21]Francois Wendel, *Calvin: The Origins and Development of His Religious Thought*, trans. by Philip Mairet (New York: Harper & Row, 1963), Part One.

[22]Martin Luther, *Temporal Authority: To What Extent It Should Be Obeyed*, LW, Vol. 45, pp. 75-129.

[23]Claus-Peter Clasen, *Anabaptism: A Social History, 1525—1618* (Ithaca: Cornell University Press, 1972), pp. 152-209 insists that Anabaptist social doctrines would have been disastrous if ever followed by a large group. Yet his analysis appears faulty at two points. First, he does not stress enough the dissimilarities of the various groups. For him (p. 171), Bullinger's statement that Anabaptism was fathered by Thomas Müntzer is still truthful enough. Mennonite historians, however, have demonstrated that such is not the case for the Swiss traditions. Second, he is too certain about the failure of such social understandings, particularly since persecuted Anabaptists were seldom allowed the possibility of setting up such communities.

[24]John Hospers, "What Means This Freedom?" reprinted in *Free Will and Determinism*, ed. by Bernard Berofsky (New York: Harper & Row, 1966), pp. 26-45. Robert Blatchford, "The Delusion of Free Will," reprinted in *Philosophy and Contemporary Issues*, 2nd ed., ed. by John R. Burr and Milton Goldfinger (New York: Macmillan, 1976), pp. 15-22.

[25]Walter T. Stace, "The Problem of Free Will," reprinted in *Philosophy and Contemporary Issues*, pp. 23-30. R. E. Hobart, "Free Will as Involving Determinism and Inconceivable Without It," reprinted in *Free Will and Determinism*, pp. 63-95.

[26]Frederick Ferré, "Self Determinism" *American Philosophical Quarterly* (July, 1973), Vol. 10, No. 3, pp. 165-176, and Roderick Chisholm, "Freedom and Action," *Freedom and Determinism*, ed. by Keith Lehrer (New York: Random House, 1966), pp. 11-45.

[27]Richard Taylor, *Metaphysics* (Englewood Cliffs: Prentice Hall, 1963), pp. 46-50 and William Frankena, *Ethics* (Englewood Cliffs: Prentice Hall, 1973), pp. 72-77 are both critical of indeterminism, even though Taylor supports free will and Frankena accepts a type of determinism.

[28]The Gnostic infancy gospels, most easily accessible in Edgar Hennecke, *New Testament Apocrypha*, ed. by Wilhelm Schneemelcher, Eng. Trans. ed. by R. McL. Wilson (Philadelphia: Westminster Press, 1963), Vol. 1, pp. 363-432, emphasize Christ's miraculous power but picture Him as a child who does what He wants when He wants.

[29]See W. K. C. Guthrie, *The Greeks and Their Gods* (Boston: Beacon Press, 1962), especially chapter 4, "God and Men in Homer."

THE IMAGE OF GOD

[30]The most perceptive is Plato's critique, which warns that Homer and Hesiod are not to be believed in their tales about the gods, The Republic, II, 17. Euripides, Xenophanes, Heracleitus, and Pythagoras had earlier voiced their criticisms of the mythology.

[31]John Ferguson, *The Religions of the Roman Empire*, (Ithaca, N.Y.: Cornell University Press, 1970), offers an interesting survey of such religions. The French series, "Études préliminaries aux religious orientales dans l'Empire romain," edited by M. J. Vermasern, offers the most up to date studies in this area.

[32]The rise of interest in Tyche, the goddess of fortune, can be well documented particularly in the Roman era. People were petrified of forces outside their control. Magic amulets and even striking representations of the evil eye in mosaics were a considerable part of religious conviction in the early Christian era. For a survey of such materials in just one city, see my "Antioch-on-the-Orontes as a Religious Center" to be published in *Aufstieg und Niedergang der römischen Welt*.

[33]Augustine, *Concerning The Nature of Good, Against the Manichaeans*, 28; Tertullian, *Against Marcion* 2.6; *On the Soul* 10.1; Origen, *On First Principles*, III, 1; John Chrysostom, *Homily 16 on Romans*. John Meyendorff, *Byzantine Theology* (New York: Fordham University Press, 1974), pp. 138-150, notes how Augustine's views on sin and free will did not penetrate the East.

[34]Augustine, *Retractions*, esp. chapters 9 and 22—25. Augustine even near the end of his life found no incongruence between affirming that God is good and that faith and salvation come through God's predestining election of certain people only.

[35]John Ferguson, *Pelagius: A Historical and Theological Study:* (Cambridge: Heffer, 1956). Robert Evans, *Pelagius: Inquiries and Reappraisals* (New York: Seabury Press, 1968). Peter Brown, "Pelagius and his Supporters," *Journal of Theological Studies*, 19 (1968), pp. 93-114. Gerald Bonner, *Augustine and Modern Research on Pelagianism* (Villanova: Villanova University Press, 1972). D. F. Wright, "Pelagius the Twice-Born," *The Churchman*, 82 (1972), pp. 6-15. William E. Phipps, "The Heresiarch: Pelagius or Augustine?" *Anglican Theological Review*, 52 (1980), pp. 124-133.

[36]Martin Luther, *Lectures on Romans*, LW, Vol. 25, particularly the comments on chapter 10, does not seem to make faith a gift of God, even though he still resists salvation by works, and insists upon dominance of grace. Benoit Girardin, *Rhetorique et Theologie: Calvin,*

Le Commentaire de l' Epître aux Romains (Paris: Editions Beauchesne, 1979), p. 327, notices how Calvin moves away from a static dependence on gracious predestination to the suggestion that the faith of the person has some bearing on salvation.

[37]Thor Hall, "Possibilities of Erasmian Influence on Denck and Hubmaier in Their Views on the Freedom of the Will"; *Mennonite Quarterly Review,* 35 (1961), pp. 149-170, demonstrates contacts and similarities of thought.

[38]Hermann Josef Vogt, "Exegese und Kirchengeschichte," *Theologische Quartalschrift* 1. Heft, 1979, p. 45, a professor in the Roman Catholic faculty at the University of Tübingen, West Germany, warns that the ancient creeds show no concern for Jesus' life between birth and death, and thus must always be viewed as having serious limitations.

CHAPTER

11

THE DOCTRINE OF SALVATION

By Ron Durham

The coming of Jesus Christ was heralded by John the Baptist, who was to "go on before the Lord . . . to give His people the knowledge of salvation by the forgiveness of their sins" (Luke 1:76, 77). The very name of Jesus reflects this central purpose of His coming: "You shall call His name Jesus (Greek *Iesous*, savior), for He will save His people from their sins" (Matthew 1:21).

Yet the idea of salvation remains obscure to many moderns. On the one hand, a materialist age looks to scientific progress to save it from its problems. With technology to turn to for new things, and psychology offering healed human relationships, what is there from which to be saved? On the other hand, there is the appeal of the radio evangelist who presents salvation in terms of a misty entity called a soul wafted magically out of an evil world into Heavenly spaces.

Against these views, the Bible offers a holistic picture of salvation. It reflects God's loving concern that people live in a secure and "safe" (Latin *salvus*, hence "salvation") relationship with Him, with their environment, and with each other. In Luke 1:77, above, Jesus' mission to bring forgiveness of sins is only the spiritual dimension of the overall "knowledge of salvation." The physical dimension of that security is reflected in His healing miracles, and in the promise of a new earth (Revelation 21:1). Jesus showed this holistic concern in such instances as the forgiveness and the healing of the paralytic in Matthew 9:1-8. When questioned about His authority to forgive sins, Jesus enabled the paralytic to walk, "that you may know that the Son of Man has authority on earth to forgive sins." The Christian's hope is not simply for his soul's salvation, but even for the "redemption of our bodies" (Romans 8:23).

Both the inner and the outer nature of salvation are implied in the Biblical language of salvation. In the Old Testament, Jahweh was a God of *yeshuah* or *yasha*—deliverance, or salvation. Bound up in this language is the concrete theme of liberation from one's enemies (Psalm 27:1); but it is unavailable to those who persist in spiritual captivity—"Salvation is far from the wicked, for they do not seek Thy statutes" (Psalm 119:155). Actually, spiritual and bodily safety are closely related throughout the Old Testament. Only as one responds body and soul to God does he or she experience *shalom*—not simply "peace," but *wholeness*.[1] Biblically, then, salvation is to be defined as living—not merely dying—in a state of wholeness, security, and safety relative to one's self, creation, others, and God.[2]

Greeks from the time of Hippocrates and the cult of Asclepius, the god of healing, spoke of salvation (*soteria, soterion*) as safety from the evils of disease, which attack the body, as well as from evil, which attacks the soul.[3] In the New Testament, Jesus was once approached by a woman with a heretofore incurable hemorrhage. "If I only touch His garment," she said, "I shall get well" (Matthew 9:21-23). The word translated "get well" (from *sozo*), regularly means "be saved"; the King James and American Standard Versions translate it "be made whole." The point is that healing and wholeness, salvation and well-being, are all inter-related in Biblical thought. It is only Western, technocratic man who has attempted to treat (save) the body apart from the soul, or the soul apart from the body, the temple of the Holy Spirit.

The Scheme of Redemption

One reason it is hard for moderns to understand salvation is that few understand sin. It is impossible to grasp the need to be at peace with God unless we are first convicted that we are estranged from Him. In Biblical theology, therefore, the doctrine of salvation is preceded by the doctrine of the fall. Not only did mankind (Hebrew, *adam*) fall, but persons fall. Knowing that our capacity to choose would mean that we sometimes choose the wrong and that wrong-doing is self-destructive, God laid out from the beginning a sweeping scheme, or plan, of salvation. True to the above definitions, it is a plan that partakes of "outer" or historical events, not merely mental or spiritual intimations of immortality. Both the Old Covenant and the New Covenant Scriptures comprise a *history* of salvation.[4] That is, they describe certain events in the "public" or historical realm, then include in the description the events' inner meaning for the salvation of mankind. It is in the stream of events that the continuity of Scripture is seen most distinctly. Many topics are not treated systematically in the Bible. For example, subjects such as the Holy Spirit, Heaven, or the people of God are best studied by contrasting the way they are treated in various types of Biblical literature, or at various moments in Biblical history. But the history of salvation comprises a continuous thread running through both Testaments. All the mighty acts of God, from creation to consummation, relate systematically to the plan by which God reconciles people to himself.

The People of God

Especially under the Old Testament, salvation is a *corporate* concept. When God calls Abram in Ur of the Chaldeans, He promises to make of him a great nation, not to save his individual soul in Heaven (Genesis 12:1-3; 17:1-5). Abraham's grandson Jacob has his name changed to Israel, the patriarch standing for the nation, the one for the many. God elects this nation as His vessel of salvation. It is for this reason that family lineage was so important among the Jews in the time of Christ. The spiritual dimensions of salvation had become overwhelmed by the material, and to be a true child of Abraham and the covenant was tantamount to having a parcel of land in the Messianic kingdom. Thus, Jesus found it necessary to remind such Jews that ultimate deliverance or salvation is not limited to tribes and nations. He broadened the concept of the people of God to include those who believed and obeyed as did Father Abraham, not merely his blood descendants (John 8:36ff).

Even under the New Covenant, salvation is wrongly viewed apart from the community of faith. In the passages used to open this chapter, Jesus came to save His *people* from their sins. It is true that individuals such as Paul—and hence individuals today—can speak of Jesus "who loved me, and delivered Himself up for *me*" (Galatians 2:20). As has been well said: Christianity is personal, but it is not private. Jesus is the Savior of the *body*, the church (Ephesians 5:23; 1:22, 23). The idea of the isolated saint or monk seeking salvation in the desert, and the concept of a sect claiming salvation for itself apart from the larger body, are both at odds with the Biblical view. Christianity as a whole and the restoration movement in particular have frequently failed to accept the cohesion inherent within the idea of the people of God.

Captivity and Deliverance

The exodus from Egypt looms as the most significant single event in the Old Testament Scriptures' history of salvation. It was predicted even to Abram in Genesis 15:13, 14:

> And God said to Abram, "Know for certain that your descendants will be strangers in a land that is not theirs, where they will be enslaved and oppressed four hundred years. But I will also judge the nation whom they will serve; and afterward they will come out with many possessions."

In the story of Joseph, son of Jacob, God's saving power is seen at work even in the depths of despair. As the chosen people move to Egypt to escape famine, the first step of a pattern of history emerges as "the descent into Egypt." Not only do God's people enter bondage in Egypt, as Pharaohs who "know not Joseph" arise and enslave the Israelites; so also does mankind descend into the bondage of sin, and so will the Savior-child Jesus repeat the descent into Egypt (Matthew 2:13-15). From that gloomy estate, however, those who cry for deliverance have a historical event, not a philosophy, on which to base their hope.

The next phase in the cycle is the exodus. As Moses leads Israel through the Red Sea, he bids them watch the destruction of the pursuing hordes of Egypt: "Do not fear! Stand by and see the salvation of the Lord which He will accomplish for you today" (Exodus 14:13). Thus, "Jahweh 'who brought Israel out of Egypt' is probably the earliest and at the same time the most widely used confessional formula" in Israel's theology of salvation.[5] And not only is Israel delivered from Egypt; so also is mankind delivered from sin, and so the Christ child returns to Nazareth, for "out of Egypt I called my son" (Hosea 11:1; cited in Matthew 2:15).

Centuries after the exodus, the continuing impact of this event is seen as a psalmist broods gloomily in a "day of trouble," then allows history to pierce the darknesss:

I shall remember the deeds of the Lord;
Surely I will remember Thy wonders of old.
I will meditate on all Thy work,
And muse on Thy deeds.
. . . .
Thou hast by Thy power redeemed Thy people,
The sons of Jacob and Joseph. [Selah.]
The waters saw Thee, O God;
The waters saw Thee, they were in anguish;
The deeps also trembled.
. . . .
Thy way was in the sea,
And Thy paths in the mighty waters. . . .
Thou didst lead Thy people like a flock
By the hand of Moses and Aaron.
                    Psalm 77:11, 12, 15, 16, 19, 20

Here, then, is a basic difference between Biblical religion and many other faiths. Hope for salvation is based not on philosophy, or good works, but on the gracious intervention of God in history.

Deliverers and the Deliverer

After the exodus, the history of salvation continues through the erratic development of the theocracy of Judaism. Moses' successor is, significantly, called Joshua (yoshua, related to yeshua, from which the name Jesus derives), meaning "Jehovah saves." Because the Jews were so often disobedient, the nations in the land of promise were a continual threat to the shalom of the elect. The book of Judges records the next cycle of saving events: "When the sons of Israel cried to the Lord, the Lord raised up a deliverer (yasha, another term for "savior") for the sons of Israel, to deliver them" (Judges 3:9). The series of judges, therefore, in this phase of Israel's history, were far more than civil or military leaders. They were concerned with the salvation or peace of Israel in the holistic sense. When a later judge, Gideon, is asked to rule over the people, he replies, "I will not rule over you, nor shall my son rule over you; the Lord shall rule over you" (Judges 8:23).

The establishment of the monarchy probably represents an erroneous shift in Israel's understanding of salvation. The cry, "Give us a king," is clearly based on the need for military safety more than spiritual, for it is based on Israel's desire to be like the surrounding nations (1 Samuel 8:4, 5, 19, 20). It is true that in Deuteronomy 17:14 God give specifications for the monarchy. It seems, however, to be based on His sovereign foreknowledge that this would be Israel's stubborn will, not His own. The point is that salvation history continues even through questionable institutions—as it does, indeed, even through nations such as Edom and Assyria, who reject God but are nonetheless pressed into the scheme of redemption.

The materialist thrust of the hope for peace is corrected by the Old Testament prophets. Military peace does not equal *shalom* or salvation:

> Woe to those who go down to Egypt for help,
> And rely on horses,
> And trust in chariots because there are many,
> And in horsemen because they are strong,
> But they do not look to the Holy One of Israel,
> Nor seek the Lord!
>
> Isaiah 31:1

Despite differing emphases in earlier and later sections of the book of Isaiah, there is a continuity of emphasis on God, not the *goyim* (the nations) as Savior (Isaiah 12:2; 43:11). In the later sections, however, the concept of salvation is changed in at least two highly significant ways. First, Israel herself is conceived not as the primary end of the saving acts of God, but the instrument with which God is to bring deliverance. Second, the possibility of salvation is expanded to include all peoples:

> Behold My servant, whom I uphold.
> . . . .
> I will appoint you as a covenant to the people,
> As a light to the nations,
> To open blind eyes,
> To bring out prisoners from the dungeon,
> And those who dwell in darkness from the prison.
>
> Isaiah 42:1, 6, 7

The "servant" here is identified now as the nation of Israel (Isaiah 41:8; 44:1, 21), then as a person, Cyrus, through whom

God works (Isaiah 45:1). Ultimately, He is one who "has borne our griefs and carried our sorrows" (Isaiah 53:4). This shift to the notion of vicarious suffering, although a stumblingblock to Jews to this day, has already been foreshadowed in the insistence that God alone—not man or sacrifices—is sufficient for salvation.

These new elements strain the Old Testament view of salvation to the point that Israel—and the modern reader—is driven to look for new interpretations and fresh fulfillment of the ancient promises. The promise of a new covenant (Jeremiah 31:31ff) led to various Messianic speculations in noncanonical intertestamentary writings. Particularly under the pressure of the Isaiah prophecies, "He who comes," Messiah, the Savior *par excellence,* becomes the focal point of Israel's hopes. None of these speculations precisely predict the way in which Jesus of Nazareth would fulfill the Messianic promises, but they point to just such a time as that when Jesus actually appeared.

Salvation in the New Covenant

The event of Jesus. When Jesus appears, the salvation themes of His Jewish heritage are immediately prominent. The aged Simeon, who was "looking for the consolation of Israel" (Luke 2:25), saw in Him the fulfillment of the two new elements of salvation history found in Isaiah 40—55: "For my eyes have seen Thy salvation, which Thou hast prepared in the presence of all peoples, a light of revelation to the Gentiles, and the glory of Thy people Israel" (Luke 2:30-32).

When Jesus himself takes up the Old Covenant Scriptures in His first recorded sermon, he turns to Isaiah. The servant through whom God will bless the nations now becomes Jesus himself. Just as Jacob stood for Israel so long ago, the Hebrew idea of corporate personality allows Jesus to stand for the new Israel and to take upon himself the saving Spirit of the Lord (Luke 4:18). Hence, the saving power of Jesus is seen, once more, in historical events—public acts of preaching, healing, praying, and serving. While Christian theology has concentrated primarily on the saving power of the death of Christ, we must not overlook the efficacy also of His life; He was the source of wholeness to all who responded in faith to His presence and message (Luke 19:9, 10).

The good news. Paul's succinct statement of the basic content of the event of Christ emphasizes His death and resurrection (1 Corinthians 15:3ff). It is this proclamation (kerygma) that formed the crucial content also of the sermons recorded in the book of Acts. The good news was that sin, death, and the grave had all been conquered in Jesus. Although His ministry had been confirmed by signs and wonders, He had been put to death by the very nation from whence He came. But God had raised Him up in the sight of witnesses, who testify both to the objective fact of this saving event and to the subjective experience of grace that has resulted from their response. Now, all people are to trust in Jesus as the fulfillment of the scheme of redemption, turn from their sins, being buried with Him in baptism and raised to walk in the joy of their salvation ministered to them by the Holy Spirit in the new age ruled over by the Messiah (see Acts 2:22-40; 3:12-26; chapter 7).

As has often been suggested, the Acts can be considered Part 2 of Luke's Gospel. The significance of the literary forms here and their sequence can hardly be overstressed. Unique in ancient literature, the Gospels are interpretive histories of the life, death, and resurrection of Jesus the Messiah. The Acts narrative shows the response of those touched by the ministry of Jesus and seized by what it implied. The public nature of the event of Jesus (as recorded in the Gospels) requires an equally historical demonstration of the impact salvation makes on whole persons (which is recorded, then, in Acts). It remained for the epistles to offer theological reflection on this event and how it should shape men and women in the community of faith.

The atonement. According to the author of the epistle to the Hebrews, Jesus "appeared once for all at the end of the age to put away sin by the sacrifice of Himself" (9:26, RSV). In a world of competing faiths, it was inevitable that this assertion would be questioned and, in turn, defended by Christian apologists. How does the death of a man in about A.D. 30 relate to the sins we commit today? Is there no offering for us to make as well? If the sacrifice of Jesus was, as in the Old Covenant, offered to God, does this make of God a tyrant whose wrath is appeased only by human blood? Or if we conceive of the sacrifice as offered to Satan, how did a sovereign God allow Satan to get the upper hand? Such questions have been addressed in Christian history in elaborate theologies of the atonement.[6]

In the light of the Old Covenant background of sacrifices for sin, it is not surprising to read in Hebrews 9:22 that "without shedding of blood there is no forgiveness" of sins. The author affirms the effectiveness of the New Covenant sacrifice, Jesus, by asserting also that "it is impossible for the blood of bulls and goats to take away sins" (10:4). It is further stated that this act is sufficient for all time (10:11-14), although Paul adds that the dedicated Christian life is required as a "living sacrifice" (*thysian zosan*, Romans 12:1).

Scripture can also speak of the sacrifice of Jesus as the "expiation" or "propitiation" (*hilasmos*) of our sins (1 John 2:2; 4:10; cf. also *hilasterion* in Romans 3:25, and the cognate verb *hilaskesthai* in Hebrews 2:17). These words are generally taken in the way of an "appeasement." From this, the doctrine of "substitutionary atonement" has been developed as the majority view among most evangelical or conservative groups. The idea is that sinners actually deserve eternal death, but Jesus bore the punishment in our stead, satisfying the divine sense of justice. The price of our salvation, in this view, was paid to God. Jesus was "a ransom for all" (1 Timothy 2:6). This understanding of the work of Christ on the cross is also called the "satisfaction" theory. It was this idea that attained the status of orthodoxy during the Middle Ages, propounded most forcefully by Anselm of Canterbury.[7]

This was not, however, the predominant view of the early church "fathers." Although they do not hesitate to use the Biblical language of sacrifice, the emphasis is rather on the way Jesus stood for us at the crucifixion as our representative before the divine court, instead of as an appeasement of the divine wrath. In this light, the atonement can be viewed as beginning not with the cross but with the incarnation. Knowing we would need a perfect representative, God himself takes on human form eventually to be killed and resurrected to plead our cause. God the Father really is at one with God the Son, and all this is done in order for man to shed his sinful human nature and put on Christ's shared divinity. As it was frequently put, God became man that man might become as God. This approach is often called the "representative" theory.

Patristic literature also stresses Jesus' triumph over Satan. The price of salvation was paid not to God but to Satan, from whom Jesus ransomed us. In a sense, Satan was tricked because, being divine, Jesus inevitably arose from the grave, "triumphing over him in it." Most contemporary theology finds some version of this approach more compatible with modern sensitivities.[8] It can be pointed out in defense of this

view that the Old Testament background of the words translated "sacrifice" in the New Testament is one in which the
sacrifice is a "covering" for sin, effectively hiding it from God's
view, rather than as a ransom fee required to appease an angry
God.[9] The same Hebrew word is often translated "reconciliation"—and the Bile asserts that man does not reconcile or appease God, but that God reconciles man to himself (2 Corinthians 5:19).

A third major way of viewing the atonement, the "exemplary"
theory, holds that Christ died not to appease God or to make
man divine, but as the supreme example of the sacrificial life.
Also called the "moral influence" theory, this view calls for us
to look at the cross and exemplify in our own lives that divine
standard of self-sacrifice. In the twelfth century, Abelard spoke
in these terms while attacking Anselm's satisfaction theory.
Although orthodoxy has never fully approved, this view has
been attractive to those who object to the idea of God as a tyrant
who would not be avenged without a blood offering. In defending God as a kindlier figure, however, this approach usually
risks infidelity to the Biblical language.

It must be noted that the Bible itself does not present a systematic doctrine of the atonement. While the language of sacrifice is certainly prominent, Scripture does not attribute to
God the qualities of the feudal lords of Anselm's day who required a pound of flesh for the transgressions of their subjects.
It is significant that the early church councils dwelt on the
doctrine of God and of Christ to the neglect of formulating an
official position on the atonement. Philosophical requirements
such as presumptions about the nature of God tend to force
Christians into one camp or another in the way they state their
convictions on the subject, but Scripture does not do so. The
Bible itself is content to assert that salvation is through the
cross without elaborating a precise explanation of just how or
why this is true.

The Nature of Salvation

From what are we saved? Concentrating on the doctrine of
the atonement brings the answer, "From sin." We recall, however, that salvation is holistic. From the vantage point of reconciliation with God, other dimensions of salvation appear. We
are saved from destructive relationships with others. Frequently, even today, a reconciled spirit contributes to physical

health. We are saved holistically in time—from past sins, sin in the present, and from the wrath of God at judgment (Romans 5:9). All these aspects of salvation have yielded various emphases in Christian history:

> For the early Greek church death and error were the things from which one needed and wanted to be saved. In the Roman Catholic church salvation is from guilt and its consequences in this and the next life (in purgatory and hell). In classical Protestantism salvation is from the law, its anxiety-producing and its condemning power. In pietism and revivalism salvation is the conquest of the godless state through conversion and transformation for those who are converted. In ascetic and liberal Protestantism salvation is the conquest of special sins and progress toward moral perfection[10]

We consider here the basis for several of these, thrust under their traditional headings.

Justification

A foundation stone in Protestantism is expressed in Romans 3:23, 24. "All have sinned and fall short of the glory of God, being justified as a gift by His grace through the redemption which is in Christ Jesus." Martin Luther's greatest contribution was the restoration of this concept as opposed to the works-salvation emphasis of late medieval Roman Catholicism. The idea here is salvation by radical surgery. No work of human merit suffices, but only the grace of God. Salvation is depicted not as a gradual growth or process, but as a sudden birth; not moral reform, but drastic change from above.

Of course, Luther's emphasis is based on Paul, who above all other writers of Scripture was concerned that salvation be freed from the works of the law of Moses or of human righteousness. Human effort could not effect the passage from godlessness to righteousness "because by the works of the Law no flesh will be justified in His sight; for through the Law comes the knowledge of sin" (Romans 3:20). Luther's famous dictum of salvation by faith alone meant for him that we are saved only by faith and not at all by works. His followers often reduced the phrase to mere mental assent, contending that no objective human response to grace was involved in salvation, a position which neither Luther nor Paul would have defended.

The main content of the *"dik-"* family of Greek words, referring to justification (*dikaiosyne, dikaois,* etc.) is of a legal or juridical nature. By grace through faith, God places us in a state safe from the accusations of the Satanic accuser. Paul adds an accounting term to the concept also. Righteousness is reckoned or "logged" (logizomai) to our account by faith in the work of Christ (Romans 4:9).

Sanctification

Traditionally, sanctification is treated as a further stage of salvation beyond justification. Actually, no dogmatic distinction can be made between justification and sanctification strictly on the basis of the Biblical language. In fact, the order is reversed in 1 Corinthians 6:11. Those who are justified are also sanctified (hagiazo) or made holy—they are the saints, those who comprise the church (1 Corinthians 1:2).

In the Old Testament, that which is "kadosh," holy or sanctified, is that which is set apart or consecrated for God's special service. It may be the sacrificial lamb (Exodus 29:42-44), the temple (1 Kings 9:3), or God's chosen people (Exodus 19:6). Always, the holiness of the article, place, or person is grounded on the holiness of God, not on inherent divinity.[11] For reasons we shall see, it is important to emphasize this meaning of the term "sanctification" instead of the idea of sinless perfection

It is in "holiness" movements that the notion of sanctification describes a work of the Holy Spirit in a "second grace" that confers perfection on the believer in this life.[12] Modern proponents of this teaching stem from the work of Wesley and his followers, although it can be traced in general terms back to Origen and Clement of Alexandria. Some hold that sanctification is an immediate state conferred on the elect by the Spirit, while others describe it as a growth, "a process which reaches its completion only when this life is over."[13] Still others would reserve the term entirely for the end of life, when God will "sanctify you entirely" (1 Thessalonians 5:23).

One way toward greater unanimity on the issue is to realize the eschatological nature of the language of salvation. Final, ultimate salvation at the end of time depends on an event that is now past—the cross. From God's timeless view, "by one offering He has perfected for all time those who are sanctified" (Hebrews 10:14). It is the nature of eschatological language for time to be "collapsed."[14] But from our time-bound point of view, salvation and sanctification are depicted in all three tenses—past, present, and future. We are saved from past sins (Acts 2:47), but we are still being saved (1 Corinthians 1:18), and it is furthermore a hope "ready to be revealed in the last time" (1 Peter 1:5). Similarly, Christians have been sanctified (1 Corinthians 6:11); they are continually being cleansed by the blood (1 John 1:7), and they have the hope that they will be, in the future, wholly sanctified (1 Thessalonians 5:23). To seize on any of these aspects as the tense of sanctification is to dwell on the Christian responsibility to remain faithful rather than on the fact that sanctification is in all tenses, each based on the holiness and perfection of Jesus, not His followers.

In summary, there is an element of truth in each of the standard positions on sanctification. It is a state in which the Christian is accredited with the righteousness of Christ, a process of growth toward the end of ultimate salvation, and the goal of final salvation.

Reconciliation

Just as salvation reconciles man with God, so it is also to heal broken relationships among persons. This "horizontal" aspect of salvation is yet another illustration of its holistic nature. The cessation of enmity between Jew and Gentile was a result of the cross, as seen in Ephesians 2:14-16:

> For He Himself is our peace, who made both groups [Jew and Gentile] into one, and broke down the barrier of the dividing wall, by abolishing in His flesh the enmity, which is the Law of commandments contained in ordinances, that in Himself He might make the two into one new man, thus establishing peace, and might reconcile them both in one body to God through the cross, by it having put to death the enmity.

The moral and ethical power of the gospel of salvation is to be stressed at this point. Unfortunately, "what God hath joined together" here—namely the races and classes of mankind—are too often put asunder by prejudice and suspicion. Salvation is "in Christ," where "there is neither Jew nor Greek, there is neither slave nor free man, there is neither male nor female; for you are all one in Christ Jesus" (Galatians 3:28). For persons reconciled to God to fail to act out their "horizontal" reconciliation in their relationships with each other is for them to deny the practical results of "vertical" reconciliation.

The above implies that ultimate salvation includes human responsibility. Its availability depends solely on the grace of God through Jesus Christ. Its applicability depends on our faithful response. Again, some of the most unfortunate divisions in Christian history have occurred over this issue. Modern controversies about "the security of the believer" were foreshadowed by two periods of intense controversy in church history, the first between Augustine and Pelagius, and the second between Calvinists and Arminians. Because of the Campbells' and other restoration leaders' emphasis on freedom of the will, against some of Augustine's and Calvin's teaching, historians usually call them "Arminian." It should be noted, however, that Campbell refused to make "the views of the Calvinists or Arminians" a test of fellowship.[15] Protagonists in the argument usually sophisticate and refine the Scriptures in support of their argument far more than they can really bear. True to their anti-creedal heritage, heirs of the restoration movement have usually been content to let passages on both sides of the argument stand on their own, without attempting to harmonize them into a philosophical system. The believer is secure: no external force can pluck the elect from God's hand. But he is enjoined to bear fruit lest he be purged from the vine (John 15:2). No works can take the place of faith, but they are to evidence our faith (James 2:14ff).[16]

It is also important to note that reconciliation is to produce the visible result of a joyful style of life—"We also exult in God through our Lord Jesus Christ, through whom we have now received the reconciliation" (Romans 5:11).

Eternal Life

Finally, the nature of salvation is to impart to the saved that quality of life that inheres in God. There is a sense in which this is reserved for the end of time, or, as Jesus puts it, "the age to come" (Mark 10:29, 30; cf. Matthew 25:46). A special characteristic of the Johannine writings, however, is that eternal life is also available in the present through Jesus Christ. "This is eternal life, that they may know Thee, the only true God, and Jesus Christ whom Thou hast sent" (John 17:3). The phrase is applied in the past tense, as something already received by Christians, in 1 John 5:11—"God gave us eternal life, and this life is in His Son" (RSV; see also vs. 13, "you have eternal life").

The language here is again "eschatological," with an

"already/not yet" duality apparent. Those who are made right with God through Christ have within them the Holy Spirit (Acts 2:38; 5:32). This is the "eternal Spirit" (Hebrews 9:14), and His indwelling thus produces an eternal *quality* of life in the Christian, not simply life unending. The Spirit's presence is a "guarantee of our inheritance until we acquire possession of it" (Ephesians 1:14, RSV) in the fullest sense, in that day when the final victory is wrought by God through Christ at the consummation of His grand scheme of redemption.

NOTES

[1]Brown, Driver, and Briggs, *Gesenius' Hebrew and English Lexicon of the Old Testament* (Oxford: The Clarendon Press, 1962), p. 1022. The authors point out a connection between *shalom* as wholeness and submission to the will of God.

[2]Cf. the etymological connection between "whole," "health," and "hale," as in *Webster's Unabridged Dictionary*.

[3]Arndt and Gingrich, *A Greek-English Lexicon* (Chicago: The University of Chicago Press, 1957), p. 806.

[4]Contemporary theology is indebted to the *"Heilsgeschichte"* (salvation-history) movement, although the restoration movement's own Robert Milligan's *Scheme of Redemption* anticipated some of the modern approach a century earlier. A basic difference is that Milligan assumed a historicist view of Biblical events, granting them basic objectivity that *Heilsgeschichte* doubts in favor of an existentialist slant. See Oscar Cullman, *Christ and Time* (Philadelphia: The Westminster Press, 1959), and G. E. Wright, *God Who Acts* (London: SCM Press, 1952).

[5]Gerhard von Rad, *Old Testament Theology* (New York: Harper and Brothers, 1962), vol. 1, p. 121.

[6]The word *atonement* appears only once in the KJV (not at all in the RSV and other modern versions), in Romans 5:11—"And not only so, but we also joy in God through our Lord Jesus Christ, by whom we have now received the atonement (Greek *katallegen*)." It is only the conventional dominance of the term that makes it useful to discuss the efficacy of Christ's death under this heading.

[7]Cf. his classic *Cur Deus Homo?* Although Alexander Campbell did not contend for a single view of the atonement, he was generally in favor of describing it in substitutionary terms (cf. *The Christian System* [Cincinnati: **Standard**, n.d.], p. 23).

[8]The most influential statement is still Gustav Aulen's *Christus Victor* (New York: The Macmillan Co., 1951).

[9]Robert B. Girdlestone, *Synonyms of the Old Testament* (Grand Rapids: Eerdman, n.d.), 129-131.

[10]Paul Tillich, *Systematic Theology* (Chicago: University of Chicago Press, 1971), vol. 2, p. 166.

[11]Otto Procksch, *"Hagios," Theological Dictionary of the New Testament*, Gerhard Kittel, ed. (Grand Rapids: Eerdmans, 1964), vol. 1, p. 88.

[12]Cf. C. E. Brown, *The Meaning of Sanctification* (Anderson, IN: The Warner Press, 1945).

[13]B. B. Warfield, *Perfectionism* (New York: Oxford University Press, 1931), vol. 1, p. 89.

[14]Cullmann, *Christ and Time.*

[15]Campbell, *The Christian System*, p. 101.

[16]A classic account of one who changed from a Calvinistic to a free-will view is Robert Shank's *Life in the Son* (Springfield, MO: Westcott Publishers, 1961).

CHAPTER

12

THE WAY OF SALVATION

By Ed Nelson

A Roman jailer cried out, "What must I do to be saved?" The missionary Paul responded, "Believe on the Lord Jesus, and you shall be saved, you and your household." What was the jailer thinking when he asked his question? Was he concerned with a physical saving from Roman discipline, hoping for a better solution than suicide, which he had contemplated only moments before? Or was he thinking now of some sort of spiritual salvation that perhaps could be effected through the two missionaries who had self-control in a desperate situation? Whatever meaning the jailer brought to the word *saved*, Paul seized upon it and connected salvation with Jesus as Lord. Obviously at that point, any belief would have been merely in a name. What was fully intended in Paul's response was explained; and the jailer and those with him believed, were baptized, and demonstrated a newness of life in the hospitality extended as well as in the joy expressed. This description of an event from Acts 16:25-34 suggests the concerns of this essay: How are we saved? What does the term salvation imply? It must be recognized that such questions can involve book-length answers, and therefore this essay is only a selection of typical materials and a partial answer to the questions.

Primal Focus: Acts of Apostles
The book of the Acts of the Apostles will be the primal focus

for this study. Though the book stands many years removed from much of the material it describes and though it was written after the Pauline epistles and probably the Synoptic Gospels, it is the only book of the New Testament that supplies us with direct descriptive information of the process people followed in securing the salvation graciously offered by God in Christ. The epistles assume that the readers have already been initiated into the church.[1] Reading the epistles supplies insight into the initiation process the readers followed, but gives no description of that process. Therefore, the Acts of the Apostles, written by Luke in the late 60s or 70s perhaps, must be studied for the description of how people became Christians. When such study is done, the findings can be augmented and confirmed by material from the epistles.

A critical problem involving Acts confronts our usage of the book as to whether it represents accurately the times it appears to represent.[2] In the 1800s, the Tübingen School of critical studies emerged around F. C. Baur, who contended that although the book of Acts was a valuable source for the apostolic age, it was generally untrustworthy. Acts was an idealized portrait of the past.[3] At the turn of the century, the work of William Ramsay[4] and Adolf Harnack[5] helped to reestablish the more traditional view of the historical reliability of Acts. Ramsay's conclusions were primarily drawn from archaeological work, whereas those of Harnack were based on literary analysis of the text. New critical approaches, however, were to be brought to Acts, and the work of Martin Dibelius[6] wielded great influence upon the scholarly world. Though he believed Luke was both the author and a historian, Dibelius concluded that the work of Acts was primarily theologically oriented, its speeches constructed by Luke for the respective setting, and generally the reliability of Acts was therefore vitiated. Dibelius' position has been expanded and expounded in work since then, represented most fully in the commentary of Ernst Haenchen.[7]

The position taken in this paper is that Acts is historically reliable. In details of names, titles, customs, and other aspects of life, it reflects a historical reliability that has been proven time and time again.[8] The problem of the speeches remains an acute question. The solution that makes these Lukan in form but accurate summaries of the earliest preaching in content finds great support.[9] Analysis of other critical problems of Acts shows Luke to be a theologian, but one faithful to his source materials and representing fairly the primitve church. Therefore, Luke's treatment of the conversion process in Acts will be here considered an accurate portrayal of the practice of the primitive Church.

The church began on the day of Pentecost around A.D. 30.[10] Luke informs us (Acts 2) that Jews had assembled in Jerusalem from throughout the Diaspora (2:8-11). Since Pentecost was one of the great pilgrimage feasts in Judaism, such a gathering could be expected. These pilgrims were astonished at what happened to a group of individuals that some of the festival crowd recognized as Galileans (2:7). When this small group was accused of drunkenness, one of them, Peter, stood to address the crowd. He witnessed that what was being seen and heard was happening not because they were filled with wine, but because they were filled with the Spirit. This coming of the Spirit fulfilled the prophecy of Joel and was proof that the last days had come upon them.

After this spirited defense, Peter began to recount the supreme work of God in the appearance of Jesus of Nazareth, whose authority and person was attested to by God's works through Him (2:22). This Jesus, though crucified, had been resurrected and exalted by God and established as Lord and Christ (2:23-36). In these events, prophecy was fulfilled, which shows this Jesus to have fulfilled the promises made to David.

Many of the hearers were convinced of the truth of Peter's claims and, being stricken in conscience, sought guidance. Peter responded by saying, "Repent and let each of you be baptized in the name of Jesus Christ for the forgiveness of your sins; and you shall receive the gift of the Holy Spirit (2:38)." Peter continued his testimony to the work of Jesus and continued to exhort his hearers to save themselves from the perverse generation that had crucified the Christ. Many "received his word," that is, they accepted the truth of Peter's testimony with its implication for their lives and were baptized and added to the group of Spirit-filled disciples (cf. 2:41f).

In his appeal, Peter used the word "save." The whole passage supplies us with the following points of information: (1) the means of salvation, which involves response to the Word about Jesus, and baptism; (2) the author of the salvation, Jesus, who is Lord and Christ; and (3) certain gifts of salvation, forgiveness of sins and the gift of the Holy Spirit. This message of salvation also created a community that adhered to the teaching of the apostles, continued in breaking of bread, prayers, and fellow-ship (2:42). The "fellowship" is concretely defined by Luke as the sharing of goods, which sprang from a mutal concern for poorer members of the fellowship of Jesus. The final note of the passage emphasizes that the ultimate agent of salvation, of the "adding," was the Lord himself.

This section of Acts is important for several reasons.

(1) It records the coming of the Spirit upon the apostles in fulfillment of Jesus' promise (1:5).

(2) It records the first message spoken in proclaiming Jesus as the Christ. Elements of the message will be picked up in other speeches in Acts, but we can justly call this a model sermon as far as basic materials are concerned.

(3) It provides us with the first description of what one must do to be saved and what are the basic gifts of that salvation.

(4) It provides us with insight into the basic life of the early church and a description that is nowhere else as succinctly expressed and is therefore, again, a model in substance.

The importance of this passage, then, provides the rationale as to why Peter's response of 2:38ff can be used as basic to the outline of "the way of salvation." While Luke is known for diversity of expression in describing the conversion process, the elements that are expressed in 2:38, as well as those that may be deduced from the passage, will be found again and again throughout the conversions of Acts. Further, the choice of the passage affords some economy of outline for the task of this essay. Therefore, this basic passage will be briefly examined for its contribution to one's understanding of the conversion process.

God's Initiative

Basic to the whole passage is the underlying initiatory work of God. He is the One who has raised up Jesus, worked wonders through Him, and when Jesus was crucified, brought Him to life and to glory, confirming Him as Lord and Christ. It is God who sent the Spirit in fulfillment of promises He made to Israel years before. That gift of the Spirit enables Peter—far different from the Peter of Passover—to stand before the people and bravely proclaim Jesus as Christ, while some in that crowd had only recently rejected Him as a fraud. It is God who directs Peter's witness and leads him to the announcement of the way of salvation, its availability and its gifts. It is God who continues His work in the mighty deeds of the apostles (Acts 2:43), which elicit wonder and praise. Finally, it is God who adds those that respond to the gospel to the infant church. The passage is eloquent testimony to the manifold meaning of that phrase in Paul—"by grace you have been saved, through faith" (Ephesians 2:8). God's grace has provided for mankind the Man of salvation, the message and means of salvation, and the gifts of salvation, which include the Spirit, who would draw believers over to that ultimate salvation. Luke's witness to the work of God (through responsive servants) is constant throughout his Gospel and Acts.

Man's Decision

The second stage of the conversion process is discerned from Peter's response to the taunts of some (2:14, 15) and his preaching of Jesus as Lord and Christ. Such action assumes that the message can be communicated with understanding and that its hearers are responsible, decision-capable individuals. Peter's sermon is couched in terms familiar to Jewish hearers. They would understand the idea of fulfilled prophecy and terms such as "Lord" and "Christ." The demand for repentance and baptism had been heard for several years from John the Baptist and his followers, as well as others. The promise of forgiveness of sins and the Holy Spirit were concepts the Jews knew well from prophetic promises. The preaching here for Jews is paralleled by the preaching to Gentiles in Acts 17:22ff, where the message is permeated by Biblical understanding, yet couched in terminology the Gentile hearers could grasp. The preaching of the message implies, then, a responsibility on the part of the preacher not only to be true to Biblical concepts, but also to be responsible to his hearers, always attempting to put the Biblical concepts in language that can be understood. The preaching thus assumes that man as man has the ability to hear and to decide. This basic assumption, common throughout Scripture, is that man is a responsible being. Alexander Campbell emphasized strongly the place of man's responsiveness through reason in the process of regeneration. He wrote, "The grand principle, or means which God has adopted for the accomplishment of this moral regeneration, is the full demonstration and proof of *a single proposition addressed to the reason of man*. This sublime proposition is, THAT GOD IS LOVE."[11]

This assumption concerning man's ability to decide is complemented by Luke's appreciation for the work of the Spirit in the conversion process. Though this is not explicit in Acts 2, the idea is found at Acts 16:14. In that passage, Paul presents the message to Lydia and "the Lord opened her heart to respond to the things spoken by Paul." The emphasis is found at John 16:8, where the coming of the Counselor "will convict the world concerning sin, and righteousness, and judgment." Through the imagery of the active power of the Word, the writer of Hebrews (4:12, 13) also suggests this emphasis of God's activity with the preached gospel. The second stage of the conversion process involves the Word of Christ, spoken with the understanding of the hearers in view but spoken with confidence in man's ability to decide (his gift of free will) and in the Spirit's work through the message spoken to bring conviction.

Receiving the Word

The next stage of the process is suggested by the word *receive* in 2:41. The people "received his word" and were baptized. The receiving represents, in the context, the hearing and decision to believe the truth of the facts spoken as well as the truth of the meaning of those facts for life. What was spoken was not only testimony about Jesus as Christ and Lord, but was also an explanation of what the hearers must do to save themselves from the perverse generation that had crucified Jesus. Therefore, receiving the word also involved the willingness of those pilgrims to repent and to be baptized, believing that God would grant the promised salvation. It should be realized that belief, or faith, was the essential element in the response. The element of faith is often emphasized in Acts (e.g., 8:12; 13:12, 48; 14:1; 16:31, 34; 17:12; 18:8, among others). At times, belief is all that is mentioned on the part of those that became disciples, while other times it is mentioned with baptism. Faith is the essential response to the proclamation. Individuals must be willing to commit themselves to the Christ and to endure the tribulation that follows (14:22). Luke can refer to Christians as simply "believers" (5:14) or as those who have believed (21:20, 25).

The importance of belief is everywhere emphasized in Scripture. The Hebrew writer succinctly states that without faith, it is impossible to please God (Hebrews 11:6). Paul, struggling against those who would tie the Mosaic law to the means of salvation, constantly emphasizes that faith is a response that brings one to right standing before God (Galatians 3:6-9, 26; Romans 5:1). Faith is important, for it precedes baptism, must accompany baptism (Colossians 2:12), and must continue throughout the life of the Christian. The type of faith here is not mere mental assent, but a responsive belief that works through love (Galatians 5:6) and is demonstrated by its work (James 2:18-26) in pure religion (James 1:5-8, 27; 4:1-4). It is faith that, within the salvation experience, responds to the instructions of Christ whether it be in repentance, baptism, putting aside the works of the flesh (1 Peter 2:11), or praying without ceasing (1 Thessalonians 5:17). The receiving of the word is a life-long experience for the Christian that begins with the basic proclamation.

The "receiving of the Word," from the context of Acts 2:38ff, also involves repentance, which in Judaism included confession of sins.[12] The demand for repentance was always part of the prophetic message to Israel. A ritual of repentance emerged in Israel that could involve tearing one's clothing, mourning, wearing sackcloth, fasting, and sitting in ashes. The prophets continually called the people to repent, to turn from their evil ways and to the ways of God (Isaiah 45:22; 55:5-8; 58:13, 14; Jeremiah 26:3; 44:4, 5; Ezekiel 14:6; 18:30-32) depreciating external forms and demanding complete change of life (Joel 2:13). The prophetic call for repentance was continued in John the Baptist (Matthew 3:1f). John also gave instruction on specific matters relating to a life befitting repentance (Luke 3:10-14). The urgency of John's demand for repentance, though, was heightened by his emphasis upon the nearness of the kingdom of God. People had to prepare for God's coming reign, which would mean wrath for the unrepentant but life for the repentant (Luke 3:7-9, 15-17). Only by repentance and baptism could John's hearers escape the certain judgment of God.[13]

Jesus continued the demand for repentance in His preaching (Mark 1:15; Luke 13:1-5). He insisted that repentance must involve the whole person's turning to the way of the kingdom. This total demand is emphasized in the sayings on discipleship (e.g. Matthew 10:24-42) and in the Sermon on the Mount (Matthew 5—7). In His coming was the exercise of the "winnowing fork" (Luke 3:17), as it continues to be exercised in the gospel. Jürgen Moltmann is only partially right when he contends that "where John proclaimed the kingdom of God as judgment, with a view to repentance, Jesus evidently proclaimed the kingdom of God as the justice of grace and demonstrated it by acts of forgiving sins."[14] Jesus indeed proclaimed in word and by His presence among the social-religious outcasts of His day that God's message was of grace to all; nevertheless that message did not exclude the element of judgment. The call to discipleship, for example, with its life or death aspect implies a judgment. The woes upon the cities of Chorazin, Bethsaida, and Capernaum (Luke 10:13-15) assume that God's judgment is present in the response to Jesus. In Luke, it is strongly suggested that the destruction of Jerusalem follows from its rejection of Jesus. The major difference between John's preaching and that of Jesus lies in the fact that John prepared for the kingdom whereas with Jesus, the kingdom was present (Luke 4:16-21; 11:20; 17:21; Matthew 12:28). Since God's reign was present, judgment was active, either unto life or unto destruction. The aspect of future judgment is also anticipated in the presence of Jesus (cf. John 3:16-18). (This understanding of the presence of judgment with Jesus is carried into the word of Jesus spoken by the church as witnessed to the now of salvation in 2 Corinthians 6:2.) However, since with Jesus the reign of God is present, repentance ushers one into acceptance before God, and into life of joyful obedience.[15]

The demand for repentance continues in the church's proclamation. Whether the preacher is before a Jewish audience (Acts 2:38; 3:19) or a Gentile audience (Acts 17:30), an essential part of the proclamation is the demand for repentance. Repentance involves a turning from the past ways of wrong and ignorance (Acts 2:38; 8:22; 17:30; 2 Corinthians 12:21; Revelation 2:22) and turning to the Christ of the Word (Acts 2:38; 20:21; 1 Peter 2:25). Repentance is demanded, and yet it is God's gift (Acts 3:26; 5:31; 11:18) as shown both in the fact that God grants the opportunity for repentance and the Spirit convicts one of the need for it. The call for repentance in the epistles reflects the fact that repentance, like faith, is an ongoing element of Christian life. As Behm comments: "To convert is not just to give one's life a new direction but in practice to reorientate oneself continually to the goal of the radical setting aside of evil."[16] The once-and-for-all decision must be followed by continual growth in the Christian life. This repentance toward God was to be expressed in one's relation toward man by a life change, demonstrated by restitution whenever possible, as seen in Leviticus 6:1-7; Numbers 5:7-9; and the example of Zaccheus, who in this same spirit (Luke 19:1-10) demonstrated the reality of his change of heart by a resolve to repay and to give. Alexander Campbell insisted that repentance is not just a feeling, but it must lead to a change in conduct. He commented: "Repentance is to reformation what motive is to action, or resolution to undertaking."[17] In regard to restitution, Campbell said, "Without repentance, and restitution when possible, there can be no remission."[18] It would not be far from the mark to suggest that the jailer's washing the wounds of Paul and Silas demonstrated the reality of his turning to the Lord (Acts 16:33). Restitution may also have been involved in the selling of goods and sharing with the poor recorded in Acts (2:45; 4:34). Restoring of relationships and righting of wrongs give testimony to the work of Christ and serve to strengthen the commitment of the individual so involved. Such action must by its nature be a personal decision, but its practice should be strongly encouraged in the church.

Baptism

Along with the preceding elements, baptism forms an integral part of conversion. The demand for baptism is repeated often in Acts, either directly (2:38; 10:48; 22:16) or by implication (8:36); and most conversions in Acts mention baptism (8:12; 16:15, 33; 18:8; 19:5). Baptism was by immersion, as indicated by the meaning of the term *baptizo* as well as what can be inferred from New Testament passages (such as Acts 8:36; Hebrews 10:22; Romans 6:2ff) and the witness of the early church writers (Didache 7:1-3; Barnabas 11:11). The New Testament witness is that baptism followed one's profession of faith, as the proper demonstration of that faith. Alan Richardson writes:

> In the Church of the New Testament, faith and baptism belong together, like soul and body in Biblical thought: the one cannot exist without the other. ... The profession of faith without the bodily action of submission in baptism is not the obedience of the whole man; a mental act which has no outward embodiment is a mere phantom of the full-blooded, full-bodied wholeness of Biblical thinking.[19]

Baptism played an important part in the initial saving process.[20]

The background for baptism can probably be traced to the many lustrations of ancient Jewish practice. In the prophetic period, the language of "washing" was utilized to express spiritual cleansing. It is not surprising that the Qumran community practiced an initiatory rite of baptism as well as frequent lustrations since they regarded themselves as preparing for the Day of the Lord. The role of proselyte baptism in relation to Christian baptism is still questioned.[21] The baptism of John serves as the nearest antecedent to Christian baptism, both in time and its place in salvation-history. John's baptism, given of God, communicated a reality to the people, for he baptized in a period of time when there were several baptistic sects. His baptism was unique in that it was with reference to a "Coming One," whose baptism would supercede his because the Messiah would baptize with the Holy Spirit and fire (Luke 3:15-17).[22]

Jesus himself came to be baptized of John and thus "fulfill all righteousness" (Matthew 3:15). At this time Jesus was anointed of the Spirit and received word from the Father that would determine the nature of His messiaship. The commission combined the royal status, "This is my beloved Son" (cf. Psalm 2:7), with that of the Servant, "in whom I am well-pleased" (cf. Isaiah 42:1). One should note that nowhere is Jesus' baptism *directly* related to Christian baptism, though one could maintain that the present narrative emphasizes elements applicable to church usage (e.g., the association of baptism with the Spirit; the definitive nature of baptism in setting Jesus apart to His ministry). The early church did make the connection, even in its painting and sculpture.[23] While baptism was part of Jesus' ministry, He himself did not baptize (John 4:2). Jesus' command to baptize had the greatest influence on Christian practice (Matthew 28:18-20). Although the present form of the Matthaen form has drawn criticism, especially its triune formula, there is little reason to doubt that it accurately reflects Jesus' words. The practice of Christian baptism ultimately rests

on the command of the Risen Lord after His achieving redemption and receiving authority over the entire cosmos; it is integrated with the commission to preach the good news to the world, and it is enforced by His own example at the beginning of His Messianic ministry. Such a charge is too imperious to be ignored or modified. It behoves us to adhere to it and conform to it as God gives grace.[24]

The book of Acts gives the account of the fulfillment of the commissioning by Jesus, that all nations should hear the gospel and be discipled through their receiving of that gospel, through baptism, and through instruction in the way of the kingdom.

Peter's sermon at Pentecost included the call to baptism, "in the name of Jesus Christ" (cf. also Acts 8:16; 10:48; 19:5). Though different Greek prepositions are used in various passages (e.g. Acts 2:38, epi; Acts 10:48, en; Acts 19:5, eis), the intent of expressing a formula is probably the same throughout.[25] The background of the formula has been sought in both Greek and Jewish sources.[26] Though the Jewish background is the more probable, the resultant meaning of either approach is basically that the baptized are dedicating themselves to Jesus. The use of the formula would have been meaningful to either Jewish or Gentile listeners. In all probability, the name was invoked by the person being baptized (cf. Acts 22:16) as well as being pronounced by the one baptizing. In any case, there was the clear sense of visibly demonstrating a turning to the Lord with a whole heart.

It must be emphasized that the physical response of baptism was an integral part of one's decision for Christ in the early church. There was nothing of our docetic mentality, which would alienate mental commitment from physical act.[27] Biblical thinking was never embarrassed by physical expression, and this is part of the strong world-accepting orientation of Biblical Christianity. Meshing of the spiritual and the physical expresses the understanding of God as Creator and His being enfleshed "in Christ." Lampe rightly contends that Luke is not antedating baptism in Acts. He says,

> The outward rite was ready to hand from the outset; early Christianity was never a religion without cultus, and, from the time when, at Pentecost, the old ceremony became the means of enlistment in the name of Jesus Christ and reception of the promised Spirit, the Church was linked with the risen and ascended Lord through the two interrelated sacraments, Baptism and the Eucharist, in back of which the action of God in Christ, accomplished once and for all, is represented and actualized for the believer. Whatever the tradition of the baptismal formula in any part of the Church, whether the Trinitarian form was employed or baptism was strictly and literally "in the name of Jesus Christ," this Christocentric significance of the sacrament seems to have been constant.[28]

Lampe's comment needs to be heard in the face of doubts raised against the probability that baptism was part of the original tradition.[29] Such a denial of baptism violates the repeated mention of baptism in Acts as well as the underlying place of baptism in argumentation throughout the epistles. Such denial usually comes from a misguided quest for "spiritual" Christianity.

Salvation as Eschatological and Historical

The purpose of the appeal for repentance and baptism was that the persons might be saved. The hearers were to be saved from the perverse generation (Acts 2:40). In Acts 2:38-47, salvation begins with acceptance of Jesus as Lord and Christ, repentance, and baptism (cf. Titus 3:5; 1 Peter 3:21). Paul's statement in Ephesians 2:8, "by grace you have been saved," uses the perfect tense, which implies that the salvation of his readers was a past and present reality. In 1 Corinthians 1:18 and 2 Corinthians 2:15, Paul speaks of Christians as those "who are being saved." He, like Peter in Acts, can appeal to readers to realize the "now" of salvation (2 Corinthians 6:2; cf. Hebrews 3:7—4:13). Our salvation is grounded in the work of Christ and in our response to it. We presently enjoy the gifts of salvation, and yet there is a strong future orientation. So Paul writes, "Salvation is nearer to us than when we believed (Romans 13:11), and Peter writes of "a salvation ready to be revealed in the last time" (1 Peter 1:5; cf. Hebrews 1:14; 5:9; 9:28). Our baptism begins life in the Spirit, who is the earnest of life to come (2 Corinthians 1:22; Ephesians 1:13ff). In baptism, we are sealed with the Spirit, looking forward to our complete redemption (Ephesians 4:30; cf. Romans 8:22, 23). Thus, salvation is a historical and yet an eschatological reality. Richardson expresses it in this way:

> To be saved is to enter even now by faith into the life of the age to come and even now to possess it eschatologically; nevertheless, we do not yet possess salvation or "life" in the full and final sense in which it will be ours hereafter; it is only he who endures to the end who will be saved (Mark 13:13).[30]

In Acts, Luke focuses on two gifts of salvation, the forgiveness of sins and the gift of the Holy Spirit. Lengthy studies have been devoted to each of these and their relation to baptism.

Therefore, of necessity, we are committed only to what appears to be the most natural meaning.

The gift of forgiveness involves both aspects of salvation, present and eschatological. The prophets wrote of the time to come when God would take away the sins of the people (Isaiah 33:24; Micah 7:18-20; Jeremiah 31:31-34; Ezekiel 36:22-28; Zechariah 13:1). Only in the Servant Song of Isaiah 53 was there hint of one bearing the sins of the people, but the Jews had not understood this to refer to a Messiah. Jesus' coming was announced with the express purpose to "save His people from their sins" (Matthew 1:21). In His ministry, He proclaimed forgiveness to solve the root problem of mankind—unresolved sin. G. E. Ladd writes,

> The presence of the Kingdom of God was not a new teaching about God; it was a new activity of God in the person of Jesus bringing to men as present experience what the prophets promised in the eschatological kingdom.[31]

This gift was granted, as seen here in Acts, in response to one's repentance and baptism. In being baptized, with faith in the working of God, sins are taken away; one is regenerated (Titus 3:5), born anew (John 3:3, 5). There is no magical nature to baptism, as if in itself it automatically conferred forgiveness and salvation. Such a viewpoint was vigorously opposed by Paul in 1 Corinthians 10, where some in Corinth had understood baptism as conferring salvation without obligation, as a magical act of itself. Baptism must be understood within the sphere of faith in God. It is not an act whereby one wrests from God His gifts; rather, it is where in trust, invoking the name and pledging obedience, we may receive. Alexander Campbell writes,

> All the means of salvation are means of enjoyment, not of procurement, . . . no one is to be put under the water of regeneration for the purpose of procuring life, but for the purpose of enjoying the life of which he is possessed.[32]

Baptism's association with gifts of salvation is not being denied. In Acts 22:16, Paul was commanded to be baptized and wash away his sins, calling on the name of the Lord. In 1 Corinthians 6:11, Paul uses what appears to be traditional language associating the "washing" of baptism with justification and sanctification. The phrase "in the name of the Lord Jesus Christ" definitely links the passage with baptismal usage.[33] The passage in Ephesians 5:26 establishes Christ as the author of the Church's cleansing, which takes place in baptism with the Word.[34] Titus 3:5 links cleansing with baptism.[35] Peter speaks of our having purified our souls through "obedience to the truth" (1 Peter 1:22), a phrase usually associated with the total response to Christ inclusive of baptism.[36] The New Testament emphasis is that baptism is a place of meeting where God is the active agent cleansing through the Word accepted, believed, and obeyed. Johannes Schneider writes,

> The rite of baptism—a rite involving the total immersion of the candidate—is naturally a sign, powerful in its symbolism; but the agent in the act itself is God, who looses the believer in Christ, who receives baptism, from his former condition of being ruled by sin and places him in a new life-context, that of Christ' community.[37]

With forgiveness, the believer can share fully with God in the present and expect to be received in the day of salvation. This emphasis on forgiveness is surely part of the strong imagery used by Paul when he speaks of being baptized into Christ's death, our old self being crucified with Him (Romans 6:3, 4, 6). In baptism, one participates in the redemptive significance of Christ's death, which was for sins. That is the reason the imagery of baptismal theology is used in ethical appeals, as in Romans 6:1-11 or Colossians 3:1ff. Schanckenburg expresses this whole idea well when he writes:

> Dying with Christ, being crucified with Christ in baptism, stamps the whole Christian existence as a being dead to sin; and rising with Christ, which is inseparable from it, is a being alive for God, and will find its last fulfillment in the bodily resurrection. That which takes place in baptism brings the Christian into so close a relation to the crucified and risen Christ, his entire way becomes fashioned after Christ.[38]

The forgiven person, the new person, emerges from the waters of baptism set on the new life ordained in Christ.

The second salvation gift that is emphasized in Acts 2:38, common throughout Luke/Acts, is the gift of the Holy Spirit. In this passage, the phrase "gift of the Holy Spirit" indicates that the gift is the Holy Spirit himself. That His coming is so closely associated with baptism in this passage is undeniable.

The coming of the Spirit is one of the eschatological gifts for which the Jews looked forward. The Spirit's bestowal by God upon His people was part of the last days (so the Joel 2:28-32 context; Jeremiah 31:31-34; Ezekiel 11:19, 20). In the intertestamental period, the Jews regarded the Spirit as having gone from Israel (1 Macc. 9:27), but He would be outpoured upon Israel in the end time (Ps. Sol. 17:37; 18:7; Jub. 1:23; 4 Esd. 6:26; Test. Judah 24:2). The Messiah was especially to be endowed with the Spirit (Isaiah 11:2; 61:1, 2). This was also emphasized in the intertestamental period (Ps. Sol. 17:37; 18:7; Eth. En. 49:3; Test. Levi 18:7). It is not surprising, then, that when the Spirit came upon the disciples at Pentecost, this was understood as the sign of the last days. Thus, in Peter's sermon, his quotation from Joel 2:28-32 begins with the phrase "in the last days" (Acts 2:17) which is not in the Hebrew or Greek text of Joel but represents the understanding of what the Spirit's coming meant. Jesus' understanding of himself as fulfilling Isaiah 61:1, 2 (Luke 4:16-30) was carried into the self-understanding of the church. The Spirit is the eschatalogical gift who seals believers for the future and enables them to live new lives in the present.

In Acts 2, the Spirit is promised to the hearers, but the passage makes no reference to a manifestation of the Spirit like that which fell on Peter and his companions. Luke may be leaving his readers to assume as much. Yet in light of Luke's reticence in speaking of special manifestations of the Spirit apart from special occasions (Acts 2:1ff; 8:14-24; 10:44-48; 19:1-7), he may be downplaying this aspect. For example, he mentions nothing of special spiritual gifts at Corinth, although the Corinthian correspondence indicates that spiritual gifts, including "tongues" were present. Luke does note that the unity of the brethren, their response to the need of others (Acts 2:42-47; 4:31-35), and the experience of joy (Acts 8:39; 16:34) are demonstrations of the Spirit.

There is a sense in which Acts is a historical commentary on the truth of John 3:8, "the Spirit blows where it will. . . ." This is borne out in major incidents in Acts where the Spirit does not come with baptism per se. In Samaria (8:14-24), although the Samaritans believed and were baptized, they did not receive the Spirit until Peter and John came from Jerusalem and laid their hands on them. The problem does not involve a different gift of the Spirit,[39] nor does it involve a problem with their faith.[40] Probably the situation was created by God so as to demonstrate not only the need for the Samaritans to give positive response to Jews and vice versa, but also the need to demonstrate the unity of the church as it moved to a new group of people. In the case of Cornelius (10:44-48), the Holy Spirit came before the command to be baptized. Such a demonstration was needed to help Peter and the early church realize that the Gentiles were to be received on the basis of faith apart from the law. Yet God demonstrates His freedom. The narrative of Apollos and the twelve disciples at Ephesus (Acts 18:24—19:7) is another problem passage; here persons knowing only John's baptism were regarded as disciples without any mention of their having been baptized into Christ. The twelve at Ephesus, however, were baptized in the name of Jesus, receiving the Spirit with the imposition of the hands of Paul. These passages, then, have disciples receiving the Spirit's coming apart from baptism, before baptism, with baptism, and with laying on of hands. Acts 2:38 still functions as a normative model; that is not being denied. But the entirety of Acts suggests a greater freedom on the part of God to respond to faith as He pleases, apart from neat formulas. In doing so, He emphasizes a point He made through His prophets, that ritual per se does not save. His people must respond to Him and not merely to prescribed practice, however significant it may be in normative theology.

The rest of the New Testament does link the Spirit with baptism. In 1 Corinthians 6:11, Paul writes that the washing, justifying, and sanctifying is done "in the Spirit of our God." This probably refers to the Spirit's agency in the conversion process of the individual (see also Romans 8:8f).[41] The references to the sealing of the Spirit (2 Corinthians 1:21, 22; Ephesians 1:13, 14; 4:30) should also be associated with baptism. Lampe comments,

> This moment [i.e., of sealing] is the reception of Baptism, or rather of the inward experience of which Baptism is the effective symbol, is made abundantly clear from a general consideration of St. Paul's baptismal theology. . . .[42]

In Titus 3:5 "the washing of regeneration and renewing by the Holy Spirit" links baptism and the Spirit, emphasizing the

Spirit as the source of new life. There is no doubt that the emphasis falls on the Spirit and the reality of His work in the believer, but baptism is integrally a part of His work. It is quite possible that even the formula "Abba, Father" was connected with Christian baptism.[43]

The process of conversion involves the interweaving of various elements: the love and work of God that permeates it all; the proclaiming of the good news about God's work in Jesus Christ; the necessity for hearing and responding to that proclamation with belief, repentance, and baptism. God grants the Savior, the Word, and the Spirit; man responds with trust and obedience; and to that God responds with the presence of His Spirit and the promise of salvation.

Salvation and the Community of Faith

One final point should not be overlooked. Much of what has been said emphasizes the place of the individual, and that is as it should be. But to enjoy the gifts of salvation involves not only an individual responsibility and experience, but also participation in a corporate reality, the community of God (1 Corinthians 12:13). The new life granted by God is lived out in the midst of the world, but especially within the "saved" community in which believers must share. Such sharing involves the devotion of both lives and goods to the benefit of fellow members of the community. This fellowship carries over into worship together, celebrating the gift of life in Jesus around His table, and His Word. The sharing extends to intercessory prayer as well as to intercessory living. Salvation involves life in the community of faith; and to work out our salvation (Philippians 2:12) includes working with and loving the people of that community.

Our salvation involves also the sharing of Jesus' care and intention for the world. We are not granted salvation to become Jonahs on a hillside in spiritual isolation, looking on the world with contempt, impatient for God to put forth His hand in judgment. Rather, we are saved for good works (Ephesians 2:8-10), for proclaiming God's mighty acts (1 Peter 2:9), and in His name "performing mighty deeds" in bringing a lost world before the throne of grace. Neither is there to be a spiritual elitism towards brethren. To separate ourselves from the community of believers because of self-styled superiority is to be blind to one of the greatest of sins, spiritual pride, and is to be blind also to Jesus' pattern of self-forgetting ministry. He who had all the right answers lived with men so long and so patiently, *leading* them to fuller insight into the truth, rather than forcing answers upon them. The saved should emulate the Savior.

Conclusion

The basic questions of this essay have been, "How are we saved?" and, "What is salvation?" The way of salvation is provided by God's grace manifest in the saving work of Christ, communicated to us in reliable testimony, and accompanied by the work of His Spirit. We must be willing to accept that testimony to the Christ, turn to Him from our lives of self-will; and demonstrate our resolve to be His and our need for the salvitic gifts He offers by submitting to baptism. Upon such a response of faith, God acts to cleanse, to grant His Spirit, to justify, to sanctify, to grant eternal life, and to grant a place among His people. We are thus enabled to fulfill the responsibilities He lays upon us, which involve ourselves, other believers, and the world. Salvation, the gift of the end, begins now, continues as we live in obedient faith, and will be granted in fullness in His coming.[44] Thanks be to God for His unspeakable gift.

NOTES

[1]This basic understanding would help keep us from certain obvious errors of interpretation. For example, we would no longer see any applicability of the use of 1 John 1:9 as describing the means by which non-Christians can be saved. The passage is clearly intended for Christians. The principle of confession may be applicable to non-Christians, but the promise of this verse is expressly to Christians.

[2]For an excellent survey, see W. Ward Gasque, A History of the Criticism of the Acts of the Apostles (Grand Rapids: Eerdmans, 1975), which is permeated by his insistence on the historical reliability of Acts.

[3]Paul: The Apostle of Jesus Christ, trans. by E. Zeller, 2 vols. (London: William & Norgate, 1873). For an excellent analysis of Baur's general historical work, see Peter C. Hodgson, The Formation of Historical Theology: A Study of Ferdinand Christian Baur (New York: Harper & Row, 1966).

[4]For example, St. Paul the Traveller and the Roman Citizen (Grand Rapids: Baker, 1962); The Bearing of Recent Discovery on the Trustworthiness of the New Testament (Grand Rapids: Baker, 1953). A full bibliography of Ramsay's work can be found in W. W. Gasque, Sir William M. Ramsay: Archaeologist and New Testament Scholar (Grand Rapids: Eerdmans, 1966). It should be noted that at times, Ramsay's work has been superceded by more modern discoveries. Yet the general value of Ramsay's work should continue to be emphasized.

[5]Especially Luke the Physician, trans. by J. R. Wilkinson (London: William & Norgate, 1907); Acts of the Apostles, trans. by J. R. Wilkinson (London: Williams & Norgate, 1911); Date of the Acts and of the Synoptic Gospels, trans. by J. R. Wilkinson (London: Williams & Norgate, 1911).

[6]Martin Dibelius, Studies in the Acts of the Apostles, trans. by Mary Ling, ed. by Heinrich Greeven (London: SCM Press, 1965).

[7]Ernst Haenchen, The Acts of the Apostles: A Commentary, revised trans. by R. Mcl. Wilson (Philadelphia: Westminster Press, 1971).

[8]See the excellent work of H. J. Cadbury, The Book of Acts in History (New York: Harper & Row, 1955); A. N. Sherwin-White, Roman Society and Roman Law in the New Testament (Oxford: Clarendon, 1963); a recent essay by W. Ward Gasque, "The Book of Acts and History" in

Unity and Diversity in New Testament Theology, essays in honor of G. E. Ladd, ed. by Robert A. Guelich (Grand Rapids: Eerdmans, 1978), pp. 54-72; also the fine commentary by F. F. Bruce, *Commentary on the Book of the Acts* (Grand Rapids: Eerdmans, 1970) as well as his earlier work on the Greek text itself.

[9]The work of Dibelius brought the problem to acute form. See also *Beginnings of Christianity*, Foakes-Jackson and Lake, eds. (reprinted by Baker as *The Acts of the Apostles*, 1979) Vol. 2, pp. 7-29 and Vol. 5, pp. 402-426. For conservative response to the position, see F. F. Bruce, "The Speeches in Acts—Thirty Years After," in *Reconciliation and Hope: New Testament Essays on Atonement and Eschatology*, presented to L. Morris on his sixtieth birthday, ed. by R. Banks (Grand Rapids: Eerdmans, 1974), pp. 53-68; W. Ward Gasque, "The Speeches of Acts—Dibelius Reconsidered," in *New Dimensions in New Testament Study*, ed. by R. N. Longenecker and M. C. Tenney (Grand Rapids: Eerdmans, 1974), pp. 232-250. Note especially their bibliographical items for fuller study.

[10]See discussion of chronology in C. S. C. Williams, *A Commentary on the Acts of the Apostles* (New York: Harper & Brothers, 1957). Also Kirsopp Lake, "The Chronology of Acts," in *Beginnings of Christianity*, Vol. 5, pp. 445-473.

[11]Alexander Campbell, *The Millennial Harbinger* (Bethany, VA: Alexander Campbell, 1833), p. 338 (italics mine).

[12]Haenchen, *Acts*, p. 184. Max Schlesinger notes that the Mosaic legislation distinguishes between offenses against God and those against man. For the former, confession of sin was required (Leviticus 5:5; Numbers 5:7) accompanied by resolve never to commit the sin again together with the offering of correct sacrifice (Leviticus 5:1-20). "Repentance," *The Jewish Encyclopedia*, ed. by Isidore Singer, Vol. 10 (New York: KTAV, 1901), p. 376.

[13]J. Behm and E. Wurthwein, "*Metanoia*," *TDNT*, Vol. 4 (Grand Rapids: Eerdmans, 1969), pp. 975-1008. Also W. A. Quanbeck, "Repentance," *The Interpreter's Dictionary of the Bible*, ed. by G. A. Buttrick, Vol. 3 (New York: Abingdon, 1962), pp. 33, 34. Otto J. Baab, *Theology of the Old Testament* (Nashville: Abingdon Press, 1949) gives a fine description of the personal impact of repentance (p. 143).

[14]Jürgen Moltmann, *The Church in the Power of the Spirit* (New York: Harper & Row, 1975), p. 234.

[15]Behm, p. 1003.

[16]*Ibid.*, p. 1004.

[17]A Campbell, *Millennial Harbinger* (1833), p. 346.

[18]*Ibid.*

[19]Alan Richardson, *An Introduction to the Theology of the New Testament* (London: SCM Press, 1958), p. 348.

[20]The question of baptism has been in the forefront of discussions, especially in the last twenty years or so. The output of published studies is enormous. Some important works are: Karl Barth, *The Teaching of the Church Regarding Baptism*, trans. by E. A. Payne (London: SCM Press, 1948), which called for a reform of baptismal practice; Oscar Cullman, *Baptism in the New Testament*, trans. by J. K. S. Reid (London: SCM, 1961), which defends infant baptism, as does Joachim Jeremias, *The Origins of Infant Baptism*, trans. by Dorothea Barton (Naperville: Alec Alleson, 1963), responding to criticism of an earlier work by Kurt Aland, *Did the Early Church Baptize Infants?*, trans. by G. R. Beasley-Murray (Philadelphia: Westminster, 1963). Another criticism of infant baptism as defended by the Reformed view is by Paul K. Jewett, *Infant Baptism and the Covenant of Grace* (Grand Rapids: Eerdmans, 1978). Perhaps the fullest statement on baptism comes from G. R. Beasley-Murray, *Baptism in the New Testament* (Grand Rapids: Eerdmans, 1962). Also see the excellent survey of denominational struggles with the whole problem in Dale Moody, *Baptism: Foundation for Christian Unity* (Philadelphia: Westminster, 1967). A good concise historical study is by Geoffrey Wainwright, *Christian Initiation* (London: Futterworth Press, 1969). On Paul's understanding, note Rudolf Schnackenburg, *Baptism in the Thought of Paul*, trans. by G. R. Beasley-Murray (New York: Herder and Herder, 1964). From within the restoration movement, still valuable is the study by Alexander Campbell, *Christian Baptism with its Antecedents and Consequences* (Bethany, VA: by the author, 1851). See also his debates with N. L. Rice in 1843 and that with John Walker, 1820. William Robinson, of the British Churches of Christ, wrote several important studies: *What Churches of Christ Stand For* (Birmingham: Berean Press, 1959; *Infant Baptism Today* (London: Carey Kingsgate Press, Ltd., 1948); *Holy Baptism and Holy Communion* (Birmingham: Berean Press, 1958); *The Biblical Doctrine of the Chruch*, rev. ed. (St. Louis: Bethany Press, 1955). Reflecting issues on the relation of baptism to church membership, see S. J. England, *The One Baptism: Baptism and Christian Unity, with Special Reference to the Relationship of Baptism to Church Membership* (St. Louis: Bethany Press, 1963). For a thorough study of the whole problem, consult the bibliographies in the above-mentioned works, especially that of G. R. Beasley-Murray.

[21]See interaction of scholars in two articles: T. T. Torrance, "Prose-lyte Baptism," *New Testament Studies*, 1 (1954), pp. 150-154; reply by T. M. Taylor, "The Beginnings of Jewish Proselyte Baptism," *New Testament Studies*, 2 (1956), pp. 193-198. Also the discussion in Beasley-Murray, *Baptism*, pp. 18-31.

[22]For general discussion on the background of baptism, see N. A. Dahl, "The Origin of Baptism," *Interpretationes ad Vetus Testamentum Pertinentes Sigmund Mowinckel* (Oslo: Fabritius and Sonner, 1955), pp. 36-52; G. R. Beasley-Murray, *Baptism*, pp. 1-44; Johannes Schneider, *Baptism and Church in the New Testament*, trans. by E. A. Payne (London: Carey Kingsgate Press, 1957), pp. 14-23.

[23]Geoffrey Wainwright, *Christian Initiation* (London: Lutterworth Press, 1969), pp. 8-96. Also the pungent comments in Marcus Barth, "Baptism and Evangelism," *Scottish Journal of Theology*, 12 (1959), pp. 35-57.

[24]Beasley-Murray, *Baptism*, p. 92.

[25]Note H. Bietenhard, "*Onoma*," *Theological Dictionary of the New Testament*, ed. by G. Friedrich, trans. and ed. by Geoffrey W. Bromiley, vol. 5 (Grand Rapids: Eerdmans, 1968), p. 276.

[26]*Ibid.*, pp. 275, 276.

[27]Richardson, *Theology*, p. 348.

[28]G. W. H. Lampe, *The Seal of the Spirit* (London: Longmans, Green & Company, 1951), p. 2.

[29]For example, Lake and Cadbury, *Beginnings of Christianity*, Vol. 4, p. 26; Vol. 1, pp. 337-344. Also F. J. Foakes-Jackson, *The Acts of the Apostles* (London: Hodder and Stoughton, Ltd., 1960), pp. 18-20.

[30]Alan Richardson, "Salvation," *Interpreter's Dictionary of the Bible*, Vol. 4 (New York: Abingdon Press, 1962), p. 181. The complete article with the bibliography is well worth study (pp. 168-181).

[31]G. E. Ladd, *The Presence of the Future: The Eschatology of Biblical Realism* (Grand Rapids: Eerdmans, 1974), p. 215.

[32]A. Campbell, *Millenial Harbinger* (1833), p. 353.

[33]Hans Conzelmann, *First Corinthians*, trans. by James W. Leitch (Philadelphia: Fortress Press, 1975), p. 107 and notes.

[34]T. K. Abbott, *A Critical and Exegetical Commentary on the Epistles to the Ephesians and to the Colossians* (Edinburgh: T & T Clark, 1897), p. 169.

[35]Martin Dibelius and Hans Conzelmann, *The Pastoral Epistles,* trans. by Philip Buttolph and Adela Yarbro (Philadelphia: Fortress Press, 1972), pp. 148-150.

[36]F. W. Beare, *The First Epistle of Peter* (Oxford: Basil Blackwell, 1961), p. 84; Js. N. D. Kelly, *A Commentary on the Epistles of Peter and Jude* (New York: Harper, 1969), p. 78; E. G. Sehwyn, *The First Epistle of Peter* (London: Macmillan, 1947), p. 149.

[37]Schneider, *Baptism and Church,* p. 28.

[38]Schnackenburg, *Baptism in the Thought of St. Paul,* pp. 154, 155. It is in light of such considerations that Beasley-Murray writes: "I am compelled to conclude that the understanding of baptism as a beautiful and expressive symbol and *nothing more* is irreconcilable with the New Testament." *Baptism Today and Tomorrow* (New York: St. Martins, 1966), p. 32. It is also insufficient to see it as having only past significance in cleansing as well.

[39]For the alternate view, see Knofel Staton, "The Holy Spirit," chapter 9 of this work.

[40]James D. G. Dunn, *Baptism in the Holy Spirit* (London: SCM Press, 1970), pp. 55-72.

[41]C. K. Barrett, *A Commentary on the First Epistle to the Corinthians* (London: Adams & Charles Black 1968), p. 143.

[42]Lampe, *The Seal of the Spirit,* p. 5

[43]T. M. Taylor, "Abba, Father and Baptism" in *Scottish Journal of Theology,* 11 (1958), pp. 62-71.

[44]An essay with important comments in relation to this last statement is Karl Paul Donfried, "Justification and Last Judgment in Paul," *Zeitschrift für die Neutestamentliche Wissenschaft,* 67 (1976), pp. 90-110.

CHAPTER

13

THE CHRISTIAN LIFE

By James G. Van Buren

Introduction: Pictures and Paradoxes

One cannot survey the various aspects of Christian teaching without giving consideration to the manner and quality of life that such a commitment seeks to inspire. As Hans Küng says in his powerful book, *On Being a Christian*, "Jesus . . . is not a name which must be constantly on your lips, but a way of life's truth which must be practiced. The truth of Christianity is not something to be 'contemplated,' 'theorized,' but 'done,' 'practiced.' "[1]

When we look at New Testament descriptions of the Christian experience, we find several paradoxical and figurative pictures. These pictures are in addition to those designations that relate to the Christian's identity with, and life in, the church. Of course, ideas that depict the individual as part of Christ's body, as being a stone in the temple of God or as being a laborer in God's work force as part of His "farm" are significant. This essay, however, will be limited to those pictures that illustrate the individual Christian life rather than including ones that represent the corporate church.

The first notable description of the actual nature of our Christian living is concerned with the fact that we are at once slaves and yet absolutely free. Our slavery is complete and our liberty is glorious. Luther was aware of this when he wrote, in his tract, *On Christian Liberty*, issued in 1520, "A Christian man is the most free lord of all and subject to none; a Christian man is the most dutiful servant of all and subject to everyone." Of course, this is qualified in that the Christian man is both free and a servant in Christ.

In Romans 6, Paul deals with the new life in Christ, which comes into being as men are raised from Christian baptism to walk in "newness of life." The contrast the new life presents to the old is vividly delineated in verses 17 and 18, where he says, "But thanks be to God that though you were slaves of sin, you became obedient from the heart to that form of teaching to which you were committed, and having been freed from sin, you became slaves of righteousness."

The word rendered "form" is *tupon* in the Greek text. It means a "copy," "image," "form," or "model." The Christian, in his baptism, has been "obedient" to that basic truth that is the essence of the proclamation. That is, Jesus died for our sins, was buried, and was raised again (1 Corinthians 15:1-4). This is a patterning of our lives in imitation of what Jesus has done for us and is expressive of our break with the slavery of sin and our entrance upon a new, liberated life of righteousness. However, this new life is one of obedience to the new Lord of our destiny—Jesus, the Messiah.

In John 8:31-36, Jesus speaks of the slavery of sin and of the liberation He came to bring to all who continue in His word of truth. Paul indicates that freedom is an inevitable part of life in Christ when he cries in Galatians 5:1, "It was for freedom that Christ set us free; therefore keep standing firm and do not be subject again to a yoke of slavery." Here he is urging that no legalistic human legislation, even in the area of religious practice, should infringe upon the freedom of life and thought a truly committed Christain should know. In a noble sense, all Christians are "liberated" persons.

In considering Christian attitudes toward the vexing question of slavery in the Roman empire, and in the lives of people involved in the fellowship of the Christian community, Paul wrote, "He who was called in the Lord while a slave, is the Lord's freedman; likewise he was called while free, is Christ's slave. You were bought with a price; do not become slaves of men" (1 Corinthians 7:22, 23). This same attitude relating to the Christian's simultaneous freedom and slavery in Christ is echoed in Colossians 3:22—4:1.

Another interesting facet of the Christian experience is that it is a condition of life and death in constant interaction. Here, again, Romans 6 presents a vivid picture. It includes the fact that if, in baptism, we are united with Christ "in the likeness of His death"—"baptized into His death" (vv. 5, 3)—we shall also be united with Him "in the likeness of His resurrection" (v. 5). This is indicated in the fact that we have been raised "as Christ was" that we might walk "in newness of life" (v. 4). The Christian is to consider himself "dead to sin, but alive to God" (v. 11).

In Colossians 2:11—3:7, Paul returns to various aspects of his theme and spells out how this death to sin works out in practical terms. God has made us "alive together with Him." Paul again relates this to baptism as picturing what has occurred (v. 12). He says if we have been "raised with" Christ, we should, therefore, seek the spiritual rather than the physical, the eternal rather than the ephemeral, and the Heavenly rather than the earthly. This involves a constant putting to death of evil qualities of life in order that the new life in Christ may flourish and grow (2:20—3:5).

We have all had experiences of being dead to certain realities of life and of knowing others who were. Sometimes we may be unresponsive and corpselike in our reaction to certain types of music or to various kinds of expressions in the visual arts. Some people seem unaware of birds or of certain kinds of flowers or of the beauties of certain shrubs, trees, insects, or rocks. Sometimes our interest becomes kindled in a certain school of architecture or a special bird or animal. Suddenly a whole area of new interest and awareness arises in our lives. We have been "made alive" to a whole new complex of experiences and expressions. In a profound way, this is the sort of thing that occurs when one begins a new life in Christ. Paul says daringly, "If any man is in Christ, he is a new creature; the old things have passed away; behold, new things have come" (2 Corinthians 5:17).

One further depiction of our Christian experience is that of dressing and undressing. As humans, we engage in this activity constantly. Not only do we clothe and unclothe ourselves each day, but often we "change clothes" several times as we prepare for certain jobs or for special occasions. The clothing we wear is often indicative of the activity in which we are to engage and, sometimes, of the mood we are experiencing or wish to evoke. In Colossians 3:8-14, Paul encourages his readers to "put off" the qualities of anger, malice, slander, lying, and "foul talk." He says this should be done because "you have taken off your old self with its practices and have put on the new self, which is being renewed in knowledge in the image of its Creator" (vv. 9, 10, NIV). From verse 12 on, the positive aspects of the new Christian's outer garb are stressed. The new nature expresses itself to the view of others in those exterior characteristics that reveal compassion, kindness, meekness, and forbearance. This section is climaxed by the admonition, "And beyond all these things put on love, which is the perfect bond of unity" (v. 14). The picture here is of a beautiful outer garment that is put on over everything else and completes and ties together the other items of clothing—just as a girl may put on various undergarments of different sorts and then, overall, put on a dress, which brings everything together into a harmony of grace, symmetry, and color. Or as a man may have on a shirt, necktie, and trousers, and then put on a coat, which brings a completion to the wardrobe. (Note the strength of this picture in the NIV and NEB, especially vv. 12-14.)

The clothing symbol is used again in Ephesians 4:20-24 and in Galatians 3:26-28. Here the Christian's new position in Christ is described as the clothing of the soul. Christian conduct is said to reveal the change within, just as outer apparel often is indicative of character. As Polonius says in *Hamlet*, "The apparel oft' proclaims the man." In the Galatians passage, Paul points to baptism as that place where the new garments of Christ are first put on. And in 1 Peter 5:5, we have another example of the use of the figure of clothing as an expression of Christian character. Peter says, "Clothe yourselves with humility toward one another, for God opposes the proud, but gives grace to the humble."

The Primary Christian Ideal—Christlikeness

The universal stress of the New Testament is on Jesus as Messiah and Lord. The greatest glory of the church is its Lord; the principal aim of its members is to be "in Christ" and to become "like Christ." His name is not just one among many, but is "above" every name. He is "head over all things to the church" (Ephesians 1:22), and is preeminent "in everything" (Colossians 1:18).

In Paul's letter to the Philippians, this obsession with Jesus is especially prominent. The names Christ, Christ Jesus, Jesus Christ, the Lord Jesus Christ, or the Lord are used nineteen times in the first chapter. In this chapter, he alleges that "the fruit of righteousness comes through Jesus Christ" (v. 11), and he asserts that "to me to live is Christ, and to die is gain" (v. 21.) In this same letter, he urges his readers to have the "attitude . . . which was also in Christ Jesus" (2:5), and states that he has counted whatever gain he had as loss "for the sake of Christ" (3:7). Indeed, everything could be lost for "the surpassing value of knowing Christ Jesus my Lord" (3:8). His great aim was that he might "know Him" (3:10).

A survey of all the New Testament letters and literature would reveal the same insistent stress on the primacy and the adequacy of Jesus for the Christian's salvation from sin, stabilization in character, and exaltation in hope. From Peter's statement that Jesus' suffering leaves us "an example" that we should "follow in His steps" (1 Peter 2:21), to the encouragement of the writer of Hebrews that we should run our life's race, "fixing our eyes on Jesus, the author and perfecter of our faith" (12:2), the New Testament points to Jesus as the Christian's guide and goal. Well does Stephen Neill write, "To be a Christian means to be like Jesus Christ."[2] Hans Küng states:

> "The criterion of what is Christian, the distinctive Christian feature—this holds both for dogmatics and consequently also for ethics—is not an abstract something or a Christ idea, not a Christology nor a Christocentric system of ideas: it is *this concrete Jesus as the Christ, as the standard.*"[3]

The fact should be noted that the church was established and that several of the letters of the New Testament may have been written before the first Gospel was produced. And, if we include the total corpus of the four, almost all of the rest of the New Testament was written before they were completed. It can therefore be seen that the early Christian community became increasingly concerned about the preservation of authentic records of the ways and words of Jesus. At first, the apostles could give their personal witness, but as the church grew and spread and as the apostles became older (and one, James the brother of John, was killed), it became evident that a durable record would be required. Since the constant stress of the apostolic proclamation was on Jesus, and since the Christian aim was to become like Him, it was vital to have a picture of what Jesus was like. It was important to know Jesus as the crucified and risen Messiah, but it was also essential to know the words and ways of the Son of man, the One who taught, healed, cared, served, and shared with men.

Some of the characteristic qualities that can be seen in Jesus' life and that Christians should be expected to exhibit follow. Of course, this is merely a sample enumeration and is not meant to be exhaustive.[4]

Simplicity

From His stable birth to His borrowed tomb, the life of Jesus was marked by a lack of ostentation and luxury. He worked as a carpenter and chose fishermen and other seemingly ordinary men as His apostles. He did not accumulate wealth. He spoke in parables that dealt with the common life of shepherding, farming, fishing, viticulture, and housekeeping. During His public ministry, He seems to have been supported by the contributions both of money and service provided by His disciples (note Luke 8:1-3). This lack of gorgeousness and display was especially noted by the Protestant reformers, beginning with John Wycliffe, who contrasted Jesus' life-style with the panoplied pomp and power of the bishops and other ecclesiastics of the Roman church. Wycliffe said,

> From this Gospel I take it as a matter of belief that Christ, during the time he walked here, was the poorest of men, both in spirit and in goods; for Christ says that he had nought to rest his head upon. . . . And thus Christ put from him all manner of worldly lordship. For the Gospel of John tells that, when they would have made Christ king, he fled and hid himself from them, for he would have no such worldly greatness.
>
> And above this, I accept it as a matter of belief that no man should follow the Pope, or any saint now in heaven, except in so far as he follows Christ.[5]

Sincerity

The lack of any deceptiveness in Jesus is immediately apparent as one looks at the Gospel records. He was always frank and open with those to whom He spoke. He told Peter vehemently that his opposition to His expected suffering and death was Satanic. Speaking to the divorcee at the well in Samaria, He referred openly to her experience with five husbands and to the fact that she was then living with a man to whom she was not married. When He was pleased, He expressed His pleasure without concealment, "I have not found such faith, no, not in

Israel"; and when displeased, He pointedly expressed it, as in His attacks on the scribes and Pharisees as "hypocrites" and "whited sepulchers."

It is evident that Jesus abhorred all pretense, all sham, and all make-believe, especially in those matters relating to the worship of God. He could not stand those who "for a pretense" made long prayers, or those who gave alms "to be seen of men." The most terrible thing about the Pharisees was that they preached but did not practice (Matthew 23:3). They outwardly appeared righteous to men, but within they were full of dead men's bones and all uncleanness.

Serenity

One of Jesus' most remarkable qualities was the central core of calm that seemed to give stability to His personality. Whether amid jostling crowds, or with His disciples in a pitching ship during a Galilean storm, He seemed the epitome of poise and self-possession. When Martha came to Him all disturbed and distraught because of her sister Mary's deficiencies, Jesus remained unagitated. There were several times when He seemed to be moved with anger and indignation—at the lovelessness of the scribes, the external ritualism of the Pharisees, and the materialistic exploitation of the temple through buying and selling. He was moved to weep over the city of Jerusalem for its unresponsiveness. Seemingly, only in the Gethsemane experience was He shaken, much distressed, and almost crushed.

When Jesus gave His followers the bequest of His peace, saying, "Peace I leave with you; My peace I give to you . . ." (John 14:27), what a surpassing gift it was! Every letter of Paul's has the greeting, somewhere near its opening, containing the twin wishes for his readers of "grace and peace." One of the primary blessings of Christian experience is the fact we can become, in some measure, possessors of the deep serenity of the Son of God in the central sanctuaries of our persons.

Sidney Lanier wrote of Jesus in the concluding stanza of his tremendous poem, "The Crystal" (first printed in 1880). In it, he contrasted Jesus with many other great figures such as Shakespeare, Homer, Socrates, and Milton, whom he had named, and whose defects he had gladly forgiven:

But Thee, but Thee, O sovereign Seer of time,

But Thee, O poet's Poet, Wisdom's Tongue,
But Thee, O man's best Man, O love's best Love,
O perfect life in perfect labor writ,
O all men's Comrade, Servant, King, or Priest,—
What *of* or *yet*, what mole, what flaw, what lapse,
What least defect or shadow of defect,
What rumor loose, what lack of grace
Even in torture's grasp, or sleep's, or death's,—
Oh, what amiss may I forgive in Thee,
Jesus, good Paragon, thou Crystal Christ?[6]

Sociability

Jesus was, indeed, as His critics charged, "a friend of publicans and sinners." It is interesting to note that many of His most memorable teachings were given at dinners where He was the guest or, as in the upper room, where He was the host. Jesus pointed out that John the Baptist was criticized because he was so austere and ascetic, while He was charged with being excessive in eating and drinking (Luke 7:31-35).

The first miracle performed by Jesus, according to John's Gospel, was the changing of water into wine while attending a marriage feast. We note He began His dealing with the tax collector, Zaccheus, by inviting himself to dinner at his house (Luke 19:1-10). He developed a deep friendship with Mary, Martha, and Lazarus in Bethany. He spent most of the time during the years of His public ministry in the company of a rather large group of men whom He had chosen and called to be His companions and helpers. Even after the resurrection, He met some of His disciples at dawn and joined them in an intimate breakfast beside the beautiful lake where they had spent so many days together.

The truly "Christlike" life must include friendship, sharing, associations, and the interflow of personality. That one can "follow Jesus" and be withdrawn, aloof, distant, and unfeeling in terms of human relationships is certainly a mistaken notion.

Spirituality

It is possible, of course, to be closely associated with our fellow man and involved in all sorts of personal interchanges without possessing the dimension of depth and an awareness of God. There are many who are social "butterflies," flitting from group to group but totally lacking in any perception of, or interest in, matters that relate to the most profound levels of life. Jesus was spiritually attuned. He prayed with great frequency and fervency, so much so that His disciples urged Him to teach them to pray (Luke 11:1). Before choosing the twelve apostles, He spent all night in prayer (Luke 6:12, 13). Prior to His appearance to His disciples on the stormy lake, "after He had sent the multitudes away, He went up to the mountain by Himself to pray; and when it was evening, He was there alone" (Matthew 14:23).

Jesus' whole life was permeated and saturated with the recognition of the reality of God. In Matthew 6, for instance, God is referred to as Father twelve times. In John 14, God as Father is spoken of some twenty-one times. From the time Jesus was in the temple at the age of twelve, when He asked, "Did you not know that I had to be in My Father's house?" (Luke 2:49), to the final cry on the cross, "Father, into Thy hands I commit My spirit!" (Luke 23:46), Jesus was in touch with His Heavenly Father. Even after His resurrection, He told His disciples, "Behold, I am sending forth the promise of My Father upon you" (Luke 24:49).

Serviceability

One of the key verses for the understanding of Jesus' life and work is Mark 10:45, "For even the Son of Man did not come to be served, but to serve, and to give His life a ransom for many." At the very beginning of His work, as Luke records it, He quoted from Isaiah 61:1, 2 in the synagogue at Nazareth. This indicated why and for what God's Spirit had "anointed" Him, or declared Him the Messiah. This was largely in terms of preaching and of service, which included releasing captives and giving sight to the blind.

John's Gospel records the dramatic incident of Jesus' washing the disciples' feet. In speaking of the meaning of what He had done, Jesus said, "If I then, the Lord and the Teacher, washed your feet, you also ought to wash one another's feet" (13:14). The intent, clearly, is to show them that all striving as to who should be greatest and all desire for dominance and authoritative command was foreign to the spirit and attitude He wished them to embody. It was an illustration of His words recorded in Mark 10:42, 43, "You know that those who are recognized as rulers of the Gentiles lord it over them; and their great men exercise authority over them. But it is not so among you, but whoever wishes to become great among you shall be your servant; and whoever wishes to be first among you shall be slave of all."

The record of Jesus' life, with His healing, concern, and compassionate outreach, is evidence of the sort of life He envisions for His disciples. It is a call, as Dietrich Bonhoeffer so eloquently pled, to be "a man for others." This is, indeed, in Jesus' kingdom, "the cost of discipleship."

The Outline of Christian Character

What we have just surveyed may be considered, in some measure, a general picture of at least some things involved in "following Jesus." To that extent, this would be a delineation of Christian character. There are many passages in the New Testament that deal with the life of the Christian. In fact, it might be argued that a large part of the New Testament is concerned with this theme. This is true, but there are a few places where there seems to be concentration of material directly addressed to such a stress. These passages are Matthew 5—7; Romans 12; 1 Corinthians 13; Galatians 5:22, 23; Philippians 4:8, 9; and 2 Peter 1:1-11. Of course, many passages dealing with "pictures and paradoxes" of Christian experience have already been considered.

Characteristic Features of Christian Living

It may be said that those acts and activities that can be considered specifically Christian are very few. However, the motivation and tenor of all of a Christian's conduct are shaped by his Christian commitment. Therefore, while little that a Christian does is utterly unique; broadly considered, it is true that everything he does is tinctured with a distinctive Christian quality. Three general categories are considered here.

Worship

New Testament passages about worship in general include John 4:19-24; Philippians 3:3; and Acts 2:42. In the first two of these passages, the main thrust seems to be that God, the Father, is the object or being worshiped and that a spiritual emphasis in such worship is primary. Further, it is to be characterized by sincerity and joyfulness. The Acts passage points out several other features that we shall note separately.

1. The Lord's Supper. In many ways, this is one of the most distinctive acts of a Christian. Eating bread and drinking the fruit of the vine in memory of Jesus' death for sin and in recognition of the "one body," the church, is not an ordinary act. Other groups of religious devotees have prayers, chanting or singing, and the reading of sacred literature. But there is nothing quite like this in most of the world religions. True, some primitive people have "divine meals," where they eat in honor of, or in some sort of fellowship with, a deity or with ancestral spirits. The unique thing about the Lord's Supper, which seems to have been the central feature of Christian worship in apostolic times, is that it finds its focus in the person and work of Jesus. It is done "in memory" of Him.

The principal passages relating to the Lord's Supper are Luke 22:19, 20; Acts 20:7; and 1 Corinthians 10:16, 17; 11:20-30. While highly figurative, John 6:48-58 would be included by many as a relevant passage. Since the Lord's Supper will be considered more fully in another section of this book, the details of its implications and applications will not be explored here.[7]

2. Singing. The early Christians usually addressed this important feature of worship to God. However, Paul indicates in Ephesians 5:19 and Colossians 3:16 that it involved elements of admonition and teaching to be addressed to fellow Christians as well. It was to be expressed in a melodious manner and in a thankful spirit. It included psalms and hymns and spiritual songs. It was not done as a matter of rote or of formal compliance with ritualistic requirements but was carried on wholeheartedly. Several New Testament scholars believe Ephesians 5:14 and 1 Timothy 3:16 contain passages from early lyrics sung by the first century Christians.

3. Giving. We know that Christians gave generously and, apparently, regularly to promote the Christian enterprise. This involved contributions for special needs during emergencies and for the support of apostolic preaching. (Note Acts 11:27-30; Philippians 4:15-18. See also the general instructions and admonitions in 1 Corinthians 16:1, 2; 2 Corinthians 8:1-12; 9:6-8.)

4. Praying. We have already noted the place of prayer in the spiritual life of Jesus. There are both admonitions in the Gospels and examples in the record of the New Testament church that indicate how vital prayer was. While the "Lord's Prayer," given in Matthew 6:9-13 and Luke 11:2-4, must have been considered a model, there is no evidence it was used as a liturgical form in the first century church. Acts 4:24-30 contains the only recorded prayer of a public, corporate nature to be found in the New Testament. It links together Biblical materials and references to the work of Jesus with specific notations of a crisis then faced by the church. It looks to the help and empowering of the church through the presence and help of God's "holy servant Jesus." In an editorial note, Luke tells us Jesus wanted to encourage men to pray always and "not to lose heart" (Luke 18:1). Paul insists Christians are to pray constantly (1 Thessalonians 5:17).

5. Scripture reading. It is apparent that Jesus placed great emphasis on the Old Testament Scriptures as "bearing witness" to himself (John 5:39). On the Emmaus road, after His resurrection, and also in a discussion with His apostles following this, He spoke of many things related to the suffering, death, and glorification of the Messiah that were fulfilled in Him (note Luke 24:26, 27; 44-47). In Romans 15:4; 2 Timothy 2:15; 3:15-17, we have references to Paul's high regard for the Scriptures. Timothy was urged to "give attention to the public reading of Scripture" (1 Timothy 4:13). While the "Scriptures" mentioned in the Pauline passages appear to refer to the Old Testament, it is still true that even in the New Testament period, the letters of Paul had begun to attain the status of "Scriptures" (2 Peter 3:15, 16). We also know that Paul desired his letters to be "read in the church," for he explicitly gave such a command (see Colossians 4:16).[8]

Service

The Christian ideal of serviceability has already been seen to be exemplified in the life of Jesus. He not only did this by His life's pattern, but specifically urged such a life-style upon His disciples. In the great judgment passage in Matthew 25:31-40, the rewards of everlasting recognition are given to those who have cared for human needs in terms of the hungry, thirsty, imprisoned, and homeless of the world. The account in Acts 9:36-42 tells about Dorcas' goodness in sewing for those who were needy. She was "abounding with deeds of kindness and charity." James 2:14-26 is only part of an insistent emphasis in that letter that genuine, vital faith issues in activities that are helpful, constructive, and blessed. Jesus' emphasis in the parable of the helpful stranger is well known. Jesus simply told how this man assisted and befriended one in need. Generations following have called him "the Good Samaritan." Jesus never called him that; He just showed us what he did, and we have decided that is what goodness is.

Meditation

It is unfortunate we give so little attention to the practice of meditation. This is the thoughtful turning over in the mind of great truths and realities we have discerned in life or in Biblical and devotional reading, or have received through Christian instruction and counsel. Several choice Christian thinkers have spoken feelingly of the significance of meditation. Jeremy Taylor said, "Meditation is the tongue of the soul . . . and the soul of prayer." Bishop Joseph Hall claimed, "It is not he that reads most, but he that meditates most on divine truth, that will prove the choicest, wisest, strongest Christian."

One often thinks that meditation really is "chewing the cud" of what one has previously ingested through reading and other life experiences. It is the reflective mental and spiritual mastication of this material until it becomes truly meaningful, applicable, palatable, and nutritious for us. As Bishop George Horne said, "Meditation is that exercise of the mind by which it recalls a known truth, as some kind of creatures do their food, to be ruminated upon till all the valuable parts be extracted."

The psalmist tells us the blessed man is the one who meditates day and night on God's law (Psalm 1:1, 2). Psalm 119 indicates that meditation should be upon both God's words and His works. Meditation is mentioned as something to be done throughout the day and in the night. There is also consideration to be given to the "testimonies" these acts and words of God bring to the enrichment of human life and to the "promises" they unfold (note verses 15, 27, 48, 97, 148).

One of the great New Testament passages in this area is Philippians 4:8, where we are encouraged to "think about" whatever is honorable, just, pure, lovely, gracious, excellent, or "worthy of praise." What a contrast the apostolic admonition is to the practice to which so many of our daily newspapers and popular literature call us. Here we are deluged with details about whatever is dishonorable, unjust, impure, ugly, and selfish. If there is anything that can be found that is faulty and worthy of denunciation, it is underscored and publicized. How essential it is to preserve oases of calm, tranquility, beauty, and peace in the midst of the "waste lands" of our era! Of course, one does not want to shun reality. But to many moderns, "reality" means rubbish but no roses, mud but no moonlight, a clear focus on entrails but no view of dawns, sunsets, stars, or rainbows.

Aids to Christian Devotion and Dedication

This section of our study will be but a brief survey of the broad spectrum covered by the topic. Time and space limit our ability to cover this field adequately.

Christian Associations

Through various formal and informal gatherings for social activity and for Bible study, much Christian helpfulness can be found. Bible classes, more formally structured, can be useful in assisting one to grow in both Biblical knowledge and the understanding of Christian personalities. Conventions whether large or small, can be both informational and inspirational. In and through all these activities, individual and family Christian friendships blossom and come to fruition in enriched lives and uplifted characters.

Christian Instruction

Christian preaching and teaching help us to be built up on our "most holy faith" (Jude 20). In speaking to the Ephesian elders, Paul tells of how he "admonished" them without ceasing night or day. He did this with a great sense of urgency and seriousness, even "with tears." Then, he commended them to God and the word of His grace, which would continue to do what Paul's instruction was aimed at accomplishing: to build them up and to help them be assured of that inheritance that is available to "all those who are sanctified" (Acts 20:31, 32). Such is the end that all Christian instruction has in view.

Christian Literature

We would certainly laud persons who are "people of one Book"—that is, who believe the Bible is the principal book Christians should read. This must not, however, be taken to mean that no other books are necessary. Of course, the Bible does constitute the central focus of a Christian's concern, yet there are many reasons other books need to be read. Paul himself showed a familiarity with literature outside the Bible; indeed, beyond the Judaeo-Christian area of life and thought. In Acts 17:28 and Titus 1:12, he evidences a knowledge of such material. In his last preserved letter, he asks Timothy to bring him, so he can use them in his prison cell, the books that he had left at Troas with Carpus (2 Timothy 4:13). Paul had received personal visions and visitations from Jesus, had written almost a third of the New Testament, and was nearing the end of his life—yet he wanted books!

Among the types of books of help to Christians in the enrichment of their lives and learning are devotional works (see Appendix B), poetry, sermons, fiction, essays, biographies and autobiographies, and church history. (For some helpful books, see Appendix C.)

Christian Music

There are great benefits to be derived from a study of hymns as statements of Christian doctrine and devotion. These values are both positive, in the strenghthening they can bring to faith in their lyrical expression of profound realities, and negative, in that some are "horrible examples" of sentimental exaggeration and intellectual vacuity. It is true also that oratorios and cantatas can bring powerful presentations of the Christian faith. The experience of singing in choirs has also been a "means of grace" for many. Anytime great church music is sung, the singers derive great benefit if they come to the task with devout spirits and alert minds. (See Appendix D for some suggestions concerning literature in this field.)

Christian Art

This involves a survey of Christian values to be found in a study of painting, sculpture, and architecture. Large numbers of significant books have been written in this field and a study of any of them cannot fail to broaden one's understanding of various aspects of Christian concern, devotion, and dedication. Art also serves to help us see various deviations from the norms of faith and works seen in New Testament Christianity. (See Appendix E for some books in this area.)

The Mutual Ministry of Christians

We might understand the phrase "mutual ministry" as referring to the ministries Christians do together or mutually undertake. In this sense, of course, various benevolent, missionary, and service activities might be thought of as mutually carried on. However, the sense in which it is used here is that considered its primary meaning in the *Oxford Universal Dictionary* as ". . . relations, feelings, actions: possessed, entertained, or done by each towards or with regard to the other; reciprocal." This is a very important, but often neglected, aspect of our Christian life and work.

We often think of the many debts we owe to God for all He has done and is doing for us. God's ministry to us is incessant and intense. We also consider, frequently, our responsibilities to serve God. What can we do that will please God, advance His kingdom, and honor His Son? Indeed, we have duties to God, and there are actions of ours in worship, service to the needy, and witness to the erring and sinful that we are challenged to carry out.

However, granting all this, let us look closer to home, to another ministry that is vital and no less a matter of Biblical exhortation and direction than these others. This is the ministry we must perform for one another. This does not demand our going to distant lands or the acquiring of special skills or expertise. It is close at hand and greatly needed, yet greatly neglected, unstressed, and often unrecognized. What we can do for one another is truly a means of demonstrating our discipleship to our Lord. Sometimes we say we can't sing or aren't musically inclined, or we can't demonstrate talent in art or public speaking. Yet here are our Christian companions, all about us, whom we can help and bless and who, in turn, can encourage, enlighten, and elevate our lives. What, then, are we to do for each other?

Love One Another

Jesus said, "This is my commandment, that you love one another, just as I have loved you" (John 15:12). The kind of love meant here is not left unclear. We do not have to seek its meaning in etymological explorations of the Greek language. Jesus defines it by saying it is the love that is similar to His love for us. He loved us unselfishly, warmly, helpfully, with a view to our greatest benefit. So we are to care for one another. We are to be constructive, self-giving, upbuilding, and redeeming.

The brief first letter of John is a regular litany on the theme of the mutual love of Christians toward each other. This it is that shows we are "in the light" (2:10); it is this that is the message we have heard "from the beginning" (3:11). This is the way we can know we have passed "out of death into life" (3:14). This mutual love must not just be expressed in words, but must be evidenced by sharing with those in physical need, never cherishing hatred at all in one's heart (3:15-18).

The essence of what God commands us is to believe in His Son Jesus as Christ and to love one another (3:23). The ones who are "born of God" and "know God" are the Christians who love one another (4:7). The call to such love is based on God's great love for us (4:11). If we want God to "abide" in us, we must love one another (4:12). The important thing is that we believe Jesus is the Christ, which makes us children of God, and we evidence this by loving God, by obeying His commandments, and this, of course, means loving His children (5:1-3).

Pray for One Another

This obligation did not begin with the New Testament period. One of the most moving speeches in the Old Testament is Samuel's, addressed to the Hebrew people after they had gone against his advice and chosen Saul to be their first king. Among many noble utterances, there are found these words: "Moreover, as for me, far be it from me that I should sin against the Lord by ceasing to pray for you" (1 Samuel 12:23).

In the New Testament, Jesus told the self-confident Peter, "Simon, Simon, behold, Satan has demanded permission to sift you like wheat; *but I have prayed for you*, that your faith may not fail" (Luke 22:31, 32). Paul wrote to the Ephesians, "I do not cease to give thanks for you, remembering you in my prayers" (Ephesians 1:16). He spoke often of praying for those to whom he wrote (2 Corinthians 13:7; Philippians 1:4, 9; Colossians 1:9; and 2 Thessalonians 1:11). He also indicates that the generosity of the Corinthians to needy fellow Christians in Jerusalem will evoke from them a harvest of prayers in behalf of, and in gratitude for, the kindness shown them (2 Corinthians 9:11-14).

But while Paul prayed for many others, he seems to have been most concerned that his fellow believers bear him up and sustain him and his helpers in their work. In 1 Thessalonians 5:25, he wrote, "Brethren, pray for us"; and in 1 Thessalonians 3:1, he urged, "Finally, brethren, pray for us, that the word of the Lord may spread rapidly and be glorified, just as it did also with you." He assured the Corinthians that they could assist in the gospel enterprise by their prayers for him, "you also joining in helping us through your prayers, that thanks may be given by many persons on our behalf for the favor bestowed on us through the prayers of many" (2 Corinthians 1:11).

As Tennyson's Arthur says to Sir Bedivere, just before his death,

> . . . More things are wrought by prayer
> Than this world dreams of. Wherefore let thy voice
> Rise like a fountain for me night and day.
> For what are men better than sheep or goats
> That nourish a blind life within the brain,
> If, knowing God, they lift not hands of prayer
> Both for themselves and those who call them friend?[9]

So the writer of Hebrews urges, "Pray for us, for we are sure that we have a good consicience, desiring to conduct ourselves honorably in all things" (13:18). James tells us, "Therefore, confess your sins to one another, and pray for one another" (5:16).

Confess Our Sins to One Another

James' statement, "Confess your sins to one another" (5:16), is rather unusual in the New Testament. The "confession" Christians made was a statement of faith in Jesus as Lord and Messiah, which was called "the good confession" (See 1 Timothy 6:12, 13; cf. Matthew 16:15-18; 1 John 4:15; 5:1; John 6:69; also note 1 John 2:22). There is also the recognition of the importance of confessing our sins to Jesus as our priest and advocate before God (1 John 1:8—2:1).

James, however, indicates we should confess our sins or "faults" (KJV) one to another as a prelude to praying for one another. Some groups, notably those involved with the "Oxford Group" or "Moral Rearmament," have made a major point of encouraging public interconfessional times. Here different members of the group recount their sins and failings in some detail as a means of spiritual catharsis and seek the help of others in prayer. This leads to many ills, such as the betrayal of confidences of other persons perhaps involved with the "confessing" one, and to a temptation to become maudlin and introspective. There is reason to believe the principle confession of our sins and faults should be in private to our Lord. The aim of "confessing" to one another should probably be admitting some offense we may have given or taken in relation to a fellow

Christian. This could be between the two persons involved, and perhaps lead to reconciliation, forgiveness, mutual understanding, and to prayers of thanksgiving, confession, and forgiveness. (This might be one aspect of the reconciliation "program" outlined by Jesus in Matthew 18:15-17.)

Sometimes, in certain situations, confessing our failings or misjudgments in public, to fellow Christians, may be salutary. If we have publicly criticized some church policy or program and later found we were wrong, it is helpful to state this, in humility, and to express regret at an error in the evaluation of the activity or project. Such statements are often constructive and upbuilding—especially if made in the proper atmosphere of love, humility and prayerfulness.

Bear One Another's Burdens

It is true that there are many life experiences that must be faced in the loneliness of one's own personal confrontation. One's reaction to the inescapable tragedies of our human lot and the frustrations of unrealistic expectations of personal resources of resiliency all too often are locked in the inner core of one's own awareness. So Hannah is said to have been "in bitterness of soul" (1 Samuel 1:10, KJV). Job says, "I will complain in the bitterness of my soul" (Job 7:11); and the wise writer of Proverbs asserts, "The heart knows its own bitterness, and a stranger does not share its joy" (Proverbs 14:10).

But there are many sorrows, anxieties, problems, and perplexities that we *can* share with our friends—especially with our friends in Christ. We are to be willing to do this, to be sure that at least we can let our brothers and sisters know of our earnest care, our genuine concern, and our deep linkage with them in the distressing hours when they yearn for words of compassion and the touch of loving hands. This is the kind of experience Jesus under went in Gethsemane. He faced a decision that only He could make. He looked ahead to torture, terror, and disgrace before men. He wanted very much to have the companionship and sympathetic concern of His apostles. He said to them, "My soul is deeply grieved, to the point of death; remain here and keep watch with Me." Later, he said sadly and with wistful reproach, "So, you men could not keep watch with Me for one hour?" (Matthew 26:38, 40). Paul urges us, "Bear one another's burdens, and thus fulfill the law of Christ" (Galatians 6:2).

Be Kind to One Another

One of the characteristics of the Christian love of which Paul speaks in 1 Corinthians 13 is that it is patient and kind (v. 4). One of the articles of Christian clothing with which our characters are to be dressed is kindness (Colossians 3:12). One of the qualities of the ideal woman, as depicted by King Lemuel in Proverbs, includes that of instructing those of her household in the practice of kindness. "She opens her mouth in wisdom and the teaching of kindness is on her tongue" (Proverbs 31:26).

Probably the finest New Testament passage on this topic is Ephesians 4:31, 32, where Paul urges, "Let all bitterness and wrath and anger and clamor and slander be put away from you, along with all malice. And be kind to one another, tender-hearted, forgiving each other, just as God in Christ also has forgiven you."

Kindness among Christians is seen throughout the New Testament—especially in the events narrated in Acts. The early Christians in Jerusalem shared with those in need, even selling some of their property to make larger gifts possible (Acts 2:44-46; 4:32-37). When Paul was on his final journey to Rome, the kindness of his fellow believers was expressed to him (Acts 27:2, 3). As he drew near Rome, a group of Christians came out to meet him on the Appian Way and journeyed into the city with him (Acts 28:13-15). It is beautiful and touching that Paul, stalwart soul that he was, firm and seemingly self-reliant, was greatly heartened by this. How simply and beautifully Luke tells it! "When Paul saw them, he thanked God and took courage" (Acts 28:15).

Exhort One Another

The writer of Hebrews urges his readers to "encourage one another day after day, as long as it is still called 'Today,' lest any of you be hardened by the deceitfulness of sin. For we have become partakers of Christ . . ." (Hebrews 3:13, 14). This note of entreaty and encouragement is one that is illustrated by the writer throughout the book. Again and again, he not only points out truths known through the record of God's dealings with His people in ancient times, but points to the tremendous realities now revealed in Jesus. These together call God's people to serious effort, and constant renewal of dedication and commitment. Notice the many times the writer combines "let us" with "since" or "therefore" (Hebrews 4:1, 11, 16; 6:1; 10:19-25; 12:1).

Many times during the heat of a football game or a basketball game, the team will take a "time out." They feel the need to encourage one another to greater effort, to check to see what's wrong, or to plan the final effort that they hope will secure victory. Christians very much need the livening, inspiriting help that comes as they speak together words of challenge and determination that they may be increasingly vital and victorious for God.

Forgive One Another

One of the most memorable sayings of Jesus is His reply to Peter's question about the number of times one should forgive a brother who has offended him. Should it be seven times? Jesus said, "I do not say to you, up to seven times, but up to seventy times seven" (Matthew 18:21, 22). In the Lord's Prayer, the only petition upon which Jesus expounded was that of asking to be forgiven as we forgive. "For if you forgive men for their transgressions, your heavenly Father will also forgive you. But if you do not forgive men, then your Father will not forgive your transgressions" (Matthew 6:14, 15).

To illustrate the need to forgive others because of what God forgives us, Jesus told Peter the dramatic story of the two debtors. One was forgiven a great debt; nevertheless, he refused to forgive the small amount owed him by a fellow servant. As a result, the "wicked" first debtor was severely punished (Matthew 18:23-35).

But we are not confined to Jesus' words in a consideration of forgiveness; we must look at His actions. He was patient and understanding, even, seemingly, giving Judas a last chance to turn in the Garden of Gethsemane when He asked Him, "Friend, why are you here?" On the cross, He prayed that those who crucified Him might be forgiven. As Paul says, "While we were yet sinners, Christ died for us" (Romans 5:8). So it is that he can write in Colossians 3:13, "Bearing with one another, and forgiving each other, whoever has a complaint against anyone; just as the Lord forgave you, so also should you." The same thought is found in Ephesians 4:32, where we are enjoined to "be kind to one another, tender-hearted, forgiving each other, just as God in Christ also has forgiven you."

Comfort One Another

There are many sources of comfort to us in our Christian

experience. The Holy Spirit is called "the Comforter" in the King James translation of the famous verse of John 14:26. The word, in the Greek text, is *parakletos*, which literally means "one who is called along side to help." It is translated, in various modern versions, as "Helper" (NASB), "Counselor" (NIV), "Advocate" (NEB), and others. Certainly, one of the ways the Holy Spirit helps us in through His comfort, and His advocacy and "standing along side us" are a source of comfort. It is interesting to note that Luke gives a summary statement of the condition of the churches in certain areas by saying, "So the church throughout all Judea and Galilee and Samaria enjoyed peace, being built up; and, going on in the fear of the Lord and in the comfort of the Holy Spirit, it continued to increase" (Acts 9:31).

Of course, God has always been a comfort to His people. The psalmist said, "Thy rod and thy staff, they comfort me" (Psalm 23:4). Isaiah was told by God to "comfort" God's people (Isaiah 40:1). Paul has a beautiful statement in 2 Thessalonians 2:16, which includes references to Jesus and the Father both as sources of comfort, "Now may our Lord Jesus Christ Himself and God our Father, who has loved us and given us eternal comfort and good hope by grace, comfort and strengthen your hearts in every good work and word."

But God's comfort is freqently ministered to us by our fellow believers. In a moving passage in 2 Corinthians, Paul passes from the concept of God as comforter to the Christian as one who shares God's comfort with others. "Blessed be the God and Father of our Lord Jesus Christ, the Father of mercies and God of all comfort; who comforts us in all our affliction so that we may be able to comfort those who are in any affliction, with the comfort with which we ourselves are comforted by God" (2 Corinthians 1:3, 4). This was evident in Paul's own experience, for he writes of Aristarchus, Mark, and Jesus "called Justus," who are, he says, among his fellow workers in the kingdom of God and who "have proved a comfort to me" (Colossians 4:10, 11, NIV).

As Paul tells of the reappearance of Jesus in an important passage in 1 Thessalonians 4, he advises, "Therefore comfort one another with these words." It is an important Christian service to remind one another of our hope in Jesus and to let the words of life and truth fall like balm upon wounded hearts and broken lives.

Be Hospitable to One Another

The word "hospitable" is derived from the Latin *hospitem*, a host, or one who entertains or lodges another in his house. To be "hospitable" is to manifest a dispostion to receive and welcome guests in a kindly manner. It involves the idea of generosity, open handedness, and good will. In Romans 12:13, there is the brief directive to practice hospitality. Both 1 Timothy 3:2 and Titus 1:8 state that being hospitable is one of the qualifications of an overseer.

Peter encourages us to be hospitable in a cluster of beautiful admonitions that illuminate the meaning of our Christian ministry toward each other. "Above all, keep fervent in your love for one another, because love covers a multitude of sins. Be hospitable to one another without complaint. As each one has received a special gift, employ it in serving one another, as good stewards of the manifold grace of God" (1 Peter 4:8-10). We are to love one another unfailingly, to be hospitable ungrudgingly, and to manage our gifts so we can benefit one another. We have different abilities and talents, and our disposition and ability to function with special competence in these areas is a gift from God. These gifts are not just for our self-serving exploitation, but for the help of our fellow Christians. So it is that the endowments that give us special competence in speech, writing, cooking, business management, farming, carpentry, teaching, music, or any other field can be utilized by the Christian community and strengthen it as a whole.

The word translated "manifold" in the phrase, "the manifold grace of God," is, in the Greek, *poikiles*. This is a word that carries the idea of "diversified," "manifold," and "of various kinds." One of its primary meanings is "variegated" or "multicolored." It was used of mosaic inlays in floors and walls, or of pictures that were polychromatic and were a marked feature of buildings in the Graeco-Roman world. A derivative of this same word, *poikilon*, is used in the Septuagint Version of Genesis 37:3, 23, and 32 of the "many-colored coat" Jacob had made for Joseph. What a lovely picture this verse makes when understood in this way! We must each use his own gift to help make up the "many colored" mosaic that is the picture of service and discipleship that pleases God. Each of us is a tiny stone but, fitted together by God's grace, we make a composite scene of devotion that has a meaning and completion none of us can achieve by himself.

NOTES

[1]Hans Küng, *On Being a Christian* (New York: Simon and Shuster, 1978), p. 410.

[2]Stephen Neill, *The Christian Character* (New York: Association Press, 1955), p. 9.

[3]Küng, *On Being a Christian*, p. 549.

[4]Some helpful and stimulating material on the nature and significance of the example of Jesus will be found in these books. (They vary in theological perspective, but each has its own value.) Henry J. Cadbury, *Jesus. What Manner of Man?* (New York: The Macmillan Co., 1947). Samuel Cartledge, *Jesus of Fact and Faith* (Grand Rapids: Eerdmans, 1968). Jack Finegan, *Rediscovering Jesus* (New York: Association Press, 1952). T. R. Glover, *The Jesus of History* (New York: Association Press, 1922). Robert E. Speer, *The Man Christ Jesus* (Old Tappan, NJ: Fleming H. Revell Co., 1898). Leslie D. Weatherhead, *His Life and Ours* (Nashville: Abingdon Press, 1933).

[5]Lewis Sergeant, *John Wycliffe* (New York: G. P. Putnam's Sons, 1893), p. 332.

[6]*Poems of Sidney Lanier* (New York: Charles Scribner's Sons, 1913), p. 30.

[7]See also the author's Walter Scott Memorial Lecture, "The Lord's Supper," delivered at Cincinnati Bible Seminary and printed in *The Christian Standard* for May 2, 9, 16, 23, 30 and June 6, 1953.

[8]For a more detailed treatment of worship in the apostolic era, see the author's "The New Testament Conception of Worship," printed in *The Shane Quarterly*, January, 1945.

[9]Alfred Tennyson, *The Idylls of the King*, "The Passing of Arthur."

APPENDIX A

Some Books Dealing With Christian Ethics

Bonhoeffer, Dietrich. *Ethics*, New York: Macmillan, 1970.

Cave, Sydney. *The Christian Way*, 1949, out of print.

Eller, Vernard. *The Simple Life: The Christian Stance Toward Possessions*, Grand Rapids: Eerdmans, 1973.

Ellul, Jacques. *The Presence of the Kingdom*, 1967, out of print.

Henry, Carl F. H., editor. *Baker's Dictionary of Christian Ethics*, Grand Rapids: Baker, 1978.

Hoyer, Theodore. *The Christian View of Life*, 1965, out of print.

King, William P. *Motives for Christian Living*, 1942, out of print.

_____ . *Right and Wrong in an Age of Confusion*, 1938, out of print.

_____ . *The Practice of the Principles of Jesus*, 1926, out of print.

Knudson, Albert C. *Principles of Christian Ethics*, 1943, out of print.

Lewis, C. S. *Mere Christianity*, New York: Macmillan, 1981.

Neill, Stephen. *The Christian Character*, 1955, out of print.

Ramsey, Paul. *Deeds and Rules in Christian Ethics*, 1967, out of print.

APPENDIX B

Some Books Helpful in Devotional Periods

Applegarth, Margaret. *Heirlooms*, 1967, out of print.

Bowie, Walter Russel, editor. *Joy in Believing*, 1956, out of print.

Gollancz, Victor. *Man and God*, 1951, out of print.

Kepler, Thomas S., editor. *The Private Devotions of Lancelot Andrewes*, 1956, out of print.

Pascal, Blaise. *Pensees (Thoughts)*. (Can be found in many editions. It is also included in the Harvard Classics set.)

Penn, William. *Some Fruits of Solitude*, Richmond, IN: Friends United, 1907.

Preyre, E-Alexis. *The Freedom of Doubt*, 1953, out of print.

Woods, Ralph. *Behold the Man: An Anthology of Jesus Christ*, 1944, out of print.

APPENDIX C

Suggested Reading List

Poetry by:

Auden, W. H. (e.g. "For the Time Being")
Browning, Elizabeth Barrett
Browning, Robert
Chaucer (e.g. "The Prologue" and "The Pardoner's Tale" in *The Canterbury Tales*)
Coleridge, Samuel T.
Cowper, William
Dickinson, Emily
Donne, John (e.g. "Holy Sonnets")
Eliot, T.S.
Fletcher, Giles
Herbert, George
Hopkins, G.M.
Langland, William (e.g. *The Vision of Piers Plowman*)
Longfellow, Henry Wadsworth
Lowell, James Russell
Masefield, John (e.g. *The Everlasting Mercy*)
Milton, John (e.g. *Paradise Lost, Paradise Regained, and Samson Agonistes*)
Pope, Alexander (e.g. "Essay on Man")
Rossetti, Christian
Smart, Christopher (e.g. "A Song to David")
Spenser, Edmund (e.g. *The Faerie Queene*)
Tennyson, Alfred
Thompson, Francis (e.g. *The Hound of Heaven*)
Van Dyke, Henry
Vaughn, Henry
Whitman, Walt (e.g. *Leaves of Grass*)
Whittier, John Greenleaf
Wordsworth, William

Sermons by:

Brooks, Phillips
Donne, John
Gossip, A. J.
Jones, J. D.
Morrison, G. H.
Robertson, F. W.
Spurgeon, C. H.
Stewart, J. S.
Taylor, Jeremy

Fiction

Bunyon, John, *The Holy War*, available in several editions.

————, *The Pilgrim's Progress*, available in several editions.

Charles, Elizabeth, *Chronicles of the Schoenberg-Colta Family*, 2 vol. in 1, New York: AMS Press, 1864.

Eliot, George, *Romola*, available in several editions.

Kingsley, Charles, *Hypatia*, available in several editions.

Lewis, C. S. *Chronicles of Narnia*, New York: Macmillan, 1970.

————, *The Pilgrim's Regress*, available in several editions.

MacDonald, George, *Annals of a Quiet Neighborhood*, out of print.

Morrow, Honore Willsie, *Splendor of God; The Life of Adoniram Judson*, Grand Rapids: Baker, 1982.

Reade, Charles, *The Cloister and the Hearth,* see *The Works of Charles Reade,* 17 vols., New York: AMS Press, 1896.

Essays

Amend, V. E., and L. T. Hendrick, eds., *Ten Contemporary Thinkers*, out of print.

Ferry, Anne Davidson, ed., *Religious Prose of Seventeenth Century England*, out of print.

Rhys, Ernest, ed., *A Century of English Essays*, Philadelphia: Richard West, 1978.

Biographies and Autobiographies

Anderson, Courtney, *To the Golden Shore: The Life of Adoniram Judson*, Grand Rapids: Zondervan, 1977.

Arant, Frances M., *"P.H.": The Welshimer Story,* Cincinnati: **Standard,** 1958, out of print.

Blaikie, W. Garden, *Personal Life of David Livingstone*, Westport, CT: Greenwood Press, 1880.

Cochran, Louis, *The Fool of God* (Alexander Campbell), Cincinnati: **Standard,** 1974, out of print.

Elliott, Elisabeth, *Through Gates of Splendor*, Wheaton: Tyndale, 1981.

Lappin, S. S., *Run, Sammy, Run*, out of print.

Marshall, C., *A Man Called Peter*, available in several editions.

Phelps, William Lyon, *Autobiography, with Letters*, New York: AMS Press, 1939.

Seaver, George, *David Livingstone: His Life and Letters*, out of print.

Ward, Maisie, *Gilbert Keith Chesterton*, out of print.

Church History
Glover, T. R., *The Christian Tradition and Its Verification*, out of print.

_____, *Christ in the Ancient World*, out of print.

_____, *The Conflicts of Religions in the Early Roman Empire*, Totowa, NJ: Cooper Square, 1909.

_____, *The World of the New Testament*, out of print.

Latourette, Kenneth Scott, *Anno Domini*, out of print.

_____, *The Christian Outlook*, out of print.

_____, *The Christian World Mission in Our Day*, out of print.

_____, *A History of Christianity*, New York: Harper & Row, 1975.

APPENDIX D

Hymn Studies

Bailey, Albert Edward, *The Gospel in Hymns*, New York: Charles Scribner's Sons, 1950.

Jackson, S. Trevena, *Fanny Crosby's Story of Ninety-four Years*, Grand Rapids: Baker, 1981.

Otis, Philo, *The Hymns You Ought to Know*, 1928, out of print.

Purcell, William, *Onward Christian Soldier: A Life of Sabine Baring-Gould*, 1957, out of print.

Rontley, Erik, *Church Music and the Christian Faith*, Carol Stream, IL: Agape, 1978.

Ruffin, Bernard, *Fanny Crosby*, New York: Pilgrim Press, 1976.

Stead, W. T., *Hymns That Have Helped*, 1904, out of print.

The Complete Works of John Newton includes an unusual commentary on Handel's "Messiah."

APPENDIX E

Christian Art

Bailey, Albert Edward, *Christ and His Gospel in Recent Art*, 1948, out of print.

———— , *The Gospel in Art*, out of print.

Crossley, Fred H., *The English Abbey*, 1943, out of print.

Hazelton, Roger, *A Theological Approach to Art*, 1967, out of print.

Johnson, James Rosser, *The Radiance of Chartres*, 1965, out of print.

Kershner, Frederick D., *The Spiritual Message of Great Art*, 1928, out of print.

Male, Emile, *The Gothic Image: Religious Art in France of the Thirteenth Century*, New York: Harper & Row, 1973.

Mans, Cynthia Pearl, *Christ and the Fine Arts*, New York: Harper & Row, 1977.

———— , *The Church and the Fine Arts*, 1960, out of print.

———— , *The Old Testament and the Fine Arts*, 1954, out of print.

Newton, Eric, and William Neil, *2000 Years of Christian Art*, 1966, out of print.

Spence, Sir Basil, *Phoenix at Coventry*, 1962, out of print.

Von Simpson, Otto, *The Gothic Cathedral: Origins of Gothic Architecture and the Medieval Concept of Order*, Princeton University Press, 1973.

Whittle, Donald, *Christianity and the Arts*, 1967, out of print.

CHAPTER

14

THE CHRISTIAN HOPE

By David R. Reagan

Blessed be the God and Father of our Lord Jesus Christ, who according to His great mercy has caused us to be born again to a living
hope through the resurrection of Jesus Christ from the dead" (1 Peter
1:3).

The Christian hope can be summarized very briefly. It is the
hope that Jesus will come back for the righteous ones of all
ages, resurrecting the dead and translating the living, and that
these people will live eternally in glorified bodies in the presence of God the Father.

Beyond this summary, however, there is little agreement.
Some believe the saints will be given glorified bodies at the
coming of Jesus. Others argue that the saved will spend eternity
as disembodied spirits. Some view eternity as being spent in a
spirit world called Heaven. Others believe they will spend
eternity on a new earth with firm soil beneath their feet. Some
teach there will be two comings of Jesus, one *for* His saints, and
the other *with* His saints. Most people lump everything into
one coming at the end of time. Some propose a thousand-year
reign of Jesus and His saints on the earth after His coming.
Others argue that the church will reign for a thousand years on
earth without the personal presence of Christ. The majority of
mainline Protestants dismiss the whole idea of any reign on
earth by Jesus or the church and take the adamant position that
Jesus will never put His foot on this earth again. Some hold that

the church, and it alone, is the kingdom. Others contend that the kingdom in its fullness is yet to come.

Confusion and Apathy

It is no wonder that Christians have shied away from the study of prophecy. Its language is technical. Its concepts are confusing. It spurs argument. It seems to divide rather than to unify.

Because of these problems, some people have written prophecy off as a lost cause—as nothing more than a play-ground for fanatics. The result is that the average Christian knows very little about prophecy, and his usual attitude toward the whole subject is one of apathy. But prophecy constitutes one-fourth of the Bible, and the Apostle Paul wrote that "all Scripture is inspired by God and profitable for teaching, for reproof, for correction, for training in righteousness" (2 Timothy 3:16). It is, therefore, a serious mistake to ignore God's prophetic word (1 Thessalonians 5:20).

But how are we to get hold of it? How can we bring any perspective to a field so broad and so full of controversy. I would suggest a chronological approach, looking at the various end-time viewpoints as they developed in history, comparing and contrasting them.

Historic Premillennial View

"Historic Premillennialism" is termed "historic" for two rea-sons: to separate it from today's most popular form of premil-lennialism and to indicate that it is the historic position of the early church. It is called "premillennial" because it envisions a

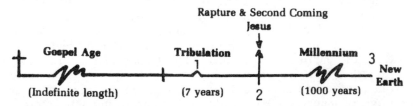

1 Revelation of the Antichrist
2 Armageddon
3 Gog & Magog

Figure 1: Historic Premillennialism

return of Christ to earth *before* (pre) the beginning of the millennium. *("Mille annum"* is Latin for one thousand years.)

A diagram of the view is presented in Figure 1. It divides the future of the world into four periods: (1) the current gospel Age; (2) a seven year period called the Tribulation; (3) a reign of Christ on earth lasting one thousand years; and (4) the eternal state of a new earth.

The Rapture

An event called the "rapture" is placed at the end of the seven years of Tribulation. The concept of the rapture is contained in 1 Thessalonians 4:13-18, although the term will not be found there in any English translation. The word comes from the Latin Vulgate translation and means "caught up" or "snatched out."

The word *rapture* vividly describes the concept. Paul says Jesus "will descend from heaven with a shout, with the voice of the archangel, and with the trumpet of God" (1 Thessalonians 4:16). The dead in Christ will be resurrected, the living will be translated, and—according to the historic premillennial viewpoint—both groups will be glorified and will instantly return to the earth to reign with Christ for a thousand years.

The Millennium

The length of Christ's reign is based upon the mention of 1,000 years six times in Revelation 20. The concept of the reign is based upon dozens of prophecies scattered throughout the Bible, from the poetic descriptions of Isaiah to the blunt statement of Zechariah that "the Lord will be king over all the earth" (Zechariah 14:9).[1]

The idea that the saints will reign with Christ comes mainly from New Testament passages such as 2 Timothy 2:12—"If we endure, we shall also reign with Him." Important, too, are the promises of Jesus in the letters to the churches recorded in Revelation 2 and 3. In one of these, Jesus says: "He who overcomes, and he who keeps My deeds until the end, to him I will give authority over the nations, and he shall rule them with a rod of iron" (Revelation 2:26, 27). In another of the letters, Jesus promises that those who overcome will sit with Him on His throne just as He has sat on His Father's throne (Revelation 3:21). The throne of Jesus is always identified in Scripture as the "throne of David" (Luke 1:32, 33), which, of course, is a throne in Jerusalem and not in Heaven. In Revelation 5, Jesus is presented before the throne of God as "the worthy Lamb." A "new song" is sung in His honor in which it is stated that those whom He has redeemed "shall reign on earth" (Revelation 5:9, 10). And in Revelation 20, the resurrected saints are pictured reigning with Jesus on the earth.[2]

The Tribulation

The time period of seven years for the Tribulation is based mainly upon passages in Daniel's vision of the seventy weeks (Daniel 9:24-27; interpreted as seventy weeks "of years," cf. RSV). Daniel states that God will complete His purpose for Israel in one final week "of years," and he goes on to state that this will be "a time of distress such as never occurred" (Daniel 12:1). He states that in the middle of this period "the prince who is to come" will desecrate the temple and stop the sacrifices (Daniel 9:27; 11:31). This concept is reinforced by the narrative in Revelation 12 and 13, which is taken to indicate that the antichrist will reveal himself at the midpoint of the Tribulation. According to this position, Jesus refers to the last three and one-half years of the Tribulation as "the great tribulation" because that is the time when the antichrist will severely persecute both Jews and Christians (Matthew 24:15-22).

The concept of a period of tribulation is seen throughout the Hebrew Scriptures. The first mention of it is in a speech by Moses when he prophesies that the sin of idolatry will cause God to scatter the children of Israel all over the world (Deuteronomy 4:15-31, esp. v. 27). Following this dispersion, he says the Jews will be brought into a time of tribulation in "the latter days," which will result in some of them turning to the Lord in faith (Deuteronomy 4:30, 31). The period is described poetically in some Scriptures as a time of refining, when the dross will be separated by the fire of God's wrath (Isaiah 1:24-26; Ezekiel 22:17-22; Zechariah 13:9; Malachi 3:1-3). It should be noted that although the Tribulation is pictured as a special time of testing for the Jews to produce a believing remnant, it is also portrayed as a time for the pouring out of God's wrath upon all people who have rejected the grace of Jesus Christ (Jeremiah 25:15-29).

Armageddon

Premillennialists believe that on the day Jesus returns, He

raptures the righteous, both the living and the dead, glorifies their bodies, and then returns with them to earth immediately to defeat the antichrist and his armies in the so-called "battle of Armageddon" Revelation 16:16; 19:17-21). We say "so-called" because there really is not a battle. The Lord will simply speak the word and the forces of the antichrist will be destroyed by a supernatural plague. (See Zechariah 14:12-15; 2 Thessalonians 2:8; Revelation 19:15.) The antichrist and his false prophet will be captured at this point and thrown into the lake of fire (Revelation 19:20). Satan is seized and bound for the duration of the thousand year reign (Revelation 20:1-3).

Jesus and His glorified saints then begin their reign over these non-believers in the flesh who lived to the end of the Tribulation. Isaiah prophesies that during the millennium, disease will be curtailed, nature will be reconciled, life spans will be extended, and the earth will be flooded with peace, righteousness, and justice (Isaiah 33:23, 24; 11:6-9; 35:1-7).

Gog and Magog

At the end of the millennial reign, Satan is released and sets out to deceive the nations, rallying them to battle against the Lord (Revelation 20:7). He and his armies are destroyed by fire from Heaven, and he is cast into the everlasting lake of fire (Revelation 20:8-10). This last battle of history is referred to in the Scriptures as the battle of "Gog and Magog, " a symbolic term used first by Ezekiel to denote those who oppose God's people (Ezekiel 38, 39).

The second resurrection, the resurrection of the unjust, occurrs at this point, and they are judged at the "great white throne." Their Judgment results in their being cast into the lake of fire, experiencing what the Scriptures term "the second death" (Revelation 20:11-15).

New Heavens and New Earth

The glorified saints are taken to Heaven while this earth is consumed with fire and a new earth is prepared for the eternal abode (2 Peter 3:7, 10-13). When the new earth is ready, the saints descend to it inside the "new Jerusalem," the glorious "mansion" Jesus has been preparing for His bride (John 14:1-3; Revelation 21:1, 2).

It is then that Jesus surrenders the kingdom to His Father, and God comes to the new earth to dwell with His children

(1 Corinthians 15:24-28; Revelation 21:3). Man and God will be perfectly reconciled, and the saints will spend eternity basking in the glory of God (Revelation 21:1—22:5).

The Church Fathers

This capsule summary of end-time events presented above is the only viewpoint that existed during the first three hundred years of the church's existence. With one exception, all the church fathers who expressed themselves on prophecy were premillennial until A.D. 400.

Justin Martyr, who was born in A.D. 100, went so far in his writings on the subject as to suggest that anyone with a different viewpoint was considered heretical. He wrote:

> I and whoever are on all points right-minded Christians know that there will be a resurrection of the dead and a thousand years in Jerusalem, which will then be built, adorned, and enlarged as the prophets Ezekiel and Isaiah and the others declare . . . and further, a certain man with us, named John, one of the Apostles of Christ, predicted by a revelation that was made to him that those who believed in our Christ would spend a thousand years in Jerusalem.[3]

Those today who have a different view of end-time events respond to the near unanimity of the early church fathers by saying they were simply wrong in their interpretation of the prophetic Scriptures.[4] It certainly should be noted that these early church leaders were not prophetic scholars. They wrote very little on prophecy, and what they wrote was sketchy. Their concern was not prophecy, but the deity of Christ, the oneness of God, the practical problems of church organization, and survival amid persecution. Yet their concept of end-time events should not be dismissed out of hand as crude and primitive, for anyone who has studied the prophetic Scriptures will have to admit that the church fathers' viewpoint presents a literal summary of the Bible's teachings about the end times.

The Spiritualizers

One exception to the consensus opinion of the early church fathers was Origen (A.D. 185-254), the leader of the Alexandrian School. Origen's approach to Scripture was to spiritualize it. He tended to deny the literal meaning of prophecy, but looked upon its language as highly symbolic and expressive of deep spiritual truths rather than of historical events.

Although Origen could not accept the premillennial view-point, he did not develop an alternative. That task fell to the greatest among the church fathers, St. Augustine (A.D. 358-434), who conceived an alternative viewpoint at the end of the fourth century.[5]

The Amillennial View

The concept formulated by Augustine is illustrated in Figure 2. It is called "Amillennialism." In the Greek language, a word is negated by putting the letter "a" in front of it. Thus, amillennial literally means "no thousand years."

The term is misleading, however, because most amillennialists do believe in a millennium, but not a literal, earthly one. They argue that the millennium is the current spiritual reign of Christ over the church and that it will continue until He returns for His saints. They thus interpret the one thousand years as a symbolic period of time.

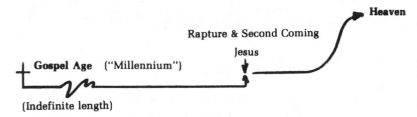

Figure 2: Amillennialism

Platonizing

Augustine "platonized" the prophetic Scriptures, reading and interpreting the words of the Bible's Hebrew writers as if they had been written by Greek philosophers.[6] The result was a radical transformation of the concept of end-time events. As Figure 2 illustrates, the Tribulation, the literal millennium, and the new earth all disappeared, as did the two resurrections mentioned in Revelation.

Using the spiritualizing principle of interpretation, Augustine argued that the binding of Satan had taken place during the ministry of Jesus. He interpreted the first resurrection of Revelation 20 to be a reference to the spiritual rebirth of the believer. He identified the millennium with the church age, stating it would be the period of time between the first and second advents of Jesus. He dismissed the new earth as symbolic language for Heaven. The kingdom was made synonymous with the church.

The Greek World View

Augustine's approach to prophetic interpretation is easy to understand when one considers the fact that he had a Greek world view, a view that clashes sharply with the Hebrew perspective. The Greeks had a creation-negating viewpoint. They viewed the material world as essentially evil. In contrast, the Hebrew view contained in Scriptures is creation-affirming. To the Hebrew mind, the creation is good, even in its fallen state. "The heavens are telling of the glory of God; and their expanse is declaring the work of His hands" (Psalm 19:1).

Whereas the Greek tended to look toward the dissolution of the universe, the Hebrew yearned for the redemption of the creation. Thus, Isaiah dreams of the "new heavens and a new earth" and Paul writes that the whole creation longs for its redemption so that it will "be set free from its slavery to corruption" (Isaiah 65:17; 66:22; Romans 8:18-21).

Acceptance of Amillennialism

Augustine's view of end-time events was adopted by the Council of Ephesus in A.D. 431 and has remained Catholic dogma to this day. It is also the current majority viewpoint among mainline Protestant denominations. In other words, the amillennial viewpoint is the one espoused today by the vast majority of all those who claim to be Christians.

The third view of end-time events, postmillennialism, did not develop until the mid-seventeenth century. This suggests that the Reformation had very little impact on prophetic views about end-time events. The reason, of course, is that the Reformation leaders had their attention riveted on the questions of Biblical authority and salvation by grace through faith.

About the only prophetic wrinkle that came out of the Reformation was the "historical" interpretation of Revelation, which saw the book as a prophecy of the apostacy of the church under the influence of the papacy. This view of the book of Revelation converted it into an anti-Catholic weapon. It prompted a response by the Jesuits, who developed and refined the "preterist" view that the book of Revelation was fulfilled in the decline and fall of the Roman Empire.[7]

The Postmillennial View

The third view of end-time events came out of the rationalistic revolution of the seventeenth century. It was developed in the mid-1600's by a Unitarian minister named Daniel Whitby.[8] It was immediately dubbed "postmillennialism" because it envisioned a return of Christ *after* (post) a literal one thousand year reign of the church upon the earth. This view is illustrated in Figure 3.

Postmillennialism spread quickly within the Protestant world, probably for two reasons. First, it gave Protestants an opportunity to differ from the Catholic position. More importantly, it was a theological expression of the prevailing rationalistic philosophy of the age, a philosophy that boldly proclaimed the ability of mankind to build the kingdom of Heaven on earth.

The postmillennial view holds that the church age will gradually evolve into a "golden age" when the church will rule the world.[9] To its credit, it can be said that this viewpoint served as a mighty stimulus to missionary efforts, as its adherents went forth all over the world to proclaim the gospel and thereby hasten the coming of the kingdom.

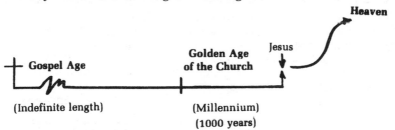

Figure 3: Postmillennialism

Campbell and Stone

Postmillennialism was the predominant viewpoint among Protestants when the Campbell-Stone restoration movement began on the American frontier in the early 1800s. It was the viewpoint Alexander Campbell adopted, and because of his enormous influence, it is the viewpoint that came to dominate the movement.

The interesting thing is that Barton W. Stone was an outspoken premillennialist. But as with many other matters on which they disagreed, like the ordination of clergy and the frequency of communion, Stone and Campbell chose to overlook their differences on prophecy in the interest of Christian unity.

Actually, neither Stone nor Campbell was particularly interested in prophecy. Their consuming passion was a return to the authority of the Bible as the basis for Christian unity. Campbell's most extensive series of articles on prophecy was written in the 1840s to counter the growing influence of the Millerites, who were predicting the second coming of the Lord in 1843.[10]

Campbell believed that he was living on the threshold of the millennium. This is one of the reasons he named his journal *The Millennial Harbinger*. Campbell believed that God would use the resources of the United States to spread the gospel all over the world and usher in the reign of what Campbell repeatedly called the "Millennial Church." Campbell also believed that a remnant of the Jews would be converted to Christ and that God would fulfill His Old Testament promises to restore this remnant to its homeland in Palestine.[11] In fact, the fundamental argument Campbell used against the Millerites was that Jesus could not come in 1843 because time will end when Jesus returns and God must yet fulfill all the promises He made in the Old Testament concerning a future age of peace, righteousness, and justice. Campbell scoffed sarcastically at the idea that these promises had already been fulfilled in some spiritualized manner in the church.[12]

Robert Milligan

The most comprehensive and penetrating writer on Biblical prophecy during the first generation of the Campbell-Stone movement was Robert Milligan. In the mid-1850s, he wrote an extensive series of articles on Bible prophecy for *The Millennial Harbinger*.[13] Like Campbell, he was a postmillennialist, and he also shared Campbell's conviction that the Old Testament promises to the Jews would be fulfilled by God during the millennial reign of the church. Wrote Milligan: "The children of Israel will yet arise from their present degraded and wretched condition, and be gathered out of all countries into the land which God gave to Abraham and to his posterity for an everlasting possession."[14]

Specifically, Milligan believed the Jews would return to their homeland in unbelief, that they would soon thereafter be converted to Christianity, and that they would then go forth "to the remotest parts of the Earth, and introduce the golden period of the Messiah's reign."[15] He even ventured to predict when these events would happen, based upon the prophecies of Daniel! He set 1892 as the year the Jews would return to Palestine; 1922 as the year of their conversion; and 1967 as the year that their mission to the world would begin.[16] He strongly reiterated these views again in his landmark book, *The Scheme of Redemption.*[17]

The Death of Postmillennialism

At the turn of this century, it could be safely said that all the branches of the Campbell-Stone heritage were predominantly postmillennial in their view of end-time events. The same could be said for Protestant Christianity at large. But the viewpoint was to be quickly dropped.

Postmillennialism died almost overnight with the outbreak of the First World War. The reason, of course, is that this great war undermined one of the fundamental assumptions of the postmillennial viewpoint—the assumption of the inevitability of progress. This had always been a fatal flaw in the postmillennial concept, due mainly to its birth in rationalistic humanism. Its visions of the perfectibility of man and the redemption of society were destroyed by the atrocities of the war.

Another fatal flaw of the postmillennial viewpoint was its lack of a consistent Biblical base. To expound the viewpoint, it was necessary to literalize some prophecies (e.g., those concerning the millennium) while at the same time allegorizing other prophecies (e.g., those concerning the personal presence of the Lord during the millennium). Also, it was necessary to ignore or explain away the many prophecies in the Bible that clearly state that things are going to get worse rather than better as the time approaches for the Lord's return (e.g., Matthew 24:4-24; 2 Thessalonians 2:1-12; 1 Timothy 4:1, 2; 2 Timothy 3:1-5).

A Vacuum

The demise of postmillennialism was so complete that its major advocates today could literally be counted on the fingers of one hand.[18] The sudden death of postmillennialism left a prophetic vacuum among Protestant groups. Since the postmillennial view was based to a large extent upon a spiritualizing approach to Scripture, and since that approach was being heralded by the burgeoning school of higher criticism that was sweeping the seminaries of this country, most Protestant groups returned to the amillennial viewpoint they had abandoned in the 1700s.

However, a new choice of prophetic viewpoint presented itself on the American scene about this same time, and some of the more fundamentalist Protestant groups opted for it. This view has since become known as "dispensational premillennialism."

The Dispensational Premillennial View

This view is called "dispensational" because its early adherents, a remarkable group of prophetic scholars among the Plymouth Brethren, taught that the history of God's dealings with man can be divided into seven distinct *dispensations*.[19] Their prophetic concept of end-time events is illustrated in Figure 4.

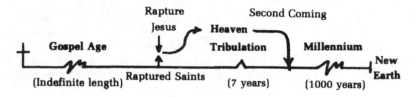

Figure 4: Dispensational Premillennialism

As can be readily seen, the dispensational view is identical to the historic premillennial view except for its concept of the rapture of the church. The Plymouth Brethren envisioned two future comings of Jesus, one *for* His church, and one *with* His church.[20] Their concept of the rapture has since come to be known as the "pre-tribulation rapture."

This view crystallized about 1830 as the result of twenty years of in-depth prophetic studies by the Plymouth Brethren, under the leadership of John Darby. The view spread rather rapidly across Europe, its most eloquent spokesman being the eminent British minister, Charles Spurgeon. Spurgeon's friend, D. L. Moody, popularized the concept in the U.S. in the late nineteenth century. But the real turning point for the view came in 1909 with the publication of a study Bible written by

C. I. Scofield, a Dallas minister, who thoroughly incorporated into its notes the dispensational concept of end-time events.[21]

A Popular View

Since that time, the dispensational viewpoint of prophecy has grown steadily in strength among Evangelicals until today it is by far the most widely accepted premillennial view. The irony is that although the Catholic church and the vast majority of all Protestant churches still hold to the amillennial view of end-time events, the dispensational view is the one that is the best known, among Christians and non-Christians alike. The reason is that the dispensational view has enjoyed some marvelously gifted communicators like Billy Graham, Hal Lindsey, and Kenneth Taylor, the writer of *The Living Bible* paraphrase. In fact, Lindsey's book, *The Late Great Planet Earth*, was certified by the *New York Times* as the number-one best-selling book of the decade of the '70s. Who would have believed in 1969 that a book on Bible prophecy would set such a record in the '70s?

The dispensational view has been attacked as being "too new to be true." But its advocates are quick to point out that the Bible teaches the principle of "progressive illumination" regarding prophecy (e.g., Daniel 12:4; Jeremiah 30:24). What they mean by this is that the Bible indicates that end-time prophecy will be better understood as the time nears for its fulfillment. Thus, say the dispensationalists, new prophetic understandings and concepts should be expected as we approach the time of the Lord's return. These will come as the Holy Spirit illuminates people's minds to understand prophecies that have previously been a mystery.

Conclusion

In looking back over the four viewpoints presented, one should note that what they have in common is far more important than their differences. Note that all four views agree on the following:

(1) that Jesus is coming back,
(2) that His return will be bodily, visible, and in great glory,
(3) that He will rapture His saints, and
(4) that He will take His saints to live eternally with God the Father.

The obvious conclusion from this observation is that differ-

CHRISTIAN HOPE

ences in prophetic viewpoints should never be allowed to divide Christians. To put it another way, what one believes about prophecy is not going to determine his eternal destiny. The eternal state will contain premillennialists, postmillennialists, amillennialists, and even a lot of "panmillennialists" (those who just expect everything to "pan out" in the end). There will be people saved who know nothing about prophecy, including some (like the apostle Paul) who have never even read the book of Revelation in this life.

Does this mean that what one believes about prophecy is irrelevant? Not at all! The study of the Christian hope is both relevant and practical. It has been abused by fanatics who have made it a playground, but when properly taught and studied, it can serve as green pastures for disciples.

Revelation 19:10 states that "the testimony of Jesus is the spirit of prophecy." That verse really sums up the value of prophetic study, for prophecy points us to Jesus as our ultimate hope. As Paul put it:

For the grace of God has appeared, bringing salvation to all men, instructing us to deny ungodliness and worldly desires and to live sensibly, righteously and godly in the present age, looking for the blessed hope and the appearing of the glory of our great God and Savior, Christ Jesus (Titus 2:11:13).

I can add only one word: "Maranatha!" (1 Corinthians 16:22).

NOTES

[1]Cf. Isaiah 2:2-4; 9:6, 7; 11:3-9; 24:21-23; 33:17-22; 61:2-7; Jeremiah 3:12-20; 23:5, 6; Ezekiel 20:33-35, 41-44; 36:22-28; 37:21-28; Daniel 7:13, 14, 18, 27; Amos 9:14, 15; Micah 5:4; Zephaniah 3:14-20; and Zechariah 9:10.

[2]Two groups are pictured as reigning with Jesus in Revelation 20. The first group consists of those to whom judgment was committed (Revelation 20:4). These are glorified saints (1 Corinthians 6:2, 3). The second group is composed of those martyred during the Tribulation (Revelation 20:4). The place of the reign is the earth (Revelation 20:9).

[3]Cited by Charles C. Ryrie, *The Basis of the Premillennial Faith* (Neptune, NJ: Loizeaux Brothers, 1966).

[4]See Oswald T. Allis, *Prophecy and the Church* (Philadelphia: Presbyterian and Reformed, 1945), and *History of the Christian Church* (New York: 1882-1910).

[5]See Augustine, *The City of God.*

[6]For a good discussion of the platonizing approach of Augustine, see Oscar Cullman, *Immortality of the Soul or Resurrection of the Dead?* (London: Epworth Press, 1958).

[7]For a fair and incisive discussion of the development and meaning of the various interpretive approaches to Revelation, see Merrill Tenney, *Interpreting Revelation* (Grand Rapids: Eerdmans, 1957).

[8]Robert G. Clouse, *The Meaning of the Millennium: Four Views* (Downers Grove, IL: Intervarsity Press, 1977).

[9]Loraine Boettner, *The Millennium* (Philadelphia: Presbyterian and Reformed, 1957).

[10]See *The Millennial Harbinger* for 1841, 1842, and 1843 for Campbell's series of twenty-six articles entitled, "The Coming of the Lord."

[11]*The Millennial Harbinger,* 1843, pp. 73-78. See also, 1841, p. 9.

[12]*The Millennial Harbinger,* 1843, pp. 73-78.

[13]*The Millennial Harbinger,* 1856 and 1857. The series consisted of thirteen in-depth articles on a wide variety of prophetic topics.

[14]The Millennial Harbinger, 1856, p. 573.

[15]The Millennial Harbinger, 1857, p. 430. See also, 1856, pp. 601-607.

[16]The Millennial Harbinger, 1857, p. 430.

[17]Robert Milligan, The Scheme of Redemption (Cincinnati: **Standard,** 1868), pp. 536-577.

[18]The foremost contemporary spokesman for postmillennialism is Loraine Boettner, The Millennium (Philadelphia: Presbyterian and Reformed, 1957). Another contemporary source for this view is J. Marcellus Kik, An Eschatology of Victory (Philadelphia: Presbyterian and Reformed, 1974). Nearly all other postmillennial books were written before World War I.

[19]For a thorough review of the historical development of dispensationalism, see Charles C. Ryrie's Dispensationalism Today (Chicago: Moody Press, 1965).

[20]Compare John 14:1-4 and 1 Thessalonians 4:13-18 with 1 Thessalonians 3:13; Jude 14; and Colossians 3:4.

[21]The Scofield Reference Bible has been published in a revised edition by Oxford Press (1967). A newer study Bible with the same viewpoint is the Ryrie Study Bible (1978) by Charles Ryrie of Dallas Theological Seminary.

PART FOUR

THE WORD INCORPORATE

"The household of God" Ephesians 2:19

SECTION OUTLINE

15. THE CHURCH, THE BODY OF CHRIST
    A. The Relation of the Church to Christ
    B. The Catholicity of the Worshiping Congregation
    C. The Nature of Christian Unity
    D. The Church and the Age

16. BAPTISM AND THE LORD'S SUPPER
    Introduction
    A. Baptism
       The Action of Baptism
       The Subjects for Baptism
       The Design of Baptism
       The Action of Baptism and Christian Unity
    B. The Lord's Supper
       The Supper—the Institution
       The Supper—as Memorial
       The Supper—the Presence of Christ
       The Supper—as Table Fellowship
       The Supper—as Covenant Renewal
       The Supper—as Sacrament

17. THE PURPOSE OF THE CHURCH
    A. The Purpose of God—the Mission of the Church
    B. Models in the Determining Purpose
       The Predestination Model
       The *Mysterion* Model
       The Apostolic Activity Model
       The "Last Will and Testament" Model
       The Consideration of Alternatives
    C. Eschatology and Purpose
       "And Then Shall the End Come"

CHAPTER

15

THE CHURCH,
THE BODY OF CHRIST

By Robert O. Fife

The Relation of the Church to Christ

Many symbols are used in Scripture to describe the Church. Among these are the "flock" of the Good Shepherd (Acts 20:28), the "kingdom" of the King (John 3:3f), the "temple of the living God" (2 Corinthians 6:16), and the bride of Christ (Ephesians 5:25).[1]

All of these models are rich with meaning. But the purpose of this chapter is to reflect upon the significance of the church as the body of Christ. To the Corinthians, Paul wrote, "Now you are Christ's body, and individually members of it" (1 Corinthians 12:27). It was through the Spirit they had all been baptized into the body (1 Corinthians 12:13).

The Colossians were reminded that Christ is the head of the body, the church. For it, Paul also suffered (Colossians 1:24). The Ephesians were exhorted to exercise the gifts of ministry for the upbuilding of the body in love (Ephesians 4:16). The Romans were taught that while there are many members, the body is one; and being members of the one body, Christians are also members of each other (Romans 12:5).

From such insights, one may discern that the church is, at least in a limited sense, "the extension of the Incarnation."[2] Identified with Him in baptism, made alive by the Holy Spirit,

359

and governed by His mind, believers are cojoined into a living organism. Ministering as He would in the world, they are in a very literal sense, "the body of Christ."

There are rich mystical overtones in such an affirmation. Even so, however, the doctrine of the church as the body of Christ is to be understood with utmost practicality. Members are called to see with His eyes, be moved with His compassion, go where He would go, and serve as He would serve. So it is that the community of faith continues to enflesh His Word in the world.

The harmony and interdependence of members and head is a profound implication of life in the body. Paul develops this most meaningfully in the first Corinthian letter. While there are many diversities among members of the body, the body is one. As each member fulfills the ministry to which he is called, the body functions in harmony. The roles of members may be varied, but each is important to the whole (1 Corinthians 12:12f). No one should consider his service in the body insignificant.

Paul shows great insight into the meaning of membership. When one member suffers, all suffer. When one is honored, all rejoice. The intimacy of true membership is thus seen to transcend any purely institutional relationship. Membership is a living relationship—not simply a formal status. It is not effected by enrollment in a record, but by the interpenetration of life with life.[3]

For this reason, the church may be defined as "the fellowship of God with His Son, Jesus Christ, shared with believers through the Covenant of Grace."[4] So Jesus prayed for His disciples, "that they may all be one; even as Thou, Father, art in Me, and I in Thee, that they also may be in Us; that the world may believe that Thou didst send Me" (John 17:21).

The church is the fellowship of the Father and the Son, extended unto men. As such, it is a gift to be received. It is rooted in Messiah Jesus, who was the faithful remnant,[5] fulfilling the promises made to pilgrims of old (Hebrews 11:39f). From Him has sprung the new remnant—the new Israel—the church (Romans 9:6; Galatians 6:16).

As the fellowship of God offered to men through Christ, the church is a gift to be received. Men do not contrive the church. Christ brings it. Men do not establish the church. He calls it. The responsibility of believers is to receive the gift, and respond to the call.

But often in the course of the church's life, the reception has fallen short of the gift. It was this that called forth several of the apostolic letters, as well as the letters of the Spirit to the seven churches of Asia (Revelation 2, 3). So the Corinthians were taught the fuller meaning of what it is to be in Christ (2 Corinthians 5:17ff). The Galatians were reminded that the gift is one of grace—not of the law (Galatians 3:1-5). The Ephesian church was charged with having left its "first love" (Revelation 2:4).

Because the church comes as God's gift, it is marked by "once-for-all-ness." It is not an evolutionary institution, set adrift amidst the tides of history. Change, indeed, has come in many ways, but the essence of the gift remains the same. For this reason, any change that obscures or neglects the gift is a deformation—not a reformation.

"Restitution," or "restoration," is that process through which the church is reformed in terms of its origins—in terms of the gift. Such reformation has always been a need of the church, as believers either fall short in their reception of the gift or allow it to be obscured.[6]

In such a view, the apostolic age marks the "creative period" in the history of the church.[7] Jesus promised that the Spirit would lead the apostolic company into "all the truth" (John 16:13), and in that is finality. This is the tradition by which all traditions are to be judged.

Through one Spirit, believers are baptized into the one body and given their functions within the organism. In such a way, the Spirit forms the members into a body suited to His ministry in the world. That order of body-relationships is portrayed in the New Testament documents, which therefore become normative for all time.

The normative nature of Scripture is not, therefore, that of a sterile code. Scripture is normative in the "biological" sense. As certain organic relationships are necessary for a human spirit to indwell a physical body, so the body of Christ must be marked by a certain order if the Holy Spirit is to indwell it freely. That order is portrayed in Scripture.

In this light, restoration is the effort to present to the Holy Spirit a body adequately suited to His ongoing ministry in the world. A spastic possesses a sound mind, but his body only marginally serves the mind. So a deformed church may hinder the free movement of the Spirit of Christ or remain unmoved by the mind of Christ.[8]

Restoration seeks ever to renew or reform the body for the Spirit's sake. This is not a legal, but a vital, principle. The order of the body—the interrelationship of head and members—is not determined by slavish imitation of a pattern. Rather, it is determined by reverence for life—the life our Lord would impart.[9]

Receiving the gift, disciples are thus exhorted to "speak the truth in love" so that all may "grow up unto Christ." In this fashion, the body of Christ continues to live in the world, indwelt by the Spirit, and effecting His will, "until we all attain . . . to the measure of the stature which belongs to the fullness of Christ" (Ephesians 4:11-16).

The Catholicity of the Worshiping Congregation

In light of these considerations, it is to be asked, "When Scripture speaks of the body of Christ, does it refer to the whole church on earth, or to the local congregation?" The answer is at once simple and profound: The Scripture applies the same term to both (Ephesians 1:23; 1 Corinthians 12:27). The worshiping congregation is the church universal in its place. The church universal exists in local congregations.[10]

In this vein, several apostolic letters were addressed to local assemblies. "In Christ" is the key phrase whereby catholicity is expressed. Thus, Paul writes to "the church of God which is at Corinth, to those who have been sanctified in Christ Jesus, . . . with all who in every place call upon the name of our Lord Jesus Christ, their Lord and ours (1 Corinthians 1:2). In similar fashion, he writes to "the saints who are at Ephesus, and who are faithful in Christ Jesus" (Ephesians 1:1). He salutes "all the saints in Christ Jesus who are in Philippi" (Philippians 1:1), and greets "the saints and faithful brethren in Christ who are at Colossae" (Colossians 1:2).

The first passage expresses the truth very well. The Corinthian congregation is a "whole Church" by virtue of the fact that it is "in Christ Jesus"; but it is not "the whole Church" because it is in Corinth.[11] The Corinthians are reminded of "all who in every place call upon the name of our Lord Jesus Christ, their Lord and ours." These are also members of the same body. Just as a cell of the human body carries the whole genetic gift, so the Corinthian congregation carries in its life the wholeness of the church. But it is a wholeness limited by time and space—the environs of Corinth. There is a larger communion of all those who call upon the name of Jesus, to whom the Corinthians also belong. The reason of that belonging is that all have the same Lord. He is both "their Lord and ours."

The content of the apostolic letters is also significant here. While often addressing local problems, they largely concern matters of universal import. Consider, for example, the great fourth chapter of Ephesians, the second chapter of Philippians, or the eighth chapter of Romans. These are not peculiar teachings for a limited time and place. On the contrary, such words are for the whole church of Christ on earth, even though they were initially addressed to particular congregations within the Roman Empire. It is for this reason that the letters were circulated and treasured. The very existence of the canon of Scripture is witness to the universal significance of that which was written to local assemblies.[12]

In short, the apostles recognized in worshiping congregations the church universal. They acknowledged the high dignity and prerogatives of these assemblies. It was to such assemblies gathered in Jesus' name that His presence was promised. It was within their fellowship that believers were baptized into the universal body. There the universal supper was shared, and the universal gospel proclaimed.[13]

At the same time, such assemblies are treated as having universal responsibility. The Romans are told that their "faith is being proclaimed throughout the whole world" (Romans 1:8). The Galatians are warned against abandoning the one gospel because of the pressure of sectarian Judaizers (Galatians 1:6f). The Macedonians are taught their responsibility for the suffering brethren of Judea (1 Corinthians 16:1f). So the reality of the "one body" was made manifest in the "genetic cells" of congregations scattered throughout the Roman World.

Thomas Campbell grasped this truth clearly when he wrote,

> that although the church of Christ upon earth must necessarily exist in particular and distinct societies, locally separate from one another; yet there ought to be no schims, no uncharitable divisions among them. . . . And for this purpose, they ought all to walk by the same rule, to mind and speak the same thing; and to be perfectly joined together in the same mind, and the same judgment.[14]

Here it is important to note that separate locality is not schism. Schism occurs when brothers do not "walk by the same rule," or "mind and speak the same thing." While it is natural that each congregation will have its own peculiar marks of the society in which it serves, such peculiarity ought never be allowed to obscure the unity of the body, which is God's gift. Such localisms as, "This is our church," or, "We do it this way here," are always to be brought under judgment of the universal gift.

This responsibility may be expressed in the following categorical imperative: "The local church ought so to believe and act that its faith and practice could be commended to the whole church of Christ on earth." The congregation is under mandate to reform any and every doctrine or practice that fails this test.

A further word is appropriate concerning American denominational thought. Denominations commonly create supracongregational structures, culminating in national centers of authority. It is often affirmed that the church is "manifested" at different "levels," each possessing more fully the essence of the church than those beneath.[15] Such thought tends to demean the dignity of the local congregation. It may well accord with American corporate structures, but hardly does it with Jesus' promise of His presence with the "two or three" gathered in His name. The presence of Jesus is the "great leveller."[16]

Does this mean that the local congregation, possessing the dignity of Christ's presence, is a law unto itself? Not at all. Congregational autonomy does not justify congregational isolation.[17] The dialogue of discipleship is incumbent on local congregations. They should teach each other and learn from each other. Such dialogue should reach far beyond denominational boundaries. It should bridge cultures and nations as well. "Speaking the truth in love" is not only an intracongregational responsibility. It is intercongregational as well.

The Jerusalem Conference (Acts 15) provides a useful model of intercongregational dialogue. The congregation in Antioch had acted in keeping with its responsibility when it obeyed the mandate of the Spirit to send Paul and Barnabas to the Gentiles (Acts 13:1-3). But the results of that mission had profound implications for the whole church. When the Gentile issue was joined, however, Antioch did not decide for itself as an "independent" congregation (Acts 15:2). It joined in counsel with the saints in Jerusalem to seek the mind of Christ. The result was a concensus of "faith-knowledge," which reflected the judgment of the "apostles and the elders, with the whole church" (Acts 15:22).

It is this "larger wisdom" that modern churches are responsible to seek. In an age of global communications, narrow parochialism is inexcusable. The "communion of saints" is God's gift to the church, reaching back to Jesus and the apostles and embracing all believers in every land. The worshiping congregation is authorized to do all that it is capable of doing, in fulfillment of the mandate of Jesus. But the insight of the "larger wisdom" cannot come in isolation. It only is gained through active cultivation of the communion of saints.[18]

Channels of communication and counsel have historically been devised to enhance realization of intercongregational fellowship. But the wholeness does not consist in these structures. This was the error of Cyprian, who was first to claim, "If any one be not with the bishop, he is not in the Church."[19]

The wholeness is in Him whom believers everywhere confess. It is in the presence promised the community of the faithful. Where Christ is, there is the church.

The Nature of Christian Unity

Unity is of the essence in the Church. Without unity, there is no church. After all, how could the community of the reconciled be divided? "Is Christ divided?" asked Paul of the Corinthians (1 Corinthians 1:13, NIV). The obvious answer is no! Men may sever themselves from Christ, but in Christ they cannot sever themselves from each other.[20]

Diversity may rightly exist within the body of Christ, but not division. Schism may only truly come when members sunder their relationship with the head. This was the danger facing the Galatians when Paul warned them about falling from grace (Galatians 5:4). The body remained one. There were not two bodies of Christ—one Gentile, the other Jewish.

The same unity prevails today, despite the manner in which modern denominational systems obscure it. Men are either in Christ or not in Christ. And those in Christ are one. The task of modern disciples is not to contrive Christian unity, but to cease obscuring it.[21] It is to be confessed, received, treasured, celebrated, and exhibited because it is God's gift.

But how can one realistically speak of the unity of the church amidst the confusion of our time? Of what denominations does that unity consist? None. Christian unity is not denominational. Mergers may be devised to combine denominations, but these do not constitute Christian unity.[22] Christian unity is of a different nature.

Christian unity is essentially *personal* and *sacramental*. It is personal because the church is the divine-human fellowship. It is sacramental because baptism and the Lord's Supper are the appointed means whereby that fellowship is entered and renewed. The personal essence of Christian unity is reflected in Jesus' prayer for His followers: " That they may all be one; even as Thou, Father, art in Me, and I in Thee, that they also may be in Us ..." (John 17:21). The sacramental means is made evident when it is affirmed that union with Christ is effected in baptism (Romans 6:4f) and sustained in the Supper (1 Corinthians 10:16f).

How is the unity that is God's gift to be recognized? Recognition depends upon an original cognition. We know the marks of Christ, the head, from the testimony of the Scripture. When we see those marks in the life of another, we recognize them, and confess that he, too, belongs to Jesus.[23]

Thomas Campbell transcended denominational fences when he dared to define the church in terms of persons professing faith and obedience. He wrote,

> The church of Christ upon earth is essentially, intentionally, and constitutionally one; consisting of all those in every place that profess their faith in Christ and obedience to him in all things according to the scriptures, and that manifest the same by their tempers and conduct. . . ."[24]

It is important to note that this was written in an era marked by bitter sectarian strife, of which Thomas Campbell had, himself, been a victim. Nonetheless, through "profession" and "manifestation," Christian faith is made visible, and the fellowship of Jesus is recognized.

But what of the obvious divisions that plague the churches today? Here it is significant that in Scripture there are two dimensions of Christian unity. The first we have already referred to as the gift; the second is the goal.

The fourth chapter of Ephesians sets this forth in a most instructive manner. We have noted that these early disciples were exhorted to "keep the unity of the Spirit." This was God's gift. Paul proceeds to state the seven marks of that unity—One body, One Spirit, One hope, One Lord, One faith, One baptism, and One God and Father.[25]

The apostle then proceeds to describe how the ascended Christ gave ministries to the church, "until we all attain to the unity of the faith, and of the knowledge of the Son of God . . ." (Ephesians 4:13).

This unity, which we may call "faith-knowledge," is thus set forth as the climactic prize to be achieved. True, not all Christians understand the implications of the faith alike. Students in the school of Jesus are not presently all in the same "grade." But having received the unity created by the Holy Spirit, they are urged toward attainment of a common faith-knowledge, which is its ultimate goal. This is only achieved as disciples, "speaking the truth in love, . . . grow up . . . into . . . Christ" (Ephesians 4:15).

Our contemporary problem is in large part occasioned by the reversal of these dimensions of unity. Many sincere disciples are unwilling to acknowledge the gift of unity until the goal has been reached. This is the thrust of the many creeds of Christendom.[26] In consequence, the gift is rejected or obscured.[27]

Such is the practical effect of much modern sectarianism. The sect hedges the unity of the Spirit by certain understandings. In so doing, it places those understandings as a prior condition to the "one Lord, one faith, one baptism" that properly constitute the ground of Christian unity.[28]

But granted acceptance of the Spirit's gift of unity, what is to be done when disciples develop different understandings or concerns? These are to be resolved *within* the communion of saints, as they share life with life and mind with mind

Because discipleship is a learning process, it is natural that communities of understanding should develop within the community of the faith. The problem comes when such communities assume to themselves the essence of the church, thus "unchurching" those who do not share their understandings. This is the error of denominationalism, for in calling themselves "churches," denominations obscure the church.[29]

How, then, may communities of understanding avoid dividing the body? By defining themselves in terms other than that of the church. Here the concept of "movement" may be most useful.[30] A movement is a community of understanding or concern that exists within the fellowship of the faith. It does not claim to be "church," but exists within and for the church. As such, it may advocate its understandings or bear witness to its concerns without dividing the body.

In this view, one is not baptized into a movement, nor does he commune as a member of it. He is baptized into the body and communes as a member of the body. For this reason, a movement makes no claim to be the body, but exists for witness within the body.

How, then, does one become part of a movement? He shares its understanding or fulfills its concern. What distinguishes a movement from the body? The body is the community of the faith; a movement is a community of understanding or concern growing out of the faith. Not all brothers and sisters may share the same understandings or concerns, but they do share the common faith. A movement is, therefore, distinguished by its witness. But as the whole body comes to share the witness, the distinction of the movement disappears. It thus "sinks into union with the Body of Christ at large."[31]

Philip's mission to Samaria may be conceived as a "movement" of one member of the body. It was later shared by others, as in the visit of Peter and John (Acts 8:14f). The first missionary journey of Paul and Barnabas was a "movement" commissioned by the Holy Spirit through the congregation in Antioch (Acts 13:1f). But it never occurred to those early disciples to limit the fellowship of the Church to those who participated in their endeavors. Indeed, Paul and Peter are specifically declared to have exchanged hands of fellowship over their diverse concerns (Galatians 2:9).

How do movements become denominations? They define the fellowship of Christ in terms of their particular understandings or concerns. For example, Methodism was for years a movement within the Church of England. Its concern was the cultivation of personal holiness. Only after the American Revolution, upon Wesley's advice, did Methodists constitute themselves a "Church."[32] In so doing, what had been a movement became a denomination.

Movements properly arise as members of the body respond to the will of the Head. But at times, movements appear more as "reflex actions" to the spirit of the age than as reflections of the mind of Christ. Gnosticism may be seen as such a movement. It was condemned because it repudiated the unique Lordship of Jesus (1 John 4:2, 3).

In its best sense, the restoration movement (or reformation of the nineteenth century) is a community of understanding and concern that reflects the will of Christ for His church. The concern of this movement is the evangelization of the world. Its understanding is that effective evangelism awaits redisclosure of Christian unity; and that unity can only be realized through reformation of the church in terms of its origins.[33]

The restoration movement is not the church. Nor is it "the brotherhood" in the Biblical sense (1 Peter 2:17). The latter consists of all the brothers and sisters of Jesus of all eras. The movement exists as a community for witness within the brotherhood.

As with all Biblical reformations, the restoration movement points to something greater than itself—the church. The movement exists within and for the church. But the restoration movement carries a special burden. It is a particular, historic community bearing witness to the unity of the church. The witness is greater than the movement. This makes the temptation to become a denomination especially critical. Only as it resists that temptation to define itself as the church may the movement exist for witness without denying the witness by its existence.[34]

The church both is, and is becoming, one. Its unity is both given by God and to be attained by men. It is for believers to claim the gift in confession and celebration, while earnestly devoting themselves toward attainment of "the measure of the stature of the fullness of Christ"—the goal.

The Church and the Age

The role of the church in the age was given by Jesus before His death, when He prayed to the Father concerning His disciples, "I do not ask Thee to take them out of the world, but to keep them from the evil one" (John 17:15). As the risen Lord, Jesus granted His peace, and honored the disciples, saying, "As the Father has sent Me, I also send you" (John 20:21). And on the Mount of Ascension, Jesus declared,

Go therefore and make disciples of all the nations, baptizing them in the name of the Father and the Son and the Holy Spirit, teaching them to observe all that I commanded you: and lo, I am with you always, even to the end of the age (Matthew 28:18-20).

Having thus called and taught the disciples, Jesus sent them

369

forth. Here we see the essential relationship of the church to the age. The church is the "called out," and the "sent forth." It is called by the gospel, embodies the gospel, and proclaims the gospel. This dynamic "event" of congregation-dispersion-congregation is the universal order of the church's life.

Karl Barth captured this sense of "eventness" when he defined the church as "The Living Congregation of the Living Lord Jesus Christ."[35] True, other forms of corporate Christian life may be devised and institutional relationships established. But these are not the essence of the church. Properties, missionary and benevolent societies, and denominational structures have often been placed at the service of the church. But the essence of the church is not in these. The essence is in the "event" of calling together and sending forth.

Persecution may deprive the church of its properties and confiscate its treasure. Leaders may be imprisoned and educational institutions closed. But even under the most barbaric conditions, the church lives, for disciples always find ways to gather in Jesus' name—and there takes place the divine-human encounter—there is the church.

In this view, the church is not a static institution set amidst other institutions of the age. It is a dynamic "presence" through which its members live in the age.

In what sense is the church called out to "be separate" (1 Corinthians 6:17f)? It is called unto the Lord and under His reign. It separates itself from those "principalities and powers" that do not acknowledge Him. This essentially involves the adoption of His teaching and way of life, and the consequent rejection of those thought-forms, values, and modes of conduct unbecoming of Him. Life-style may change—in some ways, radically (1 Corinthians 6:9-11). But the "peculiarity" of the "peculiar people" (1 Peter 2:9, KJV) is not in some particular mode of dress or rejection of a "secular" profession. The "peculiarity" is in one's obedience to the Lordship of Jesus as that is expressed in the quality of daily life. So the Christian community is sent to live "in the world," but "not of it."[36]

But being the "sent community" has not always been easy for the people of God. If comfort and encouragement are found among those of "like precious faith" (2 Peter 1:1, KJV), vulnerability and stress often mark involvement with the age. Pressures, subtle or blatant, constantly tempt the sent community to conform to the spirit of the age.

We may thus see that the central issue of the church's relation to the age is not institutional, but dynamic. It involves the flow of power. The issue may be couched in three alternatives:

1. Shall the power flow from the age through the church, unto the compromise of the radical demands of the gospel?

2. Shall there be a mutual agreement to interdict the flow of power—to "cut the switch"—so that neither the church nor the age is threatened?

3. Shall the power flow from the gospel through the church, calling the age to repentance?

Each of these three alternatives has been adopted throughout the history of the church. They appear concurrently in our own time.

The first has assumed a variety of historic forms. "Civil religion" represents such an example.[37] But even more appropriate to this discussion is the subtle way in which such American ideas as "success" compromise many congregations' responsibility to the gospel. Peter Berger calls this "culture religion."[38]

In such situations, the churches lose their prophetic voice and mute the call to repentance. Multitudes follow modern soothsayers who tell them what they wish to hear. Such evils as personal immorality, social injustice, or blatant greed are conveniently overlooked. The "hard sayings" of Jesus are seldom heard from their pulpits. Nor are those Biblical doctrines that do not fit the spirit of the age.

By the standards of the age, such churches may be deemed successful. Wealth and popularity are often their reward. Indeed, they may so adopt the materialism of the age as to depend upon the fruits of that very greed. Such churches passively allow the power to flow from the age through their corporate life, unto the compromise of the gospel. They are modern Laodiceas (Revelation 3:14f). From them, an unregenerate age has little to fear. The salt has lost its savor (Matthew 5:13).

The second alternative does not approve of the first, and fears the third. The risk of relationship implicit in "sentness" is too great. But even so, the values of a holy life are not to be abandoned. The consequent choice is withdrawal into a monastic community, isolated and self-centered.

Such monasticism may be expressed in two forms. The one is in total withdrawal from all social intercourse, as represented in the ancient desert monasteries. Economically self-sufficient and socially exclusive, holiness could be assiduously sought while the world was left to its own fate. This alternative is seldom viable in the modern world.

More common is what may be called "expedient monasticism." This form is achieved by the momentary, functional separation of life into "sacred" and "secular" spheres. Each of these is clearly defined, and neither is expected to have significant bearing upon the other. There are two kinds of "truth"— that of revelation, and that of human discovery. These two have nothing to do with each other.[39]

Christian communities adopting this style of life see the church's role only in the sphere of the sacred. Personal morality, pure doctrine, and right practice may be genuine concerns. Evils of the age may be eloquently denounced, but only within the privacy and security of the sanctuary. Such a fellowship may be rich, meaningful, and helpful. Members may genuinely care for one another in "the household of faith."

But when the "sacred" has been duly observed, the congregation scatters into the world of the "secular," where the other "truth" has dominion. Expectations and standards are different. Efficiency, anonymity, and functionality prevail.[40] Ultimate meaning is readily forgotten amidst momentary striving for success. The ethic of love is deemed impractical in the "real world," where "survival of the fittest" is the rule. Thus, the businessman who is generous with his church may drive hard bargains with his employees.

Two major problems result from "expedient monasticism." First, it tends toward a schizoid Christianity, in which personality is fragmented by intermittent loyalty to two masters. Second, it effectively annuls the mission of the church in the age.[41] The light is placed under a bushel (Matthew 5:14ff).

The third alternative—seeking the flow of power from the gospel through the church into the age—is alone consistent with the will of Christ for His people. Here, indeed, is the vulnerability of the cross. But here, also, is the power of the resurrection.

Such a flow of power can only find its source in submission to that Word of God that opens the heart to His Spirit. The gospel is "the power of God unto salvation," because it makes available to believers the power of the resurrection. That Word and that Spirit mold a congregation into the body of Christ.

But members of a human body do not exist for themselves. They exist to serve the head. So it is with the body of Christ. As the "Word became flesh, and dwelt among us" (John 1:14), so Christ's body, the church, was made to effect His will amidst succeeding generations. As the Incarnate Word was "full of grace and truth," so should it be with the church. As in the days of His flesh, the Living Word ministered unto men, so should the church present itself as a continuing servant of the Word. As the Living Word came to men in speech and deed, so is the church to speak and act in every generation. The Word is authenticated in deed.

Alexander Campbell clearly understood this when he wrote,

> That the church may have a regenerating influence upon society at large, there is wanting a fuller display of Christian philanthropy in all her public meetings; care for the poor, manifested in the liberality of her contributions; the expression of the most unfeigned sympathy for the distresses of mankind, not only among the brotherhood, but among all men; and an ardent zeal for the conversion of sinners, proportioned to her professed appreciation of the value of her own salvation, and to her resources and means of enlightening the world, on the things unseen and eternal.[42]

It is noteworthy that Campbell here draws no line between the social and evangelistic aspects of the gospel. This distinction, which has long characterized certain religious traditions, Campbell did not consider to be Biblical.[43] Unfeigned sympathy for the distresses of mankind, and an ardent zeal for the conversion of sinners, are both essentials to the mission of the church in the world.

Seen in this light, the primary role of the church in the age is that of servant community. The "basin and towel" are the effective means whereby the cross and resurrection are vindicated among men. Without the posture of servanthood, Calvary is but a distant memory. In that posture, Calvary becomes a redemptive way of life. Love authenticates discipleship; and in servanthood, love is made visible to the age.

Peter Berger sees four major aspects of servanthood: "Christian Diaconate" is the many-faceted mode of personal service that disciples may render to all men. "Christian Action" concerns institutional programs designed to meet human need. "Christian Presence" is the fellowship that shares the human predicament by simply "being there." "Christian Dialogue" is that earnest conversation with the age—the hearing and speaking whereby the Lordship of Jesus is commended to an unbelieving generation.[44] Each of these merits serious study by the concerned Christian.

In its corporate life, the servant community will bear certain marks. One of these is other-centeredness. If Jesus was "the Man for others," His church should be the "community for others." This principle has profound implications for the worshiping congregation. It means, for example, that "church growth" will never be construed as an end in itself. The church is, indeed, meant to grow—but not so that it may admire itself before a statistical mirror. The church is to grow in order to pour out its life for Christ in the world.

Such a congregation will look carefully to the ways it expends its energy and treasure. It will only cultivate those forms of "church work" that enhance the "work of the church"—in the world.[45] At the same time, what the congregation expends upon itself will only be what enables it to grow in capacity for mission. This will enable it to expend its remaining treasure beyond itself, for the sake of Christ.

Yet another mark presents a more serious question to the church in America. This concerns the willingness of the church to become the "*suffering* servant community." Nor is this a theoretical question in the twentieth century, as the daily news abundantly testifies. The relative comforts of contemporary American life ought not blind the church to the simple statement of Jesus: "In the world you shall have tribulation" (John 16:33).

Only in its willingness to suffer can the church be liberated to serve the Word of God. The apparent security of the *status quo* all too easily bribes the church into silence when it ought to speak the message of repentance. Hitler sought to capture the German church by such blandishments, and where these failed, by fear. Thus, much of the German church was caught in an intenable paradox in which its designated function in society was to be socially irrelevant.[46] It remained for the "confessing church" to accept the "costly grace"[47] of suffering, and so be liberated to serve the Word of God.

A third mark of servanthood, consequent upon the first two, is that of prophecy. Here we do not primarily refer to "foretelling" (although this is not precluded), but to "forth-telling." The servant community must be the prophetic community. The first mandate upon such a people is to conform their own lives to the Word they proclaim. This means that the prophetic community is always submissive to reformation as "further light" may break forth from the Word.

The Word exemplified in corporate life becomes the authentication of the Word proclaimed. If the Kingdom of God is "righteousness and peace and joy in the Holy Spirit" (Romans 14:17), it is vain for a congregation not possessing those qualities to proclaim the kingdom. The service of the Word roots in the continual reformation of the community that bears the Word.

Two things are requisite if the church is to speak effectively, prophetically. First, integrity, through which alone the church earns the right to be heard. Second, freedom under the Lordship of Jesus, which liberates the church from undue dependence upon the existing order. Only so may the prophetic community "forth-tell" the Word of God in the world.

The fourth mark of the servant community is its redemptive orientation toward humanity. Amidst alienation, anonymity, and indifference on every hand, the church is called to redemptive concern. In a vindictive generation, it offers forgiveness. Amidst man's disappointing quest of justice, the church proclaims God's grace. On the modern "Jericho Road," filled with travelers trying to "get ahead," it is the servant community that still sees the wounded victim and becomes his neighbor.

What is redemptive is ever true concern of the servant community. With the sure Word of God on its lips, the sweet Spirit of God in its life, the loving grace of God in its hands outstretched, let the church ever point to the Redeemer of men.

The prophetic word foretold the incarnation, saying, "A body didst thou prepare for me." To this the Son responded, "Behold, I have come . . . to do Thy will, O God" (Psalm 40:6f; Hebrews 10:5-7).

So may His mystical body, the church, say with one voice, "Behold I have come . . . to do Thy will, O God."

NOTES

[1]For a contemporary discussion, see Avery Dulles, S. J., *Models of the Church* (Garden City: Doubleday, 1974). See also Emil Brunner's provocative treatment of "The Christian Fellowship and the Holy Spirit," in *The Misunderstanding of the Church*, tr. Harold Knight (Philadelphia: Westminster, 1953), pp. 47f.

[2]"The Church is the extension in time and space of the Incarnate Word of God, crucified, ascended, glorified, operating among men through the indwelling in them of His Holy Spirit, Who mediates to it His Victorious Life." A. R. Gregg, "One Holy Catholic Apostolic Church," in *The Universal Church, The First Assembly of the World Council of Churches*, edited by W. A. Vissar T'Hooft (New York: Harper, 1949), p. 59. See also William Robinson, *The Biblical Doctrine of the Church* (St. Louis: Bethany, 1948), p. 103. For a discussion of important limitations in the concept, see Karl Barth, *Church Dogmatics*, Vol. 1, *The Doctrine of the Word of God*, Part 2, translated by Geoffrey W. Bromiley, et al, (Edinburgh: T & T Clark, 1970), pp. 214f.

[3]C. S. Lewis writes, "The very word *membership* is of Christian origin, but it has been taken over by the world and emptied of all meaning." See his perceptive essay on "Membership" in *The Weight of Glory* (Grand Rapids: Eerdmans, 1975), p. 30.

[4]At Edinburgh (1937), William Temple, then Archbishop of York declared, "The Church is not an association of men, each of whom has chosen Christ as his Lord; it is a fellowship of men, each of whom Christ has united with Himself." *The Second World Conference on Faith and Order*, ed. Leonard Hidgson (New York: Macmillan, 1938), p. 16. cf. William Robinson, *The Biblical Doctrine of the Church*, pp. 44, 45, and Emil Brunner, *The Divine-Human Encounter*, tr. Amandus W. Loos (Philadelphia: Westminster, 1943), p. 198.

[5]See William Robinson's brief but profound discussion in *The Biblical Doctrine of the Church*, pp. 31, 32. Also significant is Karl Barth's discussion of "Election," in *The Doctrine of God* (Volume 2, Part 2, of *Church Dogmatics*), pp. 211f.

[6]Speaking of the reforms advocated by Thomas Cranmer, Geoffrey W. Bromily writes, "From the standpoint of the patristic as well as the biblical age, the reforming church is the church of restoration rather than innovation. The Reformers, not the Romans, are the true heirs of the past." "Thomas Cranmer," in B. A. Gerrish (ed.), *Reformers in Profile* (Philadelphia: Fortress, 1967), p. 186.

[7]The phrase is William Robinson's, in *Biblical Doctrine of the Church*, p. 133.

[8]"Church order, like the Church itself, is not an end in itself. It is man's attempt so to serve God's Word in obedience to it, that, in face of the danger menacing the Church, the wisest, boldest and most effective steps are taken to ensure that the immediate meeting and communion of the living Lord Jesus Christ with His congregation shall take place anew. No human effort can ensure this divine encounter. But man can clear the obstacles out of the way; and this is the purpose of church order." Karl Barth, *The Universal Church*, p. 75. See also Barth, *The Doctrine of the Word of God*, Vol. 1, Part 2, p. 219.

[9]Alexander Campbell, "The Present Administration of the Kingdom of Heaven," *The Christian System* (Pittsburgh: Forrester & Campbell, 1840), pp. 172ff. Of particular interest is Campbell's observation that "In the Kingdom of Heaven, faith is, then, the *principle*, and ordinances the *means* of enjoyment; because all the wisdom, power, love, mercy, compassion, or *grace of God*, is in the ordinances of the Kingdom of Heaven; and if all grace be in them, it can only be enjoyed through them" (p. 174).

[10]For a discussion of similar import, see Robert O. Fife, "The Worshiping Congregation: Particularity and Universality," in *Essays on New Testament Christianity*, C. Robert Wetzel, ed. (Cincinnati: **Standard**, 1978), pp. 30f.

[11]Cf. Hans Küng, *The Church*, tr. Ray and Rosaleen Ockenden (New York: Sheed and Ward, 1967), p. 300. After defining the Church, Alexander Campbell writes, "This institution, called *the congregation of God*, is a great community of communities—not a community representative of communities; but a community composed of many particular communities; each of which is built upon the same foundation, walks according to the same rules, enjoys the same charter, and is under the jurisdiction of no other community of Christians; but is to all other communities as an individual disciple is to every other individual disciple in any one particular community meeting in any given place." *The Christian System*, p. 73.

[12]This is not to ignore the inclusion in the Canon of the "general" and "pastoral" epistles.

[13]See Gunnar Westin, *The Free Church Through the Ages*, tr. Virgil A. Olson (Nashville: Broadman, 1966), pp. 1, 2.

[14]*Declaration and Address of the Christian Association of*

Washington (Washington, PA: Brown & Sample, 1809), p. 16, Proposition 2.

[15]The development of such a rationale was part of the process of "Restructure," whereby The Christian Church (Disciples of Christ) was formally established. A "Panel of Scholars" appointed by the International Convention of Christian Churches provided the ideological or theological foundation for this change of polity. A three-volume series was published under the general title, *The Renewal of the Church*. Volume 1, *The Reformation of Tradition*, ed. Ronald E. Osborn; Volume 2, *The Reconstruction of Theology*, ed. Ralph G. Wilburn; Volume 3, *The Revival of the Churches*, ed. W. B. Blakemore. Of significance at this point is "The Issue of Polity for Disciples Today," by W. B. Blakemore. This is the third chapter of Volume 3.

[16]Brunner observes, "The oneness of communion with Christ and communion with man is the characteristic mark of the *Ecclesia*." *The Misunderstanding of the Church*, p. 108. See also Robert O. Fife, "Christian Unity as Reception and Attainment" in *Disciples and the Church Universal* (Nashville: Disciples of Christ Historical Society, 1967), pp. 21f. This paper, together with lectures by David Edwin Harrell, Jr., and Ronald E. Osborn, constituted "The Reed Lectures for 1966."

[17]See Alexander Campbell's series of essays entitled, "Cooperation of the Churches," which commence in *The Millennial Harbinger* (Bethany, WV, 1831), pp. 235f. Of similar import are his observations in *The Christian System*, pp. 73-77. Here Campbell draws a clear distinction between cooperation, which is a divine mandate, and the means of cooperation, which are human expedients.

[18]"No Christian Congregation can live in total independence. It is born through the witness of those who were in Christ before. It continues to need the help of other Christians for encouragement, warning, example. In all normal circumstances it needs outside help for the training and spiritual support of its ministry. And it must, if it is to be Christian, express solidarity with other Christians by acts of mutual charity." Leslie T. Lyall and Lesslie Newbigin, *The Church—Local and Universal* (London: World Dominion Press, 1962), p. 28.

[19]Ep lxvi, 7; quoted in Henry Bettenson, *Documents of the Christian Church* (Oxford, 1963), p. 74.

[20]Of contemporary significance is the *Decree of Ecumenism*, issued by the Second Vatican Council, in which Christians other than Roman Catholic are called "our separated brethren." For further discussion,

see John B. Sheerin, C.S.P., *A Practical Guide to Ecumenism* (New York: Paulist, 1967), pp. 194f. See also George Cornell, *Voyage of Faith* (New York: Odyssey, 1966), pp. 7f.

[21]As Archbishop Temple has put it, "The unity of the Church of God is perpetual fact; our task is not to create it but to exhibit it." William Temple, *The Second World Conference on Faith and Order*, p. 16.

[22]Brunner has observed, "No true *Ecclesia* can be made out of twenty ecclesiastical institutions; Christian fellowship can spring only from spiritual knowledge of Christ, which implies the will to brotherhood in Christ." *The Misunderstanding of the Church*, p. 113.

[23]This was the thrust of Alexander Campbell's Lunenberg Correspondence. In defense of his opinion that there are "Christians among the sects, " Cambell writes, "When I see a person who would die for Christ; whose brotherly kindness, sympathy, and active benevolence know no bounds but his circumstances; whose seat in the Christian assembly is never empty; whose inward piety and devotion are attested by punctual obedience to every known duty; whose family is educated in the fear of the Lord; whose constant companion is the Bible: I say, when I see such a one ranked amongst heathen men and publicans, because he never happened to inquire, but always took it for granted that he had been scripturally baptized; and that, too, by one greatly destitute of all these public and private virtues, whose chief or exclusive recommendation is that he has been immersed, and that he holds a scriptural theory of the gospel: I feel no disposition to flatter such a one; but rather to disabuse him of his error. And while I would not lead the most excellent professor of any sect to disparage the least of all the commandments of Jesus, I would say to my immersed brother as Paul said to his Jewish brother who glorified in a system which he did not adorn: 'Sir, will not his uncircumcision, or unbaptism, be counted to him for baptism? and will he not condemn you, who, though having the literal and true baptism, yet dost transgress or neglect the statutes of your king?' " *Millennial Harbinger* (1837), p. 565.

[24]*Declaration and Address*, Proposition 1. C. H. Dodd has observed, "The unity of the Church is not a unity of aggregation . . . it is a personal unity. . . ." *The Doctrine of the Church* ed. Dow Kirkpatrick (New York: Abingdon, 1964), p. 37.

[25]Lesslie Newbigin states it simply: "We must begin with the given unity." Leslie Lyall and Lesslie Newbigin, *The Church—Local and Universal*, p. 25.

[26]For this reason, Thomas Campbell declared that those "doctrinal

exhibitions" contained in the creeds belonged to the "after and progressive edification of the church." Consequently, "deductions or inferential truths" should not be made terms of communion. *Declaration and Address*, Propositions, 6, 7.

[27]Erasmus protested this process in his own day. Writing to Martin Dorp, he said, "Enumerate all the points on which the Greeks disagree with orthodox Latins: you will find nothing which has come from the words of the New Testament or which is relevant here. The whole controversy is about the word 'hypostatic,' about the procession of the Holy Spirit, about the rites of consecration, about the poverty of priests, about the authority of the Roman pontiff." *Christian Humanism and the Reformation*, John C. Olin, ed. (New York: Fordham, 1976), p. 85.

[28]Brunner criticizes the common Protestant-Catholic tendency to place theology before faith, saying, "In His Word, God does not deliver to me a course of lectures in dogmatic theology, He does not submit to me or interpret for me the content of a confession of faith, but He makes Himself accesible to me. And likewise in faith I do not think, but God leads me to think; He does not communicate 'something' to me, but 'Himself.' " *Divine-Human Encounter*, p. 85.

[29]In this light, C. C. Morrison suggested, "The way to end Protestant sectarianism is for the denominations to cease being churches." *Christian Century* Vol. 77, No. 10 (March 9, 1960), p. 281. See also, Martin Marty, *Church Unity and Church Mission* (Grand Rapids: Eerdmans, 1964), pp. 72, 137.

[30]See also Robert O. Fife, "The Neglected Alternative," *Mission*, Vol. 11, No. 5, (November, 1977), pp. 11f.

[31]John Dunlavy, *et al*, *The Last Will and Testament of the Springfield Presbytery* (1804), (Indianapolis: International Convention of Disciples of Christ, 1949), Imprimis.

[32]Wesley's letter is significant for its disavowal of the three-fold ministry. See *Minutes of the Methodist Conferences, Annually Held in America; from 1773 to 1813, Inclusive* (New York, 1813), Vol. 1, p. 51; the letter is also quoted in full in W. E. MacClenny, *The Life of Rev. James O'Kelly* (Indianapolis: Religious Book Service, 1950), pp. 46f.

[33]Alexander Campbell suggested two ways of stating this central conviction and concern:
"1st. *Nothing is essential to the conversion of the world but the union and co-operation of Christians.*

"2nd. Nothing is essential to the union of Christians but the Apostles' teaching or testimony."
Or,
"1st. The testimony of the Apostles is the only and all-sufficient means of uniting all Christians.
"2nd. The union of Christians with the Apostles' testimony is all-sufficient and alone sufficient to the conversion of the world." Christian System, p. 107.

[34]See Robert O. Fife, "Maintaining the Undenominational Plea," The Restoration Herald, Vol. 51, No. 8 (September 1977), pp. 3f. A shorter article of the same name appeared in Christian Standard, Vol. 114, No. 14 (April 8, 1979), pp. 4f.

[35]Barth, The Universal Church, p. 72.

[36]Jacques Ellul, The Presence of the Kingdom, tr. Olive Wyon (New York: Seabury, 1967), p. 7.

[37]A major analyst of "Civil" or "Civic Religion" is Robert N. Bellah, whose initial article, "Civil Religion in America" appeared in Daedalus, Vol. 96, pp. 1-21.

[38]See Peter L. Berger's provocative analysis in The Noise of Solemn Assemblies (Garden City: Doubleday, 1961), pp. 15f.

[39]See David Edwin Harrell, Jr., "Peculiar People: A Rationale for Modern Conservative Disciples," in Disciples and the Church Universal, p. 40.

[40]Harvey Cox celebrates these marks of urban life in his Secular City (New York: Macmillan, 1965). See also Daniel Callahan, ed., The Secular City Debate (New York: Macmillan, 1900).

[41]See Robert O. Fife, "The Restoration of Secularity," Mission, Vol. 12, Nos. 9, 10, 11 (March, April, May, 1979), p. 14, p. 9, p. 11.

[42]Campbell, Christian System, p. 289.

[43]This is made abundantly clear in Campbell's significant role in the Virginia Constitutional Convention of 1829-1830, and in his extensive writings concerning the problem of slavery. See the Millennial Harbinger, especially from 1832 to the Civil War. See also Christian Baptist, Vol. 7, No. 1. For the Virginia Constitutional Convention of 1829-1830, see Proceedings and Debates (Richmond: Samuel Shepherd & Co., 1830).

[44]Berger, *Noise of Solemn Assemblies,* p. 141.

[45]Ellul, *The Presence of the Kingdom,* pp. 9f.

[46]Berger, *The Noise of Solemn Assemblies,* p. 38. Berger chiefly addresses the American scene, but his analysis is significant for other societies as well.

[47]See Dietrich Bonhoeffer's remarkable book, *The Cost of Discipleship* (New York: Macmillan, 1963).

CHAPTER
16

BAPTISM AND THE LORD'S SUPPER

By John Mills

In His divine wisdom, Jesus gave the church the sacraments. The New Testament gives us ample evidence that the church's strength was in no small part due to the sacraments. Yet Paul Tillich, writing after World War II, could speak of the "death of the sacraments"[1] and express the conviction that the destiny of Protestantism depends on resolving the problem of their nature and place. Protestantism must still face this issue.

There have been reformation movements in the church's life that sought to restore the sacraments to their central place and power.[2] In time, however, this thrust has been blunted and the sacraments neglected. Only a restoration of the sacraments to their New Testament place and power will bring to the church the health it needs.

Terminology

The word *ordinance* is preferred by many groups within the church in reaction to the use of *sacrament* in some denominations. *Ordinance* means that which is ordained or commanded in reference to a religious act. For a practice to be regarded as an ordinance, it has to have been commanded by Jesus and practiced by the early church. Baptism and the Lord's Supper meet these qualifications. Jesus commanded baptism (Matthew

28:19; Mark 16:16) and the early church practiced it (Acts 2:38; 8:38; 16:15, 33; 19:5; 22:16). Jesus instituted the Lord's Supper (Matthew 26:26-28; Mark 14:22-25; Luke 22:14-23; 1 Corinthians 11:23ff) and the early church practiced it (Acts 2:42; 20:7; 1 Corinthians 10 and 11).

Sacrament implies the grace of God at work in the life of the participant. A sacrament is a sacred thing, an object drawn from the every day world and given sacred use by Christ's intention. Mystery, which Paul uses some twenty times, became the word translated "sacrament" by the church.[3] When Alexander Campbell described an ordinance as "the mode in which the grace of God acts on human nature,"[4] he was using ordinance to say what we usually mean by sacrament.

There is a reluctance in using sacrament in some quarters because of its abuse by those who treat it as a mechanical vehicle of God's grace. Indeed it is foreign to the spirit of the New Testament to say that so long as the right formula and the right elements are used, God's grace is at work, regardless of the participant's spiritual receptivity. To those taking offense at the terminology of sacrament, it must be said that the concept of ordinance may also be abused by voiding it of any real meaning through careless and mechanical observance. Our search for terminology is necessitated because the New Testament uses neither ordinance or sacrament in reference to baptism and the Lord's Supper.[5] Rather than coining a still different term, we will use both ordinance and sacrament here, preferring sacrament because we understand God to be at work in these two rites that Christ ordained.

A third term that needs definition is grace. Grace and sacrament are inextricably linked in New Testament teaching. H. J. Witherspoon declares: "Whoever says sacrament says grace, for grace is the differentia of the sacrament, by which it is more than a symbol."[6] Grace is God's favor toward us, extended without regard for merit. It is not a commodity to be received as from a vending machine, but is rather God's gracious dealing with us in the giving of himself despite our estrangement from Him. The father of the prodigal, for example, could have refused his son, but he graciously gave of himself in love and acceptance instead. He didn't even allow the son to finish his "sinner's prayer" (Luke 15:11ff). Likewise, the Holy Spirit is God's giving of himself to His children and His provision for their life (Luke 11:13).

This definition of grace opens the door for understanding the sacraments as a Christ-man encounter, established by God for the purpose of our enrichment. Faith, penitence, and submission are the necessary means for meeting our gracious Lord and receiving, in turn, a cup running over with the fullness of His blessings.

The Place of the Sacraments

A reading of church history justifies our concern for the sacraments. Wesley, being "strangely warmed" at a mid-week prayer meeting that did not include the sacraments, set the stage for a revival in which the sacraments played only a minor role. The lack of power in the worship services of the established church and sacramental abuses led George Fox to reject all "outward forms." Likewise, in the claim often made to be saved by "faith alone," baptism is stripped of its meaning. The emphasis upon experience in Augustine, and later in Calvin, led to an understanding of grace as communicated by God's direct action apart from the sacraments. Even though both Calvin and Augustine defended the sacraments and saw them filled with meaning, they did not accord them their central place in the Christian system. In our day, mass evangelism and radio and TV religious programming have led to a de-emphasis upon any vital role for the sacraments.

We must seek the restoration of the New Testament institutions if we are to be faithful to the Lord of the church. Applied to the sacraments, the question then must be, "What is God's intention?"

In the great commandment, Jesus calls for a total response to God—our heart, soul, mind, and strength (Mark 12.30). We are called to be whole persons in a broken world. Jesus knew that we must be reunited and made whole in our personal allegiance to God. The Sermon on the Mount (Matthew 5—7) is a clear call for the subjects of the kingdom to be "whole." "No one can serve two masters; for either he will hate the one and love the other, or he will hold to the one and despise the other. You cannot serve God and mammon" (Matthew 6:24). "Not everyone who says to Me, 'Lord, Lord,' will enter the kingdom of heaven, but he who does the will of My Father who is in heaven" (Matthew 7:21). Faith, to be true, must consist in total life response! James 2 is another clear call for this wholeness of life.

The institution of marriage illustrates God's concern for wholeness in the response of persons to His grace. Acts of the body express and complete faith and commitment. Thus, marriage is the union of two persons in mind, spirit, and body. The sexual relation expresses and completes this union. Hence, adultery is a breach not only of sexual fidelity, but of the union of mind and spirit as well. Moreover, it can be said that every bodily act implies a corresponding state of being. Therefore, an illicit sexual union is viewed as joining oneself to the partner in that union and, hence, a violation of one's being as a temple of the Holy Spirit (1 Corinthians 6:16, 19). In the Biblical outlook concerning man, *doing* is an aspect of *being*.

Therefore, to hold baptism and the Lord's Supper to be just "examples" or just "remembering," and devoid of power, has the effect of fragmenting the person whom God intended to be whole. To say that baptism is not a necessary aspect of the saving act of God is also to espouse the underlying principle behind the fragmentation of personality, which Jesus opposed.

The emphasis upon the validity of only inner faith opens the door to the idea of an invisible church, which holds that the church is made up of the truly elect, who are "really saved" or "born again." Such connotations are foreign to the Scriptures. One is either a Christian or he is not. One is born again (John 3), or he is not part of the kingdom. Hans Küng is correct in saying, "A real church made up of real people cannot be invisible."[7]

It is not enough to "be there in spirit." The incarnation meant the Word's taking on flesh, not just being there in Spirit. Subjectivism is a denial of the wholeness God demonstrated in the incarnate Christ and a denial of God's call for our wholeness. Made in the image of God, we are called upon to believe, repent, and be baptized. We are not called to feel and experience a spiritual high. The obedience of the whole person to Christ's saving grace will not, of course, bypass the emotions, but neither will it allow an emotional state to stand as the total response to the grace of God in Christ.

The New Testament is the church's norm for how God works to redeem man. The sacraments are God given, not man instituted. Water, bread, and fruit of the vine may mean little to some, but Jesus made them sacred instruments through which He would bless our lives. Alexander Campbell wrote: "It is as supernatural to adapt a system to man, as it is to create him."[8]

The ordinances are, then, an important part in God's plan to bless us. In the ordinances, Jesus meets us as our crucified and resurrected Lord. There He ministers to us according to His promises. We are to come in faith seeking wholeness. By His choice, the cross and the empty tomb are always the context of our meeting. As we participate with all of our heart, soul, mind, and strength in these appointed elements, He is at work within our lives. Here the God-man encounter takes place—and on His terms.

Baptism

Baptism is the God-ordained means through which a penitent believer leaves the old life and submits to Christ in obedience for the promise of forgiveness, for birth into the body of Christ (the church), and for the reception of the promised Holy Spirit. It is that particular moment that culminates one's initial response to the Savior.

As stated earlier, baptism was commanded by our Lord himself. He submitted to John's baptism (Matthew 3:13-17; Mark 1:9-11; Luke 3:21, 22) and made baptism an integral part of the Great Commission (Matthew 28:18-20). "Making disciples" and "teaching them all things" cannot be separated from the command Jesus placed between them, "baptizing them in the name of the Father and the Son and the Holy Spirit." To accept any of the three as a command of our Lord necessitates the acceptance of all three. However helpful the knowledge of the historical roots of baptism prior to John may be, Jesus' own command is paramount and sufficient for an obedient church. The early church, led by the Holy Spirit, was obedient to this command of her Lord (Acts 2:38; 8:34-40; 16:15; 16:33; 10:5; 22:16).

The Action of Baptism

The act of initiation mandated by the Great Commission is immersion "in the name of the Lord Jesus" (Acts 19:5). The Greek *baptisma* derives from *baptizein*, "to dip, immerse, sink."[9] If *baptisma* were translated, rather than transliterated, it would most commonly be rendered simply "immersion." The New Testament knows no action for baptism other than this. Sprinkling, or affusion (from *rantizein*), belongs to a later age of the church.

This matter requires but little elaboration. Jewish proselyte baptism, although differing in intent, was immersion. We are told that John was baptizing where there was "much water" (John 3:23). Narratives that describe baptism, such as that of Acts 8:38, 39, indicate that the act enjoined was immersion. Philip and the eunuch "both went down into the water," the eunuch was baptized, and "they came up out of the water." Paul undoubtedly had immersion in mind when he described baptism as being "buried with Him" and "raised up with Him through faith in the working of God" (Colossians 2:12).

The reformers of the nineteenth century, concerned with the question, "How did people respond to the gospel in the first century?" investigated the lexicons, the translations, and the commentaries of writers from all the historic traditions of Christendom. They were led to conclude that baptism is immersion. Similar agreement is registered today. For example, Hans Küng, the noted Roman Catholic writer: "In the early days baptism probably always meant total immersion."[10] Karl Barth earlier reached a similar position. In *The Teaching of the Church Regarding Baptism,* he observes that the immersion practiced in the early church had "the character of a direct threat to life" and that this act "showed what was represented in far more expressive fashion than did the affusion which later became customary."[11]

The Subjects for Baptism

In the New Testament, the subjects for baptism were always penitent believers; it was sometime later that the church began to baptize infants. Beasley-Murray examines the history of infant baptism and concludes that "the New Testament gives no evidence that infant baptism was practiced in the primitve church."[12] He contends that the application of baptism to infants resulted from the influence of paganism.[13] "The first mention of infant baptism, an obscure one, was about 185, by Irenaeus."[14] The practice did not become universal until the sixth century.[15] Many western churches are re-examining the practice of infant baptism and show evidence of slowly abandoning this tradition. More than one Protestant church that began with the Roman Catholic understanding of infant baptism has altered its understanding to the act of parental dedication. Some Roman Catholic parishes have adopted the position of requiring parental instruction before the rite is celebrated.

New Testament teaching joins baptism, as the act of initiation, to belief in Christ and determination to accept Him as Lord (Acts 2:38; 3:19; Romans 5:1; Hebrews 11:6; Colossians 2:12). Nowhere is baptism apart from faith contemplated; rather, "he who has believed and has been baptized shall be saved" (Mark 16:16). Jesus' call to wholeness of persons, referred to above, calls for a response not only of body, but of heart, soul, and mind. By their nature, faith and repentance must be personal and cannot function by proxy. The apostolic proclamation of Jesus calls for a total response of the person— hearing, faith, repentance, and baptism. The proper subjects of baptism are penitent believers. This has the further implication that the church must exercise care that candidates for baptism be old enough to enter into the experience with understanding and commitment.

The Design of Baptism

In the consideration of the purpose of baptism, the question of baptism's being a mode of God's grace confronts the church seeking to restore baptism to its place and power. Appeal to the New Testament must be the means of resolving this question; its message on this subject is quite clear, as seen in the following affirmations—each drawn from contexts containing either the command for baptism or teaching concerning the implications of baptism for the life of the believer.

"The Forgiveness of Sin." On the day of Pentecost, in response to the question, "Brethren, what shall we do?" Peter answered, "Repent, and let each you be baptized in the name of Jesus Christ for the forgiveness of your sins; and you shall receive the gift of the Holy Spirit" (Acts 2:37, 38).

The meaning of the preposition eis before forgiveness is crucial for the understanding of this passage. The consensus of scholarship overwhelmingly supports the translation, "for," as in most standard versions of Scripture. Some versions employ the phrase "so that" in expressing the meaning of eis in this passage (e.g., NIV, NEB). By this choice of terms, Peter thus links the forgiveness of sin to baptism.

Acts 2:38 does not stand alone in our consideration. The baptism of John the Baptist was "for the forgiveness of sin" (Mark 1:4). People were baptized by John "as they confessed their sins" (Matthew 3:6). John said, "I baptize you with water for repentance" (Matthew 3:11). The command of Jesus for the practice of His body, the church, was to offer no less. Saul of

Tarsus had a great experience on the Damascus Road (Acts 9) and three days later experienced a healing of his blindness (Acts 9:18; 22:13), yet he was told by the Lord's spokesman, "And now why do you delay? Arise, and be baptized, and wash away your sins, calling on His name" (Acts 22:16).[16]

The apostle Paul pictures baptism as a death, burial, and resurrection. "We . . . have been baptized into His death," and "buried," and "our old self was crucified with Him, that our body of sin might be done away with, that we should no longer be slaves to sin" (Romans 6). Obviously, baptism has reference to the old (sinful) life. Dietrich Bonhoeffer says, "It is baptism into the death of Christ which effects the forgiveness of sin and justification, and completes our separation from sin."[17] First Corinthians 6:11 indicates that the verbs *washed, sanctified,* and *justified* all refer to the same act, namely baptism.

In Titus 3:5, baptism is "the washing of regeneration and renewing by the Holy Spirit." Beasely-Murray calls this verse "the one authentic commentary" on John 3:5.[18]

Read in its proper context, 1 Peter 3:21 states that there is salvation in baptism, because baptism is for the forgiveness of sin. The New Testament leaves no doubt with its consistent message that baptism is for the forgiveness of sin.[19]

Incorporation into Christ. Baptism is not only the joyous moment in which the good news of remission of sin is realized; it is also the time when believers are incorporated into Christ Jesus. To be baptized "in the name of Jesus" (Acts 2:38) and "in the name of the Father and the Son and the Holy Spirit" (Matthew 28:19) is to participate in the divine nature, to become new creatures in Christ—"Therefore if any man is in Christ, he is a new creature; the old things passed away; behold, new things have come" (2 Corinthians 5:17).

Paul speaks of being "baptized into Christ Jesus" (Romans 6:3-5), which means incorporation into His life and hope. Galatians 3:27 says, "For all of you who were baptized into Christ have clothed yourselves with Christ." It also includes incorporation into the church; "For by one Spirit we were all baptized into one body, whether Jews or Greeks, whether slaves or free, and we were all made to drink of one Spirit" (1 Corinthians 12:13). Therefore, in baptism, we come not only under His authority, but take also His name, His promises, and the work of His body, the church. Küng calls baptism "an indispensible condition of entry into the holy eschatological community and into fellowship with the Lord."[20] We are not just baptized into a local congregation or into a denomination, but into the body of Christ, the church, of which the congregation is the concrete expression. Here we become members of His body, the means by which He works in this world. We are His royal priesthood, His ministering community.

Reception of the Holy Spirit. Peter's message on Pentecost included the promise, "And you shall receive the gift of the Holy Spirit." God is not content just to grant forgiveness and give us His name as members of His holy community. He wants us to live dynamic, victorious lives in the assurance of His divine love and guidance. To this end, His design is that we should receive nothing less than His own Spirit as His presence in our lives.

John the Baptist stated that the one who was to come after him would "baptize you with the Holy Spirit and fire" (Luke 3:16). Pentecost was ushered in with the Spirit; the Spirit's message was that those who submitted their lives to Jesus in baptism would receive the Holy Spirit. The disciples at Ephesus were baptized "in the name of the Lord Jesus" so that they might receive the gift of the Holy Spirit (Acts 19:5). Romans 6 speaks of "walking in the newness of life," of living with Him, and of being alive to God in Christ Jesus, an obvious reference to life in and of the Holy Spirit.

The indwelling Spirit provides several distinct blessings. He is the seal of our identity as sons of God (Galatians 4:6) and the guarantor of our inheritance—as the earnest of our ultimate salvation (Ephesians 1:13, 14). He aids our growth toward maturity in Christ, which is the goal of Christian living (Galatians 4:19). The fruit of the Spirit is actually a description of Christlikeness, which He is at work in us to produce (Galatians 5:22-24). Moreover, the gift of the Holy Spirit is assurance that the Father is at work in our lives to fulfill His purpose for us (Romans 8:26-31; Philippians 2:12, 13).

Several further notes on baptism may prove helpful. First, the reformers of the nineteenth century did not see baptism as a "work" toward salvation. Campbell said concerning baptism: "It can merit nothing."[21] He went on to call salvation "a perfect gratuity. The conditions, then, are not the conditions of a purchase, but of a free donation."[22] God has provided salvation in Christ; man but responds to what God offers. Man can act only because Christ has first acted. Hans Küng adds, "The believer does not baptize himself, but offers himself for baptism."[23] We come with empty hands and God blesses us with His grace.

The Action of Baptism and Christian Unity

How does this emphasis on obedience to the New Testament norm relate to our current concern for Christian unity? There is but "one baptism," as there is but "one Lord" and "one faith" (Ephesians 4:5). Alexander Campbell appealed to the ancient practice as the common ground for unity today.

> Again, as every sect agrees, that a person immersed on a confession of faith is truly baptized, and only a part of Christendom admits the possibility of any other action as baptism: for the sake of union among Christians, it may be easily shown to be the duty of all believers to be immersed, if for no other reason than that of honoring the divine institution and opening a way for the cooperation of all Christians.[24]

Stephen England sees in the above statement an indication of a shift in Campbell's views from a position he earlier held.

> In these statements Alexander Campbell went far beyond his earlier-assumed doctrinal position, that baptism is solely 'for the remission of sins.' When he faced the implications of baptism in relation to Christian unity, he could not in good conscience relegate all the unimmersed to the status of non-Christians. In principle, Campbell now admitted that the doctrine of baptism was not limited to what the New Testament displayed.[25]

Can we in good conscience immerse a pious individual who evidences the fruit of the Holy Spirit, who desires to be immersed because of only having been sprinkled, but who claims to be a forgiven member of the body of Christ? Campbell's opinion was yes, for the sake of Christian unity. Since the Spirit "blows where it will" (John 3:8) and since salvation is of God's action, our part is to be obedient to that "form of teaching to which you were committed" (Romans 6:17) and to allow God in His own way to work His needed grace.[26]

The Lord's Supper

Baptism is the door into Christ's body. The Lord's Supper is the communal meal through which that body is sustained and enjoys the continual fellowship of the Christ.

The Supper—the Institution

Jesus shared the Passover with His disciples on the evening before the crucifixion. During that meal, He instituted the Lord's Supper.[27] The occasion was the Passover. No devout Jew could forget the event in which God went through Egypt, passing over Israel and saving her firstborn, while claiming the firstborn of Egypt. In setting Israel free, God had done for her what she could not do for herself. Each observance of the Passover was not only a remembrance of what God had done, but was also a celebration of the freedom each worshiper enjoyed as a conseqeuence of God's action.[28] For this reason, the participants in the Passover reclined at the tables as free men rather than sitting at the tables or standing and eating as slaves often had to do. Jesus clearly saw himself as the Passover Lamb; He used the prayers before and after the main course to add this interpretation concerning the loaf and the cup. The Gospel of John forcefully expresses this point in its report that Jesus was crucified as the Passover lambs were being offered in the temple (John 19:14). The church clearly saw Christ as the Lamb of God (John 1:29, 36), God's Passover offering.

Jesus served as the host in the upper room. He arranged that meal and served as the leader in interpreting the meaning of the Passover. It is the divine initiative that instituted the Supper and invites us to partake. The Supper is not of human origin. As the host, Jesus declared the meaning of this Supper and set the conditions for participation.

Taking the bread at the beginning of the main course of the Passover meal, Jesus blessed it, "broke it and gave it to the disciples, and said, 'Take, eat; this is My body'" (Matthew 26:26). Notice the action verbs: took, blessed, broke, and gave. The disciples were asked to partake of this one loaf, blessed and broken. The bread clearly represented His body "the bread of life" given for us (John 6:35). Those who partook of the bread participated in the body of Christ (1 Corinthians 10:16).

Taking the "cup of blessing" (1 Corinthians 10:16), the closing of the main course of the Passover meal, Jesus gave thanks, and gave it to them, and said, "Drink from it, all of you; for this is My blood of the covenant, which is poured out for many for forgiveness of sins" (Matthew 26:27, 28). The elements clearly spoke of sacrifice and atonement. The church saw that this was a once-for-all sacrifce for all men (Hebrews 7:27; 9:25-28; 1 Peter 3:18).

Paul "delivers" the words of Jesus in conjunction with the bread: "Do this in remembrance of me," and the words: "Do this, as often as you drink it, in remembrance of me" (1 Corinthians 11:24, 25), in reference to the cup. "In remembrance of me" would be better rendered "for my recalling." *Anamnesin,* translated "remembrance," carries the idea of "bring back, to make present and real."[29] As we take the bread and lift the cup, we personally are to recall His death for our sins and His life given that we might live. Hence, it is not just remembering Jesus as we would George Washington, but being aware of what Jesus personally did for us at Calvary. He calls upon us to relive that moment and to renew our covenant as He assured us of His fellowship.

In the words of institution, Jesus links the fellowship of the table and the future manifestation of His kingdom (Matthew 26:29; Mark 14:25). Likewise, Paul writes, "You proclaim the Lord's death until He comes" (1 Corinthians 11:26). "To put it quite simply," writes Joachim Jeremias, "table fellowship with Jesus is an anticipatory gift of the final consummation."[30] Jesus wanted us to rehearse the messianic banquet and to anticipate it in the Lord's Supper. When the Lord returns, we will no longer need these elements, for we will be living in the immediate presence of the victorious Lord. Jesus, then, instituted the Supper to be perpetuated by and for His church, with himself as host.

The early church did not forget the command to "do this in remembrance of me." Throughout the book of Acts, we find the church "breaking bread," the name given to the Supper by the early church (Acts 2:42, 46; 20:7). At Corinth, we find that the Lord's Supper was a regular part of their weekly worship (1 Corinthians 11:17f). Acts 20:7 tells us that the purpose of the disciples' gathering was to "break bread."

As to the frequency of observance, the consensus of scholarship points to a weekly or perhaps even a daily observance.[31] Since the roots of the Supper were also in the daily meals with Jesus, the more frequent participation in the Supper seemed natural. Acts 20:7 tells us that the church met on the "first day" of the week to break bread. The practice of less frequent observance of the Lord's Supper has its roots in the medieval church and in the sixteenth century reformation, not within the early church. In fact, Calvin objected to the practice of annual communion:

> At least once in every week the table of the Lord ought to have been spread before each congregation of Christians and that custom, which enjoins believers to communicate only once a year, is unquestionably an invention of the devil, whoever were the persons by whom it was introduced.[32]

To what does the command, "Do this" (Luke 22:19; 1 Corinthians 11:24, 25) refer? Is it a command to remember Him or to break bread as we gather for worship? Robertson and Plummer take it to mean, "Perform this action (continue to take bread, give thanks, and break it) in remembrance of me."[33] Jeremias, after long discussion concludes, ". . . there remains only the possibility that *touto* refers to the 'rite of breaking the bread,' i.e., the rite of grace at table."[34] This is what Paul affirms in 1 Corinthians 10:16 as he refers to "the cup of blessing which we bless . . . the bread which we break." "This do" is Jesus' command to pray and break bread, to pray and to extend the cup. Can this be done in His name and not remember Him? It is from this action of breaking bread that the Supper received the name, "breaking bread," in the early church (Acts 2:42, 46: 20:7).

The Supper—as Memorial

Zwingli, the Swiss reformer, led the way in viewing the Supper as only a memorial. This position is an attractive alternative to the doctrines of transubstantiation and the "real presence" held by Roman Catholics and Lutherans respectively. Jesus did say, "Do this in remembrance of me" (1 Corinthians 11:24-26). But as stated above, this command has reference to the actions of "taking," "giving thanks," and "breaking." This does not negate the memorial aspect of the Supper, for this action is to recall Him and His actions for us. Each observance should place Jesus at its very center, for the Supper is a celebration of the gospel.

The danger of viewing the Supper as only a memorial is that insufficient emphasis is placed on the fact that He lives now. George Washington is memorialized, but he is dead. The Supper is more than just a memorial because Jesus lives. "It is no atheistic banquet at which no God is present," declares Warren Lewis. "On he contrary, He lives and meets us there."[35]

Cullman deals extensively with the impact the resurrection appearances had on the church's understanding of the Supper.

These appearances caused the church to celebrate these meals with joy: "*The certainty of the resurrection* was the essential religious motive of the primitive Lord's Supper."[36] Thus, Peter saw the meals eaten with Jesus as proof of His resurrection (Acts 10:40, 41). For Paul, participating in the Supper is proclaiming His death "until He comes" (1 Corinthians 11:26). The appeal of Revelation 3:20 is rooted in the joyful anticipation of His presence at the Supper. "Behold, I stand at the door and knock; if anyone hears My voice and opens the door, I will come in to him, and will dine with him, and he with Me."

To view the Supper as only a memorial results in speaking of "observing" the Supper. But this word lacks the idea of involvement that the Supper requires. If the Supper is only a command to obey, we can continue to "observe," but this does not lend itself to the thanksgiving and joy that should be expressed in the Supper. To reject the word "celebrate" because of fear that this might mean that He is being re-crucified, as in the mass, is to miss the joy of communion with the resurrected Lord. We need to balance our understanding of the Supper between reference to the cross and to the resurrection, and to realize that the invitation to the table is from a living Lord. This invitation calls for more than merely "observing." It is a time of celebration—of His love, His grace, His victory, His coming again, His forgiveness, our life in Him, and His presence.

The Supper—the Presence of Christ

Jesus promised to be with His disciples. He is the host of the Supper, and as such, He invites His disciples to eat with Him. To host the Supper, He must be present. He promised that where two or three are gathered together in His name, He would be present (Matthew 18:20). The church has been divided throughout much of her history over the manner of Christ's presence in the Supper. Suffice it to say that since He lives, He is present. He offers in the Supper the spiritual food we need; therefore, we accept His presence.

The question is sometimes asked: Is Jesus present in a manner different from that occasion when two or three gather in His name for prayer, and if so, what is the value of the Supper? Is there more of Jesus' presence at one occasion than the other? Such a question would not trouble the Hebrew mind. The value of the Supper lies not in how He is present, but in that He has chosen the agenda of the table encounter and that He lives to fulfill His promise. The Supper is the Christ-appointed place where He meets us for our edification. The elements and the context of the Supper determine the thought content of the encounter, and this agenda is at the very core of our salvation. In fact, the Supper is a celebration of the gospel—His death for our sin, His burial, and His resurrection. With the outward, objective form, the Supper rises above what might otherwise be purely subjective meditation on our part.

The Supper—as Table Fellowship

The breaking of break means table fellowship. "In the east, to admit a man to the table was always a sign of friendship."[37] Such fellowship has the added implication of interpersonal commitment. "Those who sit at a meal are committed to each other, and committed to their host, and their host is committed to them."[38] Jeremias expresses a similar view of the meaning of the sharing of a meal: "At every common meal *the constitution of the table fellowship* is accomplished by the rite of the breaking of bread."[39] Since common meals had this significance, how much more the meal to which Jesus invites His disciples.

Jesus, then, in the breaking of bread, deliberately offered table fellowship. He pronounced the blessing over the elements, saying that they were for the "many." Giving these elements to His disciples means "*that by eating and drinking He gives them a share in the atoning power of His death.*"[40] This meaning is indicated by the language of Paul: "Is not the cup of blessing which we bless a sharing in the blood of Christ? Is not the bread which we break a sharing in the body of Christ?" (1 Corinthians 10:16) The Supper is forgiveness offered. The Supper accepted is forgiveness accepted.

By offering table fellowship, Jesus reaches out to us that He might continue to bless us. The fourth Gospel describes that moving episode in the upper room when Jesus deliberately offered the dipped morsel to Judas. Judas accepted Jesus' friendship and fellowship, then went out to betray Him. John writes thus of Judas' treachery: "And after the morsel, Satan then entered into him" (John 13:27).

Jesus calls His people to the table weekly so that He might offer them anew His fellowship. Jesus desires to assure His disciples of their relationship in which their salvation lies. "*Everything is embraced in this one purpose of assurance.*"[41]

The Supper—as Covenant Renewal

The celebration of the Lord's Supper is also a renewal of covenant relationship with Christ. The Passover meal was a covenant meal. The Lord's Supper has its roots there, with Jesus as the Lamb of God. "This cup is the new covenant in My blood" (1 Corinthians 11:25) speaks of covenant participation by virtue of Jesus' sacrifice at Calvary. To lift the cup is to "proclaim the Lord's death until He comes" (1 Corinthians 11:26). Our participation in the Supper is renewal of the covenant accepted at baptism. Participation means acceptance of Christ's promises and standing with Him and sharing in His ministry as part of His body, the church. Jeremias calls this "the gift of the Eucharist."[42]

The Supper—as Sacrament

To see the Supper as Jesus' being present to bless, to see it as the giving and the receiving of table fellowship, and to see it as covenant renewal makes the Supper sacramental in nature. God does convey grace in the Supper. Jesus confronts us at a specific time to deal with our individual lives and our corporate life as His church. The act of a Roman soldier pledging his allegiance anew to his commanding officer was known as a sacrament,[43] a meaning not unknown to the reformers of the nineteenth century.[44] This understanding of the Supper as a sacrament calls for a faith response from the celebrant. There must be a willingness to receive what is given.

The celebration of the Supper should bring new dimensions of joy and dedication to the church. Joy flows from the awareness that the living Christ extends to His people table fellowship and assurance. New dedication comes with the call for covenant renewal with Jesus. This call for renewal in the Supper eliminates the need for special calls for "rededication" in the same services where the Supper is celebrated.

The Supper is a sacrament of the church. It was given to the church to accomplish the Lord's purposes. The unity of His followers, a personal unity centering in His person (John 17:21), was a priority with Jesus. This priority was not absent from that first Supper, and it must not be eliminated from the Supper today. The Supper has implications for the unity of the church: "Since there is one bread, we who are many are one body; for we all partake of the one bread" (1 Corinthians 10:17). As Jesus tried to include Judas in the fellowship the night in which the latter betrayed Him, we, too, should try to include rather than to exclude. We cannot be in fellowship or communion with Jesus, our host, if we are not in fellowship with those to whom He also extends the loaf and the cup. The church must hear Jesus' admonition as the Supper is celebrated, ". . . first be reconciled to your brother, and then come . . ." (Matthew 5:24). To ask for forgiveness first requires seeking the forgiveness of those who have sinned against us (Matthew 6:12, 14).

First Corinthians 11:29 calls for those receiving the elements to "discern the body" (KJV). Did Paul mean Christ's physical body, or His body the church? The weight of scholarship points to *body* in this passage as Christ's body and not the church,[45] yet Paul reflects the mind of Christ (John 17:20) as he attacks the disunity evident in the Corinthians' manner of participating in the Supper (1 Corinthians 11:17-22). "Since there is one bread, we who are many are one body; for we all partake of the one bread (1 Corinthians 10:17). Unity must prevail at the Supper because Christ has made us one. It is He who extends table fellowship. Brothers cannot be at odds with one another and truly be in fellowship with Jesus. This necessitates the worshippers' rising above the "just Jesus and me" mentality. The Supper is a sacrament of the church. It is individual but at the same time corporate and communal. We partake as members of the household of faith.

While the Lord calls each believer within a congregation to His table and the entire congregation as well, He also calls His entire body to the table and to the same fellowship. The practice of "closed communion" is a denial of another's right to accept Christ's invitation and to Paul's admonition for a believer to "examine himself and so eat of the bread and drink of the cup" (1 Corinthians 11:28). The Supper testifies to the oneness of Christ's body and to the need of that entire body to realize its unity. Since it is the Christ who calls us to unity, the total church must respond to be faithful.

This understanding of the sacraments results in a tension for the church seeking to embody the New Testament norm. Since baptism is sacramental, the church, to be faithful, will admit only the immersed believers to membership, but at the same time will welcome all believers to the table as a witness to God's grace and to the unity of the church. Thus, the church acknowledges the Lordship of Jesus at the same time it recognizes that it is by His grace and mercy men are saved.

NOTES

[1]Paul Tillich, The Protestant Era (Chicago: University of Chicago Press, 1948), pp. 94, 112.

[2]William Robinson, What Churches of Christ Stand For (Birmingham: The Churches of Christ Publishing Committee, 1926), pp. 84, 85.

[3]Henry Webb, "A Brief Historical Survey of Sacramental Theology." A paper read at the Theological Forum, North American Christian Convention, Detroit, MI, 1975.

[4]Robinson, What Churches of Christ Stand For, p. 85.

[5]Professor Joseph H. Dampier of Emmanuel School of Religion once remarked with characteristic ironic style, " We don't call baptism and the Lord's Supper 'sacraments' because the New Testament doesn't call them that, so we call them 'ordinances' because the New Testament doesn't call them that either!"

[6]H. J. Witherspoon, Religious Values in the Sacrament (1928), p. 60, cited by G. R. Beasley-Murray, Baptism in the New Testament (Grand Rapids: Eerdmans, 1962), p. 263.

[7]Hans Küng, The Church (New York: Sheed and Ward, 1967), p. 35.

[8]Alexander Campbell, Christianity Restored (Rosemead: Old Paths Book Club, 1959), p. 311.

[9]Abbott-Smith, Manual Greek Lexicon of the New Testament (London: T & T Clark, 1953).

[10]Küng, The Church, p. 207.

[11]Karl Barth, The Teaching of the Church Regarding Baptism (London: SCM Press, 1948), p. 9.

[12]Beasley-Murray, Baptism in the New Testament, p. 358.

[13]Ibid., pp. 354, 358.

[14]W. Walker, A History of the Christian Church (New York: Charles Scribner's Sons, 1954), p. 95.

[15]Ibid., p. 96.

[16]Alexander Campbell saw this relationship between baptism and forgiveness and wrote, "Peter connects these two in precept—'Repent and be baptized every one of you, for the forgiveness of sins', hence I argue, that, what God hath joined together, man ought not to separate." *The Christian System* (Cincinnati: **Standard,** 1901), p. 41.

[17]Dietrich Bonhoeffer, *The Cost of Discipleship* (London: SCM Press, 1949), p. 208.

[18]Beasley-Murray, *Baptism in the New Testament,* p. 303.

[19]For those finding it difficult to see this consensus of witness to baptism's being "for the purpose of" forgiveness, it is helpful to reflect on the origins of the various traditions. Luther and Calvin were both fighting the salvation by works doctrine of their day. Paul's epistles more readily lent themselves to this struggle than did the book of Acts. Luther's salvation "by faith alone" needed the book of Romans. The reformation of the nineteenth century in America was not fighting Rome, but asking the question, "How was baptism practiced in the early church?" The book of Acts gave ready answers which were totally consistent with the entire New Testament.

[20]Küng, *The Church,* p. 207.

[21]*The Christian System,* p. 42.

[22]Alexander Campbell, *Christian Baptism* (Bethany: Campbell, 1853), p. 114.

[23]Küng, *The Church,* p. 208.

[24]Alexander Campbell, *Millennial Harbinger* (Bethany: Campbell, 1837), p. 504.

[25]S. J. England, *The One Baptism* (St. Louis: Bethany, 1960), p. 56.

[26]William Richardson deals at length with this question and says Campbell combined a "judgment of fact and a judgment of value" and that this was "an expression of the grace that is at the heart of the gospel." *Essays on New Testament Christianity,* Robert Wetzel, ed. (Cincinnati: **Standard,** 1978), p. 114.

[27]Joachim Jeremias, *The Eucharistic Words of Jesus* (London: SCM Press, 1973), p. 87.

[28]*Ibid.,* p. 49.

[29]Oscar Cullman and F. J. Leenhardt, *Essays on the Lord's Supper* (Richmond: John Knox Press, 1972), p. 61.

[30]Jeremias, *Eucharistic Words of Jesus*, p. 262.

[31]*Ibid.*, pp. 62, 137.

[32]John Calvin, *Institutes of the Christian Religion* (Philadelphia: Presbyterian Board of Publication and Sabbath School Work, 1911), Vol. 2, p. 580.

[33]Robertson and Plummer, *First Corinthians, The International Critical Commentary* (London: T & T Clark, 1961), p. 245.

[34]Jeremias, *Eucharistic Words of Jesus*, p. 29.

[35]Warren Lewis, *The Lord's Supper* (Austin: Sweet, 1966), p. 45.

[36]Cullman, *Essays on the Lord's Supper*, p. 12.

[37]William Barclay, *The Lord's Supper* (Nashville: Abingdon, 1967), p. 95.

[38]*Ibid.*, p. 95.

[39]Jeremias, *Eucharistic Words of Jesus*, p. 232.

[40]*Ibid.*, p. 233.

[41]*Ibid.*, p. 261.

[42]*Ibid.*, p. 237.

[43]Warren Lewis, *The Lord's Supper*, p. 4.

[44]*Ibid.*, p. 4; cf. F. D. Kershner, *The Restoration Handbook*, Series 3 (Cincinnati: **Standard,** 1919), p. 58. Also *Doctrines of the Christian Faith*, Six Reports by the Study Committee of the World Convention of Churches of Christ, 1955 (Study Report 4), p. 6.

[45]F. W. Grosheide, *The First Epistle to the Corinthians, The New International Commentary on the New Testament* (Grand Rapids: Eerdmans, 1955), takes it to mean the body and blood, p. 275. Robertson and Plummer agree, p. 252, but quote Stanley, "It was the community and fellowship one with another which the Corinthian Christians were so slow to discern."

CHAPTER

17

THE PURPOSE OF THE CHURCH

By Mont W. Smith

Purpose ultimately determines all ethical and value judgments. Few would agree that the end justifies the means, but none would justify a means that did not contribute to some valued end. If, for instance, one were intending to go north, activities that took him westward would be judged as unhelpful. A foolish person in any culture is, by definition, one who chooses means that work against his own goals.

The Purpose of God—the Mission of the Church

Purpose is, by definition, mission. One's will or intent is one's purpose or mission. It is of utmost importance that the church understand its true mission or purpose. Loss of clarity of purpose, clouded purpose, or lack of agreement on purpose dissipates energy. A failure to clarify purpose for a congregation or a church movement results in segments' defining their own purposes. It gives to the individual believer or the church itself the right to declare its mission, perhaps in contrast to the stated mission of the Lord. Thus it misplaces authority; it leads to division. Goals will be set against goals, believer pitted against believer, true priority lost—all in the name of the Lord. Such difficulty can be minimized by defining clearly the purpose of the church.

The mission of the church must be rooted in the mission of God. In exercise of His own sovereign power, God has declared that "the manifold wisdom of God might now be made known through the church to the rulers and the authorities in the heavenly places. This was in accordance with the eternal purpose which He carried out in Christ Jesus our Lord" (Ephesians 3:10, 11).

The purpose of God was clearly stated many times by the apostles. The church continued Christ's mission (John 17:18-23). All ministries in the church were created to achieve the purpose of God. The covenant documents were written to restate, illustrate, and promote the one great mission. We know precisely what that mission was and is. God has clearly identified His own purpose in history.

This purpose can be summed up in any number of words, all of which assume the same situation to exist and the same mission to be accomplished. The word that we shall use is *reconciliation*. Paul, in typical Hebrew literary style, used this term in parallelism with such words as adoption, salvation, justification, sanctification, new birth, resurrection, and "having peace with." Each of these indicates God's purpose: reconciliation of all the estranged Adams of the race. Paul's finest summary of God's purpose is found in 2 Corinthians 5:17-19:

Therefore if anyone is in Christ, he is a new creature; the old things passed away; behold, new things have come. Now all these things are from God, who reconciled us to Himself through Christ and gave us the ministry of reconciliation, namely, that God was in Christ reconciling the world to Himself, not counting their trespasses against them, and he has committed to us the word of reconciliation.

Paul understood that salvation included the purpose of creating a further ministry of reconciliation. God not only gave Christ to us; He gave the church to Christ for Christ's purposes: reconciliation. Thus, a believer is called both to reconciliation with God and to the ministry of reconciliation.

The apostle Peter presented salvation the same way: it is for service to God for His purposes. One is saved and called to the *holy* (set apart) calling or purpose. "You are a chosen people, a royal priesthood, a holy nation, a people belonging to God, that you may declare the praises of Him who called you out of darkness into his wonderful light" (1 Peter 2:9, NIV). To "declare the praises of Him" was not understood as only prayer. Jesus was Peter's model. Jesus had prayed, "I glorified Thee on the earth, having accomplished the work [mission] which

Thou has given Me to do" (John 17:4). "Declaring the praise of God" to all the world is the *calling*.

Paul used another phrase that carried all the meaning of reconciliation. "In Christ" (Colossians 1:28, 29) carries the ethical value of reconciliation. To be "in Christ" is to be fully reconciled to God and becoming like Christ. Becoming like Christ is stated in Romans as God's eternal purpose (Romans 8:28, 29). To be "in Christ" is both to be reconciled to God and to be part of the body of Christ: the church. To be like Christ means to have the "mind of Christ" (Philippians 2:5-11).

The fruit of having the mind of Christ is the desire to see "every knee bow" and "every tongue confess that Jesus Christ is Lord, to the glory of God the Father" (Philippians 2:10, 11). Christ came to seek and to save the lost (Luke 19:10). Paul understood that to have been the basic purpose of the incarnation. "It is a trustworthy statement, deserving full acceptance, that Christ Jesus came into the world to save sinners" (1 Timothy 1:15).

God sees mankind in two categories: the lost and the reconciled. Those who are estranged from God shall perish (John 3:16). Jesus himself was the source of the two category analysis. He said clearly, "I am the way, the truth, and the life; no one comes to the Father, but through Me" (John 14:6).

The apostolic doctrine of "no other name" (Acts 4:12) came from the Lord.[1] Paul's theology followed that assumption to its logical conclusion. It is appropriate, therefore, to discuss the purposes of God for each of the two categories. He has a purpose for the lost: reconciliation. He has a purpose for the reconciled: the "ministry of reconciliation." Paul indicated by his use of the terms *auxesis* (growth in size) and *oikodome* (growth in love) the results accompanying a mature church (Ephesians 4:16).

The church faces two directions. It faces the world with the message of reconciliation. The activities that comprise the means to that end are called evangelism. Evangelism is making disciples (Matthew 28:18-20). The church also faces inward toward its own members. All activities toward them are called nurture or edification. The church is to grow in two ways: in size by adding recently converted pagans, and in maturity by becoming more like Christ. When a disciple is fully taught, he will be like his Master (Luke 6:40). One becomes a disciple and then becomes like Christ.

Models in Determining Purpose

It is insufficient for a theologian to select passages that support his views and announce them to be a summary of the truth. To avoid such error, one must approach the problem from a variety of perspectives. Philosophers who consider truth as one harmonious whole will welcome such an effort. An apostolic doctrine that is developed, that is, set forth with reasons and supporting argument, may be accorded a higher priority in theology than a chance remark or a once-used term or a phrase with meaning greatly limited by its context. In the section that follows, the proposition that the purpose of God is reconciliation will be shown to be a well developed theology in the Bible. The theology will be approached or analyzed from various perspectives, called models. Each model tends to draw one to the same conclusion: God's ultimate purpose is the reconciliation of the world to himself and its edification in the church of Jesus Christ.

The Predestination Model

Predestinated is a Biblical word, and the concept it bears is a Biblical concept. It has reference to God's eternal purpose in Christ. The word *predestinated* means simply planned or set in advance. Since the term was in Greek usage prior to Christ's coming, it must be some activity that men can work with other men or other things. When Paul or Luke set out on a journey by boat, they very likely sought a ship whose destination corresponded to their own. The destination was set by the owners prior to Paul's coming, that is, in advance. We may say that Paul and the boat owner were involved in human predestination. *Predestination* means planned in advance. It has reference to the destination of a category, not of individuals. God decided in eternity that Christ would die for man's sin. Christ is spoken of as having been "slain from the foundation of the world" (Revelation 13:8, KJV). All mankind who come into contact with that blood shall also have redemption from sin. The saving power of Christ's blood was predetermined "before the foundation of the world" (1 Peter 1:19, 20). All who would share in that death, who would come "in Christ" to God, were to be saved. "He chose us in Him before the foundation of the world, that we should be holy and blameless before Him. In love He predestined us to adoption as sons through Jesus Christ to Himself, according to the kind intention of His will, to the praise of the glory of His grace" (Ephesians 1:4-6). God planned in advance to adopt all who are in Christ and to present them "holy and blameless before Him."

Every individual must choose either the world or the church of Christ. The destination of each group is predetermined. One group shall be adopted as sons; they will share all things in Christ. The other group shall suffer exclusion from the presence of God (2 Thessalonians 1:8, 9). One must elect himself into the covenant (Acts 2:40, 41); he must accept the word of invitation. God calls through the gospel to all who hear it (2 Thessalonians 2:13-15). God is not willing that any should perish, but that all should come to repentance (2 Peter 3:9). God, of His own will, brings us forth "by the word of truth" (James 1:18). Predestination is, therefore, by stipulation; all who choose Christ are predestined to eternal life.

God further decided in eternity that all whom He adopted through Christ would become like Christ. "For whom He foreknew, He also predestined to become conformed to the image of His Son, that He might be first-born among many brethren; and whom He predestined, these He also called; and whom He called, these He also justified; and whom He justified, these He also glorified" (Romans 8:29, 30; cf. James 1:18).

The eternal purpose of God and the concept of predestination by stipulation are parallel concepts. God's original purpose in creating man was fellowship. The English word *fellowship* is traced to the Greek *koinonia* and, in turn, to the Hebrew *yada*. Jesus used the Hebrew understanding of *know (yada)* when He declared, "This is eternal life, that they may know Thee, the only true God" (John 17:3). To *know*, for the Hebrew, meant to have an intimate association with, not simply to know about. Thus the Scriptures say that "Adam knew his wife; and she conceived, and bare Cain" (Genesis 4:1). To *know God* means to have a personal and covenanted relationship with Him. Fellowship means the interpenetration of personality without the loss of individuality.[2] Fellowship means that each person becomes more like the other as they share life. When Adam chose power and alienated himself from God, God already had plans to restore him and all his race to fellowship (1 John 1:1-4). By covenant grace, God allowed Christ to stand in Adam's place at the cross. Reconciliation is being restored to fellowship. Christlikeness is the deepening of that fellowship by participation in God's eternal purpose.

What God intended in His creation of man must necessarily be His eternal purpose. What God wanted in Adam He demonstrated in Christ. What He wanted in the law of Moses He demonstrated in Christ. What God wants of each believer is a person like Christ. What God wants of the church is a new humanity like Christ. What God lost in Adam He is restoring through Christ, the new Adam. The gospel is the message of reconciliation. The church is the agency of reconciliation. Reconciliation is the very purpose of God. "His purpose was to create in Himself one new man out of the two, thus making peace, and in this one body to reconcile both of them to God through the cross, by which He put to death their hostility. He came and preached peace to you" (Ephesians 2:15).

By a careful study of the Biblical doctrine of predestination, one must come to the conclusion that in the purpose of God, reconciliation and Christlikeness are aspects of one process.

The Mysterion Model

Jesus first introduced the New Testament concept of the "mystery of God." By their use of mystery, the New Testament writers did not mean something unknown. Both Jesus and Paul understood that the mystery was something previously unknown or unrevealed but now completely revealed, hence a mystery no longer. The mystery of God previously unknown was God's self disclosure in Jesus Christ and the full disclosure of His purposes in the church. Jesus understood himself as the mystery revealed (Matthew 12:28). Where His Kingdom went in the person of His disciples, so went the revealed mystery of the Kingdom. As the "new humanity" emerged among all nations, the purpose of God, the eternal mystery, was being fully seen by all. The church became the "Israel of God" (Galatians 6:16). The message went out from the New Jerusalem (Galatians 4:26) to all mankind with the command, "Be reconciled to God" (2 Corinthians 5:20).

The church, as the New Israel, is to become the Canaan of every region on earth. Christ is the mystery revealed. As the church, His body, grew in each land, the mystery was being revealed there also. That spread of knowledge revealed the mystery: "Christ in you, the hope of glory" (Colossians 1:27-29). In the Ephesian letter, Paul set forth the mystery of God in two aspects. The first has to do with God's intention for the Gentiles.

You can understand my insight into the mystery of Christ, which in other generations was not made known to the sons of men, as it has now been revealed to His holy apostles and prophets in the Spirit; to be specific, that the Gentiles are fellow heirs and fellow members of the body, and fellow partakers of the promise in Christ Jesus through the gospel (Ephesians 3:4-6).

The purpose of God was to reconcile in one body all the ethnics on earth, that they may share a covenanted relationship with Christ along with that part of Abraham's children who believed (Galatians 3:29). Paul again defined the great mystery in the third chapter of Ephesians.

To preach to the Gentiles the unfathomable riches of Christ, and to bring to light what is the administration of the mystery which for ages has been hidden in God, who created all things; in order that the manifold wisdom of God might now be made known through the church (Ephesians 3:8-10).

The end, intent, or purpose of God was bound up in Christ, and was identified as Christ in you. Christlikeness, after reconciliation with God, within the church, was the mystery of God. The gospel and the church are identified as the means to the end. The church as the arena of reconciliation is an end in itself (Ephesians 3:10). In the theology of the mystery is seen a rather clear picture of the purpose of God: the reconciliation of men to God and each other in the church through the preaching of the gospel of Christ. To that purpose Paul gave himself and called upon all men to share suffering in the same commission.

In my flesh I do my share on behalf of His body (which is the church) in filling up that which is lacking in Christ's afflictions. Of this church I was made a minister according to the stewardship from God bestowed on me for your benefit, that I might fully carry out the preaching of the word of God, that is, the mystery which has been hidden from the past ages and generations; but has now been manifested to His saints, to whom God willed to make known what is the riches of the glory of this mystery among the Gentiles, which is Christ in you, the hope of glory (Colossians 1:24-27).

Does the church exist, therefore, for its own sake? Properly understood, it does. As the instrument of reconciliation and as the arena of fellowship between all ethnics, it is an end in itself. As the first body of Christ was so critical a means as to be an end in itself, so is His second body, the church. But as the first body gave itself for all mankind's salvation, so must the church, His second body, give itself to the ministry of reconciliation.

The Apostolic Activity Model

In using this model, we must admit that important presuppositions are held. The model itself is rather simple. We examine the activity of the apostles in the book of Acts and conclude their activity was the purpose of God. The assumption is that the apostles correctly understood Jesus Christ. It further assumes that Acts is authentic and can be taken at face value as the truth of what happened and why it happened.

Briefly put, the primary activity of the leadership of the ancient church was to establish churches and to edify them for the establishment of yet other congregations. They understood their commission to be "that repentance and forgiveness of sins should be proclaimed in His name to all the nations, beginning at Jerusalem" (Luke 24:47). The preaching of the message created congregations (Acts 2:42). The letters to the young church leaders from Paul can be understood only within the context of a synagogue-type church.

The nature of leadership within those Messianic "synagogues" are a further indication of the apostolic purpose (Ephesians 4:11 and 1 Timothy 3). The apostles were often before kings and governors. At no time did they admonish the official as to his governmental duty or the function of governments in general. The apostles attempted to convert the ruler to a living faith in Christ, not to lecture on perfect social structure (Acts 26:29). The church at Jerusalem attempted a type of communal living, it seems, but that model was not widespread. Even at Jerusalem, the apostles understood their highest priority to be devoting their time "to prayer, and to the ministry of the word" (Acts 6:4). The emphasis was upon the increase of numbers as well as discipleship (Acts 2:41; 4:4). As the church grew into other ethnic cells, leadership was turned over to them by the apostles (Acts 6:1ff). Believers who were scattered by persecution went everywhere "preaching the word" (Acts 8:4). The apostles preached in many towns and later returned to encourage the congregations they had established (Acts 14:21-23). The provision of leadership for new congregations was of highest priority. Paul met the leadership of the Ephesus region at Miletus, urging them to be good shepherds over "the church of God which He purchased with His own blood" (Acts 20:28). It is clear that congregations were established, for Paul addresses letters of instruction and encouragement to those very groups—the church of God "in Corinth," "in your house," "of the Thessalonians," and "to the churches of Galatia."

We are assuming that the apostles correctly understood the commission of the Lord Jesus Christ. Their activity indicated their priority system. We must conclude that the making of disciples and organizing them into congregations for the purpose of extending the Word of God was the purpose of the Lord. This conclusion harmonizes with the theology of both the predestination and the mystery of Christ models.

The "Last Will and Testament" Model

God grants to mankind certain benefits under Christ's will (Hebrews 9:16ff). The New Covenant is the administration of the eternal purposes of God and is, therefore, called the "eternal covenant" (Hebrews 13:20). Covenants that have high profile in Scripture have three aspects: parties, stipulations, and promises. The fundamental thing about Biblical covenants is that they are conditional. The conditions must be met in order to receive the benefit. Grants under a will are free, but received upon meeting stipulations, if any. To say "New Testament" is to say "New Covenant" or "the *will of God.*" *Will* denotes purpose. The Greek word for covenant is *diatheke.* It is a compound word having as its root *theke*: purpose, will, or intent.[3]

What a man declares at or near his death is held by courts to have greater significance; it is the man's last word. The last words of Jesus were held to be of greatest significance by the apostles. Matthew's account reads thus:

All authority has been given to Me in heaven and on earth. Go therefore and make disciples of all the nations, baptizing them in the name of the Father and the Son and the Holy Spirit, teaching them to observe all that I commanded you; and lo, I am with you always, even to the end of the age (Matthew 28:18-20).

In the above passage, the subject of the command is understood, "You," meaning the apostles and, therefore, the entire church. The verb is *make disciples*—in this context meaning make converts. There are three participles: *going, baptizing, teaching.* These indicate the means to the end. The end is making converts. The means are going, obtaining a commitment (baptism) and further perfecting ("teaching them to observe all that I commanded you").

Peter referred to this command when admitting the first Gentiles into the kingdom of God: "And He ordered us to preach to the people, and solemnly to testify that this is the One who has been appointed by God as Judge of the living and the dead" (Acts 10:42).

Paul viewed himself as under a "commission"; hence, he was free only to decide whether to preach with or without charge to the church. But preach he must. "For woe is me if I do not preach the gospel" (1 Corinthians 9:16). He understood the command of God to be taking the gospel to all the nations (Romans 16:26). Such was his ministry (2 Corinthians 4:5).

The stipulations of the covenant are the commands of God under that covenant. The administration of the covenant of Christ is called by Paul the ministry of the New Covenant (2 Corinthians 3:6). Paul defined the ministry of the covenant as the ministry of reconciliation (2 Corinthians 5:18). Such substitution of terms is typical Hebrew literary style. Paul first began with a discussion of covenant. He then abandoned the use of *covenant (diatheke)* and substituted in its place the word *ministry (diakonos).* He then defined clearly the word *ministry* as the *ministry of reconciliation.* Thus, the New Covenant is the ministry, and the ministry is the ministry of reconciliation; therefore the New Covenant is the ministry of reconciliation. The command is to go to all the ethnics of the world saying, *"Be ye reconciled to God."* This was just what Christ did, and as we see with unveiled faces the glory of Christ, we are being transformed into His same image (2 Corinthians 3:18). One becomes like Christ as he joins Christ in saying to God, "Behold I have come . . . to do Thy will, O God" (Hebrews 10:7). The will of God is the New Covenant being administrated to all men.

The New Covenant has parties. The parties of the New Covenant are all who are "in Christ." One can no longer be a member of the Covenant by being born of the flesh of Abraham (John 6:63). He has to be reborn, of water and the Spirit (John 3:5). Whoever responds to Christ is a full candidate for covenant keeping (John 3:36).

The New Covenant has stipulations or obligations for members of the covenanted community. The obligations of the Old

Covenant were called the law of Moses. The new command is to serve the best interests of Christ, the Master (Matthew 25:15ff). To serve means to advance the Master's best interests. The greatest in the kingdom will advance the best interests of all (Mark 10:44). The best interest of all is to be reconciled to God and be like Christ.

The Biblical doctrines of faith, hope, and love have little meaning apart from reconciliation having taken place. That is to say, faith, hope, and love have no validity in themselves. It is the object of each that gives power and meaning to each. To put it another way, faith, hope, and love (and service, for that matter) are all morally neutral. They are, as such, neither good nor bad. Whether they be good or bad depends entirely upon the object of the faith, or the hope, or the love.

For instance, Jesus said, "This is the judgment, that the light is come into the world, and men loved the darkness rather than the light" (John 3:19). Paul said, "The love of money is a root of all sorts of evil" (1 Timothy 6:10). John wrote, "Do not love the world" (1 John 2:15). It is clear that unless the object of love is sound and valid, the affection toward, or the loyalty to, that object is misplaced and may lead to death! Therefore, it is of vital importance to the very concept of love that men be reconciled to God and love Him. They can neither know Him nor love Him if they are unreconciled to Him in Christ. Love is not the salvation of the world. The love of God is the salvation of the world. Since love means, in its Old Testament root, as well as in Jesus' definition, "loyalty to" or "seeking the best interests of," it is vital that love have true content. It is necessary to know whom to love, and what is the best interests of.

As regards faith, "Some trust in chariots and some in horses, but we trust in the name of the Lord our God" (Psalm 20:7, NIV). It is clear that men can trust the wrong thing and perish. Therefore, trust itself is as able to destroy as to save. Trust is not a moral good in and of itself. Trust in God is always good. Trust in Christ will bring salvation. Trust in the will of God brings stability and honor. It is absolutely necessary that men become reconciled to God so that trust may have its life-bringing fruit.

In the same way men may hope for vain riches and have hope for gain or hope for an advantage. But hope without reconciliation is empty. It has no content. It is an unemployed emotion. It attaches to whatever passes by. It may even lead to death. The object of hope makes hope moral. There is, therefore, no love

413

for someone if his eternal future is ignored. Paul himself said, "If we have hoped in Christ in this life only, we are of all men most to be pitied" (1 Corinthians 15:19).

It is an empty love that cares for a man's body and not his soul, just as it is empty love to care for his soul alone, and yet urge him, "Go in peace, be warmed and be filled," while doing nothing about his physical needs (James 2:16). The New Covenant is, therefore, not merely based on faith, hope, and love, but faith in Christ, love of Christ, and hope in the promises in Christ.

The promises of the New Covenant do not include the vast system of immediate rewards provided for by the Old Covenant (Hebrews 8:6). The Lord allows the rain to fall on the just and the unjust (Matthew 5:45). Those in the New Covenant are asked to make God their highest priority. All men, righteous and unrighteous, have food and drink provided by God as a matter of natural law. The New Covenant asks that all who come into Christ suffer as Christ did (1 Peter 2:21).

God asks that Christ's disciples (those in covenant with Him) use all their ability and social competence to aid Christ's mission. "Do business . . . until I come back" was the command of the Master (Luke 19:13). If that commission led to suffering, as it did with Christ, they are to use that suffering to become perfect (Hebrews 5:8, 9). In a great many ways, Paul suffered for Christ's service (2 Corinthians 11:23ff). He was not deprived of comfort because he lacked faith, but because he was "filling up that which is lacking in Christ's afflictions" (Colossians 1:24). When the church suffers, it is to remain faithful. "Be faithful until death, and I will give you the crown of life" (Revelation 2:10). In lands where the church has great social or political power, it must bring, through the government, justice and peace. The promises of the covenant are remission of sin, possession of the Holy Spirit (Acts 2:38), and eternal life: to share all things with Christ (Romans 8:32).

The Consideration of Alternatives

In the following model, the reassignment of alternatives, several substitute purposes will be examined. Each alleged purpose will be identified as a reversal, which indicates the substitution of a reward, result, or by-product for God's basic purpose. None of the models below is bad. They are good things, and they are from God; but they are all results of reconciliation and ought never to replace reconciliation as the goal of the church.

According to the laws of indirection, some things are achieved only as by-products of other things. It is so with happiness. If one makes happiness his aim in life, he shall very likely be unhappy. For such a one, happiness is like a vapor, forever before him, but never attainable. If, however, he forgets about his own happiness, and seeks the welfare of others, he shall very likely find himself happy.

The following four substitute goals are misunderstandings of God's purposes. They represent the reversal of by-product to end, and downgrade the end in attentive pursuit of the by-product. They are, therefore, identified as examples of reversals, as follows: *praise of God, morality, social restructure,* and *personality development.* These four are held by some to be the actual goals of God. While recognizing that some competent scholars may disagree, we nonetheless present the diagram below to illustrate our understanding of the Biblical concept of God's purpose.

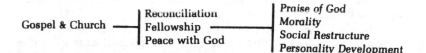

The goal of God is reconciliation, that is to say, fellowship with mankind, ending hostility, and establishing peace. The means that God has elected is the gospel and church of the Lord Jesus Christ. The by-products of peace are praise of God, true morality, gradual social uplift, and true personality development. It must be emphasized that these results are rewards resulting from the fact of reconciliation. Because each generation must be born twice, the evangelistic work of the church must never flag. What God wants is peace with all Adams of the world. To accomplish this, He has called into being the church, the continuation of the life and ministry of Jesus. The church is to announce the "good news" of God's gracious offer of reconciliation and fellowship, and to be the new humanity He envisioned when He created Adam.

The Praise of God Reversal. God created man for fellowship,

THE PURPOSE OF THE CHURCH

not simply to receive praise from him. There is no record of praise of God in Eden, but there is record of fellowship. Jesus, the very picture of God (John 14:6-9), did not seek praise, but fellowship. John declared that the mission of the church was to preach the incarnation facts and their meanings so "that you also may have fellowship with us; and indeed our fellowship is with the Father, and with His Son, Jesus Christ (1 John 1:1-4). The unreconciled do not, as a rule, praise God. Praise of God without a covenantal reconciliation is vain worship.

God seeks those who worship "in spirit and in truth" (John 4:24). True worship is to be an entire life dedicated to God and doing that which is "good and acceptable and perfect" (Romans 12:1f). The Lord Jesus is the perfect example of true worship. He said,

Sacrifice and offering Thou hast not desired, but a body Thou hast prepared for me; in whole burnt offerings and sacrifices for sin Thou hast taken no pleasure. Then I said, "Behold, I have come (in the roll of the book it is written of Me) to do Thy will, O God" (Hebrews 10:5).

In His intercessory prayer, Jesus indicated how He offered up true praise. "I glorified Thee on the earth, having accomplished the work which Thou hast given Me to do" (John 17:4).

If public "praise of God" in music, Scripture, study, and entertainment by Christian artists is emphasized as true praise of God, the church must surely fear. God has already indicated His displeasure at beautiful worship "services" that represent priority reversal.

I hate, I reject your festivals, nor do I delight in your solemn assemblies. . . . I will not even look at the peace offerings of your fatlings. Take away from Me the noise of your songs; I will not even listen to the sound of your harps. But let justice roll down like waters, and righteousness like an everflowing stream (Amos 5:21).

No individual or congregation must ever substitute mere praise for true service or worship. It is not he who worships, crying, "Lord, Lord," who enters the kingdom, but the one who obeys God's commands (Matthew 7:21). Luke understood the great command to be the last commission (Acts 1:2).

True worship was the offering up of acceptable sacrifice to God. Paul understood evangelism as true sacrifice (Romans

15:15; 16; Philippians 4:14-18). The service of Christ's best interest is true "spiritual worship" (Romans 12:1, 2, NIV). Since true worship cannot be compelled by law or statute, continued praise of God will depend upon the continued making of disciples from the unbelieving population. As church membership is limited to those who make personal profession of faith, no congregation can afford to neglect tomorrow's church: the unchurched of today. Participation in the minstry of reconciliation is true worship.

The Moral Code Reversal. The purpose of the church is not the administration of a vast moral system. There was no call by the Lord to superintend the ethics of others. It is clearly pointless to correct the morals of non-Christians, as they will be lost whether with good morals, as in the case of Cornelius (Acts 10) or with bad (Romans 1:18ff). It is faith in Christ that saves, not moral excellence apart from faith. The church is not the guardian of society's morals (1 Corinthians 5:12, 13). That is the duty of the government (Romans 13:1-7). In the Old Covenant, the kingdom of God and civic administration were one and the same thing. It is not so in the New Covenant: "My kingdom is not of this world" (John 18:36).

When a theological system allowed children to be church members by the faith of their parents, the net result was a state religion. When those same children grew up and were required to express an "experience" that indicated their own "faith," the leadership of the church became wardens of the "experiences" and morals of others. If moral conformity to a religious-civic code is the goal of the church, churchmen tend to feel their greatest contribution to God is pointing out the errors of others.

The command of Scripture is clear, "Let everyone who names the name of the Lord abstain from wickedness" (2 Timothy 2:19). The unreconciled do not depart from sin and do not praise God. They do not know how. They lack the moral strength. They are ignorant of the message of salvation. They choose only among courses of action that lead nowhere. The church that assumes that its task is to superintend the ethics of its members will soon produce an aristocracy of oversight unlike Christ. Leaders who assume their duty to be inquiry into the "experience" of members are in error. Their true duty is to equip the members for fruitful service in the Word (Ephesians 4:11, 12). The church has been brought into disrepute by the

THE PURPOSE OF THE CHURCH

excesses of some in demanding moral conformity rather than being examples of true discipleship.

Every believer is to become like Christ (Romans 8:29). Hurried conformity without proper integration of understanding and personal commitment on the part of the convert merely produces an appearance of godliness that lacks the power of Christ (2 Timothy 3:5). Everyone matures into Christlikeness at a different rate. To judge a neighbor's maturity by one or two more obvious aspects, publicly seen, is insufficient. One becomes most like Christ while doing what Christ did, seeking and saving the lost. Both Jesus (Matthew 7:1-5) and Paul (Romans 14:1-3) insisted that maturity was far too individual a matter to be overseen by immature people. While in fellowship with God in the Garden, Adam was held by only one negative law: do not eat the forbidden fruit. He enjoyed liberty in other matters. There was no massive moral system. Abraham believed God and it was considered as his righteousness (Genesis 15:6). Christians must mature into Christlikeness (2 Corinthians 3:18). Fellow believers are urged to aid the weak in a spirit of gentleness (Galatians 6:1-3). Each is urged to attend his own business (1 Thessalonians 4:11) as he becomes like his Master (Luke 6:40). Christians are not to be lawless, but under the "law of the Spirit of life in Christ" (Romans 8:2). One is most like Christ when doing what Christ did. "It is a trustworthy statement, deserving of full acceptance, that Christ Jesus came into the world to save sinners," wrote Paul (1 Timothy 1:15). We conclude that reconciliation is the proper purpose of the church.

The Social Restructure Reversal. There are many qualified theologians who advocate the reform of society as the purpose of God. The church is regarded merely as the agent used of God to usher in the kingdom of God, understood as a restructured social order where injustice, poverty, sickness, gross immorality, and denigration of the individual are eliminated. Evangelism belonged to an era in the infancy of the faith, they believe. To continue to call for "soul winning" and not attend to the pressing social errors is clinging to infancy at worst; at best, it is continuing a model of Christianity that has been a failure. To preach *soul salvation* rather than *social salvation* is an error. The priority reversal is not their error, they allege; the real reversal is the evangelism model. Mary Daly, a modern Roman Catholic thinker, urges the abandonment of such labels as

"Catholic" and "non-Catholic," "Christian" and "non-Christian." If closer attention is paid to what people actually say and do, she declares, they will be found to have "the same flame of expectation burning within them . . . the same passion for transcendance, the same desire for justice."[4]

P. Ooman Philip of India calls for a different definition of evangelism—not one of "preaching the gospel with the definite object of enlisting as many baptized adherents as possible," but of permeating the life of the country with the Spirit of Christ.[5] Michael Zeik, of Marymount College rejects the notion that "formal adherence to the Christian faith" is a requirement for salvation. "All men of good will . . . if they live by the light of their conscience will be saved."[6]

Affirming that reconciliation is the true purpose of the church is not to suggest that social concerns are not important, for they certainly are. Decisions of priority are not the choosing of the good over bad, but rather a choice between two good things. If the church had all the money and personnel it needed, both evangelism and social reform might well be advised. When there are almost *three billion* people on earth who have not heard of Christ, discussion of priority is an absolute necessity.[7]

The erosion of confidence in the apostolic message, produced by the "scientific presupposition" accepted by many philosophers in the churches, had this result: goals associated with humanism came to have a higher priority than the saving of persons. Indeed, many theologians were not sure there was a God at all. They were sure there was sickness; therefore, they helped the sick. They were not sure man had a soul. They were convinced he had hunger; so their churches fed the hungry. Such theologians lost confidence in the possibility of a life after death, and so they concentrated upon the problems of life before death. Their theology was born of their lack of faith.

This is not to imply that all scholars who believe that social action is pure Christianity are unbelievers. Far from it! Many honestly believe that the "new heaven and the new earth" (2 Peter 3:10-13) are brought in by the church and the gospel. They are urgently attempting to contribute to that end. Many competent scholars have debated the question.[8] Jesus settled it. "What will a man be profited, if he gains the whole world, and forfeits his soul? (Matthew 16:26).

If, for instance, the church could gain control of social processes and compel equality and justice, would it have achieved what God wanted of man? If the community of nations could eliminate all inequality and sickness, provide social opportunity for all, and bring equity to all areas of national life, would they have attained that for which Christ died? We think not. Similarly if the democracies of the West were able to eliminate disease, provide for the safety of all, assure equal opportunity, bring administrative justice, do away with crime and genetic defect, clear all slums, provide clean air, eliminate drug abuse, give to all an equal share of the land and its wealth, educate in the classics, and give gainful employment to all, would God have what He wants? We think not. One can have all these things and more, and if not reconciled to God may be called to the judgment and hear these words: "You fool! This very night your soul is required of you; and now who will own what you have prepared?" (Luke 12:20).

What God wanted when He made man was fellowship and mutual love. What God wants of man today is a life like Christ's and the reconciliation of the world: reconciliation to God and each other (Ephesians 2:16).

Evangelism is the world's best social action. It is better to convert a criminal than to jail him. It costs many thousands of dollars to put a man in prison and keep him there. A converted man does not go to jail. A Christian youth does not burn his neighbor's house. He does not throw homemade bombs into post office windows. He does not deface property or slash tires or terrorize the aged and helpless. He acts like Christ. The citizen who hears the Word of God and surrenders to Christ also hears the command, "Let him who steals steal no longer; but rather let him labor, performing with his own hands what is good, in order that he may have something to share with him who has need" (Ephesians 4:28).

When political reform and social or economic restructure is substituted for evangelism as the purpose of the church, a generation arises cut off from its source. A liberalism void of faith arises. Universities may flourish, justice may be championed, much upward social mobility be achieved, but the churches fail! Youth seek status in the new society. Men seek seats in the parliament, not the pulpit. Citizens demand their share of consumer goods, not caring whether the congregations, who produced the demand for equality, survive or not. One needs merely to look at England with her many qualified universities,

Christian-produced social care government, and the many empty churches to see the trend resulting from this priority reversal. If society loses its churches, from where will come the life-force to sustain an unselfish, continual social order? If each generation must be converted anew, what church dare leave off bringing in tomorrow's congregations in favor of pursuit of upward mobility?

When a state religion exists, and a child is a member of the church by statute, the sole obligation of the church is education. None have need to be converted. The trend is toward a massive program of social consciousness and moral obligation. Personal faith in God and conversion from the world, assumed by the gospel, are neglected by the third and fourth generation nominal church member-citizens. The decay of European Christianity is a result of priority reversal.

The individual Christian is the agent of social restructure. Every Christian is to act as Christ would in any given situation. The converted tax collector must collect taxes as Jesus would had Jesus been a tax collector. The governor who is converted must be the kind of governor that Jesus would have been if Jesus were a governor. A judge who is a Christian must be the kind of judge Jesus would have been. The same is true of a teacher or housewife or lawyer. The individual is the salt of the earth.

The church is charged to grow, in size and in love (Ephesians 4:16). The church does not grow generally, but only congregationally. When congregations shrink, the axe is at the root of all social gain. The duty of the church is to aid each of its members to be the kind of citizen that Christ would be. The Christian's duty as a church member is to help produce church growth. The caste system will be done away by establishing churches in all castes, each preaching the brotherhood of man in Christ. Walls fall when men no longer believe in them. Political power is related to social strength. Social strength is obtained by the church as it converts millions to Christ. A weak church makes few changes in society. A church possessing great social power is unlike Christ if it does not effect justice and equality for all.

The Personality Development Reversal. Some hold that God's goal is changed lives. They believe that each person is aided by God, as God's own goal, to attain his or her highest individual potential. Quasi-Christian psychologists add that there are means other than the Christian to do this. The value of Christianity is directly related, so these say, to its contribution to self understanding and personality adjustment. A happy individual, able to cope with life, is the goal of the church, according to these thinkers. It is our own view that conversion to God in Christ and becoming Christlike is the goal of the church. A sane and mature individual is a result of that experience.

It was never the goal of Christ to produce persons adjusted to life apart from their adjustment to God. Indeed, if God is the ultimate reality in the universe, and nature is harmonious with the will and character of God, it follows that an individual must be satisfactorily related to God to be adjusted to reality! To be adjusted to society satisfactorily may be the very source of "death," both spiritually and psychologically (1 John 2:15-17). If society is maladjusted to God, and therefore maladjusted to reality, and man is adjusted to society, then man is, in fact, ultimately maladjusted.

Normalcy means simply behaving or feeling as the average within that culture feels or behaves. What is normal in one culture is grossly abnormal in another.[9] If simple adjustment to any society is being normal, then adjustment to injustice is being normal in an unjust society!

Being like Christ is being normal whether in Manhattan or in Addis Ababa. Christianity alone has a functional definition of what is normalcy. Being like Christ is being normal. How then can one ever become well adjusted or develop his full potential unless he has been converted by the gospel and swears allegiance to Christ and obtains a model of perfect adjustment? Regardless of the culture involved, each believer is to become a child of God and act accordingly (Ephesians 5:1).

Conversion to Christ brings peace with God (Romans 5:1), but it may bring conflict with society. Jesus said, "Do you suppose that I came to grant peace on earth? I tell you, no, but rather division; for from now on . . . in one household . . . they will be divided, father against son, and . . . mother against daughter . . . " (Luke 12:51, 52). And again He said, "If the world hates you, you know that it has hated me before it hated you. If you were of the world, the world would love its own; but because you are not of the world, but I chose you out of the world, therefore the world hates you" (John 15:18).

The apostle Paul took great pains to insure that the church did not assume an anti-establishment stance as a tenet of faith (Romans 13). He obtained the requirement from Jesus that men "render to Caesar the things that are Caesar's; and to God the things that are God's" (Matthew 22:21). God is not opposed to social order. But society must not become the standard of righteousness or of what is normal. Indeed, being in "nature" without the knowledge of God is to be "dead" in sins and trespasses (Ephesians 2:1-6).

Every individual is to obtain his personality stability from Christ. He is to consider himself mature when he is behaving like Christ. He is to have the mind of Christ (Philippians 2:5). He is to heed this basic command: "And do not be conformed to this world, but be transformed by the renewing of your mind, that you may prove what the will of God is, that which is good and acceptable and perfect (Romans 12:2).

The church is to become the peer group of every convert, supporting his new personality. Approval must come from the church, not from society. The image of Christ must be fostered in all believers until they think and act as Christ would. Approval of Christlike behavior is the very task of the church. Aiding each believer to acheive true Christlikeness is true personality development. If that Christlikeness brings social disapproval, so be it. If being like Christ brings maladjustment to society, so be it. If being like Christ, or the demand to be like Christ, creates inner tensions (Romans 7:14ff), the solution is to care more for being like Christ, and less about meeting the demands of society.

The best contribution that the church can make to world sanity is to convert the world to Jesus Christ and to aid persons to become more like Christ. Obedience to God is the goal. The results are in the hands of God. We trust that He loves us and does what is best for us (Romans 8:28, 29). What is best is that we become like Christ.

Praise of God, high morality, social restructure, and personality development are excellent things. They are not, however, the goals of the church. Heaven is a great thing; but to go there is not the goal of the church. Fellowship with God is the goal. Heaven is a reward for goal achievement, for Jesus said, "Great is your reward in heaven" (Matthew 5:12). R. M. Bell, once president of Johnson Bible College, used terms similar to those in this chapter to discuss a theology advocated in the middle decades of this century.

Jesus did not commission the Apostles to go into all the world and establish charity centers. He told them to go and preach the Gospel.

Wherever the Gospel has been preached charity centers have been organized; but they are byproducts of the Gospel. Jesus did not say, "Go build hospitals," but, "Go preach the Gospel." Wherever the Gospel has been faithfully preached, hospitals have arisen; but they are byproducts. Jesus did not say, "Go build schools," but, "Go preach." Wherever the Gospel has been preached, schools have arisen; but again, they are only byproducts.[10]

Eschatology and Purpose

One's view of last events also has an effect upon his concept of purpose. If one believes that the coming of the Lord is heralded by a world becoming worse and worse, he is likely to rejoice at the appearance of social disintegration. If he believes that there is no second coming except in humanity's becoming more humane, he will tend to see reform of society as a priority. If one believes that the return of Christ is very imminent, there is little point in going to college to prepare for long-term service to Christ. There would be little point in promoting a vast building program for educational facilities for a church. There would be little incentive to rebuild slums and provide a vast system of highways. There would be little incentive, as a Christian citizen, to support a call for a constitutional convention to redress structured injustices.

If, as many "post-millennialists"[11] have advocated, the gospel will be the source of a new social order, there are many reasons for long-term and substantial commitments. If the church is so to affect government and social order as to bring in the new heaven and the new earth, there must be a rather balanced program of evangelism and instruction by the church, with a view to making a serious social impact.

"And Then the End Shall Come"

Peter taught that the church not only awaited the return of the Lord, but actually "hastened the day" (2 Peter 3:12). One could hasten the day only if an activity or other contingency could be affected by Christians. The admonition that believers "hasten" the day of the coming implied they knew what situation to promote. As always, Jesus was the source of the doctrine. He said, "And this gospel of the kingdom shall be preached in the whole world for a witness to all the nations, and then the end shall come" (Matthew 24:14). *Nations (ethne)* is best understood as language groups. The gospel must be preached to all peoples, tribes, and languages (Daniel 3:4).

Only then can the return be expected. There are in Indonesia alone more than 838 languages, in Nigeria more than 300, in Ethiopia over 250, in China over 180. It cannot be said that all *ethne* of the world have heard the gospel. The church has a massive program of world evangelism to be administrated. Less than half of all citizens in the average American community are practicing believers. The church must simply give up the notion that the task of evangelism is over. The vast majority on earth have yet to hear the gospel. If the church allows the international birth rate to exceed the conversion rate, the day of the Lord receeds further into the future. Regardless of one's view of last events, evangelism rests directly upon Christ's authority (Matthew 28:18).

Purpose and the Apostles' Doctrine

The purpose of the church is to teach and administrate the apostles' doctrine (Acts 2:42). It is insufficient for the church simply to teach "the truth" as a discipline. It is necessary that the church administrate into action what the doctrine teaches. The New Testament is the apostles' doctrine. Conformity to the apostles' doctrine produces unity. There is one body and one Spirit, one hope, one Lord, one faith, one baptism, and one God (Ephesians 4:4-6). All are brought together in the New Covenant, which provides reconciliation and growth for all who believe.

The apostles' doctrine is the core of instruction for men in every land who turn to God. There is one Lord: Jesus Christ; one faith: the gospel of the death and resurrection of Christ; one baptism: immersion in water as a pledge of covenant to God; one hope: the resurrection in glory with Christ; one calling: the participation in the ministry of reconciliation; one God: Jehovah, as exhibited in the Lord Jesus Christ; one Spirit: the messenger that defined the mission of Christ, and the author of the Bible. Every church in every land must share these truths. They are the very core of apostolic doctrine. It is the duty of the church to teach all that the apostles taught. Indigenous theology may not intrude into redefinition of these areas. Cultural conformity is not required by the church (1 Corinthians 9:16ff). Conformity to apostolic doctrine is required of all cultures (Acts 2:42). That doctrine includes the apostolic understanding of the purpose of the church. New, speculative, or nationalistic theology is unworthy of the sacrifices of the church in ages past. World evangelism, congregational multiplication, living like Christ, and transforming this world into His kingdom are worthy of the church and its Lord, Christ Jesus.

God's Call and God's Calling

The apostles were authorized by the Lord to open to all men the doors of the Kingdom (Matthew 16:16-18). Whatever the apostles bound upon men on earth would be bound upon them in Heaven. The apostles went everywhere preaching the word of the cross (1 Corinthians 1:18). By that word, God gave to mankind the invitation to fellowship (1 Corinthians 1:9). God called men out of darkness into light (1 Peter 2:9). He called to all men when upon the cross He sealed the New Covenant in the blood of His Son (Hebrews 9:17, 18). That cross was God's appeal to all men to trust Him (John 12:32). The word of the cross "pierced to the heart" those who heard it (Acts 2:37). To hear the gospel was to see Christ crucified before one's very eyes (Galatians 3:1). Although the Word of the cross seemed to be foolish to men, the Word of the cross proved to be the wisdom of God (1 Corinthians 1:24). For when men saw the cross, there awakened in them the true image of God. Confidence in God was restored, and the assurance of God's good will led them to repentance.

The gospel calls to all to surrender to God. Since the gospel is the message of the Holy Spirit, all who are called by the gospel are called by the Holy Spirit (2 Thessalonians 2:12-14). Those who believe the message have been born anew (1 Peter 1:21-23) by the Spirit and have been sanctified by the Spirit (2 Thessalonians 2:12). The gospel is God's cry in the dark night of sin. The church (the bride) and the Spirit (Christ's self in church) both unite their voices and plead, "Come" (Revelation 22:17). We are called into the kingdom (1 Thessalonians 2:12) and, like Lazarus, are called from the dead by the gospel (Ephesians 1:13; 2:5). The gospel produces in the hearts of the hearer the faith that saves (Romans 10:17).

The church is the "pillar and support of the truth" (1 Timothy 3:15). Its duty is to "preach the word" (2 Timothy 4:2). God has declared that all who call upon the name of the Lord shall be saved:

> How then shall they call upon Him in whom they have not believed? And how shall they believe in Him whom they have not

heard? And how shall they hear without a preacher? And how shall they preach unless they are sent? (Romans 10:13-15).

God's call is to eternal life. His calling is to be the body of Christ and the voice through whom He may call others. Being called and having that calling always go together (2 Timothy 1:9). All believers are both reconciled and made ministers of the message of reconciliation (2 Corinthians 5:18). We are to make our calling and election sure (2 Peter 1:10) by living a life worthy of the gospel (2 Thessalonians 1:11).

We are to be holy as He who called us is holy (1 Peter 1:15). The term *holy* means *set apart* for service to God. The calling of God is to service, a life given to God's will and purpose. None are called to status, but to God's ministry.

Conclusion

Clarity of purpose is vital to a united and vigorous church. The purpose of the church is rooted in the purpose of God. God's goal is the restoration of man to fellowship and Christ-likeness. Those who are restored to God are also reconciled in one body to each other. The church is not only the means to this goal, but is an end in itself in that it is the very arena of reconciliation.

The theology of reconciliation and Christlikeness as the purpose of God is supported by five conceptual models: predestination, the mystery of God, the apostolic activity, the New Covenant, and the elimination of alternatives. A sharp distinction must be made between means, purpose, and by-products. There exists a law of indirection: certain good things are obtained only by indirect means. Praise of God, a high morality, social reform, and true personality are the covenanted result of world evangelism. The exercise of social responsibility by the church is directly related to social strength, represented by numbers of converts and numbers of churches in every culture.

The theology of the second coming of Christ has a profound effect upon the theology of the purpose of the church. The hearing of the gospel by all language groups is the one great variable regarding the time of Christ's return.

The duty of the world is to listen to the call of God through the gospel message. The duty of the church is to contribute to God's purpose: reconciliation and Christlikeness. Paul summed it up for Timothy: "Preach the Word" (2 Timothy 4:2).

NOTES

[1]W. Adolph Vissar T'Hooft, *No Other Name,* (Philadelphia: Westminster Press, 1953). See also Alan R. Tippett, *Verdict Theology in Missionary Theory* (Lincoln, IL: Lincoln College Press, 1968).

[2]William Robinson, *Biblical Doctrine of the Church* (St. Louis: Bethany Press, 1948), p. 17.

[3]Arndt and Gingrich, *"Thelo,"* *Greek English Lexicon* (Chicago: University of Chicago Press, 1958), pp. 354, 355.

[4]Mary Daly, "Christian Mission after the Death of God," in W. T. Wilson, *Demands for Christian Renewal* (Maryknoll, NY: Maryknoll Publications, 1968), p. 17

[5]P. Ooman Phillip, "Indigenous Christian Effort," *The Christian Task in India,* John McKenzie, ed. (New York: Macmillan, 1929), pp. 212, 213.

[6]Michael Zeik, "The Aim of Christian Mission," in Wilson, *Demands for Christian Renewal,* p. 96.

[7]Ralph Winter, *The Twenty-Five Unbelievable Years* (Pasadena: William Carey Press, 1973), pp. 13ff.

[8]For instance, Peter Beyerhous, *Shaken Foundation* (Grand Rapids: Zondervan, 1972), p. 55. Donald A. McGavran, *Understanding Church Growth* (Chicago: Moody, 1972), pp. 75-150.

[9]Michael Kearney, *The Winds of Ixtepji* (New York: Holt-Rinehart, 1972), pp. 24-46.

[10]R. M. Bell, "Has the Church Lost Its Job?" *The Shane Quarterly* (Indianapolis: Butler School of Religion, 1949), p. 245.

[11]Loraine Boettner, *The Millennium* (Grand Rapids: Baker, 1975).

CHAPTER
18

THE CHURCH'S MINISTRIES

By Knofel Staton

God's Call

The church is God's people called out *(ekklesia)* of the world in order to be the continuing ministry of the risen Christ in the world. As long as the church is in the world, she is in the world for service. She is *(being)* so that she may do *(practicing)*.

Throughout the history of God's relational activities with His people, some persons have interpreted His call as a call to isolationalism. However, Jesus' incarnation demonstrated that God calls His people to involvement. Jesus declared that He came to serve (Matthew 20:28). It was through His lowly service of loving involvement in the needs of people that He interpreted God for man (John 1:18). Jesus is man's perfect exegesis of God (see *exegesato* in John 1:18); He is God's perfect exhibition of man. In Jesus, we see what God intends all humanity to be and do; and in union with Jesus, humanity is recreated as God's earthly representative (2 Corinthians 5:17-21).

The twofold dimension of being (status) and doing (service) is not a new thought for God's church, for God's call has always kept these two dimensions in balance. In the Garden of Eden, man was called to status (Genesis 1:27) for service (Genesis 1:28; 2:15). But man craved for more status ("to be like God," Genesis 3:1-7), and his service turned inward. Eventually, every thought of man was evil (Genesis 6:5)—the inevitable result when the balance of status and service is not maintained.

To emphasize status without service is to emphasize rootage without fruitage. To emphasize service without status is to call for fruitage without rootage. But God's authentic call is to keep the two dimensions in balance.

God issued the two-dimensional call through Abraham (Genesis 12:2-4):

Status	Service
And I will make you a great nation.	
And I will bless you, and make your name great;	And so you shall be a blessing;
And I will bless those who bless you,	
And the one who curses you I will curse.	And in you all the families of the earth shall be blessed.

In the same way, God chose twelve patriarchs to become the foundational leaders of God's Old Testament people *(ekklesia)*. Yet as time continued, the status dimension of God's call became desired and stressed more than the service dimension. The people of God eventually lost sight of the fact that they had privileged status for the purpose of service. Consequently, while the total population of God's people increased, the number of those who kept the two dimensions in balance diminished.

Finally, a man came who was the perfect example of how to keep status and service in balance—Jesus. And twelve men were chosen to be the foundational leaders of God's New Testament church *(ekklesia)*. From the model of Jesus, these men saw and taught that the church *is* so that she may *do*.

Extension of Jesus' Ministry

Jesus' ministry was as wide in scope as the needs of people; and because Christ could not be killed, His ministry could not be stopped. Luke made that clear in his two-volume work, Luke-Acts. In volume one, he introduced us to the earthly ministry of Jesus, tracing how Jesus crossed every human barrier to meet the needs of every type of person. In volume two, he began with the words, "The first account I composed, Theophilus, about all that Jesus began to do and teach" (Acts 1:1). Why didn't Luke say "about all that Jesus had done and taught," meaning He had completed His work? Because Jesus had not finished His doing and teaching. What Jesus began, as recorded in Luke, He continued through the church, as recorded in Acts. Luke was showing Theophilus that the activities of the church were in accordance with God's will because she continued what Jesus himself began.

The varied interests and activities of Jesus in His first-century body continue to live through His twentieth-century body—the church. The church exists to continue Jesus' ministry on earth. Thus, the church's evaluation of her activities must always go back to the life and example of Jesus.

We cannot talk about *activities* of service without also considering *attitudes* of service. Judaism's service was hindered by an attitude of selfish exclusiveness. The Jews began to categorize people as *"worthy"* and *"not worthy,"* deciding whether or not certain people were worthy recipients of their service. But Jesus broke down that barrier of exclusiveness by loving the unrighteous and calling us to do the same. Judaism's service was practically nullified by a pride that sought only to elevate her status. Jesus reversed that tendency by His humble birth, by touching lepers, by eating with riffraff, by going to tax collector's homes, and ultimately by going to the cross (Philippians 2:5-11). His final act of humility, however, is in His willingness to be the head of the church—the perfect one connected with the imperfect ones.

While Judaism was concerned that she be known for her merits, Jesus was most concerned about His ministry, and called us to share that concern (John 12:26). His teaching about who will be known as the greatest highlights the attitude of humility that He demonstrated and demands of us today: "Let him who is the greatest among you become as the youngest, and the leader as the servant" (Luke 22:26). Jesus was not ashamed to be known as a table-waiter (Luke 22:27), a foot-washer (John 13:1-16), or a friend of sinners (Matthew 11:19).

Proper attitudes are connected with proper character, which results in proper conduct. Jesus' conduct characterized the Heavenly Father, and so should the conduct of the church. Jesus' conduct is summarized in John 1:14—"full of grace and truth." Being full of grace and truth is a difficult balance to maintain. At times, the people of God have been full of grace, but had little content in their teaching. Grace (loving, caring) without truth does not meet all needs. At other times, the people of God have been full of truth, but had no grace. Many needs will remain unmet in that situation, also. God's servants must combine both in the activities of service. Paul's prayer was that the love of the church at Philippi "may abound still more and more in real knowledge and all discernment" (Philippians 1:9). The church must combine attitudes of openness, humility, and caring with the truth of God's Word to perform her ministry of service to the world. In this way, she will be continuing the work of Christ by what she is and by what she does.

Service, the Distinctive Mark of the Church
The Meaning of Service

The Greek word for "service" used in the New Testament (*diakonia*) is rarely used in the Greek translation of the Old Testament, for indeed the unselfish service of another's needs is the distinguishing mark of the New Covenant people (John 13:34, 35). It not only distinguished the church from Judaism, but also Christians from the Greeks. The Sophist declared, "How can a man be happy when he has to serve someone?" In Plato's philosophy, servers were considered inferior; the "real" man served only himself. But Jesus taught that man found himself when he lost himself in serving others (Mark 8:35).

The Greek work for the *agent* of service (*diakonos*) is used thirty-four times in the New Testament. It is the word for *minister* or *deacon*. While we today see a minister as being in a position of status, the New Testament sees him as a servant. An organizational chart of the church would better picture God's intentions if those selected to serve the whole body through designated services (such as preacher, elder, deacon, and teacher) were placed at the bottom of the chart to show the flow of service.

The words for service (in noun and verb forms) are used several times to describe waiting on tables: Matthew 8:15; Mark 1:31; Luke 4:39; 10:40; 12:37; 22:26, 27. In their general usage, however, they describe anything that is done to show caring for others. These include giving financial support (Luke 8:3; Mark 15:41; Acts 11:29), feeding the hungry, giving drink to the thirsty, clothing the naked, attending to the sick, visiting prisoners (Matthew 25:42-44; 4:11), giving up oneself to save another (Mark 10:43-45), caring for others (2 Corinthians 3:3; Hebrews 6:10; 1 Peter 4:10), personally helping a preacher (2 Timothy 1:18; Acts 19:22), and serving others in many ways (1 Corinthians 16:15; Revelation 2:19) both physically and emotionally.

Service describes a life of living for others. It calls for personal involvement and toil. In fact, the Latin cognate, *conani*, means "to give oneself trouble." The disciple of Jesus does not ask to avoid fatiguing, time-consuming service; rather, he asks, "When can I start?" It is not accidental that Paul commends the church for her toil (1 Thessalonians 1:3).

Serving others as Jesus' disciples brings us to the practical question: How can one person do all the kinds of ministries that Jesus performed? The answer is no one person has to do it all. Although each member should be growing in his service, God does not intend for him to be locked into only one ministry or expect him to do all ministries. The church is the body of Christ with many members; she is not one individual or any one congregation. *Together* the members make up a body that *collectively* should be doing the total ministry of Christ.

Unity Amid Diversity

This ministry of the church is both unified and diverse. It is unified in that there is only one ministry—the ongoing ministry of the risen Christ. Each ministry is Jesus' ministry, coming from Him as the head of the body. It is also unified in that no single individual or congregation serves independently from another. Each Christian and each congregation is interconnected with all other Christians and all other congregations, just as cells are interconnected in a body. And only as each one does his part is the entire body built up (Ephesians 4:16). It is also unified in that all genuine ministries are performed for the common good of others (1 Corinthians 12:7). To sing "He's all I need" is not Biblical. The members not only need Christ; they also need each other. The members are held together by what the other members supply (Ephesians 4:16; Colossians 2:19).

Yet the unified ministry of the church is also diverse. It is diverse in its forms. Different cultures and different times call for ministries to be rendered in different ways. God gives us freedom to move with our times. We are not locked into a Biblical blueprint for the exact way to do each service. For instance, we do not have to send someone around to the churches to collect funds for famine relief as Paul did. We do not have to select exactly seven men to minister to the needs of widows as did the church in Jerusalem. Christians in Africa may meet the need of the hungry in their midst in a way different from that done in America.

The ministry of the church is also diverse because different individuals can be involved in different expressions of that ministry. God is a God of variety. His creation is one of infinite variety. No two sets of fingerprints are alike; no two snowflakes are alike; no two stars are alike. No two individuals are alike in every way; each of us is unique, with a set of aptitudes and charisma for service related to his own individuality. We are different persons with different ways of expressing ourselves; thus our differences carry over into the work of the church. We all work for the same purpose, but we employ different methods of doing so.

Having unity amid diversity is the subject of many of Paul's writings:

> Just as we have many members [diversity] in one body [unity] and all the members do not have the same function [diversity], so we, who are many [diversity], are one body [unity] in Christ, and individually [diversity] members one of another [unity] (Romans 12:4, 5).

> For even as the body is one [unity] and yet has many members [diversity], and all the members [diversity] of the body, though they are many [diversity], are one body [unity], so also is Christ. For by one Spirit [unity] we were all baptized into one body [unity], whether Jews or Greeks [diversity], whether slaves or free [diversity], and we were all made to drink of one Spirit [unity]. For the body [unity] is not one member, but many [diversity] (1 Corinthians 12:12-14).

Paul made it very clear that the members of the body of Christ are to have different functions or ministries and yet remain unified. (Note the relation between Ephesians 4:3 and 4:7-16.)

Paul also emphasized that the differences come from God, "And since we have gifts that differ according to the grace given to us . . ." (Romans 12:6). The word *grace* is the Greek word *charis*, which is an action word. The Greeks often added the letters *ma* to the end of an action word to show what resulted from the action, creating a new word—a result word. Thus, *charis* becomes *charisma*. *Charisma* is nothing more or less than the result of grace. Anyone who has received God's grace has *charisma*. *Charisma* is used in the New Testament to refer to several different kinds of gifts, including forgiveness, mercy, and eternal life (Romans 1:11; 5:15, 16; 6:23; 11:29; 12:6; 1 Corinthians 1:7; 7:7; 12:4, 9, 28, 30, 31; 1 Timothy 4:14; 2 Timothy 1:6; 1 Peter 4:10). In Romans 12, the word refers to the different functional abilities of the various unique individuals that make up the one body of Christ. God himself has created a functional service in us. *Chrisma* is for service, and service has always been a part of God's plan.

Paul hastened to say that these functional differences should not divide Christians. As members of the body, Christians are not to be detached from each other because of their individualities, but connected to each other because of Christ (Romans 12:5). At no time should the differences in service be used to pit one member of the body against another. The differences are to be used to build up the individual members, not tear them down. Nor should members become jealous or envious because another member performs a different service. To recognize the grace of God in the functional differences of the members is to transcend the pettiness of family feuds tht might spring out of the differences (1 Corinthians 12:26; Romans 12:9-16).

The people in the church at Corinth had become trapped into doing things the world's way. They were comparing the way some members functioned with the way others functioned. This eventually caused the church to split into factions (1 Corinthians 1—4) Paul reminded the people that the functional differences should not cause discord; for even though certain members were using different methods, they were to be united in purpose (1 Corinthians 3). He reminded them that they were all servants of God. Paul then affirmed that he himself functioned as God expected him to, even though it was different from the way others functioned: "according to the grace of God which was given to me . . ." (1 Corinthians 3:10; note that this is the same phrase he used in Romans 12:6).

Members in Christ's body can differ *according to the grace* given to them. Thus, they will function differently, but without any feelings of being inferior or superior to another member of the body. Christ's body should function just like the human body, where the foot does not feel inferior to the hand, nor does the ear feel inferior to the eye (1 Corinthians 12:15, 16). Neither does the eye feel superior to the hand or the head "look down upon" the feet (1 Corinthians 12:21). Each member has a certain important function to perform. A person who feels inferior would say, "I have nothing to give to you; so I will just receive." A person who feels superior would say, "You have nothing to offer me; so I will do all the giving and serving." Both attitudes hinder the fellowship of the members and stunt the growth of the body.

It is God's intention to provide different members with different ministries, for He knows it is good for the whole body (1 Corinthians 12:18-26). If we try to put everyone into the same mold, we are thwarting God's plan for the church. We are unraveling His desires for Christians.

One of the greatest hindrances to the work of the church is the straight-jacketing of individual members by leaders of the church who are threatened to see individuals functioning differently from themselves. Leaders and members alike need to affirm that God is in the variety business. It is the *charisma*, not the appointment, ordination, or passing of a board's approval that determines the ministries in the church. We must allow the members to answer no to these questions:

> All are not apostles are they? All are not prophets, are they? All are not teachers, are they? All are not workers of miracles, are they? All do not have gifts of healings, do they? All do not speak with tongues, do they? All do not interpret, do they? (1 Corinthians 12:29, 30).

We must also realize that God is calling individuals to do certain ministries and will give them the ability and power to do them. We must not stand in God's way, but free people to serve.

The Corinthians had a difficult time handling the variety existing among them; so Paul stressed the variety but was careful to relate the variety to what they had in common.

> Now there are *varieties* of gifts, but the *same* Spirit, And there are *varieties* of ministries, and the *same* Lord. And there are *varieties* of effects, but the *same* God who works all things in all persons (1 Corinthians 12:4-6).

The varieties of ministries come from the one Lord and Spirit.

We are to be like God in character and conduct even though we are different from each other in the ways we serve God and mankind.

Paul taught that we are not to elevate certain ministries above others. The Corinthians were striving for the public and spectacular ministries, rather than the quiet ones such as giving in liberality (see Romans 12:8). They were seeking ministries that would benefit themselves rather than others. They were turning inward in their idea of service just as the nation of Israel had done many years before. Competition, jealousy, envy, and strife resulted (1 Corinthians 3:1-4). Paul told them they should seek the more benevolent services that would result from loving attitudes (1 Corinthians 13) so that they could build up each other rather than themselves (1 Corinthians 14). Paul's words in 1 Corinthians 12:31 may be translated, "But you are earnestly desiring these spectacular gifts. But I show you still a more excellent way."

It is easy to say, "My way of service is charisma, but yours is not." But we must come back to Paul's teaching:

Variety	Source
varieties of gifts (charisma)	one Spirit
varieties of ministries (services)	one Lord
varieties of effects (energies)	one God

Notice the source of these varieties is the Trinity—Spirit, Lord (the Son), and God. Which one of the Trintiy is more important? None. They are equal. Neither can we rank the designations of "charisma," "services," or "energies" above or below each other. They are equal. Each is a "grace-gift" from the divine source to enable us to function as human members in a divine body. The significance of our variety of services does not lie in the labeling of the ministry we have, but in the purpose of that functional service.

The Purpose for Service

We function differently, but we function for the same purpose—to build up the body of Christ so that the body can be well and strong enough to touch a sick world with its various ministries without getting sick itself.

Every teaching about the variety of services in the New Testament is in the broader context of unity within the body, where there was danger that the unity might be shattered. The point in these New Testament writings is that one of the ways to maintain that unity is to mature the whole body by using our various abilities for one another.

The church at Rome was diverse ethnically. The integration of Jews and Gentiles in the church had created fellowship problems that threatened its unity. Problems will always arise when we think that unity depends upon conformity in all matters, including race. Paul spent the first eleven chapters of Romans establishing the divine basis for fellowship amid the diversity of race and customs. He taught that everyone (Jew or Greek) was saved by the gospel (1:16), that God is not a respecter of persons (2:9, 11; 3:9, 22, 29, 30; 10:12), that by faith all become sons of Abraham (chapter 4), that all have peace with God in Jesus (chapter 5), and that they should pursue peace with each other (14:19). He taught that in baptism, all have been raised with Christ (chapter 6) to belong to one another (chapter 7) and to become the adopted children of God with His Spirit (chapter 8). Paul taught that God's Israel, which includes all those who accept His promise, will be saved (9—11).

After developing this foundation of why they should fellowship even though they were different, Paul told them the practical way that fellowship could be tightened and expressed— through the use of the various services that each individual could perform (12:1-8). These functions were to be done for the benefit of each other, evidenced by Paul's frequent use of the phrase "one another" in the last five chapters of the book (12:5, 10, 16; 13:8; 14:13, 19; 15:5, 7; 16:16). Unless the members of the Roman church used their various abilities for one another, there would be a loss of the richness of the fellowship reflected in the passages where this phrase, "one another," is used.

Using our abilities for others is the way we are not "conformed to this world" (Romans 12:2). The world's way is to use one's abilities to benefit himself in an attempt to be out ahead of others. But Christians are to be different. We are to be living sacrifices (Romans 12:1) by offering our abilities in service for others.

The church at Corinth was so disunited that the Lord's Supper was bathed in fussing and fighting (1 Corinthians 11:17ff). The lack of loving fellowship was taking its toll in physical illness and death among the membership (1 Corinthians 11:30).

It was in this context of disunity that Paul wrote about the church's being a united body made up of different members with different ways of functioning (1 Corinthians 12). The Corinthians were violating the purpose for their varying functions.

Paul emphasized that God gave them different abilities "for the common good" (1 Corinthians 12:7). The literal translation of the Greek is "for the bearing with" (sumpheron). The Greek word describes helping to carry another's load. It emphasizes help, aid, assistance, and yielding one's own needs to meet another's needs. God gives Christians different abilities so they can meet others' needs. Sumpheron could also be translated "bring together," picturing a bringing together of needs and the help to meet those needs. Our differences are always to be for the other person's advantage—to serve him, to build him up.

In 1 Corinthians 13, Paul talked about agape—love that is always other-oriented. When we use our abilities for self, we become self-oriented. Such an emphasis on self will always produce strife, just as it did in Corinth (3:1-4). Using our abilities for others out of an attitude of agape will always benefit others. To use them to benefit self would be to bypass God's reason for giving them to us (1 Corinthians 12:7).

The church at Ephesus was threatened with disunity; so Paul wrote the grand letter on unity—Ephesians. In the first three chapters, he developed the basis for unity. In the last three chapters, he unfolded the practical expressions of that unity. Part of that expression was the use of the different kinds of abilities and services for the building up of the body of Christ (Ephesians 4:12) to maturity (4.13-15). Paul emphasized that it is only as each part functions that the whole will be built the way God wants it built (4:16).

By the time Peter wrote, the church was being persecuted greatly for its character and conduct. In such a state, it would be tempting either to give in to the environment around the church or to give up the idea of the church altogether. Peter wrote against both those options. He said that one of the ways the church members can cling to each other for support is through the use of their different abilities to serve one another. Only then can Christians be good stewards of the variety of gifts that come from God (1 Peter 4:10). Christians should help each other by being "fervent in love" for one another (1 Peter

4:8) and by being "hospitable to one another without complaint" (1 Peter 4:9). In these contexts, we can see that the variety of services is always related to unity within the body of Christ. We must allow the members of the body the freedom to serve each other in different ways. The members must accept that freedom by serving each other in love (Galatians 5:13). The variety within the ministry of the church is to prevent division, not cause it (1 Corinthians 12:25).

The Forms of Service

The forms of service take on many different shapes. They are as varied as are God's *charisma* (1 Corinthians 12:8; Ephesians 4:8; 1 Peter 4:10). Some take on a private form, such as counseling; others are more public, such as preaching. Some, historically, have been temporary forms, such as that of the apostles. Pastors and teachers are engaged in permanent forms of service. Some forms serve the gathered community, as in the church building; others serve primarily in the scattered community, such as employees in the business world.

The New Testament has four passages listing forms of service: Romans 12, 1 Corinthians 12, Ephesians 4, and 1 Peter 4:10, 11. One listing is a category of people (Ephesians 4:11); the others are categories of functions. It is not possible to match up the functions with the people. Paul, an apostle, practiced all the functions in Romans 12:6-8 and probably all the functions in 1 Corinthians 12:8-10. While Timothy was called an evangelist, he certainly served in a variety of ways in addition to "telling the good news."

People

Some people were foundational people; they were the ones who were so inspired by God that their teachings became the foundational truths upon which the church was to be continually built. The church is built upon the "apostles and prophets, Christ Jesus himself being the corner stone" (Ephesians 2:20). While there is no apostolic or prophetic succession in people, there is apostolic and prophetic succession of truth. The church is to continue in the truth of these inspired leaders of the first century. The foundation the apostles and prophets laid is sufficient for all times. We dare not try to lay another foundation on the twentieth floor (twentieth century) of the building. The foundation holds up the church; the church can get "too wrong" to stay on its first foundation, but it can never get "too strong" to do so.

Some people were gifted to be leaders in building upon the foundation (as some are gifted today). Such leaders were (and are) called evangelists, pastors, and teachers (Ephesians 4:11). Restricting these people to certain activities is not Biblical. Evangelists were primarily traveling preachers, but they were not restricted to either traveling or preaching.

Pastors and teachers refer to the same person. The pastors were the elders (presbuteros) and overseers (episkopos). While "elder" refers to maturity, "overseer" refers to function. What kind of overseer was the elder to be? Do we go to a large corporation with its director, to a nation with its president or dictator, or to the army with its general for the appropriate model of what an overseer is to do and be? No, Jesus is our model; He is our primary overseer (1 Peter 2:25; Guardian is from the Greek word episkopos).

Any leadership in the church must get its direction from the example of Jesus. Jesus' kind of leadership can be summed up in a ministry of service—meeting the needs of people. Thus, the church's choice of the eldership must not be by popularity vote, but by the example of service each one is performing for the people. The qualifications for elders (1 Timothy 3, Titus 1) are functional qualifications. The one who has these qualities will be able to perform the functions of an elder. Those who do not have these qualities will falter in their service of the people. For instance, one who is not temperate and prudent will not listen to all sides in a counseling situation and will fail to function properly. These qualifications not only protect the church from getting the wrong type of leadership, but also protect those in leadership from getting a hurt self-image should they fail at the job. Those who do not have these qualities should not seek the job and thus open themselves to functional failure.

To understand what is involved in the job of overseer, we need to consider the New Testament's use of the verb form. It is consistently used to spotlight the humble caring for people's physical and spiritual needs. It describes someone who looks over by looking after another person (see the verb form in Matthew 25:36, 43; Luke 1:68, 78; 7:16; Acts 6:3; 7:23; 15:14, 36; Hebrews 2:6; James 1:27). Elders are not selected to a status of being commanders, but to a service of caring.

While Jesus is the personal model for the job of overseer, a shepherd is the professional model (see shepherd and overseer's being matched together in Acts 20:28; 1 Peter 2:25; 5:1-4). A shepherd's first priority is caring for the needs of the flock and acting as a guide and leader. A close study of the function of shepherds in Bible times is required to complete the picture, but that is beyond the scope of this chapter. (Note: a reading of John 10, Ezekiel 34, and Psalm 23, and relating them to practical functions in the church would be helpful. See Knofel Staton, *God's Plan for Church Leadership*, chapter 8, [Cincinnati: **Standard,** 1982], pp. 89-99).

While "pastors and teachers" in Ephesians 4:11 are referring to the same persons, they do not always have to. Every elder must be "able to teach" (1 Timothy 3:2), but not every teacher needs to be an elder. Teaching is part of continuing in the apostles' doctrine (Acts 2:42). Jesus was a teacher and commanded that the service continue (Matthew 28:19, 20).

The distinction between what is preached (*kerugma*) and what is taught (*didache*) cannot be drawn as sharply as some have thought. In the New Testament, *kerugma* is not reserved for the non-believer; neither is *didache* reserved for the believer. Prophets taught and teachers prophesied at times. Some teachers were inspired (1 Corinthians 2, 12, 14); but as the first century progressed, teachers turned to the apostolic doctrine as their content-source (1 and 2 Timothy, especially 2 Timothy 1:13—2:2). Scripture was spotlighted as being profitable for teaching (2 Timothy 3:16, 17).

Teaching requires maturity (James 3). Of course, every Christian is to mature in the faith, and the writer of Hebrews criticizes those who remained babes and thus could not teach (Hebrews 5:11—6:3). It is possible for members of the church to withdraw from serving in this capacity by saying, "I don't have the *charisma* for that." But God does not intend for us to stay locked into a set pattern or method of serving. He expects us to free ourselves to expand our ministries. As one member becomes the recipient of another's services, he not only has an immediate need met, but he also begins to develop further capacities within himself for service. As one member teaches, he not only imparts information but also develops his students into teachers (it is the same with the exposure of all of God's *charisma*). As members touch one another with service, they all grow unto the stature of Christ (Ephesians 4:13). No member has the right to "stay put" in level of growth; all must seek to grow and expand.

In addition to the apostles, prophets, evangelists, pastors, and teachers, we read about deacons in the New Testament. The word *deacon* means *servant*. Some persons were selected by a congregation to represent the church in some delegated service (1 Timothy 3:8-11); we have no other job description for deacons in the New Testament.

We cannot conclude with surety that the seven men in Acts 6 were the first deacons in the Jerusalem church. They could just as well have been the first elders, which is a distinct possibility when we consider the fact that the Jerusalem church had elders who were involved in feeding the hungry (Acts 11:30) as were the seven in Acts 6. However, the exact labeling cannot be done with accuracy; neither can the origin of deacons be pinpointed.

Deacons were probably persons chosen by churches for specific functions. They may have remained as "deacons" only as long as the specific function was necessary. Neither elders nor deacons were chosen to an "office" as much as to a work or ministry. It was service, not status, that was spotlighted. The greater the service was, the greater the leader was (Matthew 20:25-28).

Preachers were also mentioned in the New Testament. Without this function, people could not respond in faith (Romans 10: 13-15). There is no New Testament teaching that preachers were specifically called to preach. The "call" is the conviction that the world is lost and needs to hear the good news. All the Christians who scattered from Jerusalem preached (Acts 8:4)! The New Testament does not opt for a clear-cut distinction between clergy and laity; all members are considered minis ters. However, those who put aside paid occupations to preach the gospel were to receive financial help through their preaching (1 Corinthians 9:14). While Paul received no income from the Corinthians, he did receive income from others (2 Corinthians 11:7, 8; Acts 18:1-5; Philippians 4:15, 16).

We have Biblical freedom to use paid servants within the church. In our culture, it makes sense to do so. It is a ministry for the whole body to have one or a few who are free to serve various needs on a moment's notice. We cannot expect present-day employers to release their workers to help a church member who is hurting, dying, or needing immediate counseling.

At the same time, having a paid "preacher" should not give the church a practical reason for shifting the function of elders from shepherding to being administrative committee members. In too many instances, the preacher is doing the shepherding alone. All Christians are to be servants; baptism ordained us all into the ministry.

Functions

Through those leaders who laid the foundational truths, certain foundational practices were performed—confirming, certifying, and guaranteeing (Hebrews 2:4; John 10:25, 38; Acts 14:3; 2 Corinthians 12:12). These practices were the "signs and wonders" God granted to certain people to certify them as His (Exodus 4:5). Moses, Joshua, Old Testament prophets, Jesus, the apostles, and New Testament prophets were given these special gifts from God. These gifts provided the needed certification of the foundational truths upon which God's people were to build their lives. Some of these gifts or ministries are listed in Romans 12 and 1 Corinthians 12 (see chapter 9 of this work, "The Holy Spirit").

Even though such certification or confirmation of God's servants is not needed today, since we have the foundational truths intact in the Scripture, a caring concern for the needs of God's people is still very necessary. The varied ministries for meeting these needs include such broad categories as serving, teaching, encouraging, giving in liberality, leading, and performing acts of mercy (Romans 12:7, 8). These types of ministries will never cease, but they will take on varied forms. There are many ways to serve, to teach, to encourage, to lead, and to do acts of mercy. All the legitimate methods of performing these services are related to God's grace. God gives each one of us charisma in order to serve others.

The members in every congregation need to remain sensitive to the needs of those around them. Then they need to act as members in Christ's body by moving to meet that need or in enlisting someone else with the ability to do so. Many needs call for a combination of people with varied abilities who will cooperate to serve. For instance, a family whose home burns down requires the services of such people as someone who can serve through carpentry work, someone who can encourage, and someone who practices hospitality.

The ministry of the Church is varied because the needs of her people and the world are varied. Yet the purpose is one. We serve to demonstrate what the body of Christ is and does amid humanity. We do it to communicate to the world what God is like (John 1:18) and how He loves the world (John 3:16; 1 John 3:16, 17). We do it in unity, even though we are diverse in capabilities. Doing so is continuing what Christ began. Jesus' ministry is continuing through His church, and the glory of God will be shown to all (Ephesians 3:21).

Suggestions for Further Reading

Bonhoeffer, Dietrich. *The Cost of Discipleship*. New York: Macmillan, 1963.

Edge, Findley B. *The Greening of the Church*. Out of print.

————. *A Quest for a Vitality in Religion*. Out of print.

Ford, M. *Church Vocation—A New Look*. Out of print.

Getz, Gene. *Sharpening the Focus of the Church*. Chicago: Moody, 1976.

Haekendyk, J. C. *The Church Inside Out*. Out of print.

Hort, F. J. A. *The Christian Ecclesia*. Out of print.

Kirk, K. *The Apostolic Ministry*. Out of print.

Kraemer, H. *A Theology of the Laity*. Out of print.

Küng, Hans. *On Being a Christian*. Garden City: Doubleday, 1976.

————. *The Church*. Garden City: Doubleday, 1976.

————. *Signpost for the Future*. Out of print.

MacArthur, John. *The Church: The Body of Christ*. Out of print.

Manson, T. W. *Ministry and Priesthood: Christ's and Ours*. Out of print.

Minear, Paul S. *Images of the Church in the New Testament*. Philadelphia: Westminster, 1970.

Niebuhr, H. Richard and Daniel D. Williams. *The Ministry in Historical Perspective*. New York: Harper & Row, 1983.

Reid, J. K. S. *The Biblical Doctrine of Ministry*. Out of print.

Strachan, R. K. *The Inescapable Calling*. Out of print.

Staton, Knofel. *Discovering Your Gifts for Service*. Out of print.

————. *God's Plan for Church Leadership*. Cincinnati: **Standard,** 1982.

Textbooks
by Standard Publishing:

The Christian Minister
  Sam E. Stone
Introduction to Christian Education
  Eleanor Daniel, John W. Wade, Charles Gresham
Ministering to Youth
  David Roadcup, editor
The Church on Purpose
  Joe Ellis

Commentary on Acts
  J. W. McGarvey
The Equipping Ministry
  Paul Benjamin
Essays on New Testament Christianity
  C. Robert Wetzel, editor
The Fourfold Gospel
  J. W. McGarvey and P. Y. Pendleton
The Jesus Years
  Thomas D. Thurman
How to Understand the Bible
  Knofel Staton
Teach With Success
  Guy P. Leavitt, revised by Eleanor Daniel
God's Plan for Church Leadership
  Knofel Staton

Available at your Christian bookstore or

STANDARD PUBLISHING